REVISITING THE GAZE

Series Editors: Reina Lewis & Elizabeth Wilson

Dress Cultures aims to foster innovative theoretical and methodological frameworks to understand how and why we dress, exploring the connections between clothing, commerce and creativity in global contexts.

Published:

Delft Blue to Denim Blue: Contemporary Dutch Fashion
edited by Anneke Smelik

Dressing for Austerity: Aspiration, Leisure and Fashion in Post War Britain
by Geraldine Biddle-Perry

Experimental Fashion: Performance Art, Carnival and the Grotesque Body
by Francesca Granata

Fashion in European Art: Dress and Identity, Politics and the Body, 1775–1925
edited by Justine De Young

Fashion in Multiple Chinas: Chinese Styles in the Transglobal Landscape
edited by Wessie Ling and Simona Segre Reinach

Modest Fashion: Styling Bodies, Mediating Faith
edited by Reina Lewis

Niche Fashion Magazines: Changing the Shape of Fashion
by Ane Lynge-Jorlen

Styling South Asian Youth Cultures: Fashion, Media and Society
edited by Lipi Begum, Rohit K. Dasgupta and Reina Lewis

Thinking through Fashion: A Guide to Key Theorists
edited by Agnès Rocamora and Anneke Smelik

Veiling in Fashion: Space and the Hijab in Minority Communities
by Anna-Mari Almila

Wearing the Cheongsam: Dress and Culture in a Chinese Diaspora
by Cheryl Sim

Fashioning Indie: Popular Fashion, Music and Gender in the Twenty-First Century
by Rachel Lifter

Reina Lewis: reina.lewis@fashion.arts.ac.uk
Elizabeth Wilson: elizabethwilson.auth@gmail.com

REVISITING THE GAZE

THE FASHIONED BODY AND THE POLITICS OF LOOKING

Edited by
Morna Laing and Jacki Willson

BLOOMSBURY VISUAL ARTS
LONDON • NEW YORK • OXFORD • NEW DELHI • SYDNEY

BLOOMSBURY VISUAL ARTS
Bloomsbury Publishing Plc
50 Bedford Square, London, WC1B 3DP, UK
1385 Broadway, New York, NY 10018, USA
29 Earlsfort Terrace, Dublin 2, Ireland

BLOOMSBURY, BLOOMSBURY VISUAL ARTS and the Diana logo
are trademarks of Bloomsbury Publishing Plc

First published in Great Britain 2020
Paperback edition first published 2022

For legal purposes the Acknowledgements on p. xii constitute
an extension of this copyright page.

Series design by BRILL
Cover image © Matteo De Santis. Edited by Laura Perrucci.

A catalogue record for this book is available from the British Library.

ISBN: HB: 978-1-3501-5421-6
PB: 978-1-3502-4303-3
ePDF: 978-1-3501-5422-3
eBook: 978-1-3501-5423-0

Series: Dress Cultures
Typeset by Integra Software Services Pvt. Ltd.

To find out more about our authors and books visit www.bloomsbury.com
and sign up for our newsletters.

CONTENTS

List of figures vii
Notes on the editors viii
Notes on the contributors ix
Acknowledgements xii

1 **Introduction** *Morna Laing and Jacki Willson* 1

PART I Looking: The optic and the haptic

2 **Double acts: Oscillating between optical and haptic visuality in a digital age** *Mo Throp and Maria Walsh* 35

3 **The ambient gaze: Sensory atmosphere and the dressed body** *Sara Chong Kwan* 55

4 **The veiled body: The alienated system of 'looking' in post-revolutionary Iran (1979–present)** *Azadeh Fatehrad* 77

PART II Looking through neoliberalism

5 **Becoming in the eyes of others: The relational gaze in boudoir photography** *Ilya Parkins* 101

6 **The dissecting gaze: Fashioned bodies on social networking sites** *Dawn Woolley* 123

7 **Making *Lemonade?*: Beyoncé's pregnancies and the postfeminist media gaze** *Maureen Lehto Brewster* 147

PART III Looking at the 'other'

8 Looking fat in a slender world: The dialectic of seeing and becoming in Jen Davis's *Eleven Years* *Lauren Downing Peters* 175

9 Re-reading the queer female gaze in the 1990s: Spectatorship, fashion and the duality of identification and desire *Catherine Baker* 199

10 Killer looks: Marlene McCarty's *Murder Girls* *Rosa Nogués* 227

Index 253

FIGURES

1	Quilla Constance, *Pukijam* (2015)	48
2	Lucy Clout, *Shrugging Offing* (2013)	50
3	Azadeh Fatehrad, *Departure Series*, C-type Print, Tehran (2015)	77
4	*F-Magazine*, Paris (1979)	84
5	*Looking at the Pool through a Fixed Window* (1928)	90
6	Jen Davis, *Pressure Point* (2002)	179
7	Jen Davis, *Ascension* (2002)	186
8	Jen Davis, *Conforming* (2002)	187
9	Jen Davis, *Untitled No. 24* (2007)	191
10	Justine Frischmann and Elastica (1995)	209
11	Leonardo DiCaprio at the *Romeo and Juliet* Premiere (1996)	210
12	Marlene McCarty, *Marlene Olive - June 21, 1976* (1995–7)	228
13	Marlene McCarty, *Marlene Olive*, Collage (1994–6)	236
14	Marlene McCarty, *M26 Marlene Olive - June 22, 1975* (2004)	242

NOTES ON THE EDITORS

Morna Laing is Assistant Professor in Fashion Studies at The New School, Parsons Paris, France. She holds a PhD from the University of the Arts London, UK, and her current research interests include feminism, fashion media and the culture of sustainability. Her first monograph is entitled *Picturing the Woman-Child: Fashion, Feminism and the Female Gaze* and will be published by Bloomsbury Visual Arts in 2020. Her writing has appeared in journals such as *Fashion Theory*, *Sexualities* and *Critical Studies in Fashion and Beauty*. She is Fellow of the Higher Education Academy in the UK.

Jacki Willson is an academic fellow in Performance and Culture in the School of Performance and Cultural Industries at the University of Leeds, UK. She has written two monographs – *The Happy Stripper: Pleasure and Politics of the New Burlesque* (2008) and *Being Gorgeous: Sexuality and the Pleasures of the Visual* (2015). She is currently working on her third book, *Fashioning the Reproductive Body: Cultural Activism and the Bio-woman*. Her most recent articles have appeared in the journals *Porn Studies* and *Critical Studies in Fashion and Beauty*. She specializes in feminist approaches to the costumed body, performance and resistance focusing specifically on gender and sexual politics.

NOTES ON THE CONTRIBUTORS

Catherine Baker is Senior Lecturer in 20th Century History at the University of Hull, UK. Her most recent books are *Race and the Yugoslav Region: Postsocialist, Post-conflict, Postcolonial?* (2018) and the edited volume *Making War on Bodies: Militarisation, Aesthetics and Embodiment in International Politics* (2020). Her most recent articles have appeared in *Feminist Media Studies, Contemporary European History* and elsewhere. She specializes in queer and postcolonial approaches to popular culture, nationalism and conflict, especially with reference to the post-Yugoslav region and the politics of how individuals and groups narrate the past.

Maureen Lehto Brewster is a doctoral student in International Merchandising at the University of Georgia, United States. Her research interests include celebrity and influencer culture, social media, gender and the body. She holds a Master's degree in Fashion Studies from Parsons School of Design. Her writing has appeared in *The International Journal of Fashion Studies; Fashion, Style and Popular Culture; Journal of Design and Culture;* and *The Iconic.* She has also been featured on Buzzfeed News, The Business of Fashion and Women's Wear Daily. You can follow her work on Instagram at @soldbycelebs.

Sara Chong Kwan is Lecturer in Fashion Cultures and Histories (FCH) at London College of Fashion, University of the Arts London, UK, and coordinates final year FCH work in the Design school. Her research interests focus around the sensory and embodied dimensions of dress. She has convened a number of conferences, notably the 'Fashion and the Senses Symposium' at London College of Fashion. She has also co-edited a journal special edition on 'Fashion and Memory' in *Critical Studies in Fashion and Beauty* 5/2 and contributed to the *Sage Encyclopedia of Research Methods.* In her previous career Sara studied Menswear Design at Central St Martins, University of the Arts London, before co-owning an independent designer clothing store in Brighton.

Azadeh Fatehrad is Lecturer in Contemporary Art and Curating at the University of Leeds, UK, and affiliated researcher at The Artists' Writings and

Publications Research Centre. Her work has been exhibited internationally. Fatehrad received her practice-based PhD from the Royal College of Art, UK (2016), and has curated diverse public programmes such as 'The Feminist Historiography' at IASPIS, Stockholm (2016), and 'Witness 1979' at the Showroom, London (2015). Fatehrad is co-founder of 'Herstoriographies: The Feminist Media Archive Research Network' in London and is on the editorial board of the peer-reviewed *Journal for Artistic Research* (JAR). Fatehrad is also the recipient of St John's College Artist in Residence 2018 at the University of Oxford, UK (www.azadehfatehrad.com).

Rosa Nogués is Associate Lecturer in Art Theory at the Chelsea College of Arts, London, UK. Her writing has been published in *n-paradoxa*, *Revista Mundo Crítico* and the *Moving Image Review and Art Journal*, including book chapters in *Soundings: Documentary Film and the Listening Experience*, *Média Theorie* and *Transgressive Bodies: Disrupting the Canon of Corporeal Norms*. She is currently researching the work of the American film and video artist Shirley Clarke, focusing on Clarke's pioneering role in experimental film-making, radical documentary and video art, within the context of the emergence of the Women's Art Movement in the United States.

Ilya Parkins is Associate Professor of Gender and Women's Studies at the University of British Columbia, Okanagan, Canada. Her research interests include femininities, feminist cultural theory, fashion and periodical studies. She is the author of *Poiret, Schiaparelli and Dior: Fashion, Femininity and Modernity* (2012) and co-editor of *Cultures of Femininity in Modern Fashion* (2011) and *Fashion: New Feminist Essays* (2020). Her work appears in such journals as *Feminist Review, Time and Society, Biography and French Cultural Studies* as well as in various edited collections.

Lauren Downing Peters is Assistant Professor of Fashion Studies at Columbia College Chicago, United States. She holds a PhD in fashion studies from the Centre for Fashion Studies at Stockholm University. She is also the editor-in-chief of *The Fashion Studies Journal* and is a co-founding member of The Fashion Studies Alliance. Her research interests include the history of the body, plus-size fashion, the history of ready-to-wear, everyday fashion, the history of sensibilities, gender, modernity, standardized sizing, fashion media and fashion studies pedagogy. She is currently working on her first book manuscript, *Fashioning the Flesh: Fashion, Fatness and Femininity in Early 20th Century America*.

Mo Throp is Associate Researcher at Chelsea College of Arts, London, UK, where she supervises practice-based fine art PhD students. Throp is co-convener with Dr Maria Walsh of the Subjectivity and Feminisms research group, editing the book *The Performance Dinners* (2014), an account of the first three Dinners hosted by the group. Throp is the co-editor with Maria Walsh of *Twenty Years of MAKE Magazine: Back to the Future of Women's Art*. Throp's research is concerned with practice-based research and with exploring new transformative possibilities for conceptualizing identity and subjectivity especially informed by recent feminist thinking.

Maria Walsh is Reader in Artists' Moving Image at Chelsea College of Arts, London, UK. She is Reviews Editor of *MIRAJ* (*Moving Image Review and Art Journal*) and author of *Art and Psychoanalysis* (2012). Recent publications include 'Female Solidarity as Uncommodified Value: Lucy Beech's *Cannibals* and Rehana Zaman's Some Women, Other Women and All the Bittermen', in *Women Artists, Feminism and the Moving Image* (ed) L. Reynolds, Bloomsbury, 2019; and '*News From Home* the Redux Version: Amodal Perception and "la jouissance du voir"', *MIRAJ*, 8.1&2: 2019. Her current research explores the performative and critical nature of therapeutic discourses in artists' moving image.

Dawn Woolley is an artist and research fellow at Leeds Arts University, UK. Her research examines the relation between people and objects, and the impact that adverts have as producers and disseminators of social values. Her central argument is that commodity culture turns everything into adverts, including selfies and thinspiration photographs. She considers social networking sites to be *the* commercial space where commodity culture invades our social interactions. Her publications include 'Aberrant Consumers: Selfies and Fat Admiration Websites', in *Fat Studies: An Interdisciplinary Journal of Body Weight and Society*, 6(2), and *Consuming the Body: Capitalism, Social Media and Commodification*.

ACKNOWLEDGEMENTS

The editors would firstly like to thank the authors who contributed essays to this volume – the process went incredibly smoothly and this was down to the authors' professionalism, rigour and commitment to the project. We would also like to thank the delegates and attendees of the *Revisiting the Gaze* conference that was held in June 2017 at Chelsea College of Arts, University of the Arts London. The energy and ideas that flowed from the event provided the spark for this edited collection. Special thanks to the Subjectivity and Feminisms research group at Chelsea for their participation in, and support for, the project.

We would like to warmly thank the series editors – Prof. Reina Lewis and Prof. Elizabeth Wilson – who invited us to submit a proposal for the *Dress Cultures* series. We are grateful to Philippa Brewster who received our initial proposal with enthusiasm, as well as the peer reviewers for their positive comments and suggestions on the manuscript. Thank you to the University of Leeds and the School of Performance and Cultural Industries for the much-needed and greatly appreciated research time. Special thanks to Head of School Prof. Alice O'Grady and Director of Research Prof. Ben Walmsley for their continual support and positivity. Kind thanks to Caryn Simonson, Programme Director for Textile Design at Chelsea College of Arts, for her encouragement and support both for the event itself and the research activities that underpinned it. Thank you to The New School, Parsons, Paris, with special thanks to Program Director Dr Marco Pecorari for the support they provided in the final stages of the manuscript. Many thanks to the editors at Bloomsbury, Frances Arnold and Yvonne Thouroude, for their guidance and support throughout the process. Finally, we would like to express our thanks to the artists and photographers who allowed us to reproduce their work in this volume, with special thanks to Laura Perrucci and Matteo De Santis for the striking cover image.

CHAPTER 1
INTRODUCTION
Morna Laing and Jacki Willson

'Visual Pleasure at 40'

In 2015 Laura Mulvey's 'Visual Pleasure and Narrative Cinema' enjoyed its fortieth year.[1] The essay first appeared in 1975 and since then has become the most cited and referenced article in the history of *Screen* journal and seminal to debates on feminism and spectatorship.[2] To mark the essay's fortieth year the BFI hosted an event where Mulvey spoke alongside scholars and film-makers who shared their thoughts on the significance of the essay, in both personal and scholarly terms.[3] In her contribution to the panel, Mulvey emphasized that the essay was very much a 'historical document of its time' for

> it could only have been written within a narrow window of a couple of years: after the influence of the Women's Liberation Movement changed my relationship to Hollywood cinema, but before film studies came into existence, necessarily ruling out such sweeping statements and manifesto-like style of writing.[4]

Mulvey's writing was polemical, politicized, but that was her intention. For, as art historian Tamar Garb observed, the essay was about '[moving] away from the pervasive idea that looking was disinterested', in the Kantian sense, instead conceptualizing spectatorship as part and parcel of gender politics and other hierarchies of power.[5]

The 'male gaze' was mentioned just once in Mulvey's essay, and since its appearance in 1975 it has '[floated free] and become something of its own', to quote Mulvey herself.[6] The term has been mobilized by students and scholars alike, becoming central to debates on gender and the politics of looking, extending far beyond the ambit of Film Studies alone. Yet, in the process it has sometimes been detached from its psychoanalytic underpinnings, with the complexities of Mulvey's argument reductively paraphrased at times. The essay has been critiqued for its privileging of gender over other axes of identity, which are also imbricated in spectatorship, such as same-sex desire and the politics of race.[7] This speaks to critiques of Second-Wave feminism, more generally, for its failure to register the power differentials between women of different social groups and the subsequent emphasis on intersectionality in feminism since the 1980s. Finally, Mulvey herself has acknowledged that aspects of the essay have 'necessarily been rendered archaic by changes in technology'[8] and has revisited and revised it in her subsequent writing, such as *Death 24x a Second* (2006).[9]

Mention of appearance, styling and erotic spectacle in 'Visual Pleasure and Narrative Cinema' foretold how fruitful the gaze would become for making sense of the fashioned female body. Yet, in the period since the essay was published we have witnessed the evolution of Western capitalism into its current neoliberal formulation, with consumer culture absorbing the more palatable aspects of feminism in order to sell it back to women as a commodity.[10] Furthermore, with the recent resurgence of feminist activism – being termed 'Fourth Wave'[11] or 'digital' feminism[12] – debates on fashion and the gaze have evolved enormously. Blogs such as Man Repeller playfully mock the idea of the 'male gaze'[13] while women have explored the empowering potential of self-authored images of the female body. Activists on the street have used their own fashioned bodies as a site for articulating protest, through movements such as FEMEN and SlutWalk, with these protests, in turn, being critiqued on social media for their privileging of white, heteronormative, cis-gendered bodies.[14] Thus, what is new about feminist activism in the twenty-first century is the way protest on the street has converged with hashtag feminism on social media platforms, such as Twitter, Facebook and Instagram.

These social and digital changes provided the impetus for a re-examination of the fashioned female body and the politics of looking. This edited collection brings together a selection of papers that were presented at *Revisiting the Gaze: Feminism, Fashion and the Female Body*, a conference we organized in June 2017 at Chelsea College of Arts, University of the Arts London. Working from the premise that the gaze is intersectional,[15] we wanted to consider what remained fruitful in Mulvey's essay as well as thinking through new ways of theorizing fashion, the female body and spectatorship. Part of this involved addressing the relative invisibility of certain bodies – such as the ageing female body – and the hypervisibility of other bodies, such as the Muslim body or the fat body. This approach feeds into the present volume, which represents a timely contribution to scholarship on looking – in both popular and fine art contexts – with the fashioned female body being the motif connecting these two fields of visual culture. *Revisiting the Gaze* provides a fresh perspective on spectatorship in the light of digital feminism or so-called 'Fourth Wave' feminism, offering up new intersectional approaches to performative cultures where fashion, pleasure and identity interweave. That being said, we would like to acknowledge at this point the limitations of the volume. It does not include, for instance, essays on the trans body, the disabled body or the ageing body, although we invited, and endeavoured to include, as many perspectives as possible.

This introductory chapter sets the scene for the essays that follow: firstly, by mapping the ways in which scholarship on the gaze has evolved since 1975, and secondly, by turning to consider intersectional identities and the politics of looking at the fashioned female body in the digital age.

The evolution of the gaze

In the following, oft-quoted passage, Mulvey introduces the concept of the 'male gaze':

> In a world ordered by sexual imbalance, pleasure in looking has been split between active/male and passive/female. The determining male gaze projects its phantasy on to the female figure which is styled accordingly. In their traditional exhibitionist role women are simultaneously looked at and displayed, with their appearance coded for strong visual and erotic impact so that they can be said to connote *to-be-looked-at-ness*. Woman displayed as sexual object is the leit-motif of erotic spectacle: from pin-ups to strip-tease, from Ziegfeld to Busby Berkeley, she holds the look, plays to and signifies male desire.[16]

Mulvey develops her argument by building on the work of Sigmund Freud and Jacques Lacan as well as her own textual analysis of Hollywood narrative cinema. This approach, rooted in semiotics and psychoanalysis, can therefore be distinguished from that of John Berger, who studied spectatorship and the female body from a Marxist perspective in *Ways of Seeing*, published several years earlier, in 1972.[17] The tension between the body in representation and the body as theorized by Lacan is something addressed by Rosa Nogués in this volume. Her essay 'Killer Looks' explores a series of portraits by the artist Marlene McCarty, which depict young women convicted of matricide. While Mulvey looked to Lacan's discussion of the Mirror Stage to theorize the constitution of the ego, Nogués turns to Lacan's notion of Other *jouissance* in order to problematize the very concept of sex itself. Psychoanalytic approaches are less common in the field of Fashion Studies,[18] and it is therefore fruitful to see Nogués put her essay in dialogue with the work of Alison Bancroft, who theorized the female body from a Lacanian perspective in *Fashion and Psychoanalysis* (2012).[19]

Mulvey has reformulated her theory on spectatorship at several points in her career, opening up, at least theoretically, the range of viewing positions available to women and men. She did so explicitly in her 1981 essay, 'Afterthoughts on "Visual Pleasure and Narrative Cinema" Inspired by "Duel in the Sun" (King Vidor, 1946)'.[20] According to Mulvey, this second essay was prompted by 'the persistent question "what about the women in the audience?"'[21] Recognizing her own enjoyment in viewing Hollywood melodramas, Mulvey concluded that 'however ironically it had been intended originally, the male third person closed off avenues of inquiry that should be followed up'.[22] In 'Afterthoughts', Mulvey argued that female spectatorship involved an 'internal oscillation of desire' that 'lies dormant' until activated by the narrative and visual pleasures offered up in Hollywood cinema.[23] By this account, the female spectator shifts between identification with a masculine position (such as the 'active' male protagonist) and identification with a feminine position (masochistic identification with an objectified female character). The masculine position here represents a kind of temporary nostalgia for the pre-Oedipal phase of active sexuality, which is later repressed upon entrance into 'passive' adult femininity. The metaphor of transvestitism is thus invoked to characterize the unstable nature of this viewing position: 'for women (from childhood onwards) trans-sex identification is a *habit* that very easily becomes *second Nature*. However, this Nature does not sit easily and shifts restless in its borrowed transvestite clothes'.[24]

Mulvey would later reformulate the idea of 'active' female spectatorship through the concept of curiosity, which allowed for 'greater complexity' than the arguments presented in the earlier phase of her work.[25] The 'aesthetics of curiosity', and particularly the myth of Pandora, allowed for the possibility of an 'active, investigative look, but one that was this time associated with the feminine'.[26] In turn, this offered 'a way out of the rather too neat binary opposition between the spectator's gaze, constructed as active and voyeuristic, implicitly coded as masculine, and the female image on the screen, passive and exhibitionist'.[27] Curiosity, Mulvey argued, is experienced as something akin to a drive, which involves 'a desire to see' but also to know – a sort of 'epistemophilia'.[28] As such, it can be related to the feminist project of deciphering representations and their attendant myths about femininity.

In the above body of work, Mulvey is mostly concerned with the specificity of the cinematic medium yet her writing on spectatorship has always had a clear application to the study of fashion, beauty and adornment.[29] In her contribution to the panel for *Visual Pleasure at 40*, Emma Wilson, scholar of French Literature and the Visual Arts, stated: 'I love the way the essay explores overinvestment in the image of the woman on screen: the fetishization of and fascination with faces, glow, gloss, folds, silk. The essay tells me something about my own overinvestment in femininity, its stillness, its fixing, and about investment in the politics of visual pleasure and spectacle.'[30] Reflecting on Wilson's words, Mulvey stated: 'I have often felt I could have developed this (Sternberg, fetishism)[31] aspect of the essay further, especially, perhaps, in relation to recent critical writing about the "haptic" screen.'[32] Thus, in our re-evaluation of the gaze, it is worth looking to the body of writing on haptic looking that has emerged in film theory from the 1990s onwards.[33]

In Western culture since the Renaissance, vision has been privileged as the 'noble' sense.[34] This ocularcentrism can be explained, in part, by the perception of vision as a 'distance' sense, as opposed to touch, which involves direct contact between the body and the object of perception. This, in turn, maps on to Cartesian dualism and the privileging of the mind over the body, as well as the Kantian notion of 'disinterested' looking: an idea famously called into question by Pierre Bourdieu in 1979.[35] Ocularcentrism has been critiqued by feminist theorists such as Luce Irigaray for its tendency towards mastery over the object of the gaze.[36] Here the body is produced as an object of knowledge, to be surveyed, controlled and contained. Mastery of the object also applies in terms of Orientalism and the way imperialists have observed and represented non-Western cultures.[37] The recent revaluation of the senses and tactility has entailed an epistemological shift from knowing only with the mind to knowing also with the body. For as the editorial to the inaugural issue of *The Senses and Society* (2006) states: 'The senses mediate the relationship between self and society, mind and body, idea and object.'[38] This has ramifications for fashion, which sits against the body, and has historically been denigrated and feminized as a result.

In her seminal text *The Skin of the Film*, Laura U. Marks highlights the 'multisensory quality of perception' vis-à-vis intercultural cinema.[39] Building on the work of art historian Aloïs Riegl, she states that haptic visuality occurs where 'the eyes themselves function like organs of touch'.[40] Optical visuality correlates with our everyday understanding of vision, which involves the eyes perceiving objects in space and at a distance. By contrast, 'haptic looking tends to move over the surface of its object rather than plunge into illusionistic depth, not to distinguish form so much as to discern texture. It is more inclined to move than to focus, more inclined to graze than to gaze'.[41] Rather than viewing these modes of looking in strict opposition, Marks posits that 'in most processes of seeing, both are involved, in a dialectical movement from far to near'.[42] Crucially, the notion of haptic visuality emphasizes the *embodied* nature of looking.

Mo Throp and Maria Walsh open the first section of this volume with a dialogue or 'double act' on optical and haptic visuality. Drawing on the concept of masquerade, they discuss the work of video artists, such as Lucy Clout, Jennifer Ringley, Laurel Nakadate and Quilla Constance, questioning whether their digital strategies succeed in generating a productive oscillation between distance and proximity for female subjects in relation to their image. They also evaluate Laura Marks's framework in relation to Quilla Constance and the potential her work might hold for expanding spectatorship interculturally, suspending the mastery of the colonial gaze.

Moving from fine art practice to a more popular context, when it comes to the logic of the fashion system, symbolic production is sometimes said to take precedence over fashion in its materiality.[43] One could therefore be forgiven for thinking of the fashioned body in semiotic or representational terms only. However, from a phenomenological perspective, 'fashion [is] not simply an aesthetic or symbolic phenomenon but [also] a haptic experience'[44] for 'the visual and the tactile are always inextricably intertwined', as Llewellyn Negrin has argued.[45] In the present volume, Sara Chong Kwan draws upon Maurice Merleau-Ponty's account of sensory perception to theorize the sensory aspects of the dressed body. She argues that the haptic, auditory and olfactory aspects of fashion tend to be underexplored in accounts of 'appearance'. Chong Kwan's concept of the 'ambient gaze' thus makes a contribution to the emerging body of scholarship on haptic looking in the field of Fashion Studies.[46]

When considering how to define the gaze for the purposes of this volume, we found it instructive to return to an essay written by Caroline Evans and Lorraine Gamman in 1995.[47] Evans and Gamman revisited Mulvey's essays on the gaze in order to freshly situate them within a 1990s context. Students, they observed, sometimes used the 'male gaze' as a synonym for patriarchy or female objectification, often failing to read – or even recognize – the psychoanalytic texts that underpinned cinematic theory on spectatorship. Over two decades later, we find ourselves in much the same position, with the 'male gaze' frequently namechecked by students or bandied about on social media: the signifier detached from the original signified of psychoanalytic theory.

What has perhaps changed in more recent years, however, is the frequency with which the 'female gaze' is also now acknowledged. For example, in 2016 'The Female Gaze Issue' of *i-D* magazine was released (no. 344). The editorial introduction stated: 'For the first time in i-D's 36-year history, we celebrate the power of the female lens, working with female photographers only from front to back. [...] discover the myriad of ways in which women view women today.'[48] Here, the female gaze seems to be equated with any cultural text authored by a woman (thus concerning itself with the production side rather than the site of the audience). Yet, as Mulvey's 'Afterthoughts' attests, female spectatorship might nevertheless involve a masculinized way of looking; a female producer might not necessarily escape the phallogocentrism associated with the photographic lens, as Agnès Rocamora has explored vis-à-vis self-representation on fashion blogs.[49] It cannot be assumed that because a person is a woman they will necessarily have progressive beliefs or intentions – or that they will identify as a feminist. Even if the author of a cultural text *does* identify as a feminist, feminism itself has fractured into different 'waves' or factions with divergent views on what it means to be empowered as a woman in the twenty-first century, which will inevitably feed into practices of looking.[50]

While the 'male gaze' in its original formulation was framed in psychoanalytic terms, its usage in popular culture, and also in the Academy, has clearly evolved beyond this. In the present volume we were faced with the dilemma as to whether to define the term tightly, in line with Mulvey's original intention, or whether to offer up a more expansive definition of the term. We have opted for the latter, employing an interdisciplinary approach to understanding the gaze. Some of the essays remain rooted in the psychoanalytic tradition while others draw from different frameworks, such as phenomenology, Sociology, Media Studies and Cultural Studies. While the volume is interdisciplinary in scope, each author takes care to define the 'rules of the game' from the outset;[51] thus, while there might be a departure from the 'gaze' in its original formulation, this does not have to entail a loss of scholarly rigour.

Some theorists have argued that the idea of identity as discursively constructed, as per Foucault,[52] is inconsistent with psychoanalytic approaches to identity. For instance, Sean Nixon has critiqued psychoanalytic accounts of spectatorship for being 'too ahistorical and totalizing'.[53] Furthermore, the idea of universal psychic structures that govern gender and sexuality has been considered problematic in terms of the seeming incompatibility with the feminist movement, which seeks social change and a shift in relations between men and women.[54] These are complex questions, which cannot be fully unravelled here. Nevertheless, it is worth noting Judith Butler's approach on this point. Butler acknowledges that much writing on gender has been defined by essentialism versus constructionism debates, involving a 'tendency to think that sexuality is either constructed or determined; to think that if it is constructed, it is in some sense free, and if it is determined, it is in some sense fixed'.[55] However, Butler problematizes this debate, suggesting that to frame the debate in oppositional terms is not helpful. Instead she raises 'the more complex question of how "deep-seated" or constitutive constraints can be posed in terms of symbolic limits in their intractability and contestability'.[56] In this way gender performativity might be understood as 'political constraints registered psychically'[57] and the symbolic limits of intelligibility.

Ultimately, Butler argues that there 'must be a way to subject psychoanalysis to a Foucauldian redescription even as Foucault himself refused that possibility'.[58] Her intention is to challenge the heteronormativity that underpins psychoanalytic accounts of gender and sexuality, 'without dispensing with what is clearly valuable in psychoanalytic perspectives'.[59] Identification with a sexed subject-position 'is not a buried identification that is left behind in a forgotten past, but an identification that must be leveled and buried again and again, the compulsive repudiation by which the subject incessantly sustains his/her boundary'.[60] The work of psychoanalysis – and Lacan in particular – helps Butler argue that sex is also a 'symbolic position that one assumes under the threat of punishment'.[61]

Butler's points can be mobilized in response to a question posed in *i-D* (online) in 2016, which asks: 'In a world where gender is understood to be fluid, what is the relevance of concepts like male and female gazes?'[62] The idea that we now live in a gender fluid society, where femininity and masculinity are free-floating and chosen at will, is unfortunately a little too optimistic. If this were the case then there would be no ramifications for a person born female 'inhabiting' a masculine subject-position and vice versa. The threat of punishment, the constraints of intelligibility and the risk of social ostracism are fears registered both consciously and unconsciously. Looking and feeling oneself to be looked at are key to the construction of one's own gender identity and the gender identities of others. For Mulvey, the male gaze is a metaphor for the 'psychical obsessions'[63] at work in a patriarchal society: we can unpick 'patterns of fascination [...] at work within the individual subject and the social formations that have moulded him'.[64] That is not to say there is no scope for agency and subversion within this model but it is important to recognize that there remain structures that shape one's experience of gender and sexuality, and these structures can be incredibly punishing. Spectatorship and looking can involve pleasure – erotic or otherwise – but can also involve discomfort or even pain. For example, Angela McRobbie considers how fashion photography might connect the viewer with feelings of 'pain, self-punishment and loss'.[65] Using Freud or Lacan to make sense of such trauma speaks to Mulvey's assertion that psychoanalysis can be mobilized as a 'political weapon'.[66]

Intersectionality and a new politics of looking

An important motivation for opening up the present volume beyond psychoanalytic perspectives alone was the need to recognize other axes of power, besides gender and sexuality, in our account of spectatorship. Jennifer Nash in her article for the *Feminist Review* argued: 'Intersectionality, the notion that subjectivity is constituted by mutually reinforcing vectors of race, gender, class, and sexuality, has emerged as the primary theoretical tool designed to combat feminist hierarchy, hegemony, and exclusivity.'[67] The term 'intersectionality' was coined by Kimberlé Crenshaw to underscore the 'multi-dimensionality' of marginalized subjects and it gained traction within black feminism in the United States in the 1980s. This theoretical perspective – explored firstly within a legal framework – was useful in terms of understanding the plurality of lived experience in the face of inequalities. 'Woman' is not a one-axis category but is made up of what Georg Simmel's 1908 essay had earlier defined as a complicated mapping of 'intersecting social circles'.[68] With that in mind, the contributors to both the conference and this edited collection developed a range of discourses that counter normative ideals relating to 'fat', 'pregnant', 'lesbian', Muslim and black bodies.[69]

An important milestone in the developing literature on intersectional spectatorship was *The Female Gaze*, edited by Lorraine Gamman and Margaret Marshment in 1988.[70] The present volume builds upon this foundational text, in light of internet culture, new techniques of self-representation and the shifting landscape of visual culture and feminist activism in the twenty-first century.[71] 'The Gaze Revisited' (1995) by Lorraine Gamman and Caroline Evans also provided an important precedent for this current collection because of the way it foregrounded intersectional gaps in theories of the gaze. During the 1980s and 1990s these questions were broached by black feminist writers such as bell hooks,[72] Lorraine O'Grady[73] and Sander L. Gilman.[74] These essays were later collated, along with other progressive writing on the gaze, and re-published in 2003 as part of *The Feminism and Visual Culture Reader*, edited by Amelia Jones and Nicholas Mirzoeff.[75] What hooks emphasized was the fact that she had to disavow the whiteness and the lack of representational recognition in order to enjoy watching Hollywood films.[76] She could not see herself in the images being displayed; in order to experience visual pleasure she had to read them against the grain, in spite of herself, so to speak.

Catherine Baker's chapter in this volume explores this sense of marginality and exclusion but this time in relation to the lesbian gaze. Baker revisits debates on lesbian spectatorship from the 1990s, drawing on what Evans and Gamman describe as 'subcultural competences'.[77] In this mode of looking, it is 'the act of interpretation itself that is eroticized, driven in part by the thrill of detecting lesbian pleasure in the mainstream location', as Reina Lewis has argued.[78] Baker explores these ideas through an auto-ethnographic lens: namely, the lived experience of her younger teenage self. She discusses the way in which she identified with the fashioned look of Leonardo DiCaprio against the heteronormative grain. Baker's chapter thus contributes to earlier scholarship such as that of Lewis and Rolley (1996), who theorized fashion magazines as a space where women are 'tutored in consuming other women's bodies, in assessing and responding to the desirability of other women'.[79] Baker took pleasure in styling her own lesbian aesthetic, fashioned from images and 'looks' that she simultaneously desired.

What is clearly evident is that within the fashion, beauty and celebrity industries it is still an intersection of particular coordinates that are prioritized within the scopic regime. The visual economy is, on the whole, ageist and heteronormative and certain female bodies within this mapping are given validation as fashion subjects. What is articulated here therefore is that 'certain bodies matter' more than others, as Rosalind Gill has argued.[80] Even though other bodies have figured in recent fashion, beauty and celebrity trends – trans, pregnant, older, fat, black, disabled, lesbian – these bodies still have to 'pass' the judgement of the critical gaze. The recent inclusion of 'ageing femininities', for instance, has consolidated the point that it is particular ageing bodies that are given the privilege of inclusion and visibility. Deborah Jermyn points out in her essay 'Pretty Past It' (2016) that 'successful ageing'[81] is still of paramount importance. This 'success' hinges on your 'aesthetic capital' – having class privileges and being thin and able-bodied. Without these factors older women continue to endure invisibility and are disenfranchised from the fashion and beauty industries.

A pertinent example is the *Advanced Style* blog launched in 2008 by Ari Seth Cohen. The blog consists of a series of photographs documenting the style of older women. Jermyn points to the way that the 'critical gaze' within the project somehow unhinged its positive intentions towards inclusivity. The project entailed Cohen searching the streets of New York for interesting, fashion-forward older women, whom he could include in his photographic series. This was then followed up by the *Advanced Style* film in 2014. However, this is where the project falls short, as Jermyn explains:

> What of the lone woman we see Cohen tentatively checking out from behind in the street at the start of the film? This is a 'critical gaze' that evaluates (an older) woman's fitness for purpose as the subject of the look in just as crude a fashion as the objectifying sexualized male gaze on young women ranks and orders them.[82]

Older women are also party to the hierarchies that restrict and oppress younger women, with women now being 'scrutinized, elevated, or relegated alongside one another according to how they look (…) *throughout* the life course'.[83]

In the present volume, Lauren Downing Peters discusses this critical gaze vis-à-vis the fat body. Peters explores the idea of 'Looking Fat in a Slender World' in relation to the North American photographer Jen Davis. Davis directs the camera onto her own fleshy body as the fashion subject. With acute honesty, Davis also turns the camera on the merciless way that large bodies are represented in the US media. Relentlessly shorn of their heads, fat bodies are dehumanized and medicalized in representation, in a way that pathologizes 'fatness'. Peters argues that it is through the 'dressed' element of her work that Davis reveals the damage inflicted. The panoptic control of the Foucauldian gaze is felt through her own self-critical regard. The point made so pertinently by Peters is the manner in which fat bodies vacillate in the media between invisibility and hypervisibility. Indeed, this powerful assertion as regards the 'fat' body also tallies with scholars who explore the fashioned body from other intersectional perspectives, for instance, the intersection of fashion with the 'ageing body'[84] and the 'veiled body'.[85]

In terms of the veiled body, in 2015 Mulvey juxtaposed what she described as 'two completely differing social and symbolic contexts, the Hollywood of early feminist theory and post-revolutionary Iran'.[86] She argued that 'femininity is, in both cases, understood as a signifier of the sexual', thus confirming 'the centrality of female sexuality in a society that attempts to repress it as well as in one where it is commodified as a spectacle'.[87] In the present volume Azadeh Fatehrad addresses sexuality and looking in relation to the veiled female body in post-revolutionary Iran (1979–). Fatehrad argues that a complex system of looking has been developed in the name of 'protecting' the modesty of both sexes. This, in turn, has created a highly charged arena in which the partial visibility of the female body ironically intensifies its erotic visibility. This builds upon earlier work by Reina Lewis, who discusses hypervisibility in relation to modest dress and the veil. She argues that the different ways of looking and being seen are dependent on the possession of cultural competences. Different spatial contexts affect the way one is looked at – one's 'legibility'. Veiling like any dressing practice is a 'situated bodily practice'[88] and the gaze is differentiated depending on one's spatial and temporal positioning. The veiled woman actively negotiates the space through which she travels. Indeed, she argues, this places her in a strong agential position with regard to various regimes of veiling. Reflecting on these intersectional nuances to the gaze in relation to modesty, faith and the veil is an important development on theories of looking. The work extends our thinking on the gaze beyond the cinematic and beyond a purely phallocentric model in which the veiled woman is synonymous with objectification and victimhood.

However, Mulvey's early work was also generated in response to the cinematic before the advent of contemporary social media, blogs, vlogs and selfie culture. In *Death 24x a Second* Mulvey states that 'while technology never simply determines, it cannot but affect the context in which ideas are formed'.[89] Mulvey suggests that changes in technology have led to a 'feminization' of film, 'with the shift in spectatorial power relations dwelling on pose, stillness, lighting and the choreography of character and camera'.[90] This leads to an emphasis on image rather than plot. Yet, it was not just the technical nature of the medium that shifted; it was also the way the medium was consumed. 'The specificity of cinema, the relation between its material base and its poetics, dissolves while other relations, intertextual and cross-media, begin to emerge.'[91] No longer did audiences need to go to an auditorium to encounter film; they could look at it in their own homes, stopping and starting the footage as they saw fit. This heralded a new-found level of interactivity in cinematic spectatorship, which has become a hallmark of 'new media', more generally.[92]

This leads us to consider digital culture and the relationship between the public spectacle of the street and the private, more intimate space of the home. Feminist street protests now operate in tandem with the digital realm, with campaigns gaining momentum via Facebook and hashtags.[93] And similarly, intimate moments are now livestreamed. This shift has called for new political and theoretical models for understanding and interrogating this dynamic of looking. Protests such as FEMEN, SlutWalks and FreeTheNipple have revealed the extent to which digital feminism – or the Fourth Wave – seems to open itself up to the same criticisms that were used to decry Second-Wave feminists. This critique, as Hoskin et al. have outlined, was due to the Second Wave's 'history of exclusionary practices and the overlooking of spaces due to hegemonic normativity (i.e. heteronormativity, cisnormativity, normative whiteness)'.[94] Digital 'sisterhood' is similarly still seen to be a place for privileged bodies.

Digital feminism has highlighted the fractures within feminism and its exclusionary blind spots. As Aristea Fotopoulou argues, 'digital sisterhood' still retains geographical and technological barriers – activism in the UK context tends to have a physical centre in London and older women sometimes feel excluded because of their limited access to social media skills.[95] Mainstream gender equality manifestos have recently appeared online, putting the spotlight on representation and inclusivity of all genders, for instance *He For She* (2016)[96] and *Ms. Foundation* (2016).[97] However, what digital spaces have encouraged is a challenge to privileged narratives within feminism and this has occurred 'despite (or even because of) the often "toxic" environment in online spaces'.[98] The 'toxicity' makes transparent tensions and prejudice. In this way, hashtag feminism has taken privilege to task by putting attitudes under the microscope. It has also allowed for other marginalized voices, narratives and bodies to emerge, as evidenced by the discourse stemming from the Twitter hashtag #YesAllWomen.[99] Indeed, these practices extend beyond feminism alone, as is evident in movements such as Black Lives Matter, where hashtags have helped connect and mobilize communities in different geographical locations.[100]

What is becoming more evident is feminism's desire to unpick privilege, in a productive sense, and not use it 'to put others down'.[101] Contemporary feminist scholarship is also focusing on this issue with Alison Phipps poignantly asking: 'Whose personal is more political?'[102] The reaction to Beyoncé's 'hiphop feminism' is clearly a point worth mentioning in this regard. Nathalie Weidhase's article (2015) explores Annie Lennox's reaction to the Beyoncé show where she 'comes out' as a feminist. In the show in question, Beyoncé's lean black body is seen against the bright bold word 'FEMINIST'. This was described by the white singer Annie Lennox as 'feminist-lite'. Pushed further, Lennox focused in on her own objection to twerking and the way Beyoncé hypersexualizes her body. For Lennox, this was not a genuine example of empowerment but feminism being used as a publicity stunt. Weidhase argues that Beyoncé's black body was in fact contesting 'the whiteness of mainstream feminism'.[103] Her 'explicitly feminist content with performances of sexual agency signifies an exploration of black female sexuality beyond respectability politics'.[104] Exploring Beyoncé's self-sexualizing performances in relation to 'hiphop feminism' opens up a different dynamic of looking and visibility. The 'avalanche of GIFs'[105] that followed the performance amplified and supported this intersectional challenge and approach.

Beyoncé's pregnant body, as it appears in Instagram posts, is the subject of Maureen Lehto Brewster's chapter in this volume. Brewster conceptualizes Beyoncé's posts as a 'practice of the self', challenging as well as acknowledging the judgements of a postfeminist media gaze. Beyoncé deftly and performatively operates within the neoliberal discourses created by the media, the public and celebrity culture in order to create and sustain her own star image, persona and narrative. As such, her 'postfeminist pregnancy' can be read as an act of 'radical privacy' where she curates her life, style and black feminism with self-conscious artistry.

There is clearly therefore a level of filtering and control that legitimizes the visibility of particular bodies and particular kinds of activism. In her article 'Post-postfeminism?: New Feminist Visibilities in Postfeminist Times', Rosalind Gill explores the conjunction of fashion, feminism and youthfulness. With reference to the then saturation of feminism in online spaces, Gill states, 'it's worth asking not just about the amount of visibility but the *kinds of visibility* on offer'.[106] Particular kinds of feminist campaigns and hashtags are given media attention – that is feminist activity that is 'comfortable'. SlutWalks, for instance, were given a tremendous amount of coverage – for it can be trivialized as fun and accommodated within the scopic economy with ease. Another campaign was *I am Malala*, that Gill argues is similarly 'comfortable' for it is steeped in 'rescue' colonial fantasies in relation to Other cultures.

Questions of legitimization filter through into other forms of control over what is seen. The murder of Pakistani Twitter celebrity Qandeel Baloch in 2016 shows us how visibility on social media can lead to shaming and, in some cases, culminate in fatal consequences.[107] However, the posting of images on social media can be instrumental in generating further feminist discussion whether that be on a global stage or within a small-knit community or subculture. It can mould and influence the process of selection over what one posts. Reina Lewis (2015) discusses these issues of legitimization in her article on the 'female religious gaze' where images posted of veiled or unveiled Muslim female bloggers create debate within the blogging community. The act of looking and being-looked-at stimulates discussion on questions of modest dress, with Lewis presenting the bloggers' 'modified forms of self-presentation as widening, rather than quitting, the frame of modest embodiment'.[108]

This publication is concerned with representations of the female body – what it means to see and be seen as a woman in the twenty-first century – and the selfie, defined as a 'spontaneous self-portrait, taken with a [...] consumer-based device'[109] makes an important intervention into the politics of the gaze. A notable moment in the history of self-representation came in 2013, when Oxford Dictionaries hailed the 'selfie' as 2013 Word of the Year.[110] Murray argues that a distinction should be made between 'the popular notion of the selfie: the visual expression of vanity that is ubiquitous on social media sites like Facebook – and the more artistically motivated photographic self-portrait'.[111] Indeed, one of the artists Murray interviewed, Francesca Romeo, insisted on a distinction being made between selfies and self-portraiture, even though 'technically they are exactly the same'.[112] Other artists reject this difference, as Murray explores. These distinctions are worth bearing in mind when it comes to evaluating the subversive potential of such images. What the selfie does nevertheless provide is a form of 'representational agency'.[113]

In contrast to traditional portraiture, taking a selfie involves one person not two – at least in theory. Of course, turning the camera lens on oneself predates smart phones and the internet – with Cindy Sherman's self-portraits being one such example. But what has changed is the ease at which such images can be disseminated to a global audience, at least potentially. And where the selfie-taker is a woman, it cuts the man out of the picture altogether. Or does it? If our starting point is that subjects are constituted through both discourse, and discourse is influenced by or stems from psychodynamic processes of power vis-à-vis gender, sex and sexuality, then it follows that a man need not be physically present or involved in the production of a photograph for the male gaze to stake a claim in the way femininity is elaborated.

It should be noted that a lot of media discussion about selfies has, as Murray notes, tended to be 'focused (unfairly) on young women'.[114] Yet there is a disconnect between the media critique of these young women as narcissistic and the way selfie-takers themselves understand their images as 'a radical act of political empowerment: a means to resist the male-dominated media culture's obsession with and oppressive hold over their lives and bodies'.[115] In a sense this perhaps echoes some of the generational divides that certain scholars attribute to different 'waves' of feminist theory and activism. Once again, the object of fixation both in media critique and in the images posted online is the female body. A conflict is being fought out on this terrain which the public seem to have a stake in: in terms of both media commentators critiquing the body and behaviour of (young) women taking the selfies and the fact that these images are literally open to the public through new media platforms (with the public being free to leave comments below images posted, whether in a critical or celebratory mode). Some images are more obviously empowering and present more of a challenge to historical, male-authored images than others: for instance, those images displaying body hair at #bodyhairdontcare[116] challenging the taboo on body hair for women[117] or even those that show menstrual blood as a means of challenging the taboo on menstruation in mainstream culture.

These practices of self-representation sit against a backdrop of neoliberal consumer culture, with an important shift occurring in the Thatcher-Reagan era, which post-dates the publication of Mulvey's 1975 essay. Nancy Fraser notes the way in which Second-Wave feminism coincided with this new era of economic policy.[118] Neoliberalism involved policies of privatization, the deregulation of markets and competition being championed over welfare. This approach to economic policy facilitated a re-signification of Second-Wave feminist goals in the interests of capitalist society. The media played a central role in this process of re-signification since 'for the majority of people their experience of feminism is an entirely mediated one'.[119] This has led to the partial appropriation of the palatable aspects of feminism into media discourse – such as the right to consume fashion and other commodities and the right to display one's body on one's own terms – while more radical feminist content has been simultaneously emptied out.[120]

Digital media have therefore increased the significance of the body 'as a site of both self-representation and surveillance'.[121] The proliferation of social networking sites operates via an increased use of visual images that facilitates and perpetuates this self-surveillance. In this volume, Dawn Woolley argues that in order to conform to dominant body ideals, consumer culture encourages both men and women to adopt a scalpel-like gaze to critically focus in on areas of perceived imperfection. She refers to 'Thinspiration' sites in order to bring to light a self-regarding, 'dissecting gaze'. As such, Woolley argues that the increase in image sharing has intensified and magnified a fetishistic gaze or 'hyperfocalisation'. Consumers and sharers are encouraged to look at themselves – and others – with judgemental scrutiny and even self-hatred or shame.

Identity and social status are therefore inextricably linked to a body which can be 'shaped, repurposed and given value through consumer choices', as Hester Baer has argued.[122] In this volume Ilya Parkins locates boudoir photography within these neoliberal technologies of the self. More specifically she refers to what Adrienne Evans and Sarah Riley term the 'technology of sexiness', where one reproduces oneself through 'discourses of sexual liberation (as the available technologies of subjectivity provided through neoliberalism, consumerism, and postfeminism)'.[123] Parkins argues that the boudoir genre demonstrates that feminist critiques of neoliberalism do not acknowledge women's motivations. Being photographed erotically, especially for a loved one, can have a 'healing', relational aspect that can bolster confidence while acting as a form of self-care and self-love.

The selfie is seen to go hand in hand with these neoliberal tendencies as self-representation enables what Minh-Ha T. Pham (2015) refers to as the 'politics and practices of self-composure' and the positives of 'networked vanity'.[124] In her discussion, Pham posits this new form of digital vanity as a form of self-presentation that moves us beyond self-interest. These 'sartorial and corporeal displays of physical attractiveness' are, she argues, intrinsic to hashtag and digital feminism. She discusses, for instance, the Twitter hashtag campaign #feministselfie which promoted bodily acceptance as well as RAISE Our Story – a street style blog giving visibility to issues relating to immigration. As such, Pham positively argues for the agential qualities of the selfie as an activist tool: 'the networked subject-as-object has unprecedented control of the frames of vision within which they are seen'.[125]

Yet, the visibility of 'popular feminism' in online spaces has at the same time generated new forms of 'popular misogyny', with trolling being one marked example, as Sarah Banet-Weiser explores.[126] Another type of popular misogyny consists in 'creepshots': a covert form of photography whereby sexualized images of women's bodies are taken without their consent. The authors of such images are usually men, and the photographs are then shared, 'reviewed' and discussed on online platforms such as the Candid Forum, as Anne Burns has documented.[127] In January 2019 it was announced that 'upskirting', one form of such photography, was to become a criminal offence in the UK, punishable by up to two years in prison.[128] The legislation was the result of a social media campaign by Gina Martin, herself a victim of upskirting, thus demonstrating how digital feminism can have the capacity to effect genuine social change. Her experience of sexual assault led Martin to think differently about how she dressed her body in public spaces, demonstrating how these new forms of misogyny are internalized and can lead to a rolling back of one's sense of freedom and empowerment. Furthermore, in the course of her campaign, Martin experienced trolling in the form of rape threats, insults and victim-blaming.[129] This demonstrates the push and pull of competing discourses of feminism and misogyny, which play out in online spaces.

By addressing women's current relationship to spectatorship, objectification and empowerment, this volume aligns itself with the renewed sense of political purpose in Fashion Studies of late.[130] The activist inflection of such literature complements the strand of scholarship that is more oriented towards aesthetics (which is not to say that politics and aesthetics can be separated but rather that such literature engages in ideological critique to varying degrees). Feminism within the Academy has been criticized for its lack of praxis – similarly, we could argue that this has been the case in relation to Fashion Studies. In that regard our editorial position has been to mobilize theory to make a political intervention into discourses on the female body. bell hooks's stance on Cultural Studies is therefore still pertinent. She argues that a Cultural Studies approach 'challenges systems of domination' and allows us to resist and problematize 'the conventional, acceptable politics of representation'.[131] Many students of Fashion Studies go on to work in the creative industries, and we hope that the present volume will furnish them with some of the tools they might need to shape the industry in progressive ways.

We can conclude that the fashioned female body continues to generate considerable interest as a spectacle of consumption, pleasure, exploitation or violation in the current cultural context. The act of 'looking' and being-looked-at' is still politically charged and digital culture has opened up new questions when it comes to images of women and feminist activism. *Revisiting the Gaze* brings together new scholarship to address these pressing concerns and contexts. We hope therefore that as a collection the volume will both consolidate this field of knowledge within Fashion Studies and push debates forward to forge new ground.

Notes

1. Laura Mulvey, 'Visual Pleasure and Narrative Cinema', *Screen* 16/3 (Autumn 1975), pp. 6–18.
2. Alison Phipps, 'Preface', *Screen* 56/4 (Winter 2015), p. 471.
3. The event took place on 21 April 2015 at the British Film Institute in London.
4. Laura Mulvey, '"Visual Pleasure at 40" Dossier', *Screen* 56/4 (Winter 2015), pp. 481–5, p. 481.
5. Tamar Garb, '"Visual Pleasure at 40" Dossier', *Screen* 56/4 (Winter 2015), pp. 473–4, p. 473.
6. Laura Mulvey, 'Visual Pleasure at 40: Laura Mulvey in Discussion (Extract) | BFI', *YouTube*. Available at https://www.youtube.com/watch?v=IWAJdj3cPvA (accessed 7 March 2019).
7. See, for instance, bell hooks, *Black Looks: Race and Representation* (Boston: South End Press, 1992), and Jacqui Roach and Petal Felix, 'Black Looks', in L. Gamman and M. Marshment (eds), *The Female Gaze: Women as Viewers of Popular Culture* (London: The Women's Press, 1988), pp. 130–42.
8. Mulvey, 'Visual Pleasure at 40'.
9. Laura Mulvey, *Death 24x a Second: Stillness and the Moving Image* (London: Reaktion, 2006).
10. Nancy Fraser, *Fortunes of Feminism: From State-Managed Capitalism to Neoliberal Crisis* (London: Verso, 2013).
11. Kira Cochrane, 'The Fourth Wave of Feminism: Meet the Rebel Women', *The Guardian*, 10 December 2013. Available at http://www.theguardian.com/world/2013/dec/10/fourth-wave-feminism-rebel-women (accessed 21 September 2015); Ealasaid Munro, 'Feminism: A Fourth Wave?', *Political Insight* 4/2 (2013), pp. 22–5.
12. Hester Baer, 'Redoing Feminism: Digital Activism, Body Politics, and Neoliberalism', *Feminist Media Studies* 16/1 (2016), pp. 17–34.
13. In 2010, the site offered a dictionary-style definition of 'Man Repeller': 'She who outfits herself in a sartorially offensive mode that may result in repelling members of the opposite sex. Such garments include but are not limited to harem pants, boyfriend jeans, overalls, shoulder pads, full length jumpsuits, jewelry that resembles violent weaponry and clogs.' Leandra Medine, 'What Is Man Repeller', 25 April 2010. Available at http://www.manrepeller.com/2010/04/what-is-man-repeller.html (accessed 4 September 2015).
14. Baer, 'Redoing Feminism'.
15. Lorraine Gamman and Margaret Marshment (eds), *The Female Gaze: Women as Viewers of Popular Culture* (London: The Women's Press, 1988).
16. Mulvey, 'Visual Pleasure and Narrative Cinema', p. 11.

17. John Berger, *Ways of Seeing* (London: Penguin, 1972 [2008]).
18. That said, a small body of literature does exist. See, for instance, John C. Flügel, *The Psychology of Clothes* (London: Hogarth, 1933); Diana Fuss, 'Fashion and the Homospectatorial Look', in S. Benstock and S. Ferriss (eds), *On Fashion* (New Brunswick and New Jersey: Rutgers University Press, 1994), pp. 211–32; Caroline Evans, 'Masks, Mirrors and Mannequins: Elsa Schiaparelli and the Decentered Subject', *Fashion Theory* 3/1 (1999), pp. 3–32; Angela McRobbie, *The Aftermath of Feminism: Gender, Culture and Social Change* (London: Sage, 2009).
19. Alison Bancroft, *Fashion and Psychoanalysis* (London and New York: I.B. Tauris, 2012).
20. Laura Mulvey, 'Afterthoughts on "Visual Pleasure and Narrative Cinema" Inspired by "Duel in the Sun" (King Vidor, 1946)', *Framework: The Journal of Cinema and Media* 15/17 (Summer 1981), pp. 12–15.
21. Ibid., p. 12.
22. Ibid., p. 12.
23. Ibid., p. 15.
24. Ibid., p. 13.
25. Laura Mulvey, *Fetishism and Curiosity* (London: British Film Institute, 1996).
26. Ibid., p. 62.
27. Ibid., p. 62.
28. Ibid., p. 59.
29. For instance, Stella Bruzzi has suggested that female spectators might not necessarily be invested in the female body on screen but rather in the garments that adorn her body, that is, 'the art and spectacle of her clothes'. See Stella Bruzzi, *Undressing Cinema: Clothing and Identity in the Movies* (London: Routledge, 1997), p. 18.
30. Emma Wilson, '"Visual Pleasure at 40" Dossier', *Screen* 56/4 (Winter 2015), pp. 479–81, p. 479.
31. In 'Visual Pleasure and Narrative Cinema', Mulvey argues that 'Sternberg produces the ultimate fetish [...] The beauty of the woman as object and the screen space coalesce; she is no longer the bearer of guilt but a perfect product, whose body, stylised and fragmented by close-ups, is the content of the film and the direct recipient of the spectator's look' (p. 14). Such fetishization, Mulvey argues, is one way of disavowing castration anxiety (and thus displeasure) in the male spectator.
32. Mulvey, '"Visual Pleasure at 40" Dossier', p. 483.
33. This includes Jennifer M. Barker, *The Tactile Eye: Touch and the Cinematic Experience* (Berkeley, Los Angeles and London: University of California Press, 2009); Laura U. Marks, *The Skin of the Film: Intercultural Cinema, Embodiment*

and the Senses (Durham and London: Duke University Press, 2000); and Vivian Sobchack, *The Address of the Eye: A Phenomenology of Film Experience* (New Jersey and Oxford: Princeton University Press, 1992).

34. Lowe as cited in John A. Walker and Sarah Chaplin, *Visual Culture: An Introduction* (Manchester and New York: Manchester University Press, 1997), p. 20.
35. Pierre Bourdieu, *Distinction: A Social Critique of the Judgement of Taste*, trans. R. Nice (Oxon: Routledge, 1986).
36. Luce Irigaray, *Speculum of the Other Woman*, trans. G.C. Gill (Ithaca, NY: Cornell University Press, 1985).
37. Edward W. Said, *Orientalism* (London: Penguin, 2003). For discussion of women's relationship to imperialism and Orientalist discourse, see Reina Lewis, *Gendering Orientalism: Race, Femininity and Representation* (London and New York: Routledge, 1996).
38. Michael Bull, Paul Gilroy, David Howes and Douglas Kahn, 'Introducing Sensory Studies', *The Senses and Society* 1/1 (2006), pp. 5–7.
39. Marks, *The Skin of the Film*, p. 131.
40. Ibid., p. 162.
41. Ibid., p. 162.
42. Ibid., p. 163.
43. Roland Barthes, *The Fashion System*, trans. M. Ward and R. Howard (California and London: University of California Press, 1990 [1967]).
44. Llewellyn Negrin, 'Maurice Merleau-Ponty: The Corporeal Experience of Fashion' in A. Rocamora and A. Smelik (eds), *Thinking through Fashion: A Guide to Key Theorists* (London and New York: I.B. Tauris, 2016), p. 115.
45. Ibid., p. 117.
46. See, for instance, Lucia Ruggerone 'The Feeling of Being Dressed: Affect Studies and the Clothed Body', *Fashion Theory* 21/5 (2017), pp. 573–93; Marco Pecorari, *Fashion Remains: The Epistemic Potential of Fashion Ephemera*, PhD diss. (Stockholm University, 2016); Eugénie Shinkle, 'Fashion's Digital Body: Seeing and Feeling in Fashion Interactives', in D. Bartlett, S. Cole and A. Rocamora (eds), *Fashion Media: Past and Present* (London: Bloomsbury, 2013), pp. 175 –83.
47. Caroline Evans and Lorraine Gamman, 'The Gaze Revisited, or Reviewing Queer Viewing', in P. Burston and C. Richardson (eds), *A Queer Romance: Lesbians, Gay Men and Popular Culture* (London: Routledge, 1995), pp. 13–56.
48. Holly Shackleton, 'The Female Gaze Issue', *i-D* (no. 344, Pre-fall 2016), p. 36. Morna Laing has explored the way women 'read' images of women in different ways, drawing upon the method of reception studies. See Morna Laing, 'Between Image and Spectator: Reception Studies as Visual Methodology', *Fashion Theory* 22/1 (2018), pp. 5–30.

49. Agnès Rocamora, 'Personal Fashion Blogs: Screens and Mirrors in Digital Self-portraits', *Fashion Theory* 15/4 (2011), pp. 407–24.
50. Indeed, this was a point made by Shelagh Young in the late 1980s. See Shelagh Young, 'Feminism and the Politics of Power: Whose Gaze Is It Anyway?', in L. Gamman and M. Marshment (eds), *The Female Gaze: Women as Viewers of Popular Culture* (London: The Women's Press, 1988), pp. 173–88.
51. Such an approach is essential if rigour is to be maintained in interdisciplinary research, as Mieke Bal has argued. See Mieke Bal, *Travelling Concepts in the Humanities: A Rough Guide* (Toronto: University of Toronto Press, 2002).
52. Michel Foucault, *The Will to Knowledge: The History of Sexuality*, vol.1, trans. R. Hurley (London: Penguin (1998 [1976]).
53. Sean Nixon, 'Exhibiting Masculinity', in S. Hall (ed), *Representation: Cultural Representations and Signifying Practices* (London: Sage, 1997), p. 321.
54. Rosemary Betterton, 'Introduction: Feminism, Femininity and Representation', in R. Betterton (ed), *Looking On: Femininity in the Visual Arts and Media* (London: Pandora, 1987), pp. 1–17.
55. Judith Butler, *Bodies That Matter* (London and New York: Routledge, 2011 [1993]), p. 59.
56. Ibid., p. 59.
57. Ibid., p. 59.
58. Ibid., p. xxix.
59. Ibid., p. xxix.
60. Ibid., p. 76.
61. Ibid., p. 60.
62. Tish Weinstock, 'What Is the Relevance of the Male and Female Gaze in a World Where Gender Is Fluid', *i-D*, 21 November 2016. Available at https://i-d.vice.com/en_uk/article/7xvg39/reuel-lara-in-a-world-where-gender-is-fluid-what-is-the-relevance-of-the-male-and-female-gaze (accessed 18 March 2019).
63. Mulvey, 'Visual Pleasure and Narrative Cinema', p. 8.
64. Ibid., p. 6.
65. McRobbie, *The Aftermath of Feminism*, p. 99.
66. Mulvey, 'Visual Pleasure and Narrative Cinema', p. 6.
67. Jennifer C. Nash, 'Re-thinking Intersectionality', *Feminist Review* 89 (2008), pp. 1–15, p. 2.
68. See Marcel Stoetzler, 'Intersectional Individuality: Georg Simmel's Concept of "The Intersection of Social Circles" and the Emancipation of Women', *Sociological Inquiry* 86/2 (2016), pp. 216–40.
69. The conference included and attracted other fascinating intersectional approaches to looking, e.g. the ageing body, that we were unfortunately unable

to include in the present volume. Please refer to the following website for the book of abstracts: Revisiting the Gaze, 'Programme', 2017. Available at https://revisitingthegaze.wordpress.com (accessed 15 March 2019).

70. Gamman and Marshment (eds), *The Female Gaze.*

71. The debates relating to the gendered power dynamic of looking and being-looked-at are rekindled in Jacki Willson's own work on performance and feminism published in 2008 and 2015 respectively. See Jacki Willson, *The Happy Stripper: Pleasures and Politics of the New Burlesque* (London: I.B. Tauris, 2008) and Jacki Willson, *Being Gorgeous: Feminism, Sexuality and the Pleasures of the Visual* (London: I.B. Tauris, 2015).

72. hooks, *Black Looks.*

73. Lorraine O'Grady, 'Olympia's Maid: Reclaiming Black Female Subjectivity', *Afterimage* 20/1 (1992).

74. Sander L. Gilman, 'Black Bodies, White Bodies: Toward an Iconography of Female Sexuality in Late Nineteenth-Century Art, Medicine and Literature', in H.L. Gates Jnr (ed), *Race, Writing and Difference* (Chicago: The University of Chicago Press, 1986), pp. 136 –50.

75. Amelia Jones (ed), *The Feminism and Visual Culture Reader* (London and New York: Routledge, 2003). This is an important edited collection of essays exploring ways of looking. Although it was a comprehensive overview of theories of spectatorship, it was rooted in the discipline of art history so therefore excluded important work that had been developing from within Fashion Studies: e.g. Reina Lewis's 'Looking Good: The Lesbian Gaze and Fashion Imagery', *Feminist Review*, 55, Consuming Cultures (Spring 1997), pp. 92–109; Evans and Gamman's work on the gaze ('The Gaze Revisited') and Gamman's book, *The Female Gaze*, which she co-edited with Margaret Marshment. Indeed, these excluded texts form the backbone of this collection in seeking to situate the politics of looking at the female body from within a Fashion Studies context.

76. hooks, *Black Looks.*

77. Evans and Gamman, 'The Gaze Revisited'.

78. Lewis, 'Looking Good', p. 96.

79. Reina Lewis and Katrina Rolley, 'Ad(dressing) the Dyke: Lesbian Looks and Lesbian Looking', in P. Horne and R. Lewis (eds), *Outlooks: Lesbian and Gay Sexualities and Visual Cultures* (London and New York: Routledge, 1996), p. 179.

80. Rosalind Gill, 'Beyond the "Sexualization of Culture" Thesis: An Intersectional Analysis of "Sixpacks," "Midriffs" and "Hot Lesbians" in Advertising', *Sexualities* 12/2 (2009), pp. 137–60.

81. Deborah Jermyn, 'Pretty Past It? Interrogating the Post-feminist Makeover of Ageing, Style, and Fashion', *Feminist Media Studies* 16/4 (2016), pp. 573–89, p. 579.

82. Ibid., p. 580.

83. Ibid.
84. Julia Twigg, 'How Does Vogue Negotiate Age?: Fashion, the Body, and the Older Woman', *Fashion Theory* 14/4 (2010), pp. 471–90.
85. Reina Lewis, 'Uncovering Modesty: Dejabis and Dewigies Expanding the Parameters of the Modest Fashion Blogosphere', *Fashion Theory* 19/2 (2015), pp. 243–69.
86. Laura Mulvey, 'Introduction: 1970s Feminist Film Theory and the Obsolescent Object', in L. Mulvey and A. Backman Rogers (eds), *Feminisms: Diversity, Difference, and Multiplicity in Contemporary Film Cultures* (Amsterdam: Amsterdam University Press, 2015), pp. 21–2. This was a volume that sought to bring together diverse and plural perspectives on feminism and film, taking stock of changes in the cultural landscape since the 1970s.
87. Ibid.
88. Reina Lewis, 'Veils and Sales: Muslims and the Spaces of Postcolonial Fashion Retail', *Fashion Theory* 11/4 (2007), pp. 423–41, p. 426. Lewis discusses this in relation to Joanne Entwistle's ideas of 'situated bodily practice', 2000: p. 4. See Joanne Entwistle, *The Fashioned Body: Fashion, Dress and Modern Social Theory* (Cambridge: Polity, 2000).
89. Mulvey, *Death 24x a Second*, p. 9.
90. Ibid., p. 165.
91. Ibid., p. 18.
92. Kelli Fuery, *New Media: Culture and Image* (Basingstoke and New York: Palgrave Macmillan, 2009).
93. Baer, 'Redoing Feminism'; Sarah Banet-Weiser, *Empowered: Popular Feminism and Popular Misogyny* (USA: Duke University Press, 2018); Michelle Rodino-Colocino, '#YesAllWomen: Intersectional Mobilization against Sexual Assault Is Radical (Again)', *Feminist Media Studies* 14/6 (2014), pp. 1113–15.
94. Rhea Ashley Hoskin, Kay E. Jenson and Karen L. Blair, 'Is Our Feminism Bullshit? The Importance of Intersectionality in Adopting a Feminist Identity', *Cogent Social Sciences*, 3 (2017), pp. 1–19.
95. Aristea Fotopoulou, 'Digital and Networked by Default? Women's Organisations and the Social Imaginary of Networked Feminism', *New Media & Society* 18/6 (2016), pp. 989–1005.
96. He For She (2016), 'Our Mission'. Available at http://www.heforshe.org/en/our-mission (accessed 10 March 2019).
97. Ms. Foundation, 'My Feminism Is', 2016. Available at http://forwomen.org/my-feminism-is/ (accessed 10 March 2019).
98. Baer, 'Redoing Feminism', p. 18. See also Fredrika Thelandersson. 'A Less Toxic Feminism: Can the Internet Solve the Age Old Question of How to Put Intersectional Theory into Practice?', *Feminist Media Studies* 14/3 (2014), pp. 527–30.

99. This hashtag was authored by an anonymous Muslim woman of colour, following the Isla Vista shootings in May 2014. According to Michelle Rodino-Colocino, the hashtag connected women globally and 'inspired self-reflexivity among feminists regarding intersectional inclusivity, and in so doing, spawns further hashtagged discourse'. See Rodino-Colocino, '#YesAllWomen', p. 1114.
100. Nicholas Mirzoeff, 'Appearance Unbound: Articulations of Co-presence in #BlackLivesMatter' in M. Bohr and B. Sliwinska (eds), *The Evolution of the Image: Political Action and the Digital Self* (New York and London: Routledge, 2018).
101. Hoskin, Jenson and Blair, 'Is Our Feminism Bullshit?', p. 10.
102. Alison Phipps, 'Whose Personal Is More Political? Experience in Contemporary Feminist Politics', *Feminist Theory*, 17/3 (2016), pp. 303–21.
103. Nathalie Weidhase, '"Beyoncé Feminism" and the Contestation of the Black Feminist Body', *Celebrity Studies* 6/1 (2015), pp. 128–31, p. 130.
104. Ibid., p. 130.
105. Ibid., p. 125.
106. Rosalind Gill, 'Post-postfeminism?: New Feminist Visibilities in Postfeminist Times', *Feminist Media Studies* 16/4 (2016), pp. 610–30, p. 616.
107. For reportage on her murder, see Jon Boone, '"She Feared No One": The Life and Death of Qandeel Baloch', *The Guardian*, 22 September 2017. Available at https://www.theguardian.com/world/2017/sep/22/qandeel-baloch-feared-no-one-life-and-death (accessed 10 March 2019).
108. Lewis, 'Uncovering Modesty', pp. 243–69, p. 244.
109. Derek Conrad Murray 'Notes to Self: The Visual Culture of Selfies in the Age of Social Media', *Consumption, Markets and Culture* 18/6 (2015), pp. 490–516, p. 491.
110. Ibid., p. 492.
111. Ibid., p. 499.
112. Francesca Romeo quoted in ibid., p. 503.
113. Ibid., p. 512.
114. Ibid., p. 490.
115. Ibid., p. 490.
116. This hashtag was attached to 9,377 posts on Instagram on 28 June 2018.
117. Karin Lesnik-Oberstein (ed), *The Last Taboo: Women and Body Hair* (Manchester: Manchester University Press, 2006).
118. Fraser, *Fortunes of Feminism*, p. 218.
119. Rosalind Gill, *Gender and the Media* (Cambridge: Polity, 2007), p. 40.
120. Gill, *Gender and the Media*; McRobbie, *The Aftermath of Feminism.*

121. Baer 'Redoing Feminism', p. 19.
122. Ibid., p. 19.
123. Adrienne Evans and Sarah Riley, *Technologies of Sexiness: Sex, Identity and Consumer Culture* (Oxford: Oxford University Press, 2014), p. 43.
124. Minh-Ha T. Pham, '"I Click and Post and Breathe, Waiting for Others to See What I See": On #FeministSelfies, Outfit Photos, and Networked Vanity', *Fashion Theory* 19/2 (2015), pp. 221–41. Other positive perspectives of this from other disciplines include Katrin Tiidenberg and Edgar Gòmez Cruz, 'Selfies, Image and the Re-making of the Body', *Body & Society* 21/4 (2015), pp. 77–102; Valerie Gannon and Andrea Prothero, 'Beauty Blogger Selfies as Authenticating Practices', *European Journal of Marketing*, 50/9–10 (2016), pp. 1858–78.
125. Pham, '"I Click and Post and Breathe, Waiting for Others to See What I See"', ibid., p. 224.
126. Banet-Weiser, *Empowered.*
127. Anne Burns, 'Creepshots and Power: Covert Sexualised Photography, Online Communities and the Maintenance of Gender Inequality', in M. Bohr and B. Sliwinska (eds), *The Evolution of the Image: Political Action and the Digital Self* (New York and London: Routledge, 2018), pp. 27–40.
128. Katie O'Malley, 'Upskirting: What Is It and Why Has It Taken So Long to Be Made Illegal?', *The Independent*, 16 January 2019. Available at https://www.independent.co.uk/life-style/women/upskirting-explained-law-rules-criminal-offence-photos-skirt-consent-women-gina-martin-a8401011.html (accessed 24 January 2019).
129. *The Guardian*, 'Upskirting Happened to Me and Now I'm Fighting to Change the Law', *YouTube*, 15 June 2018. Available at https://www.youtube.com/watch?v=Y-ica8bbyQs (accessed 10 March 2019).
130. The year 2019 saw the publication of two political interventions in the field: *Fashion and Postcolonial Critique*, edited by Elke Gaugele and Monica Titton, and *Fashion and Politics*, edited by Djurdja Bartlett. Furthermore, identity politics have been brought particularly to the fore in the Palgrave series on Fashion and the Body, edited by Jane Tynan and Suzanne Biernoff.
131. bell hooks, *Outlaw Culture: Resisting Representations* (New York and London: Routledge, 1994), pp. 4–5.

Bibliography

Baer, Hester, 'Redoing Feminism: Digital Activism, Body Politics, and Neoliberalism', *Feminist Media Studies* 16/1 (2016), pp. 17–34.

Bal, Mieke, *Travelling Concepts in the Humanities: A Rough Guide* (Toronto: University of Toronto Press, 2002).

Bancroft, Alison, *Fashion and Psychoanalysis* (London and New York: I.B. Tauris, 2012).
Banet-Weiser, Sarah, *Empowered: Popular Feminism and Popular Misogyny* (USA: Duke University Press, 2018).
Barker, Jennifer M., *The Tactile Eye: Touch and the Cinematic Experience* (Berkeley, Los Angeles and London: University of California Press, 2009).
Barthes, Roland, *The Fashion System*, trans. M. Ward and R. Howard (California and London: University of California Press, 1990 [1967]).
Bartlett, Djurdja (ed), *Fashion and Politics* (New Haven: Yale University Press, 2019).
Berger, John, *Ways of Seeing* (London: Penguin, 2008 [1972]).
Betterton, Rosemary, 'Introduction: Feminism, Femininity and Representation', in R. Betterton (ed), *Looking On: Femininity in the Visual* Arts *and* Media (London: Pandora, 1987), pp. 1–17.
Boone, Jon, '"She Feared No One": The Life and Death of Qandeel Baloch', *The Guardian*, 22 September 2017. Available at https://www.theguardian.com/world/2017/sep/22/qandeel-baloch-feared-no-one-life-and-death (accessed 10 March 2019).
Bourdieu, Pierre, *Distinction: A Social Critique of the Judgement of Taste*, trans. R. Nice (Oxon: Routledge, 1986).
Bruzzi, Stella, *Undressing Cinema: Clothing and Identity in the Movies* (London: Routledge, 1997).
Bull, Michael, Paul Gilroy, David Howes and Douglas Kahn, "Introducing Sensory Studies"', *The Senses and Society* 1/1 (2006), pp. 5–7.
Burns, Anne, 'Creepshots and Power: Covert Sexualised Photography, Online Communities and the Maintenance of Gender Inequality', in M. Bohr and B. Sliwinska (eds), *The Evolution of the Image: Political Action and the Digital Self* (New York and London: Routledge, 2018), pp. 27–40.
Butler, Judith, *Bodies That Matter* (London and New York: Routledge, 2011 [1993]).
Cochrane, Kira, 'The Fourth Wave of Feminism: Meet the Rebel Women', *The Guardian*, 10 December 2013. Available at http://www.theguardian.com/world/2013/dec/10/fourth-wave-feminism-rebel-women (accessed 21 September 2015).
Entwistle, Joanne, *The Fashioned Body: Fashion, Dress and Modern Social Theory* (Cambridge: Polity, 2000).
Evans, Adrienne and Sarah Riley, *Technologies of Sexiness: Sex, Identity and Consumer Culture* (Oxford: Oxford University Press, 2014).
Evans, Caroline, 'Masks, Mirrors and Mannequins: Elsa Schiaparelli and the Decentered Subject', *Fashion Theory* 3/1 (1999), pp. 3–32.
Evans, Caroline and Lorraine Gamman, 'The Gaze Revisited, or Reviewing Queer Viewing', in P. Burston and C. Richardson (eds), *A Queer Romance: Lesbians, Gay Men and Popular Culture* (London: Routledge, 1995), pp.13–56.
Flügel, John C. *The Psychology of Clothes* (London: Hogarth, 1933).
Fotopoulou, Aristea, 'Digital and Networked by Default? Women's Organisations and the Social Imaginary of Networked Feminism', *New Media & Society* 18/6 (2016), pp. 989–1005.

Foucault, Michel, *The Will to Knowledge: The History of Sexuality*, vol.1, trans. R. Hurley (London: Penguin, 1998 [1976]).
Fuery, Kelli, *New Media: Culture and Image* (Basingstoke and New York: Palgrave Macmillan, 2009).
Fraser, Nancy, *Fortunes of Feminism: From State-Managed Capitalism to Neoliberal Crisis* (London: Verso, 2013).
Gamman, Lorraine and Margaret Marshment (eds), *The Female Gaze: Women as Viewers of Popular Culture* (London: The Women's Press, 1988).
Gannon, Valerie and Andrea Prothero, 'Beauty Blogger Selfies as Authenticating Practices', *European Journal of Marketing*, 50/9–10 (2016), pp. 1858–78.
Garb, Tamar, '"Visual Pleasure at 40" Dossier', *Screen* 56/4 (Winter 2015), pp. 473–4.
Gaugele, Elke and Monica Titton (eds), *Fashion and Postcolonial Critique* (Berlin: Sternberg Press, 2019).
Gill, Rosalind, *Gender and the Media* (Cambridge: Polity, 2007).
Gill, Rosalind, 'Beyond the "Sexualization of Culture" Thesis: An Intersectional Analysis of "Sixpacks," "Midriffs" and "Hot Lesbians" in Advertising', *Sexualities* 12/2 (2009), pp. 137–60.
Gilman, Sander L., 'Black Bodies, White Bodies: Toward an Iconography of Female Sexuality in Late Nineteenth-Century Art, Medicine and Literature', in H. L. Gates Jnr (ed), *Race, Writing and Difference* (Chicago: The University of Chicago Press, 1986), pp. 136–50.
The Guardian, 'Upskirting Happened to Me and Mow I'm Fighting to Change the Law', *YouTube*, 15 June 2018. Available at https://www.youtube.com/ watch?v=Y-ica8bbyQs (accessed 10 March 2019).
He For She, 'Our Mission' 2016. Available at http://www.heforshe.org/en/our-mission (link broken).
hooks, bell, *Black Looks: Race and Representation* (Boston: South End Press, 1992).
hooks, bell, *Outlaw Culture: Resisting Representations* (New York and London: Routledge, 1994).
Hoskin, Rhea Ashley, Kay E. Jenson and Karen L. Blair, 'Is Our Feminism Bullshit? The Importance of Intersectionality in Adopting a Feminist Identity', *Cogent Social Sciences* 3 (2017), pp. 1–19.
Irigaray, Luce, *Speculum of the Other Woman*, trans. G.C. Gill (Ithaca, NY: Cornell University Press, 1985).
Jermyn, Deborah, 'Pretty Past It? Interrogating the Post-feminist Makeover of Ageing, Style, and Fashion', *Feminist Media Studies* 16/4 (2016), pp. 573–89, p. 579.
Jones, Amelia and Nicholas Mirzoeff (eds), *The Feminism and Visual Culture Reader* (London: Routledge, 2003).
Laing, Morna, 'Between Image and Spectator: Reception Studies as Visual Methodology', *Fashion Theory* 22/1 (2018), pp. 5–30.
Lesnik-Oberstein, Karin (ed), *The Last Taboo: Women and Body Hair* (Manchester: Manchester University Press, 2006).
Lewis, Reina, *Gendering Orientalism: Race, Femininity and Representation* (London and New York: Routledge, 1996).
Lewis, Reina, 'Looking Good: The Lesbian Gaze and Fashion Imagery', *Feminist Review* 55, Consuming Cultures (Spring 1997), pp. 92–109.

Lewis, Reina, 'Uncovering Modesty: Dejabis and Dewigies Expanding the Parameters of the Modest Fashion Blogosphere', *Fashion Theory* 19/2 (2015), pp. 243–69.

Lewis, Reina, and Katrina Rolley, 'Ad(dressing) the Dyke: Lesbian Looks and Lesbian Looking', in P. Horne and R. Lewis (eds), *Outlooks: Lesbian and Gay Sexualities and Visual Cultures* (London and New York: Routledge, 1996), pp. 178–89

Marks, Laura U., *The Skin of the Film: Intercultural Cinema, Embodiment and the Senses* (Durham and London: Duke University Press, 2000).

McRobbie, Angela, *The Aftermath of Feminism: Gender, Culture and Social Change* (London: Sage, 2009).

Mirzoeff, Nicholas, 'Appearance Unbound: Articulations of Co-presence in #BlackLivesMatter', in M. Bohr and B. Sliwinska (eds), *The Evolution of the Image: Political Action and the Digital Self* (New York and London: Routledge, 2018), pp. 76–88.

Ms. Foundation, 'My Feminism Is', 2016. Available at http://forwomen.org/my-feminism-is/ (accessed 10 March 2019).

Mulvey, Laura, 'Visual Pleasure and Narrative Cinema', *Screen* 16/3 (Autumn 1975), pp. 6–18.

Mulvey, Laura, 'Afterthoughts on "Visual Pleasure and Narrative Cinema" Inspired by "Duel in the Sun" (King Vidor, 1946)', *Framework: The Journal of Cinema and Media* 15/17 (Summer 1981), pp. 12–15.

Mulvey, Laura, *Fetishism and Curiosity* (London: British Film Institute, 1996).

Mulvey, Laura, *Death 24x a Second: Stillness and the Moving Image* (London: Reaktion, 2006).

Mulvey, Laura, 'Introduction: 1970s Feminist Film Theory and the Obsolescent Object', in L. Mulvey and A. Backman Rogers (eds), *Feminisms: Diversity, Difference, and Multiplicity in Contemporary Film Cultures* (Amsterdam: Amsterdam University Press, 2015), pp. 21–2.

Mulvey, Laura, '"Visual Pleasure at 40" Dossier', *Screen* 56/4 (Winter 2015), pp. 481–5.

Mulvey, Laura, 'Visual Pleasure at 40: Laura Mulvey in Discussion (Extract) | BFI', *YouTube*. Available at https://www.youtube.com/watch?v=IWAJdj3cPvA (accessed 7 March 2019).

Munro, Ealasaid, 'Feminism: A Fourth Wave?', *Political Insight* 4/2 (2013), pp. 22–5.

Murray, Derek Conrad, 'Notes to Self: The Visual Culture of Selfies in the Age of Social Media', *Consumption, Markets and Culture* 18/6 (2015), pp. 490–516.

Nash, Jennifer C., 'Re-thinking Intersectionality', *Feminist Review* 89 (2008), pp. 1–15.

Negrin, Llewellyn, 'Maurice Merleau-Ponty: The Corporeal Experience of Fashion', in A. Rocamora and A. Smelik (eds), *Thinking through Fashion: A Guide to Key Theorists* (London and New York: I.B. Tauris, 2016), pp. 115–31.

Nixon, Sean, 'Exhibiting Masculinity', in S. Hall (ed), *Representation: Cultural Representations and Signifying Practices* (London: Sage, 1997), pp. 293–331.

O'Grady, Lorraine, 'Olympia's Maid: Reclaiming Black Female Subjectivity', *Afterimage* 20/1 (1992).

O'Malley, Katie, 'Upskirting: What Is It and Why Has It Taken So Long to Be Made Illegal?', *The Independent*, 16 January 2019. Available at https://www.independent.co.uk/life-style/women/upskirting-explained-law-rules-criminal-offence-photos-skirt-consent-women-gina-martin-a8401011.html (accessed 24 January 2019).

Pecorari, Marco, *Fashion Remains: The Epistemic Potential of Fashion Ephemera*, PhD diss. (Stockholm University, 2016).

Pham, Minh-Ha T., '"I Click and Post and Breathe, Waiting for Others to See What I See": On #FeministSelfies, Outfit Photos, and Networked Vanity', *Fashion Theory* 19/2 (2015), pp. 221–41.

Phipps, Alison, 'Preface', *Screen* 56/4 (Winter 2015), p. 471.

Phipps, Alison, 'Whose Personal Is More Political? Experience in Contemporary Feminist Politics', *Feminist Theory*, 17/3 (2016), pp. 303–21.

Revisiting the Gaze, 'Programme', 2017. Available at https://revisitingthegaze.wordpress.com/about/ (accessed 15 March 2019).

Roach, Jacqui and Petal Felix, 'Black Looks', in L. Gamman and M. Marshment (eds), *The Female Gaze: Women as Viewers of Popular Culture* (London: The Women's Press, 1988), pp. 130–42.

Rocamora, Agnès, 'Personal Fashion Blogs: Screens and Mirrors in Digital Self-portraits', *Fashion Theory* 15/4 (2011), pp. 407–24.

Rodino-Colocino, Michelle, '#YesAllWomen: Intersectional Mobilization against Sexual Assault Is Radical (Again)', *Feminist Media Studies* 14/6 (2014), pp. 1113–15.

Ruggerone, Lucia, 'The Feeling of Being Dressed: Affect Studies and the Clothed Body', *Fashion Theory* 21/5 (2017), pp. 573–93.

Said, Edward W., *Orientalism* (London: Penguin, 2003).

Shackleton, Holly, 'The Female Gaze Issue', *i-D* (no. 344, Pre-fall 2016).

Shinkle, Eugénie, 'Fashion's Digital Body: Seeing and Feeling in Fashion Interactives', in D. Bartlett, S. Cole and A. Rocamora (eds), *Fashion Media: Past and Present* (London: Bloomsbury, 2013), pp. 175–83.

Sobchack, Vivian, *The Address of the Eye: A Phenomenology of Film Experience* (New Jersey and Oxford: Princeton University Press, 1992).

Stoetzler, Marcel, 'Intersectional Individuality: Georg Simmel's Concept of "The Intersection of Social Circles" and the Emancipation of Women', *Sociological Inquiry* 86/2 (2016), pp. 216–40.

Thelandersson, Fredrika, 'A Less Toxic Feminism: Can the Internet Solve the Age Old Question of How to Put Intersectional Theory into Practice?', *Feminist Media Studies* 14/3 (2014), pp. 527–30.

Tiidenberg, Katrin, and Edgar Gòmez Cruz, 'Selfies, Image and the Re-making of the Body', *Body & Society* 21/4 (2015), pp. 77–102.

Twigg, Julia, 'How Does Vogue Negotiate Age?: Fashion, the Body, and the Older Woman', *Fashion Theory* 14/4 (2010), pp. 471–90.

Walker, John A. and Sarah Chaplin, *Visual Culture: An Introduction* (Manchester and New York: Manchester University Press, 1997).

Weidhase, Nathalie, '"Beyoncé Feminism" and the Contestation of the Black Feminist Body', *Celebrity Studies* 6/1 (2015), pp. 128–31.

Weinstock, Tish, 'What Is the Relevance of the Male and Female Gaze in a World Where Gender Is Fluid', *i-D*, 21 November 2016. Available at https://i-d.vice.com/en_uk/article/7xvg39/reuel-lara-in-a-world-where-gender-is-fluid-what-is-the-relevance-of-the-male-and-female-gaze (accessed 18 March 2019).

Willson, Jacki, *The Happy Stripper: Pleasures and Politics of the New Burlesque* (London: I.B. Tauris, 2008).

Willson, Jacki, *Being Gorgeous: Feminism, Sexuality and the Pleasures of the Visual* (London: I.B. Tauris, 2015).

Wilson, Emma, '"Visual Pleasure at 40" Dossier', *Screen* 56/4 (Winter 2015), pp. 479–81.

Young, Shelagh, 'Feminism and the Politics of Power: Whose Gaze Is It Anyway?', in L. Gamman and M. Marshment (eds), *The Female Gaze: Women as Viewers of Popular Culture* (London; The Women's Press, 1988), pp. 173–88.

PART I

LOOKING: THE OPTIC AND THE HAPTIC

CHAPTER 2
DOUBLE ACTS: OSCILLATING BETWEEN OPTICAL AND HAPTIC VISUALITY IN A DIGITAL AGE

Mo Throp and Maria Walsh

Prologue

In this chapter, we engage in a conversation about female subjectivity in the field of vision in relation to both optical and haptic visuality. Beginning with Laura Mulvey's 'Visual Pleasure and Narrative Cinema', we each lay out introductory terrain from which we then go on to perform our 'double act' as a dialogue that moves to-and-fro between us. Assembling examples from film, photography, the internet and digital fine art video, we claim that the issue of relating to the image for female subjects, both on- and off-screen, is one of being too close or too distant. We explore these identificatory positionalities of distance and proximity in relation to theories of the masquerade and the haptic. Our 'double act' culminates with our discussion of works by several female video artists, which enables us to go beyond the seemingly debilitating notions of the gaze. To conclude, we argue that digital strategies generate a productive oscillation between distance and proximity for female subjects in relation to their image.

> In a world ordered by sexual imbalance, pleasure in looking has been split between active/male and passive/female. [Women] connote *to-be-looked-at-ness*. [...][1] The man [...] emerges [...] as the bearer of the look of the spectator.[2]

Act I

Maria Walsh: Laura Mulvey mentions the term 'male gaze' only once in her classic essay 'Visual Pleasure and Narrative Cinema' (1975), yet this catchphrase has become everyday parlance. And while it is the case that in patriarchal social structures, the gaze may be coded and/or valued as male, feminist theorists have long argued that 'the gaze' is culturally marked and embodied in much more plural ways. Before we go on to develop this latter point in our discussion, I would like to posit two things.

Firstly, I'd like to state from the outset that the ubiquitous use of Mulvey's term dehistoricizes it and makes it seem as if the 'male gaze' is inevitably embedded in Western society. Take, for example, an article from *The Guardian* from 1999, 'She's Pregnant and He's Got His Fists Raised. Guess Who's the Victim …', by the novelist Irvine Welsh. Referring to the film adaption of his book of short stories *The Acid House*, he claims that while some of his strong female characters are doing things for themselves, they are subject to a 'male gaze' both in and outside the film. In taking this fallback position, Welsh specifically refers to Mulvey's 'seminal notion of the "gaze" of the camera being primarily male'.[3] This example of the migration of 'theoretical concepts' to popular cultural discourse underscores the general assumption that we know what the 'gaze' is, for instance, that it is synonymous with the control of the look and male empowerment and that therefore we do not need to interrogate these preconceptions. Oppositional responses to the 'male gaze', for example, a female gaze and a queer gaze, as well as positional ones, such as a surveillance gaze or a virtual gaze, replicate this notion of control, thereby setting up a counter-positional binary that I think is unhelpful.

Secondly, I'd like us to return to the letter of Mulvey's essay to see if the moments of complexity within it might offer more productive ways of considering structures and ways of looking to assist us in thinking about visibility in contemporary moving image art practices in which female bodies appear. I'm thinking in particular about Mulvey's nuancing of the structures of vision in her essay with regard to the psychoanalytic concepts of fetishistic voyeurism and narcissistic imaginary identification. While these structures of vision are both associated with control and power, in psychoanalytic thinking, they are not naturally gendered and both engender pleasures that are not necessarily 'male'.

Mo Throp: We are not, then, just concerned here with the relevance of continuing to debate the issue of an active male gaze and the passive 'to-be-looked-at-ness' of the woman but with discussing more productive ways of considering structures and ways of looking – especially in current art practices by women – rather than exploring possibilities for reclaiming the feminine as an active role or how to assert a female sensibility in order to empower the female subject trapped in this debilitating equation. Questions we might consider are: How can we revisit this debilitating scene of gender inequality and, more urgently, move beyond this binary thinking? Can we reconsider the structure of subjectivity beyond the constraints of recognition and hopefully address new forms of contestation? How might feminist interventions and these new forms of contestation by artists, rather than perpetuating Second-Wave feminist demands for a more equitable distribution of those dominant forms, continue to address these unequal operations of power and control and open up new kinds of relations? Elaborating those accounts of fetishistic voyeurism and narcissistic imaginary identification might help us begin to address this.

Maria Walsh: Mulvey is referring to the heyday of Hollywood cinema which is a different *dispositif* from artists' practices in terms of authorship, distribution, histories and reception, though both can be invested in visual pleasure and the seductive tropes of the (moving) image that are propped on fetishism and narcissism. At the time and in the context that Mulvey wrote her essay, psychoanalytic theory was seen by some socialist feminists as an analytic tool to enable a political consciousness desirous of social change. It no longer has this currency and terms such as 'fetishism' and 'narcissism' are bandied about as surface descriptors especially in relation to the fashioned body. But Mulvey, leaning heavily on Freud's 'Three Essays on the Theory of Sexuality' and incorporating a then recent English translation of Jacques Lacan's 'The Mirror-Stage' (1949),[4] was using these terms structurally to describe unconscious processes of looking and being.

In 'Three Essays', Freud refers to scopophilic pleasure as a pleasure which arises from using another person as an object of sexual stimulation through sight. A cursory reading of Mulvey equates this scopophilic pleasure, which is the foundation of voyeurism, with a male gaze, however there is nothing intrinsically male about this mode of visual pleasure. Scopophilia is a component instinct of sexuality which means that the drive to see is one mode of its expression, the desire to be seen another, and therefore the activity/passivity binary between voyeurism and exhibitionism is troubled in Freud's account.[5] Although, given his historical context, Freud did attribute fetishism to men, saying that the only possibility for female fetishism was perhaps in relation to clothes, which, while curiously interesting, is much too reductive.[6]

Narcissistic identification also occurs for both male and female spectators. In Mulvey's heteronormative analysis, narcissistic identification occurs for both sexes with the hero as the master of narrative space and controller of the look. To narcissistically identify with the woman is a masochistic identification with a seductive, though static, image that traps the female spectator in the spectacle. This consigns her to the realm of the (commodity) fetish whose destiny is either to hover eternally at a remove from social relations or be consumed in them.[7] Either case is destructive.

Mo Throp: I would like to address this issue in relation to voyeurism and exhibitionism by considering the responses when, during her junior year at Dickinson College in Carlisle, Pennsylvania, the 19-year-old Jennifer Ringley, acquiring new technology, turned the camera on herself. On 3 April 1996, she had installed the newly available webcam in her dorm room in her hall of residence and, live-streaming images of herself in that room, launched *JenniCam*, one of the first such sites that continuously and voluntarily surveyed a private life. No doubt realizing the incredible potential, Ringley exploits people's fascination in watching her, later renaming the site www.Boudoir.org[8] and charging her viewers.[9] The camera remained on twenty-four hours a day capturing one image scrolling down every three minutes. Ringley says she answered the emailed responses to her site from her followers and whatever titillation the site might suggest, she says she had very few requests to strip or perform sex acts from her viewers. In fact, she says that she installed it because she felt lonely and knowing that she was being watched made her feel more secure.

In his article about the site 'Jenni's Room: Exhibitionism and Solitude', Victor Burgin describes Ringley's exploitation of this new technology as an acting out of the familiar role of the woman – as exhibitionist – and the inevitable fascination with this by the voyeur – the traditional male role.[10] Burgin continues this interpretation of exhibitionism by likening her actions to that of the male exhibitionist who exposes his penis in the street. So what is at issue for Burgin is Ringley's supposed exhibitionism in a sexual sense. He elaborates by expounding some Freudian psychoanalytic theory.

> The small child first looks at parts of his or her own body associated with sexual pleasure. The child later develops a curiosity about the corresponding sites in the bodies of others. He or she then identifies with the look that the other gives and offers his or her own body to this other look. In effect, the exhibitionist proposes a childish exchange: 'I'll show you mine if you'll show me yours.'[11]

Though noting that it is questionable whether Ringley had any interest in such an exchange (she had no interest in seeing those who viewed her site), Burgin proposes that the screen here therefore functions as a mirror – she only sees the image of herself reflected back to her – the one captured by the camcorder; she does not see who is watching her though she knows that the image is available every three minutes 24/7 on the World Wide Web (at its peak, she has 4 million hits a day). She knows she is watched, answering the emails of those who follow her site. The camera becomes her constant companion; in seeing herself on the screen, as a mirror, she also knows that she is being observed. From the punters' side of the screen the camera becomes a window, offering us the opportunity to snoop as the Peeping Tom, taking our enjoyment in our own space knowing that we cannot be seen; we are safe from being exposed as voyeurs.

Though scopophilia, as you have outlined, has two facets – an active form in which the subject looks at an object and a passive form in which the subject desires to be looked at by some other subject – Freud claims that both these facets derive from a more primitive narcissistic phase in which the subject takes a part of its own body as its (exhibitionistic) object. In this autoerotic scopophilia, active and passive, subject and object, remain blurred, undecidedly one and the other. So Ringley, in the possibly innocent act of installing her webcam in order to feel secure, could be said to be initially more narcissistic – Freud's more primitive phase of scopophilia being acted out here. There is no initial concern for the other side of the 'window' though her security is dependent on a benign look, on being looked at in a caring manner.

Burgin continues in his essay to elaborate on this scene of the exchange (or not) of looks. Referencing psychoanalyst D.W. Winnicott's proposition that one only becomes a subject as one is recognized, he proposes that the viewer or user of *JenniCam* proffers the look that comes from the outside which functions to put the subject 'in its place', that is it bestows a subjectivity. This is the look of the mother's face, the look that the infant receives. Burgin describes two amusing examples given by Winnicott. The first is of a woman (of striking appearance) who reported, in therapy, that she had trouble in being seen in a way that made her feel she existed and another who wakes up every morning depressed until she 'puts on her face', Winnicott remarking that this '"only exaggerates what is normal. The exaggeration is of the task of *getting the mirror to notice and approve*". Jenni is noticed and approved of'.[12] The watchful face of the mother is confirmed upon her but she is still (childishly) dependent on the ability to be alone only 'in the presence of someone'. Burgin elaborates this further in relation to Winnicott's theorization of 'transitional space' as the space of play and experimentation for developing the capacity to be alone, a space which necessitates a sense of someone else being present. So Burgin suggests that in this case, under the gaze of her watchful mother, Jenni is investigating what it is to be a woman like her; she is posing the question of female sexuality. For Burgin this is staged in a place of transition between home and outside world – her dorm room.

Now this sounds all very benign until the question is raised – as many have – about a possible pornographic edge to this site – especially when Ringley renames it www.Boudoir.org and charges users. Increasingly bold, she admits to what she refers to as 'putting on shows' which entail dressing in garter belts and spike heels. Though from what information I can find she rather coyly jumps up and down on her bed in them – another child-like game, perhaps. What follows one of these 'shows', reportedly, is a death threat and a demand to perform a striptease. She closes the camera for a few days 'terrified'. It is difficult then to consider Ringley's continued use of her site as having such an innocent intention: feeling alone without it. The fact that she puts on 'shows' indicates that she is very aware of the sexual nature of the look of the other. There is maybe a shift from Freud's more primitive stage of scopophilia – an autoerotic narcissistic phase – to one of acknowledging the desire of the other: a voyeuristic demand for an exhibitionistic performance.

Act II

Maria Walsh: Your analysis of a shift from an autoerotic phase to an exhibitionist one reminds me of the dilemma identified by feminist film theorists following Mulvey. The issue for the female spectator, as Mary Ann Doane put it in the late 1980s, is the 'overpresence of the image, she is the image'.[13] In order to obviate this overpresence of the image which reduces her to a 'to-be-looked-at-ness', Doane used the concept of the masquerade as this configuration allows the female spectator both proximity to the image and the capacity to manufacture a distance from it. She says:

> The masquerade, in flaunting femininity, holds it at a distance. Womanliness is a mask which can be worn or removed. The masquerade's resistance to patriarchal positioning would therefore lie in its denial of the production of femininity as closeness, as presence to itself. […] Masquerade […] involves a realignment of femininity, the recovery, or more accurately, simulation of […] distance.[14]

One of the ways this occurs in film is through costume, as costume doubles the body akin to how the masquerade doubles representation by hyperbolizing what Doane calls the accoutrements of femininity. For instance, in Josef Von Sternberg's films, Marlene Dietrich demonstrates the representation of a woman's body via her performative veiling and unveiling of the body using paraphernalia such as hats with netting draped over the face and gloves that exaggerate the length of fingers. Masquerade offers a way for thinking of representations of the female body as a double inscription of femininity that moves between passivity and activity.

Interestingly, Mulvey moves close to Doane's articulation in her later essay 'A Phantasmagoria of the Female Body: The Work of Cindy Sherman' (1991), claiming that Sherman stages the veiling and unveiling characteristic of the process of fetishism as the oscillation between two contradictory views, that is anxiety and curiosity. Although Mulvey is ultimately pessimistic about Sherman's self-fetishization,[15] she also sees her citation of Hans Bellmer and art history as a means of creating a perspective on the proximity of the female artist/spectator to the image of woman. She says, 'The viewer looks, recognizes a style, doubts, does a double take, then recognizes that the style is a citation, and meanings shift and change their reference like shifting perceptions of perspective from an optical illusion.'[16] It is as if citation is operating as a kind of masquerade that might generate what John Fletcher writing on the masquerade calls a 'relay of alternative wishes and demands that re-routes the gaze of mastery'.[17] This would thereby open onto another scene of desire that would be more fluid. I think this re-routing of the gaze might be of interest today when the ability to manufacture a distance is in question in relation to digital image technologies which are all-pervasive. Although, as you point out, the position of power associated with voyeurism is more likely to be chosen. That said, the desire to exhibit oneself is also a powerful subject position. It is a demand to be looked at.

Mo Throp: Elizabeth Grosz notes that the subject is defined as that which is capable of being seen without necessarily being able to see either the observer or itself.[18] The possibility of being observed is always primary, the result of being placed in the field of the other, and this is equally open to both sexes. Vision, as you have already remarked, cannot therefore be only masculine; nevertheless, it must be noted, certain ways of using vision (for example, to objectify) may confirm and help produce patriarchal power relations. This is the line women have to negotiate daily with any form of sexual expression. The benign watchful look of the mother (or primary caregiver) can shift to the repressive regard – a judgemental gaze – of the father (the law of the father) to keep her in check – and as we know this can have catastrophic and traumatic outcomes for some women, for instance domestic violence, honour killings, even practices such as female genital mutilation (FGM). Jenni finds herself acting on the edge of such prohibition; we could say that she is testing out the borders of the cultural restrictions and rigid regulations which mark female sexuality in a patriarchal society. In this regard, *JenniCam*, named as the first life-caster, still remains open to both empowering and possibly debilitating possibilities for women. However, exploring the possibilities of a mutual exchange of gazes in the act of looking as a feminist goal might remain problematic with the continued use of the internet as it retains the same techno-sphere for the procurement and trade in women. There are increasingly frequent cases of online abuse of women who use the technology to express and explore their own subjectivity and this will remain so until some kind of responsibility is taken for those boundaries that the technology itself fails to regulate.

Maria Walsh: This seems pessimistic and perhaps forecloses the possibilities for re-routing 'the gaze of mastery' that I mentioned. While online conduct needs to be regulated further, this does not overrule the attraction of this space for women artists who are interested in performing their subjectivity.

Mo Throp: Well, *JenniCam* does represent possible uses and engagements with a medium within which women might find possible ways of producing erotic imagery to counter mainstream pornography and its stereotypical messaging. Even though Ringley failed to make such attempts, by keeping in email contact with those who watched her, she possibly kept a certain amount of control over this and exerted a certain amount of agency over her own identity. This site, though, hardly presented any evidence of possible transgressive enactments which might challenge structures of power and so ultimately ends up, I would suggest, reinforcing the usual patriarchal constructions of the female exhibitionist and the voyeuristic male consumer. However, the way in which *JenniCam* allowed us to see sexuality and gender being performed in daily life opened up a practical space in which the performativity of gender (as a cultural construct) can be more easily grasped.

Maria Walsh: There is another aspect to Burgin's analysis which I find potentially productive. Yes, there is voyeurism, but he also suggests that there is a re-enactment of transitional space in which Jenni's QuickCam becomes a transitional object for both Jenni and its viewers, male and female. Because the download speeds were inordinately slow, there being a three-minute delay before an image would have scrolled down fully, oftentimes the *JenniCam* screen was blank. Some people might wait obsessively for Jenni's reappearance, but Burgin proffers that the *JenniCam* window would be open along with other windows, for instance, other activities such as spreadsheets and banking. The *JenniCam*, therefore, provided a kind of comforting background. So, in a sense Jenni becomes like the mother who controls her absence and presence for the 'child', the *JenniCam* acting as a transitional space of play that enables the 'child' to tolerate 'her' absence.[19] In the case of internet behaviour, this 'child' is a community of diverse users, so the stasis and solitariness of voyeurism and exhibitionism are distributed in a networked field of relations where they are potentially more mobile. This impetus towards community-building is much greater in current internet practices which are built around identifications that can be shared and are both comforting and empowering for fans and performers alike, for example Ann Hirsch's YouTube video series *Scandalishious* (2008–9) – a series of webcam videos on YouTube in which she appears as a character called Caroline Benton. On the one hand, she could be said to update the masquerade as a double inscription of femininity in that she combines close-up flirtatious toying with the imagined audience on the other side of the webcam window with an ironic distance that allows her to perform some 'risky play'.[20]

In one vlog diary she writhes and shimmies to Bonnie Tyler's 'Total Eclipse of the Heart' wearing a skimpy pink bikini tube top and white skirt slip; in another, she splays her legs wearing a skintight leotard. Costume is important as is the location of her performances, which mainly take place in her bedroom, an intimate space in which she confesses her latest anxieties about her appearance and sexual desires. What makes Caroline's song and dance performances different from many of the millions of other young girls who offer their bodies to the anonymous gaze of online audiences is the fact that she is doing it as part of an art practice whose goal is to examine the conditions of contemporary representations of femininity partly by parodying them and partly by inhabiting them. However, not only does she risk being subject to the same conditions of reception as any other YouTube videos, for instance, garnering insulting comments and/or 'likes', but she also uses the platform and her persona as both a critique of the tropes of femininity and a means of self-help. Hirsch states:

> While I was growing up and becoming a woman, I hated myself. I knew I was smart but other than that I thought I was just a disgusting girl that no one could be sexually interested in. I started performing as *Scandalishious* because I was tired of feeling that way. Or at least, I was tired of appearing as though I felt that way. So I started pretending

> I thought I was sexy and I quickly learned that if I pretended to be confident, people would believe it. And then I actually became more confident as a result.[21]

Performing this character to address her own anxieties, Hirsch would receive response videos from 12-year-old girls imitating her, which, on the one hand, worried her in case it might make them vulnerable to exploitation, but which, on the other hand, she recognized as an important means of sexual self-expression that could be shared with other girls.[22]

Maybe Hirsch's work offers another example of an exploration of a narcissistic mobility that is open to transitional play and the multiplicity of sexual expression which later devolves into more stable voyeuristic positionalities? Although much of her later work is very literal, for example her video *vaginal canals* (2015), in which she superimposed her vagina onto footage of the canals of Venice in a conflation of (female) sex and art as commodity,[23] *Scandalishious* to my mind incorporates both a distance – in the adoption of a character or persona – and a discomforting narcissistic proximity to the female image. She is playing with the boundaries that you mentioned earlier in relation to *JenniCam*, but unlike Ringley, and this is in part due to the speed and ubiquity of vlogging technology today, Hirsch has a community of female fans who want to be like her. Hirsch is no benign mother but, on the other hand, her performed humorous naiveté gives others courage. It is ok to fail. You will still be liked.

Mo Throp: Yes, and it is also easy to argue that experimentations such as these could easily be reduced to the sum of their sexually explicit moments indirectly reinforcing patriarchal constructions through our acceptance of the interpretations of the voyeuristic male consumer. Ringley's site can also be seen as offering a counterpoint to beauty myths perpetuated in mainstream media that undermine the confidence and self-perceptions of many girls. The issue of how the woman might circumvent this relation to the subject's desire to be recognized by the other might be taken further by considering Laurel Nakadate's video work where she also turns the camera on herself and at the same time uses it as a way to make contact. Nakadate has also said that as a Japanese girl growing up in Iowa she felt an outsider, her feelings of loneliness increasing with her move to New York to begin her MA studies. There she became aware of lonely older men in the streets who would proposition her; she decides to turn the tables on them by inviting them to take part in a series of video works where she nevertheless remains in control of this 'collaboration'.

In an interview in *The Believer*, October 2006, Nakadate describes her video work and this 'collaborative' relationship:

> The *Birthday Party* video is one of the first that I made with strangers I met on the street. I wanted to make believe with them, to play pretend. These are men who live by themselves, who don't have anyone to care for them or anyone to care about. I wanted to put them in a situation where they were really in over their heads or out of their depth or just where they felt uncomfortable and didn't know how to deal with what was happening … I also like the idea of turning the tables – the idea of them thinking that they're in charge or that they're in power and they're asking me for something and then I turn it on them, where I'm the director and the world is really my world.[24]

The camera then, in Nakadate's case, is also acting as an empowering mirror; for instance, in another early video she performs Britney's song and dance routine to the camera in identification with the singer, mimicking her dance moves in a highly sexualized manner. Empowering though this may be, I have an anxiety about this flaunting of femininity and the possibility of a double-inscription that you mentioned as advocated by Doane. Nakadate has described her intentions to disarm the viewer by enacting a vulnerability which could be read as being difficult to control: turning the camera on herself to create what she insists is a fantasized character operating between real-life situations and fantasy – what she describes as hybrid spaces. However, Nakadate's imagery nevertheless remains all too close for me; where is that necessary distance? Maybe my discomfort as a viewer is the issue of the mastery of the gaze. I still seem to be caught up in this impossible power struggle. I remain implicated here as the voyeur. Is there, though, a self-fetishization at work here by Nakadate? Am I, as viewer, experiencing here the process of fetishism as an oscillation between two contradictory views: anxiety and curiosity, which you mentioned earlier with Mulvey's description of Sherman's images? Can Nakadate's video works be understood as this performance: as masquerade – as a citation – which might allow meanings to shift and become unstable? Is this the possible re-routing of the gaze we are seeking here which actually might open up to other scenes of desire which you referred to? The work we have discussed thus far raises the question of how might it be possible for women to act as powerful agents over their own identities without referencing or considering the stark reality of patriarchal constructions that continue to scupper such attempts. Grosz in her more recent book *Becoming Undone* tackles the problematic question of female subjectivity proposed by these debilitating theorizations. Antagonistic to any egalitarian project which might be directed to the equalization of the relations between the sexes, or between races, or ethnicities, as that would invariably reflect the values of the dominant position/order, Grosz remarks: 'We wait to be recognized instead of making something, inventing something, which will enable us to recognize ourselves, or more interestingly, to eschew recognition altogether.'[25]

Act III

Maria Walsh: I do not know what making something new yet recognizable might entail but one way of approaching the politics of the gaze from an angle other than recognition would be that of haptic visuality. Initially, the haptic turn in 1990s visual culture was seen as a way out of the problematics of representation that you outline, for instance, that images of the woman are inevitably circulated as commoditized objects. It was also perhaps a response to the deadlock of the masquerade whereby its effectivity – 'to manufacture a distance from the image, to generate a problematic within which the image is manipulable, producible and readable by the woman'[26] – can, as you have outlined in relation to Nakadate's work, be co-opted for other ends. Laura U. Marks, who did not invent the term 'haptic' but who is credited for importing it from art history into visual culture in her analyses of electronic video, was interested in expanding spectatorship interculturally and acknowledging different value systems of perception. For Marks, proximity to the image is a mode of perception generated by those who are in opposition to or excluded from the gaze of mastery and its links to the project of colonialism. She defines haptic visuality as a mode of seeing in which the eyes themselves function like organs of touch, comprising other forms of sense experience such as the kinaesthetic and the proprioceptive. Marks borrows the term from the nineteenth-century art historian Alois Riegl, who referred to his appreciative viewing of Persian carpets, Egyptian and Islamic painting as a haptic gaze spread out over a flatly two-dimensional textured surface rather than penetrating in depth. These non-perspectival textiles and forms of painting engender a surface looking, a tracing of pattern, in which the viewer's sensory gaze is in proximity to what it is looking at.[27] Haptic visuality, then, is very different to the manufacturing of a distance operative in masquerade which is dependent on optical vision. While Marks refers to a dynamic movement between optical and haptical ways of seeing 'in which it is possible to compare different ways of knowing and interacting with another', there is a question for me of how this can happen if there is no distinction between figure and ground in a haptical looking that 'is so intensely involved with the presence of the other that it cannot step back to discern difference'.[28] In fact, this reminds me of Doane's 'overpresence' of the image for the woman.

The other thing to note is that Marks's theorization of haptic visuality is propped on the blurry electronic video signal, suggesting that perceptual forms determine vision. This reduction of sensory experience to form ignores contexts of reception. It also does not reckon with the fact that haptical seeing in film is by contrast associated with a sense of being able to touch space in the depths of the image.[29] I wonder if there is something to be gained by keeping both surface and depth modes of haptic reception in mind in relation to a strategy of a 'non-mastering visuality'[30] vis-à-vis the projected image of woman.

Mo Throp: Perhaps we can come back to this as I'd also like to approach the question of the gaze in another way and examine artistic tactics or strategies that might lead beyond the desire for recognition that Grosz suggests. Artist Jennifer Allen, in her performance as Quilla Constance in her video work *Pukijam* (2015), has, I think, created a more affirmative strategy through which to address debilitating operations of power. *Pukijam* moves beyond the goals of identity politics which seek to affirm what we are and what we know through. Quilla Constance's exaggerated re-enactments of a female identity as golliwog, pole dancer and artist – with images of afro hair combs, pineapples, cakes, glamour models, wigs, fried chicken all thrown in as cultural signifiers – shift and dislocate. This is a repetitive collage that undercuts any fixed meaning, thereby destabilizing identity, particularly in this case, from its colonial context. Allen's performances are not traumatic nor essentialist re-assemblages of identities as fixed truths but, rather, they put into motion the unfixed and prescribed nature of all forms of identity.

There is an anti-normative inscription at work here which precludes any possibility of a close identification. Could we argue that there is a kind of citation which operates here as a masquerade, enacted in this over-identification, creating a distance which is necessary for a re-routing of identification (a holding of these signifiers at a distance) and one which might more easily lend itself to our quest for a practice that might open up onto another scene of desire? I would like to propose that in this constant flow of pleasurable dis-identification, *Pukijam* enacts a scene where we

Figure 1 Quilla Constance, *Pukijam* (2015). Digital video still, courtesy of the artist.

might recognize more productive ways for reconsidering structures and ways of looking which do not return us to the debilitating scenario of self-identification.

Maria Walsh: I'd like to know more about how and for whom this dis-identification might be pleasurable, as dis-identification, as I understand it, is a painful experience. Also, is there any connection to be made between what you are claiming here for *Pukijam* and Marks's notion of the haptic as a strategy of 'non-mastering visuality [...] that offers its object to the viewer but only on the condition that its unknowability remains intact'?[31] This positionality would be counter to the colonial project of classification from which racism ensues. I'm curious as well to know how you see the possibilities for embodiment in relation to *Pukijam* as the signifiers seem more discursive and dependent on cultural readings rather than being open to the bodily absorption of the haptic.

Mo Throp: As you have said, Marks's notion of the haptic does have an intention to expand spectatorship interculturally and to acknowledge different value systems of perception. In Quilla Constance's over-identification with specific cultural signifiers maybe there is actually a proximity to the image which in this case is concerned with a mode of perception, as you explained earlier, which is generated by those who are in opposition to, or excluded by, the gaze of mastery and here especially as linked to the project of colonialism. This is certainly Allen's agenda for an over-identification of categories, a re-inhabiting of those images in an exaggerated form in order to allow for what I would call a dis-identification with their original constructions. In *Pukijam* Allen puts the proximity of these exaggerated forms, which could be aligned with Marks's haptic visuality as an almost too-close bodily absorption, into parenthesis through her manipulation of digital montage. The repetitious assemblages of these forms, alongside the rhythmic sound, especially Quilla Constance's highly emotional verbal nonsensical utterances, do draw an embodied response from the viewer – a powerful emotional response, which finally allows one to acknowledge what one sees critically – its racial, sexual, colonial gaze – and then relocates it via this fast-moving, digital, rhythmic, tactile seeing as a sensory engagement for the viewer. Something of a haptic proximity might be created by a certain Punk aesthetic at play in this work. In this way, might it finally, through this rhythmic repetition of image and sound as digital montage, allow a dis-identification with its patriarchal, colonial origins and so 'unmaster' the image by putting identification itself at a distance in an oscillation between optic and haptic visuality?

Maria Walsh: You seem to be suggesting that this oscillation might be a way of undoing debilitating identifications? Perhaps the experimental use of digital technology gives female artists more room for manoeuvre. Its composite techniques, its visual and sonic layering and the fluidity of movements – like scrolling and inserting multiple windows – seem to offer potential for confusing the rigid binaries of visuality that are socially inculcated. Your discussion of *Pukijam* reminds me of Lucy Clout's video *Shrugging Offing* (2013), which seems to me to incorporate both surface and depth haptic spatiality, as well as referring to the fashioned body.

The video's 'mise-en-scène' is a clothing factory.[32] Empty of workers, it opens on a central cutting table surrounded by paper garment cut-outs that infer the female body. While composed of a number of montage sequences, some culled from the internet, the main body of the work oscillates between close-ups of the artist's arm and/or leg, both clad in high-visibility green sportswear, that enter the frame by flopping down on the floor and shots of an item of clothing, such as an animal print blouson or a fine-knit cardi-wrap, suspended on a hanger above the cutting table. An off-screen presence knocks these surrogate bodies off their precarious perches by throwing balled up socks at them. Towards the end of the video, the cardi-wrap 'character' reappears on a hanger. The thrown socks this time miss their target and the garment, poised half on, half off, its hanger, conjures the image of coy flirtation akin to the play of masquerade. A voice-over from an ASMR (autonomous sensory meridian response) practitioner role-playing

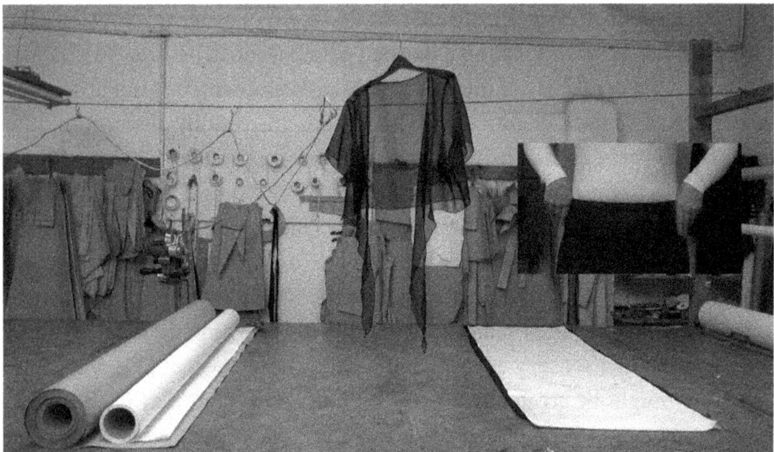

Figure 2 Lucy Clout, *Shrugging Offing* (2013). Digital video still, courtesy of the artist.

a dermatologist, whose video window had earlier opened up in the factory shot, softly gives out skincare instructions throughout the work. ASMR is compared with auditory-tactile synesthesia and with having a direct bodily impact on the viewer, thereby doubling the sensory engagement of the close-ups of the green-clad body parts onto which highly mobile, more abstract footage evocative of skin is projected. Once one has identified that what is going on in this YouTube footage is spot-squeezing, there is an instant recoiling both at the tactile proximity of the gaze to the on-screen activity and to the abject nature of pus – one of the video's sequences is called 'Flying Pus'.[33] But unlike, say, Mulvey's critique of Sherman's unveiling of the fetish to reveal the uncanniness of the abject, which is so horrific that it requires a re-fetishization, here the abject nature of the body has a humorous lightness of touch.

Almost as a motif of the set of double acts we have been engaged in during this discussion, there is a shot in which two pairs of legs shown from the knee down perform a simple dance routine to an electro-beat. Footage of spot-squeezing is projected on one of the pairs, the combination of surface and depth eliciting a complex reading of the performance as oscillating in a haptic space both near and far. It seems to me that this video attempts to resist the cultural modelling of femininity that masquerading as a woman entails. I could go on but my main point here is that while the internet is a space of discipline, abuse and voyeurism, it also provides opportunities for redistributing bodily affects and actions. In both *Pukijam* and *Shrugging Offing*, the technology itself allows for the layering of a multiplicity of sign systems which bounce off one another, putting rigid structures of looking into question.

Mo Throp: I think they do; and they do that by allowing a space for the viewer to open up to other narratives than those which the colonial and patriarchal gaze continues to fix and control.

Maria Walsh: I am optimistic in thinking that these kinds of practices enable a productive combination of kinaesthetic looking and the curious gaze that Mulvey claims is associated with feminism.[34] While haptic viewing can end up reifying an ahistorical body, these digital video art practices allow us to move in and out of bodily identifications that are both stereotypical and unfamiliar. No one single field of vision is privileged, instead there is a continual mixing up of the codes of looking to create 'libidinally resonant'[35] bodies that are not equal but are equally open to anyone who desires to give up the gaze of mastery.

Notes

1. Laura Mulvey, 'Visual Pleasure and Narrative Cinema', *Screen* 16/3 (Autumn 1975), p. 11.
2. Ibid., p. 12.
3. Irvine Welsh, 'She's Pregnant and He's Got His Fists Raised. Guess Who's the Victim…', *The Guardian*, 16 January 1999, p. 4.
4. Jean Roussel prepared the first English translation of Lacan's essay 'The Mirror Stage as Formative of the Function of the I as Revealed in Psychoanalytic Experience', which appeared in *New Left Review* 51 (September/October 1968), pp. 63–77.
5. In Freud's account of scopophilia, rather than either simply subjecting another to a controlling gaze or being subjected to the gaze of the other, the phenomenon is conceived of as a four-part process, whereby the initial autoerotic taking by the subject of its own body as the object of desire is redirected towards an extraneous object. This leads to voyeurism per se, but then this energy is redirected back to the subject's own person resulting in a new aim – to be looked at – which, in turn, constitutes a new subject to whom one displays oneself (as subject) in order to be looked at (as object). See Julie Levin Russo, 'Show Me Yours: Cyber-exhibitionism from Perversion to Politics', *Camera Obscura* #73, 25/1 (2010), pp. 131–59, p. 137.

6. Baudrillard says that if women are not fetishists, it is because they perform the labour of continual fetishization on themselves. Jean Baudrillard, *Symbolic Exchange and Death*, trans. Iain Hamilton Grant, intro. Mike Gane (London, Thousand Oaks, New Delhi: Sage, 1993), p. 110.
7. [Editors' Note: In her contribution to this volume, Dawn Woolley explores commodity fetishism in relation to fashion advertising and the hashtag 'thinspiration'.]
8. [Editors' Note: See also Ilya Parkins's chapter in this volume on boudoir photography, 'Becoming in the Eyes of Others: The Relational Gaze in Boudoir Photography'.]
9. Sarah Banet-Weiser, 'Branding the Post-feminist Self: Girls' Video Production and YouTube', in M.C. Kearney (ed), *Mediated Girlhoods: New Explorations of Girls' Media Culture* (New York: Peter Lang, 2013), pp. 51–71.
10. Victor Burgin, 'Jenni's Room: Exhibitionism & Solitude', *Critical Inquiry* 27/1 (Autumn 2000), pp. 77–89.
11. Ibid., p. 79.
12. Ibid., p. 82.
13. Mary Ann Doane, *Femmes Fatales: Feminism, Film Theory, Psychoanalysis* (New York and London: Routledge, 1991), p. 22.
14. Ibid., p. 25. Doane is referencing Joan Rivière's essay 'Womanliness as a Masquerade' (1929), published in *The International Journal of Psychoanalysis* 10, pp. 303–13.
15. 'The wordlessness and despair in her work represents the wordlessness and despair that ensues when a fetishist structure, the means of erasing history and memory, collapses, leaving a void in its wake.' Laura Mulvey, 'A Phantasmagoria of the Female Body: The Work of Cindy Sherman', *New Left Review* 188 (July–August 1991), p. 150.
16. Ibid., pp. 146–7.
17. John Fletcher, 'Versions of Masquerade', *Screen* 29/3 (1988), pp. 43–70.
18. Elizabeth Grosz, *Becoming Undone: Darwinian Reflections on Life, Politics and Art* (Durham and London: Duke University Press, 2011), p. 84.
19. Burgin, 'Jenni's Room', p. 87.
20. Burgin contrasts 'risky play' to childish exhibitionism. Ibid., p. 84.
21. Hirsch in Karen Archey, 'Artist Profile: Ann Hirsch', *Rhizome*, 2012. Available at http://rhizome.org/editorial/2012/mar/7/artist-profile/ (accessed 19 October 2015).
22. Hirsch in Ana Cecilia Alvarez, 'Ann Hirsch Is the Fairy Godmother of Young Artists Who Grew Up on Reality TV', *Vice*, 7 June 2014. Available at http://www.vice.com/read/ann-hirsch-is-the-godmother-of-young-artists-who-grew-up-on-reality-tv-and-porn (accessed 2 April 2015).

23. This video was publicly available on YouTube in 2015, but now it is password protected on Vimeo.
24. Laurel Nakadate interviewed by Scott Indrisek in *The Believer* 4/8, October 2006.
25. Grosz, *Becoming Undone*, p. 84.
26. Fletcher, 'Versions of Masquerade', p. 56.
27. Laura U. Marks, 'Video Haptics and Erotics', *Screen* 39/4 (Winter 1998), pp. 331–47.
28. Ibid., p. 345.
29. The main reference here would be Walter Benjamin, 'The Work of Art in the Age of Mechanical Reproduction' (1935)', in H. Arendt (ed), *Illuminations*, trans. Harry Zohn (New York: Schocken Books, 1969), pp. 217–51.
30. Marks, 'Video Haptics and Erotics', p. 347.
31. Ibid.
32. The North London clothing factory specializes in older women's garb.
33. Apparently, these YouTube spot-squeezing videos are mostly, but not solely, by men with women doing the squeezing.
34. Mulvey in Martine Beugnet and Laura Mulvey, 'Film, Corporeality, Transgressive Cinema: A Feminist Perspective', in L. Mulvey and A. Backman Rogers (eds), *Feminisms: Diversity, Difference and Multiplicity in Contemporary Film Cultures* (Amsterdam: Amsterdam University Press, 2015), p. 197.
35. Anu Koivunen, 'The Promise of Touch: Turns to Affect in Feminist Film Theory', in L. Mulvey and A. Backman Rogers (eds), *Feminisms: Diversity, Difference and Multiplicity in Contemporary Film Cultures* (Amsterdam: Amsterdam University Press, 2015), p. 109.

Bibliography

Alvarez, Ana Cecilia, 'Ann Hirsch Is the Fairy Godmother of Young Artists Who Grew Up on Reality TV', *Vice*, 7 June 2014. Available at http://www.vice.com/read/ann-hirsch-is-the-godmother-of-young-artists-who-grew-up-on-reality-tv-and-porn (accessed 2 April 2015).

Archey, Karen, 'Artist Profile: Ann Hirsch', *Rhizome*, 2012. Available at http://rhizome.org/editorial/2012/mar/7/artist-profile/ (accessed 19 October 2015).

Beugnet, Martine and Laura Mulvey, 'Film, Corporeality, Transgressive Cinema: A Feminist Perspective', in L. Mulvey and A. Backman Rogers (eds), *Feminisms: Diversity, Difference and Multiplicity in Contemporary Film Cultures* (Amsterdam: Amsterdam University Press, 2015), pp. 97–110.

Burgin, Victor, 'Jenni's Room: Exhibitionism & Solitude', *Critical Inquiry* 27/1 (Autumn 2000), pp. 77–89.

Doane, Mary Ann, *Femmes Fatales: Feminism, Film Theory, Psychoanalysis* (New York and London: Routledge, 1991).
Fletcher, John, 'Versions of Masquerade', *Screen* 29/3 (1988), pp. 43–70.
Grosz, Elizabeth, *Becoming Undone: Darwinian Reflections on Life, Politics and Art* (Durham: Duke University Press, 2011).
Koivunen, Anu, 'The Promise of Touch: Turns to Affect in Feminist Film Theory', in L. Mulvey and A. Backman Rogers (eds), *Feminisms: Diversity, Difference and Multiplicity in Contemporary Film Cultures* (Amsterdam: Amsterdam University Press, 2015), pp. 97–110.
Marks, Laura U., 'Video Haptics and Erotics', *Screen* 39/4 (Winter 1998), pp. 331–47.
Mulvey, Laura, 'Visual Pleasure and Narrative Cinema', *Screen* 16/3 (Autumn 1975), pp. 6–18.
Mulvey, Laura, 'A Phantasmagoria of the Female Body: The Work of Cindy Sherman', *New Left Review* 188 (July–August 1991), pp. 137–50.
Nakadate, Laurel, Interviewed by Scott Indrisek in *The Believer* 4/8 (October 2006).
Welsh, Irvine, 'She's Pregnant and He's Got His Fists Raised. Guess Who's the Victim …', *The Guardian*, 16 January 1999.

CHAPTER 3

THE AMBIENT GAZE: SENSORY ATMOSPHERE AND THE DRESSED BODY

Sara Chong Kwan

The sensing and sensuous body amounts to more than the visual term 'appearance' would suggest. Georg Simmel alluded to this sensuous atmosphere of the dressed body in his writing on adornment:

> The radiations of adornment, the sensuous attention it provokes, supply the personality with such an enlargement or intensification of its sphere: the personality so to speak, is more when it is adorned.[1]

In their seminal definition of 'dress', Mary Ellen Roach-Higgins and Joanne B. Eicher propose that dress, which sits at the interface between the body and the macro-physical environment, is perceived by all the senses, not just sight[2] but also, in varying degrees, touch, sound, smell and to a lesser extent taste. This chapter reconsiders, or rather complicates, 'the gaze' in relation to the dressed body from the phenomenological perspective of the wearer. It challenges conventional approaches to 'male gaze' theory that tend to overstate the power of the gaze and the importance of appearance in forming dressed experience for the wearer. Such approaches fail to account for the actual lived agency of the wearer in resisting this social gaze and constructing their own sense of self through other sensory aspects of dress. A theory of the 'male gaze' tends to assume that this is the main system that defines how women dress and feel when dressed, yet empirical evidence presented in this chapter suggests that dressed experience for the wearer is much more complex than this – rather it is a multi-sensory act of self-creation, in which other meanings of dress also have importance. It departs from a notion of the wearer as passive object, moving the focus towards acknowledging the experience of the dressed self as subject: active in the process of meaning-making. Alternative notions of 'dress as a sensory atmosphere for the body' and the 'ambient gaze' are proposed. These frameworks recognize the multi-sensory impressions that a dressed body makes in social life and the way in which all sensory modalities are in play when 'gazing' upon and interpreting the dressed appearance of others.

Dress is a practice, where social relations are played out, negotiated and constructed within different spaces and situations. It is, as Joanne Entwistle terms it, a 'situated bodily practice'[3] but furthermore, as will be argued in this chapter, it is a multi-sensory practice. Visual appearance is only one element, which together with other sensory dimensions contributes to an overall 'atmosphere' or multi-sensory surround for the body. This notion of 'atmosphere' attends more holistically to the way clothing and the body mingle, in movement, through everyday life. In this context, atmosphere is constituted through appearance, movement, texture and touch, aromas and sounds, deportment, gestures and more intangible aspects such as the wearer's attitude, emotional mood, memories and imagination. Approaching the dressed body as atmospheric and the gaze as 'ambient' enables a consideration of these more intangible sensory aspects of dressed experience which also shape the meanings of dress for both wearer and observer.

The opening section of this chapter outlines the development of the theoretical framework that underpins this approach, one that integrates embodied, phenomenological and sensory theory, alongside an understanding of atmosphere as central to social life. Here the sensory gaps in Fashion and Dress Studies are highlighted, providing a critique to ocularcentric approaches that have tended to overlook the subjective perspective of the wearer. The following section discusses feminist critiques of the 'male gaze': a notion that privileges the visual over other senses – such as touch – in addition to devaluing the sensuous experience of women. Here the importance of understanding the senses as culturally constructed and in particular as gendered is stressed. The final section discusses how managing the sensory dimensions of everyday dress enables the wearer to negotiate the social gaze and mediate the impressions they make on others. Furthermore, it considers the contradictions between how the wearer may feel when dressed and how they may appear to others – problematizing the notion of fashion and dress as visual communication and questioning the power of the 'male gaze'. At the boundaries of the body, dress is positioned as providing a sensory atmosphere for the wearer, one that negotiates the tensions between private and public experience, between the meanings of dress for the observed and the observer.

Throughout this chapter, but particularly in the final section, the arguments will be underpinned with examples from interviews undertaken as part of my doctoral study into sensory engagement with everyday dress in a contemporary UK context.[4] This study was based on individual testimony, collected using life-world interviews with twenty participants both men and women, incorporating material culture analysis. I will highlight some of the ways in which the female and male participants expressed a self-conscious awareness of 'seeing and being seen' in particular social situations and public environments. Multi-sensory engagement with dress, involving visual but also tactile, auditory and olfactory elements, played a role in the participants' negotiation of the gaze of others and the social structures, such as gender, that regulate rules of dressing. For example, the participants employed sensory dress strategies of inviting and deflecting the attention of others, such as hiding and/or revealing parts of the body or managing the body's scent and sound. These strategies provided an element of control over how 'visible' or 'invisible' they were to others and helped to mediate the 'impressions' that they made in social life. Additionally, more hidden, intimate and non-visual aspects of sensory dress experience, for example the touch of clothing on the skin, at times gave the participants a private sense of agency and resistance to perceived social expectations around appearance. This approach relies on two, interlinked understandings of the term 'sense': firstly as a specific 'sensation or feeling' and secondly as the action of 'making sense'. According to Vannini, Waskul and Gottschalk, 'The sense(s) is (are) both a reaching out to the world as a source of information and an understanding of the world so gathered.'[5]

Developing a sensory theoretical framework

Dress is the first physical point of contact, the interface between the 'self' (as contained in the body) and the material, social and cultural world. Since the 1990s, Fashion and Dress Studies has demonstrated how through dress and appearance, notions of the self and identity are explored by the wearer. Aspects of identity are expressed to others through clothing choices – constructed in accordance with or as a form of resisting, socially structured rules of dressing that link to cultural categories such as gender, age and class. The overwhelming focus of these studies has been towards only one of the five Western senses: sight.[6] They have tended to theorize fashion and dress as a means of visual communication, in which dressed bodies are gazed upon, their meaning and 'identities' interpreted by others. Roland Barthes[7] proposed that fashion can be understood as a complex system of signs and following this, Alison Lurie[8] argued that clothes can be read as one would read a language. All of these accounts are based on visual aspects of dress – observations of either the item of dress or the appearance of the wearer when dressed. These approaches have privileged the perspective of the observer gazing upon the dressed bodies of others. The notion of 'the gaze', attended to in this volume, has been an important tool for critically unpicking the politics of dressed appearance and the implicit power of spectatorship. In particular this has been applied to gender politics in order to understand how the appearance of women is regulated through a disciplinary male gaze.

What these theoretical approaches have tended to overlook, however, is the perspective of the wearer – the 'other side' of the power of looking. That is, how the wearer experiences the gaze and, moreover, how they might employ individual agency to negotiate this disciplinary gaze. Dress and appearance form part of a social system that constructs and disciplines the body.[9] As a result, being dressed in everyday social life can be a highly self-conscious act, often involving a level of anxiety[10] as the wearer attempts to construct a look that will both fit in with the required norms of dressing to suit that situation while also expressing individual preferences. However, the wearer can never be sure how their appearance will be interpreted by others, nor can the observer be sure of how the wearer feels.

More recently, a body of work within fashion theory has established the importance of investigating the wearer's perspectives on dress. The work of Efrat Tseelon,[11] Joanne Entwistle,[12] Shaun Cole,[13] Lou Taylor,[14] Sophie Woodward[15] and Lucia Ruggerone,[16] among others, has begun to challenge purely visual interpretations of dressed appearance, addressing more fully the wearer's embodied perspective and experience. This departure contributes to a broader shift within the social sciences, arts and humanities towards an understanding of the body as the seat of perception and social and cultural meaning-making.[17] This has its philosophical basis in phenomenology, in particular, that of Maurice Merleau-Ponty. This century has seen increased interest in phenomenology, which when combined with continental philosophy has acted to critique the notion of Cartesian dualism – the separation and privileging of the mind over the body. By contrast, a phenomenological philosophy of embodiment views the mind as part of the body – as one 'unified person' – and knowledge as an integral aspect of bodily experience. In this way, knowledge of the world and the self is understood to come through lived experience.[18] Within sociology, a 'social constructivist' approach emerging from historical and anthropological work concerning the body has also challenged Cartesium dualism. This approach positions the body as a social and cultural phenomenon (as opposed to a biological entity), historically shaped by, and shaping, cultural and social life and has established the body as a valid object of study within the social sciences and Cultural Studies.[19]

Colin Campbell's[20] critique of Lurie's positioning of clothes as a 'language' suggests that observed meanings of dress are ambiguous and subjective, not necessarily shared between wearer and perceiver. Therefore, attempts to read what people wear as a form of language are unreliable and based on the observer's assumptions. Campbell argues that the focus on the visual pins 'meaning' to a singular visual appearance.[21] Arguably, this has led to a denial or marginalization of other accounts of meaning, in particular the wearer's own account, and their embodied, sensory experience. When dressed the wearer is seen and aware of being seen, but simultaneously feels the touch and movement of dress upon the body and is similarly sensitive to their body's scent and sound. As Entwistle has argued in her work on dress and embodiment, 'dress in everyday life cannot be separated from the living, breathing, moving body it adorns'.[22]

As a form of material culture, what we wear is both a social, public activity and an intensely personal one, primarily due to its physical proximity to our bodies – we are in constant touch with our clothes. As previously stated, within Fashion and Dress Studies Merleau-Ponty's particular approach to phenomenology, which presents the sensory body as the seat of all perception and experience, has been increasingly influential in articulating the embodied nature of worn clothing. His influence is discussed by Llewellyn Negrin who argues that his work provides 'the theoretical tools with which to address fashion not simply as an aesthetic or symbolic phenomenon but as a haptic[23] experience' producing 'certain modes of bodily demeanour'.[24] This understanding of experience as centred in the lived – that is the 'feeling' and 'moving' – body acknowledges the corporeality of being dressed. The logical progression from this embodied approach is to ask how the body experiences and perceives dress. Although fashion and dress scholarship has begun to increasingly focus on the phenomenological lived body (utilizing Merleau-Ponty in this respect), it has not fully engaged with his articulation of the nature of sensory perception in which the senses are interconnected and the body experiences a duality of seeing and touching. As Merleau-Ponty states: 'My body simultaneously sees and is seen. That which looks at all things can also look at itself and recognise, in what it sees, the "other side" of its power of looking. It sees itself seeing; it touches itself touching: it is visible and sensitive for itself.'[25]

Arguably, approaching dress as embodied practice necessitates an attention to how the wearer's body perceives dress and that is through all the senses. There are hidden, sometimes taken for granted, sensory aspects of dressed experience – such as the smell of a perfume or the texture of a garment that have particular meanings, emotions or memories for the wearer. These aspects are usually not accounted for, particularly within theories of the gaze. How it feels to be dressed in all its dimensions and in particular situations is an intrinsic, though not always easily researched or represented, aspect of daily life. Additionally, fashion and dress scholarship has not until very recently engaged with the collection of interdisciplinary work around the senses which began to emerge at the end of the twentieth century. Initially funded by a grant from the Research Council of Canada, and based at Concordia University in Quebec, Anthony Synnott and David Howes, later joined by Constance Classen, were central in developing the cultural history, anthropology and sociology of the senses, brought together through the establishment of the Centre for Sensory Studies in 2012.[26] In Howes's account, the body experiences, comprehends and constructs the world through all its senses,[27] thus culture shapes the senses and sensory activity shapes culture. How we use our senses and how we value the different senses and sensory behaviour and experience are culturally constructed and hierarchically arranged. The body's social and cultural experience, of which dress is one aspect, can in this way be seen as mediated through all sensory modalities. Following Howes, I argue that visual dimensions and visual perceptions of the dressed body are predicated on the other senses, which can work in tandem or at times in conflict with the visual.

At the turn of the twentieth century, the sociologist Georg Simmel was one of the first to theorize the 'relationship of aesthetic and social forms'[28] and also the relationship between the individual and social structures. This informed his work on the changing 'style' of fashionable clothing that articulated, for him, the 'paradox of fashion, of belonging and standing out simultaneously via sartorial methods and techniques'.[29] Simmel also theorized the senses and at times these two areas of fashion and the senses collide in his writing. Simmel highlights the importance of sensation in social life, positioning micro-sensory interaction as the building blocks or 'pulsating life' of larger social structures, as 'agents connecting individuals to social existence'.[30] This leads him to consider the sensory impressions a person makes through their 'radiations of adornment' – by which he means extraordinary dress that is designed to impress. Simmel's use of the term 'radiations' is suggestive of how all sensory aspects of dress – visual but also haptic, auditory and olfactory aspects – surround the wearer's body, creating a dressed atmosphere that is perceived by both wearer and observer and which plays into this sense of 'belonging' and of 'standing out'. In his writing on the senses, Simmel explicitly outlined how a 'person's atmosphere' which makes a 'sensory impression' on others is integral to social interaction. He argues that atmospheres pull people towards others, through instigating an 'instinct' or 'desire' to get to know them better through talking and interacting with them, and that this combination of sensory impression and knowledge 'become[s] cooperatively, and in practical terms inseparably, the foundation of our relationship to that person'.[31] In her sociological research into everyday 'atmospheres', Jennifer Mason has similarly argued that atmospheres in general play an integral part within social life:

> A smell, a taste or a snatch of music that 'literally' (I use the term advisedly) transports you to another time and place and conjures its atmosphere in your mind, body and senses. Atmospheres bring into play not only human interactions, imaginaries, and sensations, but a wider more-than-human world of things, lives, rhythms, energies, elements, forces, places and times. Atmospheres are conjured and perceived in multisensory, extra-sensory, and ineffable ways. They can feel simultaneously tangible and intangible.[32]

Dress both reveals and conceals the body, changing its appearance and shape, but also its deportment and other sensory dimensions such as how it smells and sounds. In this way, appearance always involves a complex intertwining of sensory aspects and the perception of the onlooker is never purely a visual one. The gaze upon the dressed body employs vision but also an understanding of these other sensory aspects – an empathy towards the sensory experience of the wearer. When we observe another's dress, through drawing upon our own experience, we also bring to our gaze other sensory understandings. For example, we can imagine how the weight of the fabric and the cut of the garment might feel upon the body. This is embodied, sensory knowledge constructed from our own memories and lived experience of the sensory properties of clothing alongside understandings and associations that are socially constructed and mediated according to our individual culture, background and experience.[33] Arguably, then, a more holistic and accurate way of conceptualizing how these atmospheres of the dressed body are perceived by others, and the 'sensuous attention' they provoke, is through the notion of an 'ambient gaze'.

Photographs of clothing can also invite the viewer to imagine how they might feel to touch or to wear. As sensory ethnographer Sarah Pink argues, even images have sensual qualities beyond the visual because they ignite the viewer's prior, embodied and sensory knowledge of the subject:

> Photographs have the capacity to bring textures, surfaces and sensory experiences they evoke right up close to the reader: they both invoke embodied reactions and offer routes by which, via our own memories and subjectivities, we might anticipate what it feels like to be in another place.[34]

In relation to images and the sensory materiality of clothing, this empathetic and ambient gaze was nicely articulated by the feminist philosopher Iris Marion Young in her critique of the 'male gaze'. Young describes how, when looking at an advertising image of a woman in a wool suit, she imagines the feel of the wool swishing around her legs.[35] As will be discussed in the following section, feminist philosophy, such as Young's, has played an important role in critiquing the notion of the 'male gaze' through reclaiming the sensory pleasures (and pains) that frame women's understanding of dress and fashion as part of their identities.

Feminist philosophy, the gaze and the senses

Drawing on continental philosophy, such as the writing of Luce Irigaray,[36] Young, in her seminal essay on women's embodied experience, considers women's intimate and emotional relationship with clothing and how an alternative and more representative way of talking about this might, for example, embrace the sense of touch more than sight.[37] The exclusive focus on 'the gaze', and more specifically a 'male gaze' that acts upon women, denies the subjective perspective and agency of women – who are more than passive objects on whom meaning is imposed but are themselves active agents in the process of meaning-making. Young questions how hierarchical values are imposed upon different types of sensory experience. There are parallels here between the hierarchical structuring of gender and that of the senses. The way that sensory aspects of dress are discussed in a Western cultural context and in fashion theory is hierarchically structured, with vision taking prominence. This privileging becomes self-perpetuating. Because non-visual aspects of dress have been assigned less cultural importance, they are less often articulated and therefore become more difficult to articulate. Ruggerone has proposed that a new paradigm is required to investigate the everyday affective (material and immaterial) encounters with clothing, arguing that 'because these practices are continually flowing events (becomings), their meaning can only be partially captured by interpretative/linguistic discourses'.[38] In my study, at times the participants struggled to clearly explain in words non-visual aspects of their sensory engagement with dress, often reverting to hand gestures, such as rubbing their fingers together, to denote a texture or looking upwards as they 'imagined' the sensation but could not find the right words.

In Daniel Miller's view, the gendering of clothing is related to a 'denigration of surfaces' (clothing being a surface or covering for the body) as 'superficial', in contrast with the profound nature of the 'real' person inside or abstract and 'deep' political thought:

> This denigration of surfaces has been part of the denigration of clothing and, by extension, of those said to be particularly interested in clothing, often seen as women, or blacks or any other group that thereby come to be regarded as more superficial and less deep.[39]

Here, there are also parallels to be made between the gendering of 'fashion' as female and the gendered hierarchy of sensory modalities that Howes describes as follows:

> In the West the dominant group – whether it be conceptualized in terms of gender, class or race – has conventionally been associated with the supposedly 'higher' senses of sight and hearing, while subordinate groups (women, workers, non-Westerners) have been associated with the so-called lower senses of smell, taste and touch.[40]

There is a contradiction apparent between these two examples of gender hierarchies, one that reveals them as nonsensical constructs, which as Miller suggests, can be used by one group to put down another. On the one hand, as Miller points out above, women are still denigrated as superficial, linked to an over concern with appearance, yet if sight is designated a 'higher' sense, it would logically follow that appearance should be highly valued. However, this contradiction is then overcome through further layering of hierarchies, such as the denigration of 'surface'.

While Young does not deny the existence of a patriarchal gaze that positions women as objects to be admired and denigrated in equal measure, she nevertheless argues that female experience of dress and fashion is much more than this: 'There is a certain freedom involved in our relation to clothes, an active subjectivity not represented in the male gaze theory.'[41] Rather, female experience of dress employs the pleasures of touch, bonding and fantasy in the active reimagining of the self. The way that dress touches and shapes the body is not merely expressive of cultural ideas or social structures, nor is it purely a pursuit for sensory and aesthetic pleasure. It is, as fashion theorists such as Elizabeth Wilson,[42] Young and Agnès Rocamora[43] have argued, a complex mix of the two. As Wilson points out, the control of women's bodies through fashion and dress and their resulting subordination has been a 'source of concern to feminists, both today and in an earlier period', but she also acknowledges that this concern needs to be balanced with fashion's role as an active and liberating form of creative, self-expression, albeit an ambiguous one.[44]

To give an example that illustrates this complexity, one of my participants, Pamela, described how the touch of dress can indeed be a liberating force. She had a vivid, sensual memory of the first, flimsy silk bra she wore as a young woman in the 1950s. This signalled a profound sensory change from the girdle style 'roll-on' rubber underwear that she had previously worn (and her mother's generation still wore). She said:

> This feeling of just two thin bits of fabric over your boobies, you know, which was caressing you actually. I mean, it was really lovely. It was sumptuous. Once you put those on you couldn't go back to the others, so that also had something to do with the clothes, the freedom.

Having described the initial tactile pleasure of wearing the bra, Pamela then reflected on its loose, free structure and as a result, the more intangible and emotional sense of 'freedom' she experienced when wearing it. Pamela suggested that this might link to a social and moral sense of moving away from what she described as the 'chastity' and 'control mechanism' of the girdle. As Mark Paterson points out in his historical work on touch, tactile and haptic knowledge relates to objects but also to the space around the body: 'The feeling of cutaneous touch when an object brushes our skin is simultaneously an awareness of the materiality of the object and an awareness of the spatial limits and sensations of our lived body.'[45] Pamela's sensation of breaking free from the boundaries restricting and disciplining her body alludes to wider sociocultural changes that were taking place at the time as social rules relaxed and some of the younger generation began to reject previous social conventions and styles of dressing. It further demonstrates the importance of haptic aspects of clothing in both restricting and liberating the social body and the role of sensuous pleasure in enabling the wearer to know – and then potentially to transform – the way in which they position themselves in society.

Fashion, in the second half of the twentieth century, has provided a means for resisting social structures and dominant identities. Research into these sartorial forms of resistance, such as subcultural style, has demonstrated the role fashion and dress play in enacting change in individual subjectivities and, in turn, in broader social life. As Kaja Silverman states: 'If [...] clothing not only draws the body so that it can be seen, but also maps out the shape of the ego, then every transformation within a society's vestimentary code implies some kind of shift within its ways of articulating subjectivity.'[46] Deviant appearance is the visual enactment of social change. If, then, as Simmel argues, sensory micro experience provides the building blocks of larger social life, we can begin to consider how the multi-sensory experience of clothing, not just its appearance, can also provide a means of resisting and negotiating the disciplining social gaze of others, which ultimately affects social and cultural change. Paul Sweetman has argued, in relation to subcultural identity, that fashion and style are not purely visual statements. The feel of clothing against the body, the way it makes the wearer move and act, that is, how clothing shapes a 'particular habitus' also helps 'to shape both individual and group subjectivities'.[47]

Remaining open to a fuller range of sensory knowledge and experience allows us to move beyond the focus on dress and fashion as appearance and therefore explore the complexities of the relationship between the wearer and their clothes. This relates to male as well as female experience. As will be demonstrated in the following empirical examples, while gender shapes particular sensory experience, it is not only women who have a complex multi-sensory relationship with their clothing.

Sensory dress strategies: Negotiating the social gaze

How dress items looked and their own appearance when dressed were important daily considerations for the participants in my study, framed by aesthetic preferences and a self-conscious awareness of how others might perceive them within social situations. All of the participants acknowledged the need to dress appropriately and to take into account how other people might interpret their outfits in relation to social conventions and expectations of what they should look like, but they did not always comply with this need and sometimes challenged or subverted it.

Related to this body consciousness, in my interviews dress was, at times, used by the participants to pull in their bodies, to reshape them in an attempt to make their bodies both look and feel good. Managing these haptic sensations of dress could provide – like managing appearance – a means of conforming to but also negotiating the pressures from wider social structuring forces and discourses, which included normative and ideal notions around body shape and appropriate dressing. For example, one participant, James, collected and loved to wear American workwear. He talked in detail about the fabrics and how they felt to the touch, the structure of the garments and how they felt on. In this way, touch was central to how these items connoted, for James, a rather nostalgic sense of 'authenticity', 'toughness' and 'masculinity'. He told me that he often wore a particular pea coat – a heavy woollen double breasted coat traditionally worn by sailors – for smarter, social occasions:

> When I put it on, it's got shape. It's almost like *you* have to fit the coat. The coat is not particularly forgiving to you. 'No. This is the shape I'm gonna be' (Laughter). And you kind of sort of have to deal with that … It's almost like it's made out of cast iron. I love the rigidity of it.

Here, James's body is affected. He changed to 'fit' the coat, not the other way round. The coat transformed the way he moved about the world, his deportment and attitude. It made him feel, act and possibly appear more contained and formal – and more 'masculine'. His body is disciplined not only through the perceived gaze of others, relating to how he thinks he should look, but also by the structure and feel of the coat on his body. Yet, while James's body is being disciplined, this is a physical sensation that he experienced as pleasurable.

In a different example, Robert illustrated the importance of haptic sensation in relation to his sense of self. Here I am using the term 'haptic' to describe how the whole body experiences and is affected by the feel of dress moving against, touching or pressing upon the body. Robert, who was born in the 1950s, remembered being forced to wear shorts as a schoolboy – which he hated with a passion – how the sensation of pulling on long trousers for the first time felt like a transition into manhood. He described how the very fabric itself seemed softer and of a better quality against the skin, which contributed to the physical sensation of having grown up and gained importance in the world. This is a type of sensory experience, in this instance haptic, that was felt intimately by Robert and had personal significance within his life relating to his specific social, cultural and life situation at the time. Wearing shorts had both private haptic and public visual meaning – he looked more grown up to others within society and he himself could sense this transition to adulthood. In this instance, both the visual and the haptic aspects of his dressed body are confirming the social rules that are guiding Robert's bodily sense of transition. This experience became a powerful sensory memory for Robert that framed his appreciation of the agency clothing could hold for him.

One of the main strategies employed to negotiate the gaze was through inviting and deflecting the attention of others by managing the sensory dimensions of their dress, such as hiding and/or revealing parts of the body or changing the body's scent and sound. These strategies provided an element of control over how 'visible' or 'invisible' they were or to put it in a multi-sensory way, helped to mediate the 'impressions' that they made on others in social life. For example, the sound of shoes was at times used by various participants to create impact or blend in within a social situation. Ryan illustrated this, when he discussed his brogues: 'Yeah. I've got a pair of brogues that I sometimes wear for work. Sometimes I love the noise that they make. And sometimes I hate it.' He said he liked it when 'I've got a spring in my step and I'm feeling bold and I'm in a look-at-me mode'. In this way, aural dimensions of clothing, like visual dimensions, can be seen to contribute to an individual's 'presentation of self'[48] providing a means to manage feelings of self-confidence and self-consciousness. As a result, the sound of clothing can have an important effect on how a person inhabits a social space, whether making them stand out or blend in, garner negative, positive or a confused response from others. Another participant, Corin, stated that he did not want to draw attention to himself, so he was happy that his shoes were quiet. He said, 'I like to creep around unnoticed so I kind of – they (the soles) are quite soft.' Karen also echoed a similar sentiment when she stated:

> Not in England, but when I was in Poland, I already attracted loads of attention from people because I wear colourful stuff, and I was bullied and making sound would make it even worse so yeah, I never really wear stuff like dresses that make sound.

Alternatively, the sound of clothing can intensify the impression a person makes on others. One participant, Pamela, remembered how the sound of her clothing helped to signal her 'arrival' and domination at an important fashion awards event in Milan. In order to make an impression, she had purchased for the occasion an unusual raffia jacket. She described it as 'perfect' and 'magical', standing out against the classic, conservative style favoured by many Milanese. Pamela described the jacket in all its sensory dimensions, how the shiny black raffia 'sparkled', and was 'crunchy' yet 'malleable'. She expanded on the sound, 'It rustled, it rustled. So, particularly if you were doing the arm business, it rustled.' When I asked her how that made her feel, she said, 'I loved that. You know. Again, it's like, we used to wear large, clanking bracelets and they'd drive you mad.' Pamela, who worked in fashion, is aware that within fashion circles great emphasis is placed on dressing well and in an interesting way, wanting others to notice their clothes, and through this, establish their status. Therefore, to make an impact within this context requires something that will make an extraordinary impression and sound can provide that. She remembers:

> The noise, you know. But that was a terribly fashion-y thing because, eventually, when I got to know fashion editors, they liked making noise. You know it's like, they liked showing people they were in the room and clank, clank on the table or the desk is just part of it, you know? It's like, 'I've arrived. You can hear me coming down the corridor'. It's the shoes. And it's the bracelet. You know. Of course, it's on the phone as well but, you know … but that's the … all those things.

Additionally, more private and intimate aspects of sensory dress experience, for example the touch of clothing on the skin, at times gave the participants a private sense of pleasure and resistance that contradicted how others perceived their appearance and the degree to which they were conforming to the social expectations and gaze of others. The need to conform to these expectations could be balanced out through a choice of outfit that had particular sensory properties with personal meanings for the wearer. This was apparent in one participant's, Susan, description of a wedding she recently attended and the outfit she eventually chose to wear.

Susan, by her own admission, had a conflicted relationship with clothes, particularly around the tension between social expectations and her own enjoyment of dress. She was quite ethically minded and disliked high street shopping, both on a practical and a moral level, but loved to find a second-hand bargain. I met her at a local clothes swap. The wedding that she described was a large family affair, taking place abroad and her daughter wanted her to buy a new outfit for it. In this instance, Susan resisted her daughter's suggestion and instead suggested wearing an old dress that she had picked up at a previous clothes swap, one she was not particularly fond of and had never worn because she disliked the synthetic fabric. To Susan's surprise her daughter thought it would be 'perfect'. Susan explained:

> I just felt like laughing because it was so ridiculous. I wore that and I was actually reading a poem out at the wedding in the cathedral and she thought it was all fine ... Here's a dress that I have never worn, never really wanted to wear particularly – I didn't think it looked particularly nice, but she did – and it was a clothes swap (laughter).

Susan realized:

> It was her idea of what I looked like [...] it was perfectly ordinary, short-sleeved, polka dot. It was awful material I remember, Crimplene type stuff, but it didn't matter because nobody was going to come up and feel it, nobody cared.

Susan was aware of the conflict between how she appeared to others (including her daughter) and how she thought she looked, but also how the fabric felt to wear. The feel of the Crimplene against her skin was unpleasant and symbolized the artificial. Susan did not feel this was appropriate for a wedding nor was it something she liked to wear: in fact she did not even think she looked particularly good. There is a tension here between Susan's experience and interpretation and that of her daughter, who thinks she looked perfect and assumes that her mother likes the dress. But Susan is not anxious, rather she is aware of the playful irony inherent in the situation. Both conforming yet privately resisting, Susan appeared to have made an effort, to have worn something smart and appropriate, something that was 'her', yet she would never normally have worn it. In a double irony, she loves the fact that only *she* can feel the Crimplene, only she knows the dress came from a clothes swap, which is in fact a private expression of her inner beliefs. Susan experiences this tension as a positive and satisfying revelation and confirmation of her own agency, subjectivity and positioning within the situation and life more generally. In this instance, she has successfully drawn upon her sensory and emotional relationship to the dress to balance out the negative pressure she felt from the social requirements of the wedding and the social gaze of her daughter and others. In this way, it is argued that private sensory aspects of dress, such as touch, can have important meanings for the wearer, meanings that may be hidden from observers and that challenge the power of the gaze.

Mark M. Smith, a sensory historian, has highlighted the historical importance of non-visual sensory dimensions of clothing, intimate aspects – such as the touch of clothing against skin – that make up the experiential minutiae of daily life. These aspects may seem trivial or mundane, but can nonetheless have wider political, as well as personal, value and meaning for the wearer and for those observing them. He points out that historically, 'clothing was not simply and singularly visual; it was also tactile by definition, suggesting something important about the wearer's skin and, ergo, about his or her worth or social standing'.[49] Smith outlines how the wearing of luxuriously soft materials like fur was, at certain moments in history, confined to the powerful classes in a number of cultures, yet historians have failed to appreciate the importance of this due to a focus on the 'visual'. He identified clothing as having two points of perception and meaning-making, the inside which is sensed by the body of the wearer and the outside which is perceived by the observer. Tim Dant, in his writing on material culture, similarly observes:

> It is through experiencing the inside of a thing, through sensing and responding to its 'pushiness', that we are able to collaborate with material objects, recognizing from their inside something about the rest of the world, including ourselves as physical objects.[50]

The participants in my study described both sensory dress strategies and complex meanings related to the sensory dimensions of their dress. I have highlighted some of these here, but there are many more pertaining to all the senses, including vision, sound and smell that emerged in my study. This demonstrates the importance of paying attention to how garments feel on the inside to the wearer, sitting against the body, and how they sound and smell, as well as how the dressed body appears. These sensory elements work together to constitute the public presentation of self and the negotiation of individual subjectivities within social life. As previously stated, this moves away from approaching the dressed body as an object to be gazed upon and towards an appreciation of the embodied and dressed self as a meaningful, active subject. Theorizing the dressed body as having a 'sensory atmosphere', and considering how an empathetic, 'ambient gaze' might complicate how dressed bodies are understood and interpreted, can enable a more nuanced understanding of the role dress plays in everyday social life. It questions the effect of the social gaze and the importance of appearance within the experience of being dressed in everyday life. Importantly, it gives agency to the wearer and values alternative experience and perspectives that challenge dominant and potentially limiting understandings of dressed experience and its social and political implications.

Notes

1. Georg Simmel, 'Adornment', in D. Frisby and M. Featherstone (eds), *Simmel on Culture* (London, Thousand Oaks, New Delhi: Sage, 1997 [1908]), p. 207.
2. Mary Ellen Roach-Higgins and Joanne B. Eicher, 'Dress and Identity', in M.E. Roach Higgins, J.B. Eicher and K.K.P. Johnson (eds), *Dress and Identity* (New York: Fairchild Publications, 1995), pp. 7–18.
3. Joanne Entwistle, *The Fashioned Body* (Cambridge, Maiden: Polity Press, 2000).
4. Sara Chong Kwan, *Making Sense of Everyday Dress: Integrating Multi-sensory Experience within Our Understanding of Contemporary Dress in the UK*. PhD diss., (London College of Fashion, University of the Arts London, 2017). The names of all interviewees have been changed.
5. Phillip Vannini, Dennis D. Waskul and Simon Gottschalk, *The Senses in Self, Society and Culture: A Sociology of the Senses* (New York, Oxon: Routledge, 2012), p. 123.
6. For a discussion of non-Western sensory cultures, see David Howes's edited collection of essays. David Howes (ed), *Empire of the Senses: The Sensual Culture Reader* (Oxford, New York: Berg, 2005).
7. Roland Barthes, *The Fashion System* (London: Cape, 1995 [1967]).
8. Alison Lurie, *The Language of Clothes* (New York: Henry Holt, 2000 [1981]).
9. See Michel Foucault, *Discipline and Punish: The Birth of the Prison*, trans. Alan Sheridan (London, New York, Victoria, Ontario, New Delhi, Auckland, Rosebank: Penguin Books, 1977).
10. Sophie Woodward, *Why Women Wear What They Wear* (Oxford, New York: Berg, 2007). See also Alison Clarke and Daniel Miller, 'Fashion and Anxiety', *Fashion Theory* 6/2 (2002), pp. 191–214.
11. Efrat Tseelon, *The Masque of Femininity: The Presentation of Woman in Everyday Life* (London, Thousand Oaks: Sage, 1995).
12. Joanne Entwistle, 'Power Dressing and the Fashioning of the Career Woman', in L. Goodman, R. Allen, L. Janes and C. King (eds), *Buy This Book: Studies in*

Advertising and Consumption (London: Routledge, 1997). See also Entwistle, *The Fashioned Body*, pp. 311–23.

13. Shaun Cole, *Don We Now Our Gay Apparel: Gay Men's Dress in The Twentieth Century* (London: Berg, 2000).
14. Lou Taylor, *The Study of Dress History* (Manchester: Manchester University Press, 2002). See also Lou Taylor, *Establishing Dress History* (Manchester: Manchester University Press, 2004).
15. Woodward, *Why Women Wear What They Wear.*
16. Lucia Ruggerone, 'The Feeling of Being Dressed: Affect Studies and the Clothes Body', *Fashion Theory* 21/5 (2016), pp. 573–93.
17. The following section on the turn towards embodiment is developed from my earlier writing on 'Embodied Research Methods', published in the SAGE Research Methods Foundations series, part of *The SAGE Encyclopedia of Research Methods* (Sage, 2019).
18. Don Welton (ed), *The Body: Classic and Contemporary Readings* (Massachusetts, Oxford: John Wiley & Sons, 1999).
19. Entwistle, *The Fashioned Body*, pp. 12–13.
20. Colin Campbell, 'When the Meaning Is Not a Message: A Critique of the Consumption as Communication Thesis', in M. Barnard (ed), *Fashion Theory: A Reader* (Oxon, New York: Routledge, 2007), pp. 159–69.
21. Ibid., p. 166.
22. Entwistle, *The Fashioned Body*, p. 9.
23. Here 'haptic' describes how the body experiences and is affected by the feel of dress moving against and touching or pressing upon the body.
24. Llewellyn Negrin, 'Maurice Merleau-Ponty: The Corporeal Experience of Fashion', in A. Rocamora and A. Smelik (eds), *Thinking through Fashion* (London, New York: I.B. Taurus, 2016), pp. 115–16.
25. Maurice Merleau-Ponty, 'Eye and Mind', in G.A. Johnson (ed), *The Merleau-Ponty Aesthetics Reader* (Illinois: Northwestern University Press, 1993 [1964]) p. 124.
26. www.sensorystudies.org (accessed 20 November 2019).
27. Howes, *Empire of the Senses.*
28. Peter McNeil, 'George Simmel: The 'Philosophical Monet', in A. Rocamora and A. Smelik (eds), *Thinking through Fashion: A Guide to Key Theorists* (London and New York: I.B. Taurus, 2016), p. 66.
29. Ibid., p. 71.
30. Ibid., p. 109.
31. Ibid., p. 111.
32. Jennifer Mason, *The Socio-atmospherics of Weather* (2015) [Internet]. Available at http://www.socialsciences.manchester.ac.uk/morgancentre/events/atmospheres/ (accessed 29 April 1996).

33. Susan Bordo, *Unbearable Weight: Feminism, Western Culture and the Body* (Berkeley, Los Angeles, London: University of California Press, 2003 [1993]), p. 35.
34. Sarah Pink, *Doing Sensory Ethnography* (London, California, New Delhi, Singapore: Sage, 2009), p. 136.
35. Iris Marion Young, *On Female Body Experience: 'Throwing Like a Girl' and Other Essays* (New York: Oxford University Press, 2005 [1988]) p. 643.
36. Luce Irigaray, *Speculum of the Other Woman*, trans. G.C. Gill (Ithaca, NY: Cornell University Press, 1985).
37. Luce Irigaray quoted in Young, *On Female Body Experience*, p. 68.
38. Ruggerone, 'The Feeling of Being Dressed: Affect Studies and the Clothes Body', pp. 573–593.
39. Daniel Miller, 'Introduction', in S. Kuchler and D. Miller (eds), *Clothing as Material Culture* (Oxford, New York: Berg, 2005). p. 3.
40. Howes, *Empire of the Senses*, p. 10.
41. Young, *On Female Body Experience*, p. 73.
42. Elizabeth Wilson, *Adorned in Dreams* (London, New York: I.B. Taurus, 2003 [1985]).
43. Agnès Rocamora, 'Fields of Fashion: Critical Insights into Bourdieu's Sociology of Culture', *Journal of Consumer Culture* 2/3 (2002), pp. 341–62.
44. Wilson, *Adorned in Dreams*, p. 13.
45. Mark Paterson, *The Senses of Touch: Haptics, Affects and Technologies* (Oxford, New York: Berg, 2007), p. 2.
46. Kaja Silverman, 'Fragments of a Fashionable Discourse', in S. Benstock and S. Ferriss (eds), *On Fashion* (New Jersey: Rutgers University Press, 1994 [1986]), p. 193.
47. Paul Sweetman, 'Shop-window Dummies?', in J. Entwistle and E. Wilson (eds), *Body Dressing* (Oxford, New York: Berg, 2001), p. 67.
48. Erving Goffman, *The Presentation of Self in Everyday Life* (London, New York, Victoria, Toronto, New Delhi, Albany, Rosebank: Penguin Books, 1990 [1959]).
49. Mark, M. Smith, *Sensory History* (Oxford, New York: Berg, 2007) p. 106.
50. Tim Dant, *Material Culture in the Social World: Values, Activities, Lifestyles* (Buckingham, Philadelphia: Open University Press, 1999), p. 123.

Bibliography

Barthes, Roland, *The Fashion System* (London: Cape, 1995 [1967]).
Bordo, Susan, *Unbearable Weight: Feminism, Western Culture and the Body* (Berkeley, Los Angeles, London: University of California Press, 2003 [1993]).
Campbell, Colin, 'When the Meaning Is Not a Message: A Critique of the Consumption as Communication Thesis', in M. Barnard (ed), *Fashion Theory: A Reader* (Oxon, New York: Routledge, 2007), pp. 159–69.
Chong Kwan, Sara, *Making Sense of Everyday Dress: Integrating Multi-sensory Experience within Our Understanding of Contemporary Dress in the UK*. PhD diss., (London College of Fashion, University of the Arts London, 2017).
Chong Kwan, Sara, 'Embodied Methods in Qualitative Research', in P. Atkinson, S. Delamont, A. Cernat, J.W. Sakshaug, and R.A. Williams (eds), *SAGE Research Methods Foundations* (online: Sage, 2019).
Clarke, Alison and Daniel Miller, 'Fashion and Anxiety', in *Fashion Theory* 6/2 (2002), pp. 191–214.
Cole, Shaun, *Don We Now Our Gay Apparel: Gay Men's Dress in The Twentieth Century* (London: Berg, 2000).
Dant, Tim, *Material Culture in the Social World: Values, Activities, Lifestyles* (Buckingham, Philadelphia: Open University Press, 1999).
Entwistle, Joanne, 'Power Dressing and the Fashioning of the Career Woman', in L. Goodman, R. Allen, L. Janes and C. King (eds), *Buy This Book: Studies in Advertising and Consumption* (London: Routledge, 1997), pp. 311–23.
Entwistle, Joanne, *The Fashioned Body* (Cambridge, Maiden: Polity Press, 2000).
Foucault, Michel, *Discipline and Punish: The Birth of the Prison*, trans. Alan Sheridan (London, New York, Victoria, Ontario, New Delhi, Auckland, Rosebank: Penguin Books, 1977).
Goffman, Erving, *The Presentation of Self in Everyday Life* (London, New York, Victoria, Toronto, New Delhi, Albany, Rosebank: Penguin Books, 1990 [1959]).
Howes, David (ed), *Empire of the Senses: The Sensual Culture Reader* (Oxford, New York: Berg, 2005).
Irigaray, Luce, *Speculum of the Other Woman*, trans. G.C. Gill (Ithaca, NY: Cornell University Press, 1985).
Lurie, Alison, *The Language of Clothes* (New York: Henry Holt, 2000 [1981]).
Mason, Jennifer, *The Socio-atmospherics of Weather* (2015) [Internet] Available at http://www.socialsciences.manchester.ac.uk/morgancentre/events/atmospheres/ (accessed 29 April 1996).
Miller, Daniel, 'Introduction', in S. Kuchler and D. Miller (eds), *Clothing as Material Culture* (Oxford, New York: Berg, 2005), pp. 1–20.
McNeil, Peter, 'George Simmel: The 'Philosophical Monet', in A. Rocamora and A. Smelik (eds), *Thinking through Fashion: A Guide to Key Theorists* (London and New York: I.B. Taurus, 2016), pp. 63–80.
Merleau-Ponty, Maurice, 'Eye and Mind', in G.A. Johnson (ed), *The Merleau-Ponty Aesthetics Reader* (Illinois: Northwestern University Press, 1993 [1964]), pp. 121–49.

Negrin, Llewellyn, 'Maurice Merleau-Ponty: The Corporeal Experience of Fashion', in A. Rocamora and A. Smelik (eds), *Thinking through Fashion* (London, New York: I.B. Taurus, 2016), pp. 115–31.

Paterson, Mark, *The Senses of Touch: Haptics, Affects and Technologies* (Oxford, New York: Berg, 2007).

Pink, Sarah, *Doing Sensory Ethnography* (London, California, New Delhi, Singapore: Sage, 2009).

Roach-Higgins, Mary-Ellen and Joanne B. Eicher, 'Dress and Identity', in M.E. Roach Higgins, J.B. Eicher and K.K.P. Johnson (eds), *Dress and Identity* (New York: Fairchild Publications, 1995), pp. 7–18.

Rocamora, Agnès, 'Fields of Fashion: Critical Insights into Bourdieu's Sociology of Culture', *Journal of Consumer Culture* 2/3 (2002), pp. 341–62.

Ruggerone, Lucia, 'The Feeling of Being Dressed: Affect Studies and the Clothes Body', *Fashion Theory* 21/5 (2016), pp. 573–93.

Silverman, Kaja, 'Fragments of a Fashionable Discourse', in S. Benstock and S. Ferriss (eds), *On Fashion* (New Jersey: Rutgers University Press, 1994 [1986]), pp. 183–96.

Simmel, Georg, 'Adornment', in D. Frisby and M. Featherstone (eds), *Simmel on Culture* (London, Thousand Oaks, New Delhi: Sage, 1997 [1908]), pp. 206–10.

Simmel, Georg, 'The Sociology of the Senses', in D. Frisby and M. Featherstone (eds), *Simmel on Culture* (London, Thousand Oaks, New Delhi: Sage, 1997 [1908]), pp. 109–19.

Smith, Mark, M., *Sensory History* (Oxford, New York: Berg, 2007).

Sweetman, Paul, 'Shop-window Dummies?', in J. Entwistle and E. Wilson (eds), *Body Dressing* (Oxford, New York: Berg, 2001), pp. 59–78.

Taylor, Lou, *The Study of Dress History* (Manchester: Manchester University Press, 2002).

Taylor, Lou, *Establishing Dress History* (Manchester: Manchester University Press, 2004).

Tseelon, Efrat, *The Masque of Femininity: The Presentation of Woman in Everyday Life* (London, Thousand Oaks: Sage, 1995).

Vannini, Phillip, Dennis D. Waskul and Simon Gottschalk, *The Senses in Self, Society and Culture: A Sociology of the Senses* (New York, Oxon: Routledge, 2012).

Welton, Don (ed), *The Body: Classic and Contemporary Readings* (Massachusetts, Oxford: John Wiley & Sons, 1999).

Wilson, Elizabeth, *Adorned in Dreams* (London, New York: I.B. Taurus, 2003 [1985]).

Woodward, Sophie, *Why Women Wear What They Wear* (Oxford, New York: Berg, 2007).

Young, Iris Marion, *On Female Body Experience: 'Throwing Like a Girl' and Other Essays* (New York: Oxford University Press, 2005 [1988]).

CHAPTER 4
THE VEILED BODY: THE ALIENATED SYSTEM OF 'LOOKING' IN POST-REVOLUTIONARY IRAN (1979–PRESENT)

Azadeh Fatehrad

Figure 3 Azadeh Fatehrad, *Departure Series*, C-type Print, Tehran (2015). Courtesy of the artist.

Introduction

Following the announcement of the compulsory dress code in Iran in 1979, Ayatollah Khomeini (the founder of the Islamic Republic of Iran and the country's supreme leader[1]) drew on the Quran to support his idea that veiling was a form of protection for women. He proclaimed that 'woman is a pearl that is best hidden in an oyster shell'[2] and that the veil would protect her (woman) from being sexually objectified when out in public. It is because of this momentous decree that in post-revolutionary Iran, women's bodies are mysteriously covered and inaccessible at all times. Yet, the strict segregation of men and women actually significantly charges the act of 'looking', thereby having the opposite effect that Khomeini purportedly intended. This is because the 'moral police' and its avatars create the fantasy of an omnipresent and omniscient gaze that shames a woman who shows what she should not be showing.

This chapter reflects on the highly charged arena in which women's bodies are watched, whether by the police, the government or the general public. It builds upon traditional theories of looking, such as Laura Mulvey's Male Gaze Theory and Hamid Naficy's 'Veiled Vision' (1999), and aims to draw a clearer picture of the act of looking in the context of contemporary Iran by referring to theoretical texts on practices of veiling, combined with my own autobiographical accounts. In addition, the chapter goes on to explore feminist strategies of resistance to the compulsory dress code introduced during the 1979 revolution.

The hijab in Iran: An overview

I remember that when I was very young, I would play volleyball in our front garden. Occasionally, my ball would inadvertently go over the garden wall. Once, I wanted to go outside, just a few steps beyond the gate of our house, to retrieve my ball. My mother warned me to put on something appropriate before stepping out onto the street. I was frustrated and did not wish to be delayed. My indignant reply was, 'No, Mother, there's no-one there!' but my mother insisted that I change before going out. While it was true that there was no one in the street, the fact that I was going outside the house meant I was entering the public space. This action for my mother, like many other Iranian adults, meant that there was always someone watching. The historical context of the hijab clearly hinges on this idea of surveillance. My story ties into broader regime changes in Iran and subsequent activism that enunciated and politicized women's embodied experience of living within such a regime of looking.

During the twentieth century in Iran, the meaning of 'hijab' went through several transformations. Unveiled women symbolized the secular and westernized regime of Reza Shah's son and successor, Mohammad Reza Shah (1941–79). Then, 'wrapped in a black chador', women became icons of the Islamic Revolution (1979–96) and, two decades later, their more relaxed, colourful and vibrant hijabs became the symbol of a new era of progress and reform in the Islamic Republic (1997–present).

Before 1936 (a momentous point in time for Iranian history when the Shah gave a speech in support of women at a graduation ceremony) middle- and upper-class women would wear full-length head-to-toe clothing and, occasionally, an additional face covering called a *pichih*. The hijab for peasant and tribal women who worked mostly in the fields consisted of a colourful *rusari* (headscarf) and loose clothing, which provided them with more freedom of movement than the floor-length chador and, therefore, with greater comfort. For the younger generation who had been brought up without the veil, the headscarf was generally considered unfashionable and a sign of backwardness and devout religiosity, all of which they were keen to distance themselves from, so for them it was not a consideration. At the turn of the twentieth century, the more covered a woman was, and the more modesty in her behaviour and demeanour, the higher her social status was deemed to be.[3]

This hierarchy of women was somewhat eroded during the reign of Mohammad Reza Shah because women were allowed to wear what they wanted. As a result, different and unexpected forms of fashion such as a short chador with high heels emerged, as revealed by videos in the US National Library that depict the lives of women in Tehran in 1943. A question which started to arise is, to what extent can fashion express an oppressive or liberated social condition? Here, Reina Lewis's work is relevant, in terms of fashion and modesty and the relation between the current currencies of modest fashion, faith and representation. This point will be returned to later.

During this era (the mid-twentieth century), slowly but surely, progress was made in terms of women's rights and status in Iranian society, but this progress was not consistent. For instance, while women readily had access to the birth control pill and abortions, they still needed written permission from their husbands to travel abroad.[4] Reza Shah and, later, Mohammad Reza Shah pushed through quick dramatic changes without any real platform that would allow women to negotiate their lives outside of the home. On the surface, these changes might appear progressive, but the core structure was not stable and much still needed to be done for women's rights. It was only in 1963 that the right to vote was granted for women in Iran and in that same year the first woman was elected to Iran's parliament, Dr Farrakhroo Parsay. Under the iron rule of Reza Shah, the judiciary was secularized in 1931, but family law was left to the jurisdiction of the clergy and the dictate of Sharia law. That said, one great achievement during Mohammad Reza Shah's reign was the passing of the Family Protection Law in 1967, which set up special courts to deal with family law matters and put useful safeguards in place with regard to the minimum marriageable age, divorce and child custody.[5]

The Iranian Revolution (1979) called for the foundation of an Islamic state based on Islamic principles and the upholding of Islamic law. It imposed a strict dress code on women, with veiling being a visible symbol of that commitment. Islamic fundamentalists believe that this is necessary in order to prevent sexual tension in society because men are deemed incapable of controlling their sexual desire.[6] Women must cover themselves so that men are not tempted and are free to go about their business.

In terms of etymology, in Farsi, *poshesh* ('clothing') is derived from the verb *pushidan*, meaning to cover up or conceal from view, whereas the English term 'dress' refers to, among other things, decorating or adorning. On the other hand, the word 'hijab' is derived from the Farsi word *hojb*, meaning modesty and shyness, and *bi hejab* refers to a woman who lacks such modesty. From this, a concept known as the 'hijabisation of behaviour' has been coined, which applies regardless of whether a woman is actually wearing a veil and is apparently essential for the construction and maintenance of virtue, respect and social acceptability.[7] At the heart of the concept lies the *hijab-i-iffat* itself, which is not just 'a piece of cloth external to the female body' but 'a veil to be acquired through modern education, as some internal quality of self, … a disciplined modern body that obscured the women's sexuality, obliterated its bodily presence'.[8] In fact, the understanding of the specific requirements of the hijab has been, and continues to be, a point of argument among legal traditions and individual jurists (there is no real consensus here).

In post-revolutionary Iran, the covering took two forms: the first was the full black veil that stretched from head to toe and the second a headscarf accompanied by a loose long-sleeved garment in a dark colour such as dark blue, black or grey. Therefore, while 'black from head to toe' is an expression that is commonly used to describe a woman wearing a veil, in reality, this is not always the case, particularly among the younger generations, and the expression perhaps more accurately refers to the idea of the Islamists encouraging women to wear dark colours rather than referring strictly to the veil. In addition to these stipulations, with regard to clothing, women could not 'wear … make-up, perfume, or anything that might attract the attention of the Basij or moral police'.[9]

To understand the reasons behind the Women's Uprising that occurred in response to the compulsory dress code on 8 March 1979 (as discussed below), it is necessary to understand how much women had struggled prior to the revolution. Their strong feelings had nothing to do with how they would look; rather, it reminded them of the backwardness and narrow-mindedness that they had fought so hard to get rid of, and the knowledge and independence that they had secured for themselves. They feared the 'hidden curtains' would once again make women useless and invisible in Iran, where they had been kept behind closed doors until 1925. This is because Iranian women had greatly benefited from the changes that had occurred under the reigns of the two Pahlavi monarchs (1925–79), Reza Shah and Mohammad Reza Pahlavi, in that they had educated women and enabled them to enter the workforce. At the same time, there was considerable debate about the loss of tradition that modernity had inevitably caused, but women enjoyed key achievements during this time, including securing the right to vote and seeing the passing of the Family Protection Law (mentioned above), both of which occurred around 1963 and 1965.

Badr ol-Moluk Bamdad calls the first Pahlavi monarch 'the Daybreak' and points to a momentous speech in support of women, given by the Shah at a graduation ceremony at the University of Tehran on 7 January 1936.[10] In it, he recognized women as valued members of society, encouraging them to take a more active role, particularly when it came to participation in education. He believed that since women made up half of the Iranian population, their education would not only benefit them but also society as a whole.[11] He set out a vision for the future in which women were as active and powerful as men, giving them a higher status than they had ever enjoyed before. At this point, it seemed that Iranian women would emerge out of a situation where they had been kept in ignorance to one where they would become suddenly enlightened. In fact, following the ceremony, Reza Shah actually changed the rules regarding women's attire in public (1936), imposing a Western-style dress code of skirt and blouse while banning the veil/hijab.

However, this meant that following the decree, any woman found covered in public was to be forcibly uncovered. One must remember that for many years prior, women had been covered, and this sudden change was perceived by some as an act of violence against women. Indeed, feminists like Badr ol-Moluk Bamdad noted the verbal and physical harassment that veiled women were subjected to as Reza Shah's soldiers forcibly unveiled them.[12] As a result, the 1936 'Unveiling' ultimately ensured that women who had spent their entire lives wearing the veil would remain in the private confines of their homes since, for them, walking the street unveiled was tantamount to walking the street naked.[13] After this seminal day in Iranian history, women became policed by men, and their bodies became a site of enforcement. This situation is very similar to contemporary Iran, except that now, as a result of Khomeini's 1979 decree, women must cover themselves. Whoever is in power, it seems that women's bodies are perpetually a site of state control.

Despite the level of violence and aggression surrounding the 1936 'Unveiling', the dominant feminist response at the time was celebratory. It was seen as such an important milestone that Reza Shah made 7 January 'National Women's Day', replacing the 8 March International Women's Day. In essence, the Shah was modernizing the country by destroying the boundaries between the *andaroni* (the private and inner domain) and the *bironi* (the public and outer domain); in other words, women were required to appear in the street as they would at home, that is uncovered.

Alternatively, the 'Unveiling' can be seen as having the effect of at least widening the boundaries of the domestic into the public sphere. One of Reza Shah's aims was, in fact, to democratize gender roles in imitation of the Western model by unveiling women and encouraging mixed social gatherings. Prior to this decision, 'outside the home' was very much a male-dominated area; only a very limited number of women were to be found in public spaces, such as the workplace, educational settings and shops. Unveiling thus forced women to become active participants in life outside the home, for example through visiting shops, entering schools, joining the workforce and generally being outside the home in the same way as men. In this way, women gradually became more independent and participated alongside men in the public realm, meaning that society became a more balanced and mixed-sex environment.

Returning to the 1979 revolution, the day after the compulsory dress code was announced (i.e. 8 March), thousands of men and women spontaneously marched on the streets of Tehran in opposition to the decision. The demonstration continued for six days. During the first few days, people were holding up barely visible protest signs made of paper, but by days four and five, they were using curtains and marker pens and being far more effective.

Female subjectivity was the core power behind this protest, which can also be seen in relation to clothing, ornament/decoration and public appearance. At the time of the protest, the American feminist author Kate Millett was in Iran, attending a conference at Tehran University, ironically, for International Women's Day. She stated that she was extremely affected by the Women's Uprising, noting in an interview[14] that in America, a demonstration of that scale would require many years of planning and writing to women to try to persuade them to take part. She was surprised that such a large number of people had, seemingly overnight, simply taken it upon themselves to meet at a particular location the following day.

Many journalists arrived in Iran on the third day of demonstration to capture the momentous event. A fascinating documentary titled *Mouvement de libération des femmes iraniennes – année zéro* was made by four French journalists (Michelle Muller, Sylvina Boissonnas, Claudine Mulard and Sylviane Rey) from the group Psychanalyse et politique, part of the Mouvement de libération des femmes (MLF). In the video, journalists are seen/heard asking protesters the reason they are out on the streets.

This video documents a pivotal moment in the history of Iran and politicized women's embodied relationship with regimes of looking therein. For instance, one woman explains passionately: 'We are here for freedom. We are as many men as women. With or without the veil, we fight for freedom, for us and for the people.' Even if the price she pays is to forego her religion, the woman says she prefers to be free and not be under the control of an enforced order. A much older veiled woman gives a different reason for being there: 'I have been wearing the chador for years now for my own personal reasons. I'm not here to try to stop wearing the chador; rather, I'm the mother of six daughters and I'm protesting because I don't want them to be forced to wear the chador if they don't want to. I'm here to defend my daughters from the enforcement of the chador by men.'

The aim of the remarkable six-day protest was not just to reject the compulsory dress code or even just to protect the rights and autonomy of women away from the authority of the men who sought to force them to cover (although that was obviously a big part of it). More than that, however, the objective of the protest was also to draw people's attention back to the initial purpose of the revolution, that is to secure greater freedom and equality for all people in Iran. The protesters were fighting for equal pay for men and women, for freedom of the press and for freedom of speech and assembly, among other things.

In 2015, at Comité des femmes contre la lapidation in France, as part of the 8 March International Women's Day celebrations, Shahin Nawai[15] presented her poignant account of the demonstration she herself had taken part in more than thirty-five years prior. Nawai was one of the founders of the feminist movement in Iran, which effectively created the National Unity of Women's Associations during the 1979 uprising. On 8 March 1979, Nawai and her friends decided to support the Iranian women's movement in order to try to stop the rolling back of women's rights as society became Islamized. They believed they were protecting the future of women in Iran, and were joined by feminists from France, Germany, Egypt and many other countries, all of whom were anxious to lend their support to Iranian women. This led to the creation of a Solidarity Committee (CIDF) headed up by French writer Simone de Beauvoir (Figure 4). Nawai notes that the uprising became calmer on the fourth day when Mahmoud Taleghani from the government came to talk to the people and tried to persuade them that Khomeini was not, in fact, enforcing the wearing of the hijab but was rather merely suggesting that women should be encouraged to wear it for the purposes of public order and decency. This, of course, turned out to be a subterfuge and, by April 1983, the compulsory veil was in full force, applying to all women in Iran regardless of nationality, and women's rights were gradually eroded.

Upon close examination, it does appear that the focus of the feminist movement in Iran has always been about reclaiming human dignity for all people.[16] Nawai argues that feminism and Islam are unable to exist in harmony because Islam does not really provide for equality, open discussion and individual choice or prerogative (by its nature, this is the core of feminism).[17] It is, in any case, instructive to note that it was women who first noticed the totalitarian threat of the Islamic government.

Figure 4 *F-Magazine*, Paris (1979).

'Looking' in Iranian society

The religious dress code aims to provide modesty but, at least to a certain degree, it encourages the invisibility of women, due to the uniform dress code and the shapeless, unfashionable attire women are required to wear. Reina Lewis notes that even though faith-related fashion (for Muslim women, Jewish women, etc.) may convey a certain sense of solidarity and unification, in the current context of online platforms such as 'My Stealthy Freedom',[18] covered women have become highly visible to the point of being overexposed.[19] This kind of hypervisibility is, in fact, just another way to deny people recognition and the right to be truly seen, which is why the gaze here is a negative and judgemental one.

Iranian women today publicly express their resistance to the authorities and the conditions imposed on them in an aesthetic way, appropriating the very object of oppression (the veil) and turning it into an object of aesthetic pleasure and beauty. In this way, the hijab is turned into a fashion accessory, that is something that can be added to complete or complement an outfit. This element will typically have a young, modern, perhaps Western feel to it; this mix or combination of fashions is not unique to Iranian women but can be seen among all Muslim women who are 'modest dressers'. As Reina Lewis states in *Modest Fashion: Styling Bodies, Mediating Faith*, modest dressers tend to be regarded as 'representatives of essentialized, unchanging collective religious identities'.[20] Lewis goes on to raise an interesting question about modest fashion: 'Does this help to keep people in the faith … Or does it dangerously dilute religious identifications?'[21]In other words, Muslim women might ask themselves if they want to blend in and become part of the secular fashionscape.

The global media certainly seems quite fixated on the 'mystery' behind the veil and enjoys printing images not only of women wearing the veil but of them removing it.[22] This is arguably unhelpful and serves only to highlight the differences between Muslims and Westerners. There is also very much a sense of the veiled woman being inferior but becoming superior once her veil is removed. It is crucial to note that the values expressed by veiling are related not only to a woman's concealment (as the international press will often suggest) but to much broader moral, sexual, political, economic and aesthetic considerations on the part of both men and women. It is not for nothing that the subject of the veil is a constant preoccupation for everyone in Iran.

Today, the traditional equation of veiled = sexualized is no longer as clear or as immutable as it once was. Now a woman can be veiled and also have a public voice and presence,[23] meaning that the situation today is double-edged. There is no state of full or absolute 'veiled-ness' or 'unveiled-ness'; whether veiled or unveiled, there is a constant duality. The question, however, is whether concealing the body in this way empowers the woman or whether it is by revealing herself and being seen that she is empowered.

The hijab is governed by an Islamic conceptualization of space that is divided into two categories: *mahrem* and *namahrem*. In this context, *mahrem* ('unlawful') refers to a father, brother, uncle or other close male family member whom a woman is permitted to be seen by without her veil (chador) but whom she is forbidden from marrying (hence 'unlawful'). By contrast, *namahrem* (not *mahrem*) refers to any other man around whom women must be covered and veiled at all times. The *namahrem* men are considered 'lawful' because there is potential for sexual union between them (unlike the potential for incestuous union between family members which is thus unlawful).[24] This separation and categorization of space as *mahrem* or *namahrem* is, therefore, based on what type of male 'looker' (forbidden or permitted) is present in the space. In this way, veiling can be said to construct social space – and vice versa.

French philosopher Henri Lefebvre describes a similar creation of space in *The Production of Space*,[25] referring to space as socially produced (i.e. it does not exist of its own accord). In this context, space lies in-between the 'scene' that can take place there and the 'obscene' that cannot, with the two existing at the same time.[26] Lefebvre recognizes three forms of space – that which is conceived, that which is lived in and that which is perceived. Following this line of thinking, the chador can be said to be a space that is conceived, a space that is lived in (by the woman wearing it) and, while the woman is moving around in this private territory and interacting with others, the space is also being perceived and interpreted by others.

The cloak worn by women in Iran is known in Persian as the 'chador', a word derived from the Turkish word *chadir*; in modern Turkish, this word means 'tent' as Çagla Hadimioglu notes.[27] In this way, the chador (cloak) can be seen as a kind of mobile home around a woman's body, which facilitates her movement around the city and her dealings with men. The accessibility of a space in Iran is, as mentioned above, related to the category of male looker (permitted or forbidden) found there. However, it is important to note that public space in Iran is geared towards permitted male lookers.[28] Even though a woman may be walking alongside a forbidden male looker (i.e. a father, brother or other close relative), she must still remain covered and inaccessible in outdoor spaces. Thus, the two categories of forbidden male lookers and permitted ones merge into one in public spaces in Iran where the concern is solely on keeping women hidden from men they are not closely related to.

The overall sense of self (the individual) in Iranian society is conditioned between an outer shell (the public self) and an inner core (the private self). Psychologically, the core is supposed to be private, stable, intimate and reliable, while the exterior is perceived to be unstable and unreliable, the domain of surfaces, corruption and worldly influences. In a practical sense, people and their feelings and behaviours are, of course, disjointed and operate in both the *zaheri* (external) and *bateni* (internal) spheres. Abstraction supplants concreteness, generality replaces specificity and indirection becomes common practice.[29]

This self-duality necessitates a barrier which, like a veil or screen, can protect the core from contamination from the outside. This boundary, which can consist of walls, words and/or veils, can mark, mask, separate and confine both women and men alike.[30] This segregation of the inner and outer space of self has been cautiously practised in various forms throughout history such as in architecture, dress, behaviour, voice, eye contact and relationships. Iranian scholar Farzaneh Milani notes the hijab is also a reflection of the two parts found in an affluent Iranian house: the *andaruni* (inner part) and *biruni* (outer part).[31] The position of women inside the Iranian home is similar to that described by Laura Mulvey in *Fetishism and Curiosity*, in which she refers to 'inside' space as womanly as it carries connotations of maternal femininity (the womb, the home) while also perhaps being linked to the enclosed, concealed space of secrecy (a box, a room).[32]

The protection zones and boundaries created by veils and walls suggest a general lack of trust between Iranian men themselves. In this sense, the veil or wall expresses their 'possession' of the particular woman's body concerned and, as such, their masculinity drives them to protect or hide it from other men.[33] However, these traditional beliefs are no longer held by the new generation and many youngsters have found a way to transgress these barriers, albeit strictly underground. Indeed, my visit to Tehran in 2015 differed greatly from the picture I had in my mind of my previous visits. I encountered open and relaxed male/female relationships being conducted behind closed doors in homes and in private companies. Parties in the lobbies of the modern tower blocks and buildings in West/North Tehran are now attended by men and women alike, who will dress up for the occasion. Comparisons can be made to London's Soho on a Saturday night, the only difference being that in Tehran, these parties take place clandestinely, out of sight from the moral police.

There is drinking, dancing, flirting and sometimes even kissing at these mixed-sex parties. The male gaze on these occasions might, therefore, be lustful and seductive, fuelled by lavish libidinal encounters. This is arguably harmless and merely a case of men enjoying women's company and vice versa (it is certainly the norm in the Western world). It is in stark contrast to the gaze of the moral police who sometimes violently and aggressively break up these gatherings. Their contemptuous disdainful gaze is typically directed at the women in the group, rather than the men, as the moral police believe these women have shamed and humiliated themselves.

Despite this potential danger, it seems as though the middle-class youth is able to enjoy quite an extreme, albeit secret, private life. All this makes me wonder what barriers really exist in Iran today. When inside people's homes, I was reminded of the London lifestyle, but its Islamic counterpart does continue to prevail on the streets of Tehran. Each time I visit my home city I seem to encounter more and more conflicting and bizarre combinations of fashion, trends and lifestyles. It seems that there is a duality between being inside and outside the home, a lavish rebellious life led underground away from the moral police and a parallel life in line with Islamic rules conducted above ground.

Religious scholars such as Khomeini and Musavi Khoi have, over the years, established and refined a set of rules based on Quranic texts that provide instruction on the act of looking to ensure that it is appropriate at all times. Under *Ahkam-e Negah Kardan* ("The commandments for looking"), men and women are forbidden from looking, with or without lustful thoughts or intentions, at naked bodies or body parts of people of the opposite sex to whom they are not closely related. In addition, men are forbidden from looking at women's hair and women are obligated to cover it. Looking at the sexual organs of others is forbidden, whether done directly or indirectly through a glass, in a mirror, reflected in water or in a film.[34] The strict dress code is obviously supposed to facilitate this.

In reality, men and women obviously look at each other all the time, with or without lust and desire, so in order to satisfy the rules of modesty, a certain accepted set of terminology has been created to refer to the first-degree 'direct look' and the second-degree 'averted look'.[35] The Quran warns Muslims against the danger of the direct gaze – we should lower our gaze and guard our sexual organs at all times.[36] When meeting, people tend either to look down or at the other's face in an unfocused way, so as to avoid making direct eye contact. Notwithstanding this, it is common to see a person gazing at another intently until they get noticed, at which point they will quickly look away. The type of look here lies somewhere between the evasive and aggressive furtive look. It seems that a complex system of looking is in operation, one which involves a combination of controlling the look and being controlled by it. In this case, there is no full dominance or authority by the 'looker' over the 'looked at'.

In parallel with the system of looking that operates between ordinary men and women in Iran, there is another system of looking between the authorities and the people. An example of this would be the moral police busting into private mixed-sex parties, as mentioned earlier, but it does not have to involve face-to-face interaction; rather, in a totalitarian society like Iran, one's personal or private life is open to scrutiny and control regardless of whether the powers that be are actually there or not. If we use Jeremy Bentham's Panopticon prison[37] as an analogy, in the prison, the power of looking is fully in the hands of the privileged jailers who are positioned in a tower in the middle of the building observing the cells around them day and night. They will, of course, be unable to observe each individual cell without interruption, but for the prisoners there is certainly the sense of being under constant surveillance, and this is the same in Iran also. Aside from breaking up parties or gatherings at which unrelated men and women are present, the moral police have the power to confront you in the street when they believe you have breached the strict dress code. They can also stop your car to confirm the relationship between you and the man sitting next to you, as well as many other things.

The Iranian system of looking can be understood through the metaphor of the unbuilt house that Adolf Loos designed. Within personal and collective experience, it has not been easy to demonstrate the alienated system of looking that exists in Iran. Perhaps the closest contextualization that can be offered is related to Loos's design in 1928 for Josephine Baker, in that the architectural piece provides an interior space through which the Iranian system of looking can perhaps be understood. As seen in Figure 5, Loos has placed a swimming pool at the very centre of the house with large horizontal fixed windows. Whatever direction a visitor enters the house from, their gaze is immediately directed through the glass at the pool and beyond. For instance, one can be in the living room and see, across the glazed pool, the dressing room that is on the other side of the house.

What is particularly unusual about this design is that unlike in Loos's other buildings where the occupant sees before being seen as he masterfully

Figure 5 *Looking at the Pool through a Fixed Window* (1928). From Adolf Loos's design for Josephine Baker's house.

links the corridors in the house and the staircase in the main hall, in such a way that the occupant is in full control of the look from the moment of arrival of the guest, here, to the contrary, it is the occupant who immediately becomes the object or focus of the look.

In Josephine Baker's house, the visitor is invited to look through the window that frames him in the act of looking into this inner sanctum that he himself cannot enter.[38] The swimming pool is lit from above by a skylight, so inside it the windows actually appear as reflective surfaces, impeding the swimmer's view of the visitor approaching the pool. However, the swimmer might catch a reflection of their own wet body framed by the window and over-layered on the disembodied eyes of the vague figure of the visitor, whose lower body is also framed and cut out by the window. Thus, the swimmer is not entirely unaware of the voyeur. As Beatriz Colomina notes in *Publicity and Privacy*, 'The occupant is aware of being looked at by another: a narcissistic gaze superimposed on a voyeuristic gaze. The erotic complex of looks in which the occupant is suspended is inscribed in each of the four windows opening onto the swimming pool. Even if there is no-one looking through them, each window constitutes, from both sides, a gaze.'[39]

The distance between subject and object that is necessary for the act of looking to take place is realized by Loos's use of glass and reflections and this, therefore, amounts to an alienated system of looking, as in the Iranian context. As Oswald Ungers writes, 'Entertainment in this house consists in looking, but between this gaze and its object – the body – is a screen of glass and water, which renders the body inaccessible.'[40] The position of the spectator is not fully authorized; it lies somewhere between seeing and not seeing. The system of looking actuated in the architecture behind Josephine Baker's house evokes aspects of the particular gaze upon the covered woman in Iranian society. The water and glass, just like the veil, function to abstract the viewer from direct and sustained looking, but neither the veil nor the water or glass fully conceals the body. In Iranian society, women cannot hide from nor can they return the gaze, which is paradoxically omnipresent as in Josephine Baker's house.

Regardless of the intent, historian Ludmilla Jordanova notes that the veiled woman conveys ideas of femininity, secrecy and deception.[41] Therefore, the veiled woman is alluring, exciting and maybe even dangerous, and all this mystery allows men's imagination to run wild. Applying this, a Western woman, who displays herself more than a Muslim woman, is arguably less enticing, precisely because there is less to be curious about when more is revealed. Aside from having to wear the veil, Iranian women actually have a great deal of latitude in how they present themselves to the gaze of male lookers, in terms of body language, eye contact, type of veil, clothing worn underneath the veil and what they do with the veil. As Hamid Naficy explains in *Veiled Visions/Powerful Presences: Women in Post-revolutionary Cinema: The New Iranian Cinema*, a woman might fan open or close her veil at a strategic moment to lure or to mask, to reveal or to conceal the face, the body or the clothing underneath.[42] Iranian philosopher Dariush Shayegan also notes that a veiled woman can make herself look more attractive by walking gracefully.[43]

This leads to Freud's concept of scopophilia, which is a form of voyeurism that is contingent on distance between the subject and the object because 'it is through the play of distance that desire is activated'.[44] This distance is created by a woman's veil; the looker (the subject) might actually be in close proximity, but the veil keeps the woman hidden and inaccessible, creating that distance. In this way, the object of the look (the woman) becomes highly sexualized and eroticized, which is, again, ironic given the supposed thinking behind the Islamic fundamentalist principle of veiling. It certainly seems that the veil draws more attention to the woman wearing it than she might receive if she was not wearing it.

Not surprisingly, Iranian women are frequently accused of violating the strict Islamic dress code, not just because of this use of the veil as a weapon of protest but for many other reasons. Masserat Amir-Ebrahimi, Iranian feminist and sociologist, remarks, 'In the past two decades, gradual transgressions of Urf and Shari'a have become a sign of modernity and resistance for many women and young people who wish to generate changes in their situation.'[45] She further explains: 'If "improperly veiled" women in urban public spaces are considered a challenge to Sharia and the rules of public conduct in the Islamic Republic, the acts of self-narration and self-disclosure in "Weblogistan" are considered a transgression of Urf and the rules of patriarchy.'[46]

Sociologist Christopher Jenks defines transgression as 'that conduct which breaks rules or exceeds boundaries'.[47] As such, he considers it an indicator of modernity: 'A feature of modernity, accelerating into postmodernity, is the desire to transcend limits – limits that are physical, racial, aesthetic, sexual, national, legal and moral … Modernity has unintentionally generated an ungoverned desire to extend, exceed, or go beyond the margins of acceptability or normal performance.'[48] I have witnessed that level of transgression in Iranian society in the last few years. On each of my visits I have encountered a new, higher level of openness in the underground life of the younger generations, who are doing what they want and participating in activities which would have been impossible for the older generations, communicating in ways that would simply have been inappropriate during my time.

Even though women are fighting on this common and shared web platform (Amir-Ebrahimi's 'Weblogistan' above refers to the new path of self-expression that has emerged online), the movement is more or less based upon individual acts of pushing the boundaries in terms of the restrictions imposed on women. In both the case of veiling and the writing (blogging) that has become so popular, a woman expresses/exposes herself publicly. Both are a means of expression and communication: 'One gives her voice a body, the other gives her body a voice.'[49] Through both, an absence becomes a presence.

Conclusion

In this chapter, I have discussed the concept of looking and the history of the veil (chador) in Iran. Having seen the chronological stages of veiling (1907), unveiling (1936) and re-veiling (1979), one could conclude that the state has had massive power and authority over women's bodies over the last two centuries. The fashionable female body was certainly one of the first targets of the Islamic Republic of Iran when, twenty-four days after the revolution, the compulsory dress code was announced.

In recent years, there has been a major shift in the way the veil is perceived by women. No longer solely an instrument of their segregation, it has come to facilitate women's access to the public arena and given them a means to renegotiate boundaries. For instance, there are numerous advisory roles for women as many governors need an advisor on women's affairs, so many women use the chador to gain access to leadership roles in government.[50] By discussing different forums in which the veil is perceived (and judged), such as online platforms and public spaces, we could conclude that veiling actually amounts to a highly charged dress code for women.

The concept of looking and how it is perceived in Iranian society are not only limited to digital (online) and physical (public) spaces. There are, in fact, several contextualizations of space that are held within Iranian culture, as seen with *mahram/namahram*. However, the two categories of forbidden male lookers (*namahram*) and permitted ones (*mahram*) merge into one in public spaces in Iran. The most contemporary discovery of mine in relation to looking and the female body relates to the alienated system of looking which I grew up with myself, an omnipresent state gaze over your everyday life activities, which is invisible yet powerfully present, causing immense paranoia.

At the same time, one can conclude that the veil no longer protects a woman from the outside gaze, but rather overexposes her as is the case with online platforms and the notion of hypervisibility. Veiled women in non-Muslim countries (a minority) are certainly subject to this hypervisibility and an often scrutinizing look. It therefore seems that, paradoxically, the veil draws more attention to the woman wearing it than she might receive if she was not wearing it.

Notes

1. The highest-ranking political and religious authority of Iran, which he held until his death in 1989.
2. KING-slave of ALLAH, 'ISLAM – World's Greatest Religion!' Available at https://islamgreatreligion.wordpress.com/2010/12/04/hidden-pearls/ (accessed 20 April 2017).
3. Badr ol-Moluk Bamdad and Nasrin Rahimieh, *From Darkness into Light: Women's Emancipation in Iran* (California: Mazda Publishers, 1980), pp. 7–23.
4. Haideh Daragahi and Nina Witoszek, 'Anti-totalitarian Feminism? Civic Resistance in Iran', in L. Trägårdh, N. Witoszek and B. Taylor (eds), *Civil Society in the Age of Monitory Democracy* (Oxford: Berghahn Books, 2013), pp. 231–54.
5. Ibid.
6. Morteza Motahhari, *The Problem of Hijab* (Tehran: Basir Publication, 1986), p. 29.
7. Fataneh Farahani, *Gender, Sexuality and Diaspora* (New York/Oxon: Routledge, 2018), p. 169.
8. Ibid., p. 148.
9. Masserat Amir-Ebrahimi, 'Transgression in Narration: The Lives of Iranian Women in Cyberspace', *Journal of Middle East Women's Studies* 4/3, Special Issue – Innovative Women: Unsung Pioneers of Social Change (Fall 2008), p. 92.
10. Badr ol-moluk Bamdad, *From Darkness into Light: Women's Emancipation in Iran*. Introduction by N. Rahimieh. Translated from Persian and edited by F.R.C. Bagley (California: Mazda Publishers, 2013), pp. 7–23.
11. See Taj Al-Saltana, *Crowning Anguish: Memoirs of a Persian Princess from the Harem to Modernity*, trans A. Vanzan, ed. E. Abbas (Washington DC: Mage Publishers, 2003), p. 200.
12. Ibid., p. 20.
13. Bamdad, *From Darkness into Light*, pp. 7–23.
14. *Mouvement de libération des femmes iraniennes – année zéro*. Produced by Des Femmes Filment. France (Distributed by Des Femmes Filment, 1979). Short. 13 min.
15. Jamileh Nedai, *Le Comité des Femmes Contre la Lapidation* [Online Video]. 2015. Available at https://www.youtube.com/watch?v=_7mnB_exy9I (Part 1) and https://www.youtube.com/watch?v=gP9NrL6Y5kA&list=UUYCQJkRR9Py D3HXJZ8 STlZg (Part 2) (accessed 14 December 2018).
16. See Daragahi and Witoszek, 'Anti-totalitarian Feminism?', pp. 231–54.
17. Nedai, *Le Comité des Femmes Contre la Lapidation*.

18. My Stealthy Freedom was founded in 2013 by London-based Iranian journalist Masih Alinejad. The impetus behind the site was to promote Iranian women's right to choose whether or not to wear the hijab. Iranian women use the Facebook page to share photos of themselves not wearing the hijab, in defiance of the state-imposed dress rule. The majority of posts are in Farsi but with all the online translation tools available these days, they could potentially be accessed by all.
19. Reina Lewis, *Gendering Orientalism: Race, Femininity and Representation* (London: Routledge, 1996).
20. Reina Lewis, *Modest Fashion: Styling Bodies, Mediating Faith* (London: I.B. Tauris, 2013).
21. Ibid.
22. Ibid., p. 39.
23. Farzaneh Milani, *Veils and Words: The Emerging Voices of Iranian Women Writers* (New York: Syracuse University Press, 1992), p. 9.
24. Çagla Hadimioglu, 'Black Tent', *TEXT Revue*, 2010. Available at http://www.text-revue.net/revue/heft-8 (accessed 12 November 2015).
25. Ibid.
26. Christian Schmid, 'Henry Lefebvre – Theory of the Production of Space towards a Three Dimensional Dialectic', in K. Goonewardena, S. Kipfer, R. Milgrom and C. Schmid (eds), *Space, Difference, Everyday Life: Reading Henry Lefebvre* (London: Routledge, 2008), pp. 27–30.
27. Hadimioglu, 'Black Tent'.
28. To clarify, a permitted male onlooker is a person whom a woman can *potentially* marry (i.e. not a family member) but unless she is in actual fact married to said man, she is forbidden to be seen by him without her veil.
29. Nima Naghibi, *Rethinking Global Sisterhood: Western Feminism and Iran* (Minneapolis: University of Minnesota Press, 2007), p. 39.
30. Milani, *Veils and Words*.
31. Ibid., p. 235.
32. Laura Mulvey. *Fetishism and Curiosity: Cinema and the Mind's Eye* (London: British Film Institute, 2013), pp. 67–9.
33. Hamid Naficy, 'Veiled Vision/Powerful Presence: Women in Post-revolutionary Iranian Cinema', in R. Issa and S. Whitaker (eds), *Life and Art: The New Iranian Cinema* (London: NFT/BFI, 1999), p. 53.
34. Ruhollah Khomeini, *Towzihol Masa'el* (n.p.), Kho'I Sayyed Abolqasem Musavi, *Resaleh-ye Towzih al Masa'el*, Tehran, Entesharat – e Javidan (extract from Hamid Naficy, 'Veiled Vision', p. 141).
35. Naficy, 'Veiled Vision/Powerful Presence', p. 56.
36. Qu'ran Surat al-Nur Verse 31. Available at http://quran.com/24/31 (accessed 28 September 2015).

37. Naficy, 'Veiled Vision/Powerful Presence', p. 60.
38. Beatriz Colomina, *Privacy and Publicity: Modern Architecture as Mass Media* (London: MIT Press, 1996), pp. 234–81.
39. Ibid., p. 260.
40. Ibid., p. 261.
41. Ludmilla Jordanova, *Sexual Visions: Images of Gender in Science and Medicine between the Eighteenth and Twentieth Centuries* (Madison: University of Wisconsin Press, 1993).
42. Naficy, 'Veiled Vision/Powerful Presence', p. 58.
43. Dariush Shayegan, *Asiya Dar Barabar Gharb (Asia Confronting the West)* (Tehran: Amir Kabir Publishing, 1977), p. 29.
44. Ibid.
45. Amir-Ebrahimi, 'Transgression in Narration', p. 89.
46. Ibid., p. 93.
47. C. Jenks, *Transgression* (London: Routledge, 2003), p. 8.
48. Ibid.
49. Milani, *Veils and Words*, p. 6.
50. Elizabeth Bucar, *Pious Fashion: How Muslim Women Dress* (Harvard University Press, 2017), p. 48.

Bibliography

Al-Saltana, Taj, *Crowning Anguish: Memoirs of a Persian Princess from the Harem to Modernity*, trans A. Vanzan, ed. E. Abbas (Washington, DC: Mage Publishers, 2003).

Amir-Ebrahimi, Masserat, 'Transgression in Narration: The Lives of Iranian Women in Cyberspace', *Journal of Middle East Women's Studies* 4/3, Special Issue – Innovative Women: Unsung Pioneers of Social Change (Fall 2008), pp. 89–118.

Bamdad, Badr ol-Moluk and Nasrin Rahimieh, *From Darkness into Light: Women's Emancipation in Iran* (California: Mazda Publishers, 1980), pp. 7–23.

Bucar, Elizabeth, *Pious Fashion: How Muslim Women Dress* (Harvard University Press, 2017).

Çagla Hadimioglu, 'Black Tent', *TEXT Revue*, 2010. Available at http://www.text-revue.net/revue/heft-8 (accessed 12 November 2015).

Colomina, Beatriz, *Privacy and Publicity: Modern Architecture as Mass Media* (London: MIT Press, 1996), pp. 234–81.

Daragahi, Haideh and Nina Witoszek, 'Anti-totalitarian Feminism? Civic Resistance in Iran', in L. Trägårdh, N. Witoszek and B. Taylor (eds), *Civil Society in the Age of Monitory Democracy* (Oxford: Berghahn Books, 2013), pp. 231–54.

Des Femmes Filment, 'Mouvement de Libération des Femmes Iraniennes – Année Zéro', 1979. Available at https://www.youtube.com/watch?v=ulJwXHji6f4 (accessed 20 April 2017).

Doy, Jen, *Drapery: Classicism and Barbarism in Visual Culture* (London: I.B. Tauris, 2001).

Farahani, Fataneh, *Gender, Sexuality and Diaspora* (New York/Oxon: Routledge, 2018).

Jenks, Christopher, *Transgression* (London: Routledge 2003).

Jordanova, Ludmilla, *Sexual Visions: Images of Gender in Science and Medicine between the Eighteenth and Twentieth Centuries* (Madison: University of Wisconsin Press, 1993).

KING-slave of ALLAH, 'ISLAM—World's Greatest Religion!', 2008. Available at https://islamgreatreligion.wordpress.com/2010/12/04/hidden-pearls/ (accessed 20 April 2017).

Lewis, Reina, *Gendering Orientalism: Race, Femininity and Representation* (Routledge, 1996).

Lewis, Reina, *Modest Fashion: Styling Bodies, Mediating Faith* (London: I.B. Tauris, 2013).

Milani, Farzaneh, *Veils and Words: The Emerging Voices of Iranian Women Writers* (New York: Syracuse University Press, 1992).

Motahhari, Morteza, *The Problem of Hijab* (Tehran: Basir Publication, 1986).

Mulvey, Laura, *Fetishism and Curiosity: Cinema and the Mind's Eye* (London: British Film Institute, 2013).

Naficy, Hamid, 'Veiled Vision/Powerful Presence: Women in Post-revolutionary Iranian Cinema', in R. Issa and S. Whitaker (eds), *Life and Art: The New Iranian Cinema* (London: NFT/BFI, 1999), pp. 43–65.

Naghibi, Nima, *Rethinking Global Sisterhood: Western Feminism and Iran* (Minneapolis: University of Minnesota Press, 2007).

Nedai, Jamileh, 'Comité des Femmes Contre la Lapidation', 2015. Available at https://www.youtube.com/watch?v=_7mnB_exy9I(Part1)andhttps://www.youtube.com/watch?v=gP9NrL6Y5kA&list=UUYCQJkRR9PyD3HXJZ8STlZg(Part2) (accessed 14 December 2018).

Qu'ran Surat al-Nur Verse 31, 'Islamic Rules of Modesty for Women', 2015. Available at http://quran.com/24/31 (accessed 20 April 2017).

Schmid, Christian, 'Henri Lefebvre's Theory of the Production of Space: Towards a Three-dimensional Dialectic', in K. Goonewardena, S. Kipfer, R. Milgrom and C. Schmid (eds), *Space, Difference, Everyday Life: Reading Henry Lefebvre* (London: Routledge, 2008), pp. 27–45.

Shayegan, Dariush, *Asiya Dar Barabar Gharb (Asia Confronting the West)* (Tehran: Amir Kabir Publishing, 1977).

PART II

LOOKING THROUGH NEOLIBERALISM

CHAPTER 5
BECOMING IN THE EYES OF OTHERS: THE RELATIONAL GAZE IN BOUDOIR PHOTOGRAPHY

Ilya Parkins

Since the new millennium, boudoir photography has seen a surge in interest. This is a sub-genre of suggestive intimate photography, especially popular in North America, that focuses almost exclusively on women.[1] It features naked, semi-naked or lingerie-clad subjects and relies on a variety of visual tropes of sexual invitation and availability. Often positioned as an erotic form well suited to gifting to a lover, and especially as a wedding-day gift to the spouse-to-be, the form has increasingly come to be sought out by women for their own uses. Boudoir thus offers an ideal forum through which to examine the instrumental application of an external gaze in the contemporary moment. As Michele White puts it, 'Women's participation in boudoir sessions is an expression of their desire to be erotically evident.'[2] The resulting photographs tend most often to conform to conventional ideas of feminine sexual desirability and objectification, with some exceptions. Yet a notable negotiation between photographer and subject frequently characterizes the textual matter surrounding the genre, complicating commonplace assumptions about the violence of the gaze by presenting a vision of the gaze as *healing* in relation to women's pervasive feelings of shame and hatred of their bodies.

In many ways this is not surprising; women increasingly commission the form in order to generate body confidence through the construction and solicitation of a gaze – sometimes in relation to an event such as their wedding and sometimes in a more general context, which might include navigating the effects on the body of experiences of pregnancy, childbirth, illness, ageing and gender transition. From a feminist critical perspective, boudoir can be firmly located as a neoliberal 'technology of sexiness', to borrow the term elaborated by Adrienne Evans and Sarah Riley.[3] Reading Foucault's technologies of self and subjectivity alongside Butler's theory of performativity, Evans and Riley define technologies of sexiness as 'technologies of self in which one works upon oneself and one's body (as an expression of agency) to reproduce oneself through discourses of sexual liberation (as the available technologies of subjectivity provided through neoliberalism, consumerism, and postfeminism)'.[4] As the following analysis shall indicate, women's motivations for, and framing of, their boudoir experiences clearly indicate some investment in the potential of sexually charged photographs to contribute to the production of a sexually liberated and generally confident self.

Indeed, boudoir photography is ripe for a feminist analysis, especially in terms of its relationship to the sexualization of the feminine body, the commodification and circulation of new visual forms in the last two decades, along with the gazes they enable. Notwithstanding the visual character of the form and the way that the internet has enabled its proliferation, this chapter dwells on the online *text* surrounding the photos: client testimonials, photographers' promotional material and journalistic accounts of the boudoir shoot. This is part of a wider interest I have in reading text alongside or against image in discourses of fashion and beauty. In working with women's fashion and style magazines, I have consistently found that text in this genre, which is characterized by its visual spectacularity, often works against its own visual messaging.[5] Closely reading text thus attunes us to a discursive richness and complexity that we might miss if we were to dwell only on the pictorial representations. In relation to the current analysis, the ways that subjects conceive and narrate the visual relations of boudoir photography have much more to tell us than the photographs alone, which speak rather one dimensionally of a vision of the sexualized feminine. Inquiring after the formulation of the gaze in this body of work prompts us to consider the relational frameworks within which the gaze operates in the present moment. And attending to text alongside image calls us to ask different, more complex questions about its consequences for new femininities. In the context of this feminized and sexualized – and thus trivialized – genre, this becomes particularly important.

These images and much of the text surrounding them affirm what many scholars have identified as the hallmarks of neoliberal femininity – individualism, invocations of an ill-defined 'empowerment' tied exclusively to sex and aesthetics and the fetishization of 'confidence'. Yet I also find the textual matter revealing of an ambiguity at the heart of the boudoir enterprise: what is being narrated is, in fact, a model of relational looking and even of self-making that challenges our understanding of the gaze as objectifying and instead points to it as relationally subjectifying. It reveals, I suggest, an under-acknowledged alternative model *inside* neoliberalism, pointing to the complexity of neoliberal cultural formations, including the incubation of their own alternatives. As such, a close reading of this textual matter has much to offer to a reconsideration of the gaze in neoliberal times. Rather than remaining locked in a binary between powerful subject and powerless object, from which gaze theory has had a difficult time extricating itself, this chapter advances a vision of networked gazes that queers such approaches. While it must be acknowledged as a commercially mediated and thus entirely aspirational medium, this work nonetheless bears within it the seeds of a different understanding of visuality. Furthermore, there is an embedded acknowledgement that the subject comes to be, and is transformed, in visual relation, meaning it has implications for the way we make sense of the feminine body and subjectification.

This chapter offers a close examination of the textual matter surrounding boudoir, beginning from the recognition that it is a commercial production in its entirety. That is, much of what is written about it is strategically curated (with the possible, partial exception of some blog comments and some journalism) and commercially mediated. I do not read these as 'authentic' expressions of feeling, as affect-saturated as they might be. Yet this does not invalidate the work – far from it. In fact, it gives us access to the content of a widely shared set of fantasies: about what it means to be feminine, what it might mean to look and be looked at. Ultimately, in its narration of a visually mediated process of authentic subjectification, the form offers an idealized account of an anti-individualist becoming that works *against* some of the other logics that clearly animate it.

The text I analyse comes mostly from the United States, with a small minority from the UK and Canada, published online between 2012 and 2017. The most significant source is photographers' websites, which tend to contain both photographers' statements of philosophy and client testimonials. Some sponsored posts – essentially, advertorials – on blogs such as the popular *Offbeat Bride* were also included in the analysis. So, too, were some blog posts or journalism that purported to get behind the scenes of this emerging trend by offering a first-person account of a shoot. Most of the subjects seemed to be heterosexual, cisgender (non-transgender) women, though there are certainly a few photographers who specialize in queer boudoir and frame their work in terms of inclusion and equity. For example, a lesbian photographer who posted boudoir photos of her spouse on a same-sex wedding blog writes, 'As lesbian women, I think it's hard sometimes to feel our own uniqueness is sexy or attractive.'[6] She took these photos in order to contribute to the development of a specifically queer aesthetic in boudoir as an affirmative act. Likewise, some photographers directly address racial, ethnic, gender and body diversity, and argue that their work challenges white supremacist and fat-phobic beauty standards. These photographers, however, tend to share a general orientation towards body positivity with the vast majority of boudoir photographers – intriguingly, there are few differences between the way more overtly politicized photographers imagine their work as contributing to body acceptance, and the way mainstream photographers do, which indicates the pervasive reach of discourses of body positivity and embodied self-affirmation.

Boudoir photography and the confident selfhood narrative

My analysis of this work is framed by the literature on new femininities since the millennium. Scholars have been tracing the ways that the figure of the young woman has, to use Angela McRobbie's term, been 'endow[ed] with capacity'.[7] I follow the lead, for instance, of Elias, Gill and Scharff, who 'situate the continuing focus on appearance within … *neoliberalism*, with its relentless exhortation to be active, entrepreneurial, self-optimising subjects'.[8] The stress on the discursive production of the feminine subject as confident and agentic, especially around sexuality, is of course particularly relevant to this analysis, as the texts I will trace epitomize the association of sexual pleasure, opportunism and fitness with power. Feminist scholars have argued that this amounts to a widespread substitution of individual experiences of a nebulously defined empowerment for actual social transformation, a critique that is being extended to recent popular reconstructions of feminism.[9] Boudoir might be said to epitomize this kind of individualist, choice-oriented feminism, as Michele White's analysis has shown. For instance, a photographer, in a blog post called 'Boudoir Is a Feminist Issue', writes that boudoir is about 'equality and the right to choose' and that it 'is not a passive subservient thing, but a powerful self celebration of strong women'.[10] Another photographer writes that boudoir can 'unleash' 'a powerful, feminist side'.[11]

The narrative that emerges across these sources illustrates the intersection of boudoir with a 'choice'- and 'empowerment'-steeped post-millennial femininity. It suggests that women do boudoir for themselves. The impetus for the shoot might be to offer the photos as a gift for a lover or fiancé, but this is roundly disavowed. As one woman commented on a wedding blog post about boudoir, 'I went into it thinking, "Oh, this is just a present for my soon-to-be husband," but I came out of it with a completely new sense of myself and my body.'[12] Photographers corroborate this view – which of course helps in turn to create a new market. They often suggest that women are always doing the shoot for themselves but using their partner as a cover. One, for instance, writes, '99% of women who have walked through my studio doors have confessed, "Well, I'm giving them to him for his birthday … but I'm really doing it for me."'[13] Of course, the individual subject's sense that she is doing it for 'herself' might well be overlain or constructed by the lover's gaze, following Laura Mulvey's foundational work on the male gaze as internalized by women. Is it possible to separate what one wants from the looks and desires of the person one is intimately entangled with?

These relational dimensions surface more clearly in an analysis of the writing about the logistics of the shoot itself. One of the most commonly employed descriptions of the shoots is 'confidence boost'. As one photographer notes, 'Boudoir is a celebration of yourself. It's liberating, confidence-building.'[14] In the comments section of this post, the term 'confidence boost' is repeated by nearly every commenter. In these cases, the women do boudoir for what we might call utilitarian reasons: it is used for pre-wedding reassurance. As one commenter writes, 'I was starting to have real concerns about everybody looking at me walking down the aisle and how I would photograph etc, and this really reassured me that I could and would look beautiful on my wedding day.'[15] We see here the first hint that there is more at stake than just individual self-regard. This is a crucial acknowledgement that self-concept is entwined with an external gaze.

There are undeniable echoes here of what Gill and Orgad call the 'confidence cult', which they trace through discourses about women in the workplace and body positivity movements. They identify confidence as a technology of neoliberal self-making that has appropriated the language of feminism.[16] It invites women and girls to internalize blame for their own lack of confidence and body hatred, a point elaborated in Laura Favaro's related analysis of what she names 'confidence chic'.[17] Gill and Orgad suggest that in displacing blame for systemic inequality and symbolic violence onto women themselves, the confidence cult 'makes over … feminism into a neoliberal feminism that is complicit with rather than critical of patriarchal capitalism'.[18] Their analysis crystallizes some of what is at work in the textual matter surrounding boudoir, which ultimately abjects women's feelings of grief: subjects' body hatred exists in these texts only as something to be overcome, paradoxically encouraging women to be silent about their experiences of bodily unease or self-loathing. The lack of negative or mixed experiences is not surprising when we consider that the bulk of the material is tightly curated and promotional – it is obviously not in photographers' interest to share traces of boudoir disturbing people. Yet the pervasiveness of this story forecloses, to use Gill and Orgad's terms, the pervasiveness of gendered pain and grief – conditions that require political engagement and community for their resolution, many feminist readings would say. In other words, what is being rendered unintelligible in these textual archives is any number of collaborative labours – of advocacy, protest, therapy and network-forging – that exist or could exist in the subject's life, connecting her to others, be they humans or systems in which she is embedded. The significant actor in the boudoir text, and the confidence cult it epitomizes, is the feminine individual, triumphant over her supposedly irrational body hatred and warped self-perception. This side of the story accords with Michele White's general finding on boudoir, which is that boudoir clients 'continue rather than break from previous cultures of sexual objectification and subjectification'.[19]

Boudoir portrait as relational encounter

And yet, there is another story embedded here, one that centres the other's gaze or more precisely a network of multiple gazes. For as White writes, boudoir subjects' 'negotiation of visibility and invisibility, especially their control of the means through which men will see their boudoir photography, are different than society's more usual positioning of women as visual and objects of the "male gaze"'.[20] Reading a different body of textual matter surrounding the genre, White effectively queers boudoir. In the spirit of her suggestion that the form is queerly ambiguous, I offer a reading of the relational visuality that becomes so apparent in the text. Work on what it means to pose for a camera and an imagined gaze becomes relevant here, in particular, Roland Barthes's conception of the experience of the self as split in the act of posing. As he writes, at work in this moment are multiple conceptions of self: 'In front of the lens, I am at the same time: the one I think I am, the one the photographer thinks I am, the one I want others to think I am, and the one [the photographer] makes use of to exhibit his art.'[21] Barthes thus establishes the multiple lines of relation that condition a posed photographic encounter, allowing us to think about the shoot as characterized by a relational networking, implicitly countering the profoundly individualist account of self-making that I have just described. And it is a relational quality that is conditioned by the acts and technical apparatus of looking. This is what the textual matter I have located overwhelmingly features, and it complicates the assumptions that a feminist analysis might bring to boudoir if only engaged with the visual archive. This is not a story of the gaze as alienating and disembodying, and the installation of a subject-object binary between photographer and client. Rather, in text what emerges is an account of the photographic encounter as intimate and even healing, and the multiple gazes that are mediated through the encounter, and in viewing the final photographs, are loving and nourishing of the subject.

Tracing the narrative structure that attends almost all published accounts of boudoir helps us locate this story of the compassionate gaze. The narrative is remarkably similar across the genre and can be gleaned even from short testimonials about one part of the experience, which implicitly allude to the whole. The structure hinges on the client's transformation. We are told that clients start off nervous and insecure, are guided to comfort and confidence by a deft photographer and end up having an enjoyable and even joyful experience. When they see the results, the photos, they are shocked and transformed, moving from misrecognition to recognition. On one level, of course, this account lines up with the fetishization of confidence that I discuss above; it might be described as the disciplining of the self-conscious feminine subject, with the sexually confident woman triumphant at the end. But closer scrutiny reveals ambiguities in the account as it stresses relational implications of each stage in the process and foregrounds the implicit other actors involved in the labour of self-making.

The first thing that is narrated is the transformation of the model from uneasy to joyful and playful. This is a process facilitated by the photographer, according to both photographers and subjects. As one client testifies, 'I really never thought I would want to get in front of a camera again. Melissa changed all that. She will help you love yourself a little more.'[22] Photographers themselves routinely describe their work in similar terms: it's a calling, a higher purpose, almost always framed as contributing to women's well-being, such as 'Justine's main goal is to show everyone … how awesome *and* bad-ass *and* beautiful they are' in a sponsored post on *Offbeat Bride*[23] or in an editorial piece, 'she sees beauty in all women, and it is her objective to make them feel great about themselves.'[24] To be sure, we can note a paradox, which is that such representations both reinforce and undercut the valuation of beauty: this both locates well-being in aesthetics and strategically repositions photographers' work outside of the trivialized and feminized realm of glamour and aesthetics by giving it a moral purpose that trumps the aesthetic one. In this sense, it reinforces the wearisome double bind that requires women to be beautiful yet to disavow their investment in beauty.

Yet it also inadvertently re-centres self-making as a collaborative enterprise. Another sponsored post on *Offbeat Bride* says that client and photographer will 'be co-creating this experience based on your interests, personality, and how you want to be seen.'[25] This is a clear description of sexualized depiction as identity project, which has been traced by a number of Foucauldian scholars, particularly around pornography.[26] Here, though, it is a joint project – the photographer gets involved with both what is imagined to be your 'essential' self – interests and personality – and your identity projection. Another photographer stresses the intimacy of this relationship: 'I will get to know you very well … By the time you are done with the process we will be like old friends.'[27] Still others frame the relationship pedagogically: 'Angelica coached me pose by pose, telling me how to lean and angle my head and give the camera the best view of my assets.'[28] Another variation is the portrayal of the client-photographer relationship as therapeutic, as in 'I want you to know and practice self-love, self-acceptance, and body-positivity.'[29]

A range of linked relationships between photographer and client is thus sketched. And what is striking is how closely these detail the collaborative labour of self-making: the photographer is a key actor in what could be merely a self-transformative process. Laura Favaro calls confidence chic 'an exemplary neoliberal technology … structured by a violent ethos of self-determination that repudiates notions of social/external constraints, pressures, or influences.'[30] But the narration of the boudoir genre seems to acknowledge the entanglement of selves in the production of this confidence. Perhaps this is because of the intimate-to-sexual nature of the genre: a number of photographers stress that what they love about their work is that it requires and then visually depicts vulnerability. The act of undressing for the camera, and the resulting photos, constitutes a kind of opening to another – or in fact, to a series of others, from photographer to viewers.

Further, whereas the suggestive or lightly pornographic aspect of boudoir could easily lend itself to claims of an objectifying, anything but reciprocal, gaze, the full or partial nudity that characterizes the genre seems to enable the reciprocity that is described as part of the photographic encounter. The ingredient of revelation that comes into play through full or partial nudity in this particular genre seems to ease the path to opening to another. As a client puts it, 'Somehow it's a lot less awkward taking clothes off in front of people you just met with a camera than strangers at a doctor's office.'[31] In these narratives, nudity takes on some of the positive associations it has long held in the 'Western' cultural imaginary: honesty, authenticity, openness.[32] Nudity facilitates the forging of a compassionate relationship, rather than preventing it through objectification. And this narration of nudity as promoting compassion describes not only the relation of subject to photographer but the relationship of subject to herself: a consistent theme across the works is that the opportunity to be naked and in the camera's frame facilitates a newly loving gaze at herself, as well.[33] As a client testimonial puts it, after testifying that the photographic experience leads to a new honesty in relation to her body, 'getting naked does stuff'.[34] The relations that appear at the heart of boudoir extend to a new relation to self, as the client so frequently recounts an experience of coming to know herself differently through the process.

A kind of reciprocal erotics of the photographic encounter emerges. A client testifies about her photographer: 'Her photos … are her, advocating you! She loves you and you can feel it. And therefore, she is loved by anyone that she touches.'[35] And in a blog post on 'emotional connection', a photographer who works in a team of two details the three layers of intimacy involved in a boudoir shoot, beginning with that between photographer and model: 'In just a couple hours, you know us; and we know you … There's no shyness, no holding back. [We] believe in honesty, so we are full-frontal with you. No secrets. We want you to be the same.'[36] This is about the photographer's affect, to be sure – client testimonials often testify that photographers act to put them at ease. It is also engaging with the ethos of transparency that has come to be so meaningful in the new millennium[37] – a tense engagement, since the posing that is at the heart of boudoir is in opposition to the values associated with transparency, at least as the latter is typically conceived.

Along with the photographer's affect and the question of revelation, it is also about the apparatus of the camera and the moment of the photographic encounter, a relational meeting that is technologically enabled and mediated. Consider again the client's assertion that the photographer's 'photos are her, advocating you'. The elision of the difference between photographer and her photos shows what is at stake here: the collaborative intimacy of the boudoir encounter is enabled by its nature as photographic. In such accounts, the camera does not negate reciprocal relation in its rendering of the subject by reflecting only the consuming gaze of viewer and photographer, as feminist accounts of an objectifying gaze might suggest. Rather, the presence of the camera and the context of the photographic encounter produce a continually reciprocal relation. The 'full-frontal' meeting that the above-cited photographer calls for is derived not only from interactions with clients but from the fact that they are being photographed half-clothed, with all the posing this entails, and the coaxing and inducement to comfort that the photographer must engage in.

It is not surprising that photography has the capacity to activate an intimate relationship between photographer and subject. As Ariella Azoulay points out, 'Collaboration always already lies at the basis of the event of photography.'[38] This insight threatens to be lost in the recognition that, as the literature on portraiture has made clear for decades now, posing for the camera is an act of self-making: on a surface level, there seems no more individualist representation than a portrait of a singular individual. Yet as Amelia Jones, Craig Owens and others have made clear, portraiture is always an opening to another and demands of the viewer an encounter, rather than simple mastery. Jones writes, 'While the photographic portrait in general has historically been mobilized as a way of solidifying the making and viewing subject (the centered, Cartesian, Western "individual") [...] it can only do this, as more recent practices have seemed to stress, by *passing through the object*.'[39] She applies a Lacanian reading of subject formation to (self-) portraiture, as Lacan theorized subjectification as a process of *screening*, whereby the subject is brought into being through the screen as a 'locus of mediation' between subject and gaze.[40] Read against this backdrop, the boudoir portrait becomes legible as a relation between the photographer and the subject, and later between the subject and other viewers (as I shall describe). Though Jones's work locates this argument in transgressive, critical, self-representational work by women artists, her discussion of the ways that self comes into being through the gaze speaks directly to the narration of boudoir photography by clients and photographers.

Looking in relation

This experience of revaluing the body occurs in relation to several elements of the boudoir process. I have so far been talking about the photo shoot itself, the photographic encounter as event. But the collaborative, relational nature of boudoir's framing – and its ability to prompt a changed relation to the self – is also evident in the narration of looking at the results, the photos, themselves. Before exploring the gaze as relational, it is important to establish that it seems the images function as a kind of 'proof' of women's beauty, more real than women's own flawed perceptions of their bodies. Clients testify, over and over again, that they never believed they were beautiful until they saw the photos. One journalistic account notes that 'I didn't sign up for this shoot so someone else could look at me. I signed up to see myself clearly'.[41] A client is grateful because she 'finally was able to see the beauty and sexiness in myself'.[42] Another writes that 'this experience showed me an image of myself as a complete individual', intimating that that it had helped her to see herself fully or authentically.[43] Often this is expressed in terms of misrecognition – as one photographer puts it, 'At first you'll look at the pictures and say "Is that me?" because the person you see you don't recognize immediately … but then after a moment, your eyes will adjust, and the person in the photograph becomes less of a stranger.'[44] Clients echo this repeatedly; one writes, 'I stared at the screen wondering how that could be me.'[45] When we pair this with the constant assertion that the photos capture some truth, it is hard not to see this as a dressing down of women for their failure to see themselves properly – the trope of misrecognition blames *them* for their erroneous self-regard instead of acknowledging that their own gaze is constituted in what is paradoxically a deeply anti-corporeal cultural context. In addition to the important echoes of what Gill and Orgad, and Favaro, identify as the perniciously self-blaming culture of body positivity discourse, this resonates with Susan Bordo's foundational work on mainstream representations of anorexia: anorexia is seen as an individual pathology rather than a perfectly reasonable response to a deeply misogynist and fat-phobic culture.[46] The trope of misrecognition is deeply individualizing in its location of responsibility for the gaze in the subject herself.

And yet, once again, this individual gaze is enfolded in layers of relation. The woman's gaze at herself is enabled by others, both human and mechanical: the photographer and the camera, as well as her lover, who very often 'ghosts' the boudoir experience and narration. One photographer writes that boudoir allows you to 'see yourself through another person's eyes. You get to see the magnificence that someone else sees in you when you look at your photos'.[47] According to another photographer, 'Boudoir shoots and glamour shoots are a good idea because [they] enable you to see the angles and views of yourself that you can't normally see. When you see every inch of yourself … then you can love every inch of yourself.'[48] It is more complex than it appears, then. The looking relations being described here involve an exchange between model and photographer, in which the model is not chastised for her failure to see correctly but guided to see differently – and often in a language of benevolence and even love, as we have seen. Surely this is not an innocent exchange; as Paul Frosh and other photography theorists have made clear, everyone from the subject to the viewer recognizes that the photograph is a document of the photographer's power over the subject.[49] And there is a commercial benefit to the photographer in successfully guiding the subject to see 'accurately', of course. Nevertheless, while most of the work about the neoliberal feminine subject and her empowered relationship to embodiment mines the Foucauldian literature on discipline, something different is being narrated here. Rather, there is a movement away from an internally directed discipline to an embodied ethics. While a notion of self-care undergirds these texts, and this is also central in representations of the neoliberal feminine subject, the model that emerges in these textual accounts suggests that self-care is challenging if not impossible if conceived of in isolation.

In fact, I would suggest that boudoir is narrated as a relational coming into being – this is about being seen, by another, into selfhood. It narrates a relational and specular becoming. As Liz Conor writes about the transformation of feminine visibility in the 1920s, 'by turning themselves into spectacles women could enter new feminine categories'.[50] New visibilities enabled new ontologies, that is. The litany of client testimonials shows that the boudoir model understands the photographs to instantiate a new self, one that is confident and secure. Yet this is shown to be entirely contingent on the gaze of others, including the photographer. The transformed self comes to be only in relation.

The others that are required to see oneself into new forms of feminine being in this genre also include the technical apparatus of the camera, which has been likened to the – penetrating, dominating – phallus in some psychoanalytic photography theory. Photographers often attach their own gaze to the possibilities enabled by the mechanical eye, suggesting, as one does, that women have been 'looking at yourself through [a] tainted lens'[51] and that the camera's lens will capture them more accurately. Here, the subject is once again implicitly called out and her own self-knowledge subordinated to that of a supposedly more objective – because less socially embedded? – lens. As it is mediated in the photographer's words, there is a latent tension, here, between 'objectivity' brought by the camera – an impersonal and mechanistic function – and the love that photographers are said to bring and enable. On the other hand, several clients also compare the camera to a mirror, suggesting that the camera is the better, kinder technology, inseparable as it is from the loving gaze of the photographer and thus somehow humanized as an other. For example, one woman writes in a comment on an article about boudoir, 'Sometimes it takes seeing an image of ourselves rather than a reflection from a mirror – which allows us to see something new.'[52] And in a client testimonial on a photographer's site, another exclaims that 'mirrors (and my brain) do lie!'[53] Given the ways that the camera gets transposed on to the photographer in this body of work, it seems likely that the greater accuracy of the camera than the mirror is a result of both the camera's deep and physical link to the photographer, and the inextricability of the process of looking at the final photos from the generally compassionate gaze that is said to circulate in the encounter itself.

Finally, there is the complexity of the lover's gaze. Though the photos are so often framed as being for oneself rather than anyone else, their other status as gifts for a lover or fiancé or spouse comes through strongly. Even in compulsively naming the boudoir shoot as happening under the guise of gifts for a lover, but really being for oneself, the accounts – whether by clients or photographers – implicitly interpellate the lover. The lover becomes the foundation or ground for the act of self-creation, thereby revealing the boudoir's production of confidence as less individualist than it might seem. Though this is at one level simply a logistical reality – the photos are occasioned by, or imagined as for, the lover – it has implications for the complex visuality that is narrated in the textual archive of boudoir.

The role of the lover in the circuit of gazes that characterizes the genre is signalled in various ways, ranging from implicit to overt. At times the presence is ambiguous. One photographer writes that a benefit of boudoir is that 'you get to see the magnificence that someone else sees in you.'[54] Here, I suggest, the photographer is ghosted by the lover. This 'someone else' could be both. The shoot and the experience of looking at the resulting photos enable a kind of transposition of the subject into the eyes of at least *two* others, in all but the rarest cases. One photographer names this transposition with remarkable directness: 'When you take a photo at the Boudoir Café, we remind you of this connection you have with the person [the loved one]. You look at me … behind the camera and I'm there to support you and [the photographer's male colleague, who is also her lover] is right next to me, to remind you of this bond.'[55] A noteworthy network of gazes is invoked here, one which certainly exceeds the possibilities attached to the normative heterosexual romantic dyad. This accords with White's reading of women's discussions of boudoir on online wedding forums as exceeding the commonplace figuration of heterosexual unions by interpellating (ambiguously eroticized) other gazes.[56]

This becomes more complex when the lover is directly invoked. Frequently, the photos act as confirmation of the lover's gaze. For example, one woman writes, in a piece on *Huffington Post* that asked readers to share boudoir experiences and photos, 'When I met my husband, I was shy of my average body. But I quickly learned that he loved me for me, regardless of wrinkles, lumps, or scars. The pictures were for him, to show him that I have come a long way in loving myself because of him.'[57] This quotation frames the vaunted self-love of the empowered woman as requiring the loving gaze of another. So does this: 'It feels so fulfilling to finally believe my husband when he looks into my eyes and tells me that I'm beautiful.'[58] Implied here, again, is the woman's own misrecognition of herself – and potentially the suggestion that the (male) lover knows better. But the other point obliquely being made here is that self-constitution is a fiction: the will of one person in isolation will not be enough to dislodge self-hatred. We may rightly challenge the way that boudoir narratives most often locate this gesture at the fiction of unfettered selfhood in the frames of heterosexual romance, but it nonetheless stands as a partial recognition that looking – including self-regard – is complexly networked.

Also at work in the invocations of the lover, whether ghostly or fully present, is a desire for greater intimacy between the self and the lover. Boudoir testimonies are almost invariably used to suggest that the experience of relearning to look, to see what the lover sees, intensifies and renews the romantic relationship by facilitating openness, as much as it adds erotic excitement. Here again, a kind of yearning for deep connection – and even transposition – seems to animate the writing and is another testament to the power of the photographic apparatus not to objectify and alienate but to enable intimacy. This point is crystal clear in the occasional description of couples' boudoir, not surprisingly: both clients and photographers suggest that a boudoir session as a couple prompts greater closeness because clients 'see their partner in vulnerability and in love'.[59] What is notable, however, is the way that this vulnerability is said to translate even across the supposedly objectifying medium of photography, permeating even solo shoots, and that it is figured as a yearning towards deeper bonds.

This question of a yearning-towards is what is most striking in the admittedly ambiguous writing I have traced here. To what extent might we characterize the primary impulse in this commercially structured set of texts as a desire for and an incubation of communal possibility, including networked forms of the gaze that acknowledge their own relationality? As I have argued throughout, the textual matter associated with the promotion of boudoir is ambiguous: it at once affirms and challenges the ubiquitous stress on individual discipline and imperatives to unfettered self-transformation in neoliberal cultures of feminine beauty and sexuality. I read these traces as counter-currents in the discursive structures of neoliberalism, which paradoxically gain their vitality from the very positions and technologies that are seen as most damaging to women, such as the apparently alienating photographic apparatus. How and why is capitalism incubating its own desires for another world, one that accommodates a desire for connection and prioritizes the self in relation? To what extent is this, itself, commodifiable? Altogether, a textual analysis of the recent archive surrounding boudoir is startling in its location of possibilities for transformation in the very structures of capitalism. Scholars of the intersection between capitalism and culture have extrapolated from Wendy Brown's brief mention of 'extramarket morality' to analyse sites in which relations produced by neoliberal capitalist marketplaces exceed the frames of the market.[60] Theorists of those feminized forms, fashion and dress, have produced a compelling analysis of the ways that dress, with its affective resonance, seems to give rise to forms of relation that are not reducible to market logics.[61] It may be that boudoir, with its ambiguous yearning towards the other, is another such site, prompting us to wonder what it is about deeply feminized cultural forms that lead them to facilitate the currents of an extramarket morality.

Notes

1. Recently, a genre of men's boudoir has emerged and been christened 'dudeoir'. Notably, dudeoir is often a form characterized by jokiness, featuring jocund men in deliberately ridiculous poses. This can be read as the ridiculization of an objectifying gaze at sexualized men, which contributes to the naturalization of the sexualized feminine.
2. Michele White, 'Concerns about Being Visible and Expressions of Pleasure: Women's Internet Wedding Forum Considerations of Boudoir Photography Sessions', *Interstitial Journal*, October 2013, 1. Available at https://interstitialjournal.files.wordpress.com/2013/10/white-concerns.pdf (accessed 14 April 2018).
3. Adrienne Evans and Sarah Riley, *Technologies of Sexiness: Sex, Identity and Consumer Culture* (Oxford: Oxford University Press, 2014).
4. Ibid., p. 43.
5. See Ilya Parkins, 'Domesticating Enchantment: Mediating Feminine Magic in the Interwar French Fashion Magazine', *French Cultural Studies* 28/4 (2017), 344–59; Ilya Parkins, '"Eve Goes Synthetic": Modernizing Feminine Beauty, Renegotiating Masculinity in *Britannia and Eve*', in C. Clay et al. (eds), *Women's*

Print Media and Periodical Culture in Britain, 1918–39: The Interwar Years (Edinburgh: Edinburgh University Press, 2017).

6. 'Something a Little Different', *A Bicycle Built for Two*, 7 February 2016. Available at http://www.onabicyclebuiltfortwo.com/2016/02/something-a-little-different-nsfw.html (accessed 26 April 2018).
7. Angela McRobbie, 'Top Girls? Young Women and the Post-feminist Sexual Contract', *Cultural Studies* 21/4–5 (2007), p. 722.
8. Ana Sofia Elias, Rosalind Gill and Christina Scharff, 'Aesthetic Labour: Beauty Politics in Neoliberalism', in A.S. Elias, R. Gill and C. Scharff (eds), *Aesthetic Labour: Rethinking Beauty Politics in Neoliberalism* (London: Palgrave Macmillan, 2017), p. 5.
9. See, for example, Nancy Fraser, 'Feminism, Capitalism and the Cunning of History', *New Left Review* 56 (2009), pp. 97–117; Angela McRobbie, *The Aftermath of Feminism: Gender, Culture, and Social Change* (London: Sage, 2009); Rosalind Gill, 'From Sexual Objectification to Sexual Subjectification: The Resexualisation of Women's Bodies in the Media', *Feminist Media Studies* 3/1 (2003), pp. 99–106; and Rosalind Gill, 'Critical Respect: The Difficulties and Dilemmas of Agency and "Choice" for Women: A Reply to Duits and Van Zoonen', *European Journal of Women's Studies* 14/1 (2007), pp. 69–80.
10. Mrs Smith, 'Boudoir Is a Feminist Issue', 23 July 2014. Available at https://mrssmithboudoir.com/2014/07/23/boudoir-is-a-feminist-issue/ (accessed 26 April 2018).
11. Cherie Steinberg, 'The Boudoir Café Talks Photography and Feminism!!!', 27 August 2015. Available at http://www.theboudoircafe.com/the-boudoir-cafe-talks-boudoir-photography-and-feminism/ (accessed 26 April 2018).
12. Jillian Nicole, Comment on Annabel, 'Laid Bare Week – Boudoir Photography, Would You?', 27 February 2012. Available at http://www.lovemydress.net/blog/2012/02/baring-all-a-curious-minds-guide-to-boudoir-photography.html (accessed 26 April 2018).
13. Natalie Kita, 'Boudoir and Feminism – The Truth as I See It', 20 March 2013. Available at http://www.boudoirphotographyeastcoast.com/boudoir-and-feminism-the-truth-as-i-see-it (accessed 26 April 2018). Also see Muse Mneme Photography, 'From Pin-Ups to Commercial Photography: Boudoir and Feminism – Is Boudoir Photography Objectifying or Empowering for Women?', 27 June 2015. Available at https://themusemneme.com/2015/06/27/from-pin-ups-to-commercial-photography-boudoir-and-feminism-is-boudoir-photography-objectifying-or-empowering-for-women/ (accessed 26 April 2018).
14. Ibid.
15. Ibid., comment by Rebecca.

16. Rosalind Gill and Shani Orgad, 'The Confidence Cul(ure)', *Australian Feminist Studies* 30/86 (2015), p. 325.
17. Ibid., pp. 331, 333. Laura Favaro, '"Just Be Confident Girls!" Confidence Chic as Neoliberal Governmentality', in A.S. Elias, R. Gill and C. Scharff (eds), *Aesthetic Labour: Rethinking Beauty Politics in Neoliberalism* (Basingstoke, 2017), pp. 288–9.
18. Ibid., p. 341.
19. White, 'Concerns', p. 6.
20. White, 'Concerns', p. 1.
21. Roland Barthes, *Camera Lucida: Reflections on Photography*, trans. Richard Howard (New York: Hill and Wang, 1981), p. 13.
22. Megan Finley, '10 Images That Will Change the Way You Think about Boudoir Photography', *Offbeat Bride*, n.d. Available at http://offbeatbride.com/denver-boudoir-photographer/ (accessed 26 April 2018).
23. Catherine Clark, 'Boudoir Photography as Love Potion', *Offbeat Bride*, n.d. Available at http://offbeatbride.com/maine-boudoir-photography/ (accessed 26 April 2018).
24. Olga Barsky, 'Girl Crush Dreams Come True: A Boudoir Shoot with Scarlett O'Neill', *She Does the City.com*, 9 April 2013. Available at http://www.shedoesthecity.com/girl-crush-dreams-come-true-a-boudoir-shoot-with-scarlet-oneill (accessed 26 April 2018).
25. Catherine Clark, '"Getting Naked Does Stuff": Finding Yourself with Body-Positive Boudoir Photography from Jezebel VonZephyr', *Offbeat Bride*, n.d. Available at http://offbeatbride.com/seattle-body-positive-boudoir-photography/ (accessed 24 April 2018).
26. See Danielle De Voss, 'Women's Porn Sites – Spaces of Fissure and Eruption and "I'm a Little Bit of Everything"', *Sexuality and Culture* 6/3 (2002), pp. 75–94; Fiona Attwood, 'No Money Shot? Commerce, Pornography and New Sex Taste Cultures', *Sexualities* 10/4 (2007), pp. 441–56.
27. Shondy Studios, 'The Experience'. Formerly available at https://shondystudios.com/info/ (accessed 21 June 2017). Link broken.
28. Katie Oldenburg, 'Frisky Q&A: Award-Winning Boudoir Photographer Talks Photoshoot Tips, Common Questions', *The Frisky*, 14 April 2014. Available at http://www.thefrisky.com/2014-04-14/frisky-qa-award-winning-boudoir-photographer-angelica-roberts-talks-photoshoot-tips-common-questions/ (accessed 26 April 2018).
29. Laura Rahel Crosby, 'The Reason Why I Do Boudoir Photography'. Available at http://www.laurarahelphotography.com/blog/why-i-do-what-i-do (accessed 26 April 2018).
30. Favaro, 'Just Be Confident Girls!' p. 289.

31. Katy, testimonial. Available at http://www.breathlessboudoir.com/testimonials/ (accessed 24 April 2018).
32. See Ruth Barcan, *Nudity: A Cultural Anatomy* (London: Bloomsbury, 2004), pp. 83–8.
33. [Editors' Note – This discovery of body confidence through photography is also discussed by Lauren Downing Peters in her analysis of Jen Davis's self-portraiture elsewhere in this volume.]
34. Clark, 'Getting Naked Does Stuff', n.p.
35. Simply Boudoir, 'Overcoming Odds', 8 February 2017. Available at http://www.simply-boudoir.com/dark-sultry/overcoming-odds/ (accessed 26 April 2018).
36. Cherie Steinberg, 'Emotional Connection!!!', *The BoudoirCafe*, 9 June 2015. Available at http://www.theboudoircafe.com/uncategorized/emotional-connection/ (accessed 24 April 2018).
37. Clare Birchall, 'Radical Transparency?', *Cultural Studies<->Critical Methodologies* 14/1 (2014), pp. 77–88; Clare Birchall, 'Transparency, Interrupted: Secrets of the Left', *Theory, Culture, and Society* 28 (2011), pp. 60–84; Mark Fenster, 'Transparency in Search of a Theory', *European Journal of Social Theory* 18/2 (2015), pp. 150–67.
38. Ariella Azoulay, 'Photography Consists of Collaboration: Susan Meiselas, Wendy Ewald, and Ariella Azoulay', *Camera Obscura* 31/1 (2016), p. 189.
39. Amelia Jones, 'The "Eternal Return": Self-Portrait Photography as a Technology of Embodiment', *Signs* 27/4 (2002), p. 960.
40. Ibid., pp. 957–8.
41. Ostarello, 'From Plain Jane to Boudoir Babe'.
42. Summer, testimonial. Available at http://www.breathlessboudoir.com/testimonials/ (accessed 24 April 2018).
43. Sarah, testimonial. Available at http://www.breathlessboudoir.com/testimonials/ (accessed 24 April 2018).
44. Marisa Leigh, '50 Shades of Gorgeous – The Art of Boudoir and the Beauty of Women', *Huffington Post*, 23 September 2013. Available at http://www.huffingtonpost.com/marisa-leigh/50-shades-of-gorgeous-the_b_3963296.html (accessed 26 April 2018).
45. Katy, testimonial.
46. Susan Bordo, *Unbearable Weight: Feminism, Western Culture and the Body* (Berkeley: University of California Press, 2003), pp. 45–70.
47. Laura Rahel Crosby, 'Benefits of Having a Boudoir Shoot'. Available at http://www.laurarahelphotography.com/blog/benefits-of-doing-a-boudoir-session (accessed 26 April 2018).
48. Cherie Steinberg, 'Empower and Love Yourself with a Boudoir Shoot', *Boudoir Café*, 25 August 2016. Available at http://www.theboudoircafe.com/

uncategorized/empower-and-love-yourself-with-a-photo-shoot/ (accessed 26 April 2018).

49. Paul Frosh, 'The Public Eye and the Citizen-Voyeur: Photography as a Performance of Power', *Social Semiotics* 11/1 (2001), p. 50. Also see Halla Belloff, 'Social Interaction in Photographing', *Leonardo* 16/3 (1983), pp. 165–71.
50. Liz Conor, *The Spectacular Modern Woman: Feminine Visibility in the 1920s* (Bloomington: Indiana University Press, 2004), p. 29.
51. Leigh, '50 Shades of Gorgeous'.
52. Comment by Jacqueline. Available at http://www.lovemydress.net/blog/2012/02/baring-all-a-curious-minds-guide-to-boudoir-photography.html (accessed 26 April 2018).
53. Ms. E., testimonial. Available at http://www.simply-boudoir.com/testimonials/ (accessed 23 April 2018).
54. Crosby, 'Benefits of Having a Boudoir Session'.
55. Steinberg, 'Emotional Connection'.
56. White, 'Concerns', pp. 18–19. Also see pp. 22–3.
57. 'Boudoir Photos: Readers Share Pictures from Their Sexy Shoots', *Huffington Post*, 25 June 2013. Available at http://www.huffingtonpost.com/2013/06/25/boudoir-photos_n_3497897.html (accessed 26 April 2018).
58. Kim, testimonial. Available at http://www.breathlessboudoir.com/testimonials/ (accessed 25 April 2018).
59. Marisa Leigh, 'Couple's Boudoir: Re-Ignite Your Passion', *Huffington Post*, 1 September 2015. Available at https://www.huffingtonpost.com/marisa-leigh/couples-boudoir-re-ignite-your-passion_b_8049226.html (accessed 25 April 2018). Also see Dustin Cantrell, 'Life Hack for Bonding with Your Partner: An Intimate Couple's Session (and How to Rock It!)', *Offbeat Bride*, n.d. Available at http://offbeatbride.com/intimate-couples-session-guide/ (accessed 25 April 2018); and Amy, testimonial. Available at http://www.breathlessboudoir.com/testimonials/ (accessed 25 April 2018).
60. Wendy Brown, *Edgework: Critical Essays on Knowledge and Politics* (Princeton: Princeton University Press, 2005), p. 53.
61. E.g. Thuy Linh N. Tu, *The Beautiful Generation: Asian Americans and the Cultural Economy of Fashion* (Durham: Duke University Press, 2011), p. 94; Minh-Ha T. Pham, 'Blog Ambition: Fashion, Feeling and the Digital Raced Body', *Camera Obscura* 26/1 (2011), pp. 1–37.

Bibliography

Attwood, Feona, 'No Money Shot? Commerce, Pornography and New Sex Taste Cultures', *Sexualities* 10/4 (2007), pp. 441–56.

Azoulay, Ariella, 'Photography Consists of Collaboration: Susan Meiselas, Wendy Ewald, and Ariella Azoulay', *Camera Obscura* 31/1 (2016), pp. 187–201.

Barcan, Ruth, *Nudity: A Cultural Anatomy* (London: Bloomsbury, 2004).

Barthes, Roland, *Camera Lucida: Reflections on Photography*, trans. Richard Howard (New York: Hill and Wang, 1981).

Belloff, Halla, 'Social Interaction in Photographing', *Leonardo* 16/3 (1983), pp. 165–71.

Birchall, Clare, 'Transparency, Interrupted: Secrets of the Left', *Theory, Culture, and Society* 28 (2011), pp. 60–84.

Birchall, Clare, 'Radical Transparency?', *Cultural Studies<->Critical Methodologies* 14/1 (2014), pp. 77–88.

Bordo, Susan, *Unbearable Weight: Feminism, Western Culture and the Body* (Berkeley: University of California Press, 2003), pp. 45–70.

Brown, Wendy, *Edgework: Critical Essays on Knowledge and Politics* (Princeton: Princeton University Press, 2005).

Conor, Liz, *The Spectacular Modern Woman: Feminine Visibility in the 1920s* (Bloomington: Indiana University Press, 2004).

De Voss, Danielle, 'Women's Porn Sites – Spaces of Fissure and Eruption and "I'm a Little Bit of Everything"', *Sexuality and Culture* 6/3 (2002), pp. 75–94.

Elias, Ana Sofia, Rosalind Gill and Christina Scharff (eds), *Aesthetic Labour: Rethinking Beauty Politics in Neoliberalism* (London: Palgrave Macmillan, 2017).

Evans, Adrienne and Sarah Riley, *Technologies of Sexiness: Sex, Identity and Consumer Culture* (Oxford: Oxford University Press, 2014).

Favaro, Laura, '"Just Be Confident Girls!" Confidence Chic as Neoliberal Governmentality', in A.S. Elias, R. Gill and C. Scharff (eds), *Aesthetic Labour: Rethinking Beauty Politics in Neoliberalism* (Basingstoke: Palgrave Macmillan, 2017), pp. 283–300.

Fenster, Mark, 'Transparency in Search of a Theory', *European Journal of Social Theory* 18/2 (2015), pp. 150–67.

Fraser, Nancy, 'Feminism, Capitalism and the Cunning of History', *New Left Review* 56 (2009), pp. 97–117.

Frosh, Paul, 'The Public Eye and the Citizen-Voyeur: Photography as a Performance of Power', *Social Semiotics* 11/1 (2001), pp. 43–59.

Gill, Rosalind, 'From Sexual Objectification to Sexual Subjectification: The Resexualisation of Women's Bodies in the Media', *Feminist Media Studies* 3/1 (2003), pp. 99–106.

Gill, Rosalind, 'Critical Respect: The Difficulties and Dilemmas of Agency and "Choice" for Women: A Reply to Duits and Van Zoonen', *European Journal of Women's Studies* 14/1 (2007), pp. 69–80.

Gill, Rosalind and Shani Orgad, 'The Confidence Cul(ure)', *Australian Feminist Studies* 30/86 (2015), pp. 324–44.

Jones, Amelia, 'The "Eternal Return": Self-Portrait Photography as a Technology of Embodiment', *Signs* 27/4 (2002), pp. 947–78.

McRobbie, Angela, 'Top Girls? Young Women and the Post-feminist Sexual Contract', *Cultural Studies* 21/4–5 (2007), pp. 718–37.

McRobbie, Angela, *The Aftermath of Feminism: Gender, Culture, and Social Change* (London: Sage, 2009).

Parkins, Ilya, 'Domesticating Enchantment: Mediating Feminine Magic in the Interwar French Fashion Magazine', *French Cultural Studies* 28/4 (2017), pp. 344–59.

Parkins, Ilya, '"Eve Goes Synthetic": Modernizing Feminine Beauty, Renegotiating Masculinity in *Britannia and Eve*', in C. Clay et al. (eds), *Women's Print Media and Periodical Culture in Britain, 1918–39: The Interwar Years* (Edinburgh: Edinburgh University Press, 2017), pp. 139–52.

Pham, Minh-ha T., 'Blog Ambition: Fashion, Feeling and the Digital Raced Body', *Camera Obscura* 26/1 (2011), pp. 1–37.

Tu, Thuy Linh N., *The Beautiful Generation: Asian Americans and the Cultural Economy of Fashion* (Durham: Duke University Press, 2011).

White, Michele, 'Concerns about Being Visible and Expressions of Pleasure: Women's Internet Wedding Forum Considerations of Boudoir Photography Sessions', *Interstitial Journal*, October 2013, 1. Available at https://interstitialjournal.files.wordpress.com/2013/10/white-concerns.pdf (accessed 22 January 2019).

CHAPTER 6
THE DISSECTING GAZE: FASHIONED BODIES ON SOCIAL NETWORKING SITES

Dawn Woolley

Introduction

In 'Visual Pleasure and Narrative Cinema', Laura Mulvey says the gender inequality that favours men and disadvantages women also structures how we look. Women are passive objects of the look and men are active agents of it. Fetishistic scopophilia exaggerates and emphasizes the physical beauty of a woman so she is pleasurable to look at, but at the same time it reduces her to a non-threatening fragment, a part-object without subjectivity. In reference to Marxism and psychoanalysis, this chapter will argue that contemporary culture, characterized by the predominance of social networking sites and selfies, produces a particular type of fetishistic look: a magnifying, dissecting gaze. This mode of looking is an internalized gaze that compels the individual to work on the body so it more closely resembles social body ideals. It is not the pleasurable scopophilia described by Mulvey but a judgemental, disciplining gaze.

An examination of feminine and masculine ideals from the 1980s and 1990s demonstrates how advertising rhetoric has incorporated some aspects of feminist discourse while still shaping our codes of desire in accordance with patriarchal consumer culture ideology. Selfies and 'thinspiration' are discussed in this chapter, as a way of examining how the aesthetic tropes of fetishism have been used in consumer culture to emphasize the surface appearance of the body so as to compel individuals to consume commodities and fashion the body so that it conforms to dominant body ideals. The structure of fetishism is used to identify how gendered subjects are caught and instrumentalized by capitalism, and not in order to pathologize individual consumers. Similarly, when interpreting selfies and thinspiration images from social networking sites, the individual selfie-takers are not analysed. Visual trends, alongside blog posts and comments that accompany the photographs, are interpreted to understand the self-portraits as signs of an acceptance or rejection of consumer culture ideals.

Contemporary consumer subjectivity will be explored using the figure of the 'Young-Girl', an exemplary type of consumer described in *Preliminary Materials for a Theory of the Young Girl* by Tiqqun, an anonymous collective of writers and cultural theorists. The Young-Girl is an ideal, eroticized consumer who is defined by her or his surface and who seems to be without interiority. Tiqqun argue that consumers are turned into Young-Girls through their purchasing habits and the alienation that results from the neoliberalization of social relations. Although they designate this ideal consumer and propagator of neoliberal values a Young-Girl, Tiqqun argue that anyone, including mature males, can become Young-Girls. They write:

> Women's magazines breathe new life into a nearly-hundred-year-old wrong by finally offering their equivalent to males. All the old figures of patriarchal authority, from statesmen to bosses and cops, have become Young-Girlified, every last one of them, even the Pope.[1]

In the *New Inquiry*, Moira Weigel and Mal Ahern criticize Tiqqun's gender choice, arguing that the anonymity of the collective allows Tiqqun to claim to have female members and justify ideas that are misogynistic.[2] Nina Power also questions the validity of claiming that the Young-Girl could be male, saying 'and yet the book is precisely not called "Theory of the Wizened-Pope"', suggesting that the choice of appellation is gender specific and perpetuates the stereotype that women are narcissistic consumers.[3] However, Tiqqun offer this explanation:

> Young people, because adolescence is the 'period of time with none but a consumptive relation to civil society' (Stuart Ewen, *Captains of Consciousness*). Women, because it is the sphere of *reproduction*, over which they still reign, that must be colonized. Hypostasized Youth and Femininity, abstracted and recoded into *Youthitude* and *Femininitude*, find themselves raised to the rank of ideal regulators of the integration of the Imperial citizenry. The figure of the Young-Girl combines these two determinations into one immediate, spontaneous, and perfectly desirable whole.[4]

In *The Consumer Society*, published forty-two years before Tiqqun's text, Baudrillard made similar statements. He described how 'woman', 'youth' and 'sex' were potential forces of disruption and would be rigorously controlled by consumer society. Tiqqun quote Baudrillard: 'Women are given Woman to consume, the young are given the Young and, in this formal and narcissistic emancipation, their real liberation is successfully averted.'[5] Tiqqun further emphasize this idea by saying:

> By investing young people and women with an absurd symbolic surplus value, by making them the exclusive carriers of the two new kinds of esoteric knowledge proper to the new social order – consumption and seduction – Spectacle has effectively emancipated the slaves of the past, but it has emancipated them AS SLAVES.[6]

Both texts question why consumer society subjugates some members of society to a greater extent than others. It is controversial to designate the 'infantry, the rank-and-file of the current dictatorship of appearances' a Young-Girl.[7] However, the Young-Girl captures the idolatry of young, beautiful and highly sexualized woman that is predominant in consumer culture. She is an ideal image that produces a strong compulsion to consume. In this chapter, Tiqqun's descriptions of the Young-Girl are used to elucidate the methods of indoctrination and discipline that female consumers are subjected to in contemporary neoliberal capitalist society.

However, in specifying that a small number of descriptions in the text refer to male Young-Girls, Tiqqun imply that the text predominantly describes female consumers. This differentiation between genders produces gender-stereotypical descriptions of a disciplined masculine consumer who is 'alienated by contagion' and a feminine consumer who is a 'non-being', engaging in meaningless 'chatter'.[8] Therefore, this chapter argues against the suggestion that Young-Girlification offers a form of gender equality via enslavement to the Spectacle and examines how gender difference is reinforced by this process of subjection.

The old new patriarchal same[9]

Since the publication of 'Visual Pleasure and Narrative Cinema', the impact that feminism has had on visual and consumer culture has been noticeable. In the 1980s, lifestyle and fashion magazines aimed at male consumers produced growing markets for male grooming and fashion commodities. The variety of representations of male bodies also changed in response to feminism. In her essay Mulvey described that female bodies were frequently represented using the aesthetic codes of sexual fetishism:

close-ups of female body parts. Mulvey says: 'One part of a fragmented body destroys the Renaissance space, the illusion of depth demanded by the narrative; it gives flatness, the quality of a cut-out or icon, rather than verisimilitude, to the screen.'[10] The fetishized body part does not contribute to the realism or narrative of the film. It is outside of time and space because it exists solely to excite an eroticized look. In the 1980s, adverts depicted the figure of the 'new man' using some of the aesthetic codes of fetishism described by Mulvey. The adverts showed male subjects in isolation, fully absorbed in the pleasures of clothing and consumption. Describing the models in the 'Laundrette' and 'Bath' adverts by Levi 501, Sean Nixon writes:

> Arms, chest, face, bottom and thighs, together with a focus on the unbuttoning of the jeans and (in the case of 'Bath') a cut of the water seeping over the model's jean-clad crotch, undermined more conventional significances of power and aggression associated with displayed masculine bodies.[11]

The close-up crops of male body parts not only fetishized the bodies, turning them into fragments for the pleasure of spectators; they also intensified the viewing pleasure, because the 'spectatorial eye was brought up much closer to the surface of the masculine body'.[12]

However, as Rosalind Gill describes, these depictions of male bodies are selective in their use of the visual motifs of the objectified female body. The male bodies in adverts are usually muscular, hard bodies connoting strength and phallic power. The models do not smile invitingly or pout alluringly and they are rarely depicted using gestures that have come to signify the passive and subordinated female. Frequently 'they look back at the viewer in ways reminiscent of street gazes to assert dominance or look up or off, indicating that their interest is elsewhere'.[13] The 'new man' is coded in a manner that challenges some conventions without undermining dominant gender assumptions. Gill says that 'sexualized representation of the male body has not proved incommensurable with male dominance'.[14]

Feminist discourse and the 'new man' produced another figure that reinforced pre-Second-Wave feminist stereotypes of gender representation. In the 1990s, as a reaction against the 'new man', the 'new lad' was championed as the ideal masculine character. In *Arena* magazine Sean O' Hagan described the 'new lad' as

> educated, stylish, more often than not well groomed and totally in tune with the shifting codes of contemporary culture [...] [H]e is well versed in the language, and protocol, of post-feminist discourse and he will never ever, even after a few post-prandial brandies slip into Sid the Sexist mode like a regular (Jack the) lad might.[15]

However, the 'new lad' is 'a rather schizoid fellow. He aspires to New Man status when he's with women, but reverts to old man type when he's out with the boys'.[16]

Despite claims that the 'new lad' would never slip back into 'Sid the Sexist' mode, the description implies that this individual would only act like a postfeminist enlightened man when in female company. New 1990s men's style magazines such as *Loaded*, alongside existing magazines including *FHM*, *Arena* and *GQ*, brought highly sexualized images of women back into mainstream visual culture. The magazines also contained articles and editorials that scrutinized women using derogatory sexist language. Nixon describes the 'new lad' as a return of the repressed:

> While the moral language of antisexism associated with the sexual politics of the new social movements clearly impacted on the debates about the 'new man' (putting a limited block on the more trenchant sexualized scrutiny of women within magazine publishing, for example) no alternative sexual scripts were fully elaborated [...] [Because] no new hetereosexual scripts were articulated – scripts that were both sexy and antisexist – the opportunity for established scripts to re-emerge was always left open.[17]

The 'new lad' is characterized by pre-'new man' sexism and a heightened interest in fashion and body-maintenance: he embodies Tiqqun's description of the feminized masculine consumer who is 'alienated by contagion' and 'both the victim and the object of its own alienated desire'.[18]

While representations of male bodies were going through these transformations, representations of female bodies were also being affected by feminism. Prior to Second-Wave feminism, female consumer practices were described as a form of oppression and a means of distraction from oppression. In 1792 Mary Wollstencraft wrote: 'Taught from their infancy that beauty is woman's sceptre, the mind shapes itself to the body, and, roaming round its gilt cage, only seeks to adorn its prison.'[19] Almost 200 years later, Wolfgang Fritz Haug described female consumer practices as 'goddess-packaging' that functions as a 'glittering straitjacket, a glossy recompense for subjection and degradation to a second-rate existence. Furthermore, maintaining the packaging is not only expensive but it keeps one occupied'.[20]

Throughout the 1980s and 1990s, many women experienced financial independence because they were able to take up more lucrative paid employment. This transformed advertising in a number of ways. Angela McRobbie says the disposable income enjoyed by women produced an 'exponential growth of the female beauty, cosmetics, fashion and media industries'.[21] The consumption of pampering and body maintenance commodities was promoted as

> an archetypal female leisure activity, often carrying with it a kind of faux feminist legitimacy. It is coded as a new kind of women's right or entitlement on the basis of having become a wage earner and thus of having gained certain freedoms [...].[22]

In consumer culture, female empowerment became inextricably linked to consumption and body maintenance. Similar to the figure of the 'new lad', the empowered women in the 1990s were characterized by stereotypical gender traits, modified to accommodate feminist discourse. Rosalind Gill describes the empowered young woman from the 1990s as 'a young, attractive, heterosexual woman who knowingly and deliberately plays with her sexual power and is always "up for" sex'.[23] Feminist discourse and ideas of sexual liberation are incorporated into advertising rhetoric: 'New hair, new look, new bra. And if he doesn't like it, new boyfriend' (Triumph); 'Discover the power of femininity. Defy conventions and take the lead' (Elizabeth Arden); and 'Empower your eyes' (Shiseido mascara).[24] Gill describes how empowerment is reduced to a type of sexual power over men that is achieved by having a young, slim and beautiful body.[25]

Gill used the term 'midriff' to refer to the generation of girls and young women in their teens and twenties in the 1990s.[26] The 'midriff' is exemplified by Trevor Beattie's 1994 Wonderbra campaign and the slogan 'Hello Boys'. The advert caused controversy in the UK when first displayed, with some viewers claiming it was derogatory and others suggesting it had caused traffic accidents because it was distracting drivers. The advert was voted the 'most successful campaign of all time' in 2011.[27] The woman in the advert knowingly and humorously addresses the viewer; she knows she is desired and flaunts her attractive body as a source of power. Gill writes that 'today women are presented as active, desiring sexual subjects who choose to present themselves in a seemingly objectified manner because it suits their (implicitly "liberated") interests to do so'.[28] Liberation becomes a 'new form of tyranny, an obligation to be sexual in a highly specific kind of way'.[29]

The woman on display in the Wonderbra advert is powerful, but her power derives from a heteronormative sexual display of an idealized body type. Not only does this depoliticize the original political intent of the feminist aim for empowerment but also provides an alibi for sexist content. Gill notes a contradiction in this 'empowering' type of advertising, in which 'the more closely an image borrows from the vocabulary of heterosexual soft porn, the more the advertisement's written or verbal text will stress women's empowerment'.[30]

However, in the Wonderbra advert, the text 'hello boys' emphasizes the sexual nature of the image and 'empowerment' is not overtly stated as in the advertising campaigns listed above. The Wonderbra image employs the aesthetic codes of fetishism described by Mulvey. The central focus of the image, and the model's attention, is her breasts. There is no narrative or discernable location, taking the image 'into a no man's land outside its own time and space', in which the body is an object of pure scopophilic pleasure.[31] Her 'empowerment' derives from her desirable body and the enhanced cleavage produced by the commodity. She does not pose a challenge to patriarchal order.

In 'Visual Pleasure and Narrative Cinema', Mulvey says a female film star becomes 'reassuring rather than dangerous' when her appearance is enhanced: she is turned into an icon instead of a unique person with desires and demands.[32] By removing imperfections and increasing surface appeal through commodification, the body is simultaneously idolized and dehumanized. In his account of fetishism Sigmund Freud referred to the Chinese custom of 'lotus feet', in which women's feet were mutilated by tight binding and then revered like fetish objects. He suggested that 'the Chinese male wants to thank the woman for having submitted to being castrated'.[33] Through the sacrifice of mobility and comfort the Chinese woman gained an elevated social position; she was deemed to be an extraordinary object of desire.

Disguised as empowerment, women in contemporary consumer society are coerced into becoming reassuring and docile sex objects. This form of fetishization is more insidious than the one described by Mulvey because it is presented as a personal choice and a pleasure. Gill says this connotes a change of spectatorial power from an external, judgemental male gaze to a 'self policing narcissistic gaze'.[34] Gill continues:

> Power is not imposed from above or from outside, but constructs our very subjectivity. Girls and women are invited to become a particular kind of self, and endowed with agency on condition that it is used to construct oneself as a subject closely resembling the heterosexual male fantasy that is found in pornography.[35]

Fetishistic depictions of bodies are prevalent in contemporary consumer culture. Although masculine and feminine bodies are displayed in adverts using similar fetishistic tropes, the masculine models retain signifiers of mastery and dominance but the feminine models do not. Contemporary gender ideals continue to be coded to the dominant patriarchal order, despite the incorporation of Second-Wave feminist discourse into advertising rhetoric. Feminist rhetoric is used to sell products in a sexualized way. It has been incorporated, depoliticized and relegated to a moment in history.

The Young-Girl and selfie subjectivities

The conflation of empowerment with sexualization and commodification has also produced a feminine subjectivity that is ideally suited to neoliberal values. The pseudo-feminist discourse in advertising implies that because women are empowered by consumption there is no need for collective feminist action. The power to achieve success resides in the individual, who can choose to work at her appearance and use her assets to get what she wants. There is no place to blame sexism, racism, classism and structural inequality for lack of success because all of life's problems can be solved with the consumption of commodities. The empowered 'midriff' embodies the ideals of individualism and entrepreneurialism that characterize neoliberal capitalism.

The following description of the Young-Girl shows how female consumers are subordinated with the promise of limited social power:

> The symbolic privileges accorded by the Spectacle to the Young-Girl are her dividends for absorbing and diffusing the ephemeral codes, the updated user's manuals, the general semiology that THEY have had to dispense in order to render politically harmless the free time enabled by 'progress' in the social organization.[36]

By spending time on self-improvement and body labour in order to gain social power, the Young-Girl is neutralized as a disruptive political force. She is beautiful and docile. The Young-Girl is an ideal neoliberal subject because she 'defines herself in terms fixed by extraneous judgment'[37] provided by the Spectacle (advertising) and uses numerical systems to measure her success. She says:

> How much beauty have you got? No, beauty is not a question of subjective appreciation. Unlike charm, much too fluid a notion, beauty is calculated in centimeters, divided into fractions, weighed, examined by magnifying glass, evaluated in its thousands of sly details. Stop hiding behind neo-hippy principles, like 'inner beauty, that's what counts', 'I've got my own style', and dare to measure yourselves in the court of the greats!!![38]

Physical attractiveness is a quantifiable value and a form of labour. In Tiqqun's words, the Young-Girl's 'appearance entirely exhausts her essence, as her representation does her reality'.[39] Like Mulvey's fetishized film star, there is a form of erasure implicit in the commodified body, a loss of individuality that comes from copying a template. The Young-Girl is reduced (or elevated) to the status of an image.

The unsmiling expressions of the models in the Dolce and Gabbana Autumn/Winter 2015[40] campaign bring to mind the Young-Girl as commodity par excellence who 'pursues plastic perfection in all its forms, in particular, her own'.[41] In each advert the model is posing to take a selfie using her mobile phone, transfixed by her image. She appears to be captivated by the spectacle of her own beauty as it is enhanced by dazzling Dolce and Gabbana accessories. She stands with a handbag held close to her face, suggesting they are comparable and complementary objects. The adverts bring to mind Tiqqun's description of the relation between the Young-Girl and commodities:

> The Young-Girl covets commodities with an eye filled with envy, because she sees the model of herself in them, which is to say, the same thing that she is, only more perfect. What remains of her humanity is not only what keeps her in default of commodity perfection, it is also the cause of all her suffering. It is this remaining humanity, therefore, that she must eradicate.[42]

In the Dolce and Gabbana adverts, the models have achieved the perfection of the commodity and no longer view them with envy. The model and commodity are objects of equal value and appeal.

In the Dolce and Gabbana adverts, the models pose for selfies. The viewer cannot see the image the model sees. This arouses a desire to view the model and her commodities from the position of the screen. Identification with the model is increased by the imagined position and produces a fantasy of possession: of the dress, the handbag, the body, the face. The Dolce and Gabbana adverts reduce the gap between ideal and consumer, levelling social differences onto a single lateral plain of 'selfie-producer', further increasing identification with the model. The adverts also suggest that the consumer will improve the quality of their selfies if they purchase the commodities. The selfie in the advert functions as a mode of address that can be viewed as aspirational because it heightens the viewer's identification with the model and disciplinary because it can induce the viewer to try to achieve a similar glamorous look. Agnès Rocamora describes the dual viewing position produced when looking at selfies on fashion blogs as follows:

> The viewer is simultaneously placed in the position of the one doing the looking, and, through identification, the one being looked at [...] The screen/mirror shows an idealized self the viewer can identify with and therefore appropriate to work on her own identity construction, whilst also indulging in the pleasure of voyeurism her status as a spectator grants her.[43]

The viewer is positioned both inside the image and external to it, taking the fantasized position of the selfie-taker and viewing the other as an object. When looking at a selfie I view the individual from the position of the screen and her image; however, in the Dolce and Gabbana adverts I view the model from a third position and I am required to project myself, in fantasy, into the space between the model and her image. It seems that I will gain access to the self-regarding gaze of the model if I purchase Dolce and Gabbana accessories.

In fashion blogs and the Dolce and Gabbana adverts, selfies link identification and voyeurism with the consumption of commodities. In *Hard Looks* Nixon says that consumer subjectivities are produced by the way we view commodities. Drawing on Walter Benjamin's discussion of the flâneur in nineteenth-century Paris, he says:

> The consumer subjectivity not only established a series of looks at the displays of goods and the detail of the shop interiors, but also invited the consumer to look at themselves amidst this spectacle – often literally, through catching sight of their reflection in a mirror

> or shop window. A self monitoring look was implicit, then, in these ways of looking.[44]

The consumer subjectivity of the flâneur was constructed by fleeting glimpses of the self, between glances of commodity displays and other consumers. Self, commodity and other are part of the spectatorial experience. Nixon says that the interior design of clothes shops in the 1980s produced a similar consumer experience. By catching glimpses of their own bodies in the shiny chrome surfaces of the shop interior, the individuals are encouraged to critically appraise their bodies and imagine themselves in the clothes.

Social networking sites also offer users the opportunity to browse commodities and other people in posts containing selfies, snapshots and adverts. The shiny surface of the computer or mobile phone screen places the viewer's reflection in the scene. The popularity and ubiquity of selfies mean that users are encouraged to put their own image into the environment, increasing the propensity to identify with other user's selfies, make comparisons and adopt a self-monitoring look.

The selfie plays a prominent role in consumer subjectivity construction. It is conceptualized as the intersection of two 'technologies of the self': photography and 'a contemporary space of individual expression: the computer screen.'[45] In academic discourse, the selfie is analysed as a symptom of the negative impact of globalized social networking sites and an empowering form of agency. For example, Rocamora says women's desire to represent themselves online followed a historical period in which women's capacity to represent themselves was 'restrained by men's ownership of the tools of artistic production such as the brush or the camera as well as of the spaces of display such as galleries and museums.'[46] She says that social media and mobile camera technology are tools that women can use for self-representation, 'thereby appropriating the power of representation that has often eluded them.'[47] In his article interpreting the function of selfies produced by female artists, Derek Conrad Murray echoes this sentiment with even greater optimism:

> Viewed individually, they appear rather banal, commonplace, and benign. Taken en masse, it feels like a revolutionary political movement – like a radical colonization of the visual realm and an aggressive reclaiming of the female body. Even if there is no overt political intent, they are indeed contending with the manner in which capitalism is enacted upon their lives.[48]

Murray views the prevalence of 'pin-up' style selfies online as a reaction against the unattainable beauty ideals perpetuated in popular culture. The sexualized selfies are 'not meant as titillation for the male gaze, rather it is designed to embrace femininity and sexuality; celebrate the history of women; reject unhealthy beauty standards promoted by the media; and advance a body-positive attitude'.[49] However, he goes on to say the images explore 'formulaic female sexualities' that reiterate patriarchal ideals and do so as a form of empowerment.[50] Pin-up selfies reiterate the commodified empowerment of 'midriff' advertising and suggest nostalgia for beauty ideals that reference a time prior to Second-Wave feminism.

Despite the potential to represent the self in any number of ways, selfies tend to conform to a narrow set of gestures and poses that are derived from advertising and reinforce gender stereotypes. In 1976 Erving Goffman analysed the pose, position of the body, facial expression and clothing of female and male subjects in over 500 adverts. He identified several ways that gender ideals are enacted and reinforced through gesture and positioning.[51] In 2015 Nicola Döring, Anne Reif and Sandra Poeschl conducted content analysis of 500 selfies found on Instagram to determine if selfies conform to the gender stereotypes identified by Goffman. Not only were the same gender stereotypical behaviours found in adverts repeated in selfies, but the stereotypical gender display categories were present more frequently in selfies than in adverts in magazines, suggesting that an intensification of gender stereotypical behaviours has taken place.[52]

In reference to Sarah Gram, a social media blogger, Mehita Iqani and Jonathan E. Schroeder say that selfie-takers turn the self into a commodity to 'claim themselves as valuable in a cultural system (capitalism) that considers them valuable only in certain ways (as sexy bodies and pretty faces)'.[53] By taking selfies and sharing them online, the individual becomes an object of exchange. Although the phenomenon enables an individual to produce the image of their choosing, selfies also increase self-surveillance and foreground the value of appearance. Social networking sites support consumer culture by producing technologies and practices that create ideal consumers while homogenizing gendered behaviours and body ideals. Despite her positive attitude towards selfies on fashion blogs, Rocamora describes the screen as 'one more instrument imposing on woman the panoptic control which mirrors and the masculine gaze subject them to [...] computer self-control is the more pernicious in that it is inscribed in a playful, banalized, and voluntary logic'.[54] The selfie, as a technology of the self, reinforces the self-policing gaze as something that is self-chosen and deemed to be fun.

The selfie can be viewed as a tool that disciplines individuals into a consumer subjectivity of the Young-Girl. Social networking sites reproduce the Spectacle as 'a mirror that shows the Young-Girl the assimilable image of her ideal'.[55] Tiqqun could be referring to the selfie when they say:

> The Young-Girl possesses her reality outside of herself, in the Spectacle, in all of the doctored representations of the ideal that it traffics, in the fleeting conventions it decrees, in the mores through which it commands mimesis. She is simply the insubstantial concretion of all these abstractions, which precede and follow her.[56]

The magnifying, dissecting gaze

The proliferation of mobile telephones with cameras and the development of social networks to disseminate the photographs have led to the increase in opportunities to be photographed and instantly share the image with wide networks. The increase in self-surveillance causes an intensification of the self-policing gaze, producing a magnifying and dissecting gaze. As Tiqqun say: 'Beauty is calculated in centimeters, divided into fractions, weighed, examined by magnifying glass, evaluated in its thousands of sly details.'[57]

This self-regarding gaze encourages me to perceive my body as fragments corresponding to areas of imperfection: I focus on an area of my body to be improved by commodities. This is a fetishistic mode of looking, similar to that described by Emily Apter as 'hyperfocalization', in which 'the fetishist does indeed refuse to look, but in refusing to look, he stares. It is a "not looking" sustained paradoxically through visual fixation on the substitute [...].'[58] Fetishistic hyperfocalization dissects the body into parts that can be improved. When the individual focuses on a small area of imperfection, the appearance and experience of the whole body are obscured from comprehension. This mode of looking is a repetition of the view of the body disseminated in consumer culture. As commodity markets become overcrowded, products are produced to target increasingly small areas of the body. Face products specify which part of the face they are produced to improve, and moisturisers are now made for the face, hands, feet and body. As commodity producers scrutinize the body for new parts to problematize, the consumer also intensifies their hyperfocalizing self-regarding gaze. Mike Featherstone describes the contemporary view of the body as a 'cool surgical gaze measuring the body for cutting' produced by 'the "cutting scalpel eye" of the consumer culture body maintenance and transformation professionals, whose gaze assesses and marks the re-fashionable potential of our bodies'.[59] Featherstone says the relation between body and image in contemporary consumer society encourages us to compare ourselves with the bodies we see in images and view the images as evidence of what we are not but wish to become. This propensity supports the ideology of transformation exemplified in 'before-and-after' photographs of diet products and cosmetic surgery procedures.

Issue 932 of *Heat* magazine features an interview with Malin Andersson, a British reality TV star. The interview is titled 'Love Island's Malin "I had £7K of Surgery to Look Good on Social Media": She had it *all* done for Instagram and Snapchat'. Andersson says that self-consciousness about her body led her to have cosmetic surgery. The relation between social networking sites, visibility and imperfection is clear:

> If you look at my Instagram, there are no pictures with my boobs out or bikini shots. I absolutely hated them – even selfies in the mirror. I used to wear baggy jumpers, but now I can wear everything tight. I'll be like, 'Damn!' and now I'm taking selfies left, right, and centre.[60]

Having cosmetic surgery enables Andersson to present herself to the scrutiny of others. Surgery disciplines her body to social norms, making herself '*recognizable* in the vitreous eyes of the Spectacle', so she can participate in the social interactions that are enabled by selfie-taking and sharing.[61]

An article that immediately follows Andersson's interview announces 'Snapchat Surgery Hits the UK'. A cosmetic surgeon referred to as 'Dr Miami' the 'Snapchat surgeon' describes how images of perfect faces and bodies achieved using digital filters and disseminated on Snapchat are driving people to surgery. Dr Miami says that 'since Snapchat took off, my surgery schedule is booked out solid for two years'.[62] He publishes Snapchat posts of cosmetic surgery operations that are viewed 'a million and a half' times by his 576,000 followers. 'Imperfect' selfies sit alongside Instagram posts advertising cosmetic surgery procedures that claim to erase imperfections. The ideal body is described and disseminated on social networking sites. Followers are repeatedly told how they can become perfect with the aid of commodities and cosmetic procedures. The body of the contemporary consumer is never complete and never good enough. Featherstone says that the availability of affordable surgery, which has been normalized by television programmes such as *Extreme Makeover* and *10 Years Younger*, produces a 'particular view of the body, as bounded and compartmentalized into separate domains, each of which can be renovated or upgraded'.[63] It is a vicious cycle: the increased expectation of perfection causes increased scrutiny and greater sensitivity to what constitutes an imperfection. Susan Bordo quotes a cosmetic surgeon: 'Plastic surgery sharpens your eyesight. You get something done, suddenly you're looking in the mirror every five minutes – at imperfections nobody else can see.'[64] The dissecting gaze is also a magnifying gaze that turns small flaws into glaring aberrations. This way of looking also shapes the way the body is viewed as a fetish object.

Psychoanalyst Louise Kaplan describes the visual character of the fetish as 'a glaring lie and fetishistic tropes as blunt metaphors, vividly bright, iconic images that blind us'.[65] She continues: 'The hyperpigmented image is a sham, the false gold that distracts the viewer by glittering up the perceptual field.'[66] The glittering of the fetish is a lure and a distraction. Janine Chasseguet-Smirgel, who is also a psychoanalyst, says that fetish objects often have an attractive shiny surface and an unpleasant smell. For example, a highly polished shoe and a pair of satin knickers are simultaneously 'grotesque and excremental, ideal and pristine' because they are visually alluring and, once worn, emit body odour.[67] The fetish object has a dual character; one aspect of it is idealized and revered and another aspect is detested and debased.

The fetishized bodies of others on social networking sites and in adverts function as 'bright, iconic images that blind us',[68] but under a self-regarding gaze the body isn't glittering false gold but a defective object. The revered and hated fetish is split in two: the ideal body of the other is prized and the consumer's own body is denigrated. Rather than 'glittering up the perceptual field' with an object that is reassuring and pleasant to view, this gaze produces a degraded and despised object that is a source of anxiety and guilt.[69] The carefully posed and digitally enhanced selfie offers the consumer a compromise solution between the desired perfect bodies viewed online and their real 'imperfect' body.

This alienated relation between self and body can be viewed in #thinspiration. Thinspiration or pro-ana (pro-anorexia) sites are blogs and websites created by individuals with eating disorders. The writers share stories about their own weight loss regimes and provide tips on how to lose weight and how to evade detection by doctors, family members and friends. They frequently contain thinspiration or thinspo pages of images of their own emaciated body, images of other eating disorder sufferers or very thin celebrities. Thinspiration and thinspo are also hashtags used on social networking sites to denote the type of images posted and enable pro-ana users to search for and share the material.

Although eating disorders are commonly perceived to be female illnesses, it is estimated that men showing signs of eating disorder account for up to 25 per cent of cases in the UK.[70] A study by David Giles and Jessica Close found that exposure to male body ideals in 'lads' magazines led to a drive for muscularity and eating disturbance, particularly in single men.[71] Mike Featherstone calls this new disorder 'athletic nervosa'.[72]

The internalization of consumer society ideals is seen in thinspiration blogs where individuals reward their suffering with shopping trips and beauty treatments. Many pro-eating disorder websites suggest methods of distraction or rewards for resisting food couched in terms of consumption and body labour. Visitors to one website are encouraged to undertake some of the following activities to prevent them from giving in to hunger pangs:

> Exfoliate your entire body, take a long hot bath, pluck/wax your eyebrows, paint your finger and toe nails, use crest white strips, apply self tanner, try a new hairstyle, have your hair cut, straighten your hair, give yourself a make over with totally, [*sic*] different makeup, shave/wax your legs, put a face mask on, go for a manicure or pedicure.[73]

The creator of this website suggests readers search online to 'find something you love, and get it once you go x number of days without bingeing'. Another proposes that readers calculate how much money they have saved by not buying food and reward themselves with a shopping trip for smaller sized clothing.[74] These recommendations turn self-starvation into an activity that enables consumption of commodities and produces value for the body.

In contrast to the enticing 'self-advertisement' of the selfie-producer, the thinspiration-producer presents the self as a disturbing image, fixating on a slender ideal but distorting the value of the body in the process. The anorexic way of looking 'hyperfocalizes' on parts of the body, searching for areas that are imperfect. As the body diminishes and fat is almost imperceptible, the magnifying gaze enables the individual to identify additional areas for improvement. The bodies in thinspiration photographs are rarely shown in their entirety: the photographs reproduce a dissecting, magnifying gaze to more clearly show the body's emaciation. Individuals post a series of images to draw the viewer's attention to the chest, rib cage, spine, thighs, knees, arms, hips, shoulder blades and collarbone.

In thinspiration photographs, the body is not presented as an idealized, commodified body that conforms to social ideals but as an imperfect object produced when the body is viewed with a dissecting, fetishizing gaze. The photograph presents the body as a separate, degraded thing, demonstrating the tyrannical rule of the mind over the body. The individual in the photograph has dissociated the body, presenting it in a way that says 'look at the transformations I have produced with the body that I have' rather than 'the body that I am'. The subject reigns supreme, demonstrating and asserting its agency through the destruction of the object. The individual views the body as a dehumanized object: a fetish that must be reduced to a fragment to prevent it expressing threatening wants or desires.

In their description of the Young-Girl, Tiqqun say destruction of the body of the anorexic demonstrates 'the desire to free oneself from a body entirely colonized by commodity symbolism, to reduce to nothing a physical objectivity the Young-Girl wholly lacks'.[75] The emaciated body functions as a demonstration of the logical end point for the aestheticized body as a commodity and a fetish. If commodity fetishes emphasize surface appeal to conceal the dehumanizing effect of commodification, the anorexic body presents the surface as a paper-thin veneer. The skin is translucent and the skeleton beneath captures my attention. The dazzling surface is overemphasized to the point that it fails to conceal the destruction caused by commodification.

Conclusion

In 'Visual Pleasure and Narrative Cinema', Laura Mulvey used psychoanalytic theory as a 'political weapon, demonstrating the way the unconscious of patriarchal society has structured film form'.[76] In this chapter, I have examined contemporary consumer culture to determine if the aesthetic codes of the fetishized female star, indicative of patriarchal control of the codes of desire, are still prevalent. I also ask, do patriarchal social codes structure self-presentation on social networking sites?

Second-Wave feminism produced a number of changes in consumer culture. Adverts now contain a greater variety of representations of male bodies, including imagery that fetishistically crops the body into fragments. However, the selective use of the visual codes of fetishism present the masculine body as sexualized but not subordinated. For the female consumer, emancipation is packaged as the freedom to buy cosmetics and beauty products, and empowerment is achieved when her body conforms to patriarchal codes of desire. In the introduction of *Preliminary Materials* Tiqqun state: 'Women's magazines breathe new life into a nearly-hundred-year-old wrong by finally offering their equivalent to males. All the old figures of patriarchal authority, from statesmen to bosses and cops, have become Young-Girlified [...].'[77] To encourage them to buy body maintenance and grooming products, male consumers are objectified and sexualized in adverts. However, the different forms that fetishization takes in adverts depicting male and female subjects demonstrate that the subjugation of male consumers is not equivalent to that of female consumers. The masculine and feminine Young-Girls are not the same. Furthermore, the existence of a form of eating disorder that predominantly affects young men and is characterized by a drive for muscularity and athleticism suggests that strength and action are still dominant masculine stereotypes in consumer society.

In the twenty-first century, the development and popularity of social networking sites have increased the dominance of gender stereotypical representations produced in adverts. Their gestures and styling are reproduced in selfies, reinforcing the fetishizing gaze, in its gender-specific forms. The selfie also functions as a technology of the self that further stresses the need for body maintenance, with 'likes' being a visible and quantifiable system of reward for conformity to patriarchal body ideals. A self-policing gaze instituted by social networking sites is exacerbated by selfie-production and contributes to the consumer culture view of the body founded on an ideology of comparison and transformation.

The dissecting gaze initiates a vicious cycle of body improvement in which 'problem areas' of the body are produced by the intense scrutiny of a magnifying gaze. This endless pursuit of perfection brings to mind the Young-Girl: 'As the Young-Girl formatting becomes more widespread, competition hardens and the satisfaction linked to conformity wanes. A qualitative jump becomes necessary; it becomes urgent to equip oneself with new and unheard-of attributes: One must move into some still-virgin space.'[78]

Snapchat surgery demonstrates the role that social networking sites play in hardening competition and producing unheard-of attributes for the body. The increased visibility caused by selfie-taking and comparison of one's own body with people in adverts and other selfies produces anxiety. It also provides an ideal model to aspire to. The adverts for products and procedures that claim to transform the body into the ideal are interspersed in the news feed, offering a solution to anxiety.

The thinspiration body interrupts the repetitious order of commodified body ideals found in selfies on social networking sites. It demands a look that is specifically created for its form. As Susie Orbach writes:

> She demands to be related to originally. Reflexive responses – for example, flirtatious or patronizing ones from men, or the 'once over' from another woman who needs to position herself [...] – are confounded. She defies easy, comfortable definition [...] She is now looked at, not as someone who is appealing, but as some-body one cannot take one's eyes off.[79]

The disciplinary modes of looking common to social networking sites are brought to a halt. Orbach describes the experience of viewing an anorexic body where 'anguish and defiance combine in the most curious way to make the observer passive and motionless in response. There is a simultaneous desire to retreat and move in closer. The conflict renders one immobile'.[80] The viewer is horrified by the corpse-like figure but cannot look away. The anorexic body disrupts the magnifying, dissecting gaze and produces a look akin to that of abject fascination.

The anorexic body of thinspiration exposes the destructive end point of the fetishistic commodification of consumer culture. It shows that the relentless pursuit of perfection does not produce the mannequin-like perfection of models in Dolce and Gabbana adverts but the fragmented, skeletal form of the thinspiration body. The dissecting gaze is laid bare and the corpse-like body that is proudly displayed in thinspiration images exposes the true desire of the fetishist: to produce a dehumanized dead object.

Notes

1. Tiqqun (Collective), *Preliminary Materials for a Theory of the Young-Girl* (Los Angeles, CA: Semiotext(e), 2012), p. 17.
2. Moira Weigel and Mal Ahern, 'Further Materials toward a Theory of the Man-Child', *The New Enquiry*, 2013. Available at https://thenewinquiry.com/further-materials-toward-a-theory-of-the-manchild/ (accessed 12 May 2016).
3. Nina Power, 'She's Just Not That into You', *Radical Philosophy* 177 (2013). Available at https://www.radicalphilosophy.com/reviews/individual-reviews/rp177-shes-just-not-that-into-you (accessed 12 May 2016).
4. Tiqqun (Collective), *Preliminary Materials*, p. 16 (emphasis in original).

5. Jean Baudrillard, *The Consumer Society: Myths and Structures*, trans. Chris Turner, 2nd edn (London: Sage, 1998), pp. 46–7.
6. Tiqqun (Collective), *Preliminary Materials*, p. 23, p. 43, p. 25.
7. Ibid., p. 106.
8. Ibid., p. 25.
9. In response to Tasker and Negra's 2005 assertion that the commodification of feminism did not result in a continuation of the patriarchal oppression experienced prior to the 1990s, McRobbie counters that it results in 'not simply the old, but rather the new "patriarchal same"'. p. 539. Yvonne Tasker and Diane Negra (eds) (2005) 'In Focus: Postfeminism and Contemporary Media Studies', *Cinema Journal*, 44/2 (Winter, 2005), pp. 107–10. Angela McRobbie, 'Young Women and Consumer Culture', *Cultural Studies* 22/5 (2008), pp. 531–50.
10. Laura Mulvey, *Visual and Other Pleasures*, 2nd edn (Basingstoke: Palgrave Macmillan, 2009), p. 20.
11. Sean Nixon, *Hard Looks: Masculinities, Spectatorship and Contemporary Consumption* (London: UCL Press, 1996), p. 119.
12. Ibid., p. 192.
13. Rosalind Gill, 'Beyond the "Sexualisation of Culture" Thesis: An Intersectional Analysis of "Sixpacks," "Midriffs" and "Hot Lesbians" in Advertising', *Sexualities* 12/2 (2009), pp. 137–60, p. 146.
14. Ibid., p. 147.
15. Sean O'Hagan, *Arena* 27 (Spring/Summer 1991), p. 22, quoted in Nixon, *Hard Looks*, p. 204.
16. Ibid.
17. Ibid., p. 206.
18. Tiqqun (Collective), *Preliminary Materials*, p. 23, p. 25.
19. Mary Wollstonecraft quoted in Virginia Sapiro, *A Vindication of Political Virtue: The Political Theory of Mary Wollstonecraft* (Chicago: The University of Chicago Press, 1992), p. 126.
20. Wolfgang Fritz Haug, *Critique of Commodity Aesthetics: Appearance, Sexuality and Advertising in Capitalist Society* (Cambridge: Polity Press, 1986), p. 76.
21. Angela McRobbie, 'Reflections on Feminism and Immaterial Labour', *New Formations* 70 (2010), pp. 60–76, p. 67.
22. Ibid.
23. Gill, 'Beyond the "Sexualisation of Culture" Thesis', p. 148.
24. Ibid., pp. 148–9.
25. Ibid.
26. Rosalind Gill, 'Empowerment/Sexism: Figuring Female Sexual Agency in Contemporary Advertising', *Feminism and Psychology* 18/1 (2008), pp. 35–60.

27. Daniel Farey-Jones, 'Hello Boys Voted Greatest Poster Ever Created', 31 March 2011. Available at http://www.campaignlive.co.uk/article/hello-boys-voted-greatest-poster-ever-created/1063405# (accessed 26 August 2016).
28. Gill, 'Empowerment/Sexism', p. 42.
29. Ibid., p. 53.
30. Gill, 'Beyond the "Sexualisation of Culture" Thesis', p. 154.
31. Mulvey, *Visual and Other Pleasures*, p. 20.
32. Ibid., p. 22.
33. Sigmund Freud, 'Fetishism' in A. Richards (ed) *On Sexuality: Three Essays on the Theory of Sexuality and Other Works*, trans. James Strachey (London: Penguin Books, 1991), pp. 345–57 ['Fetischismus', *Almanach* (1929), pp. 17–24], p. 357.
34. Rosalind Gill, 'Postfeminist Media Culture: Elements of a Sensibility', *European Journal of Cultural Studies* 10/2 (2007), pp. 147–66, p. 151.
35. Ibid., p. 152.
36. Tiqqun (Collective), *Preliminary Materials*, p. 102.
37. Ibid., p. 107.
38. Ibid., pp. 59–60.
39. Tiqqun (Collective), *Preliminary Materials*, p. 33.
40. Domenico Dolce [photographer], *Dolce and Gabbana*, Autumn/Winter Collection (2015). A selection of the adverts can be viewed at https://fashionista.com/2015/06/dolce-gabbana-fall-2015-campaign.
41. Tiqqun (Collective), *Preliminary Materials*, p. 60.
42. Ibid., p. 110.
43. Agnès Rocamora, 'Personal Fashion Blogs: Screens and Mirrors in Digital Self-portraits', *Fashion Theory* 15/4 (2011), pp. 407–24, p. 417.
44. Nixon, *Hard Looks*, p. 64.
45. Rocamora, 'Personal Fashion Blogs', p. 414.
46. Ibid.
47. Ibid., pp. 418–19.
48. Derek Conrad Murray, 'Notes to Self: The Visual Culture of Selfies in the Age of Social Media', *Consumption Markets and Culture* 18/6 (2015), pp. 490–516. Available at http://dx.doi.org/10.1080/10253866.2015.1052967 (accessed 13 August 2015), p. 1.
49. Ibid., p. 495.
50. Ibid.
51. Erving Goffman, *Gender Advertisements* (New York: Harper Torchbooks, 1976).

52. Nicola Döring, Anne Reif and Sandra Poeschl, 'How Gender-Stereotypical Are Selfies? A Content Analysis and Comparison with Magazine Adverts', *Computers in Human Behaviour* 55 (2016), p. 955, p. 62.
53. Mehita Iqani and Jonathan E. Schroeder, '#Selfie: Digital Self-portraits as Commodity Form and Consumption Practice', *Consumption Markets and Culture* 19/5 (2016). Available at http://dx.doi.org/10.1080/10253866.2015.1116784 (accessed 5 January 2016), p. 7.
54. Rocamora, 'Personal Fashion Blogs', p. 418.
55. Tiqqun (Collective), *Preliminary Materials*, p. 71.
56. Ibid., p. 66.
57. Ibid., pp. 59–60.
58. Emily Apter, *Feminizing the Fetish – Psychoanalysis and Narrative Obsession in Turn-of-the Century France* (Ithaca, NY: Cornell University Press, 1993), p. xiii.
59. Mike Featherstone, 'Body, Image and Affect in Consumer Culture', *Body and Society* 16/1 (2010), pp. 193–221, p. 210.
60. Kelly Allen, '*Love Island*'s Malin "I had £7K of Surgery to Look Good on Social Media": She Had It *All* Done for Instagram and Snapchat', *Heat* 932 (22–28 April 2017), pp. 12–14, p. 14.
61. Tiqqun (Collective), *Preliminary Materials*, p. 79 (emphasis in original).
62. Kelly Allen, 'Snapchat Surgery Hits the UK', *Heat* 932 (22–28 April 2017), p. 15.
63. Featherstone, 'Body, Image and Affect in Consumer Culture', p. 205.
64. Dr Randal Haworth, quoted in Susan Bordo, *Unbearable Weight: Feminism, Western Culture, and the Body*, 2nd edn (Berkeley and Los Angeles, CA: University of California Press, 2004), p. xvii.
65. Louise J. Kaplan, 'Fits and Misfits: The Body of a Woman', *American Imago* 50/4 (1993), pp. 457–80, p. 462.
66. Ibid., p. 469.
67. Apter, *Feminizing the Fetish*, p. 182.
68. Kaplan, 'Fits and Misfits', p. 462.
69. Ibid., p. 469.
70. Beat Eating Disorders, 'Statistics for Journalists', n.d. Available at https://www.beateatingdisorders.org.uk/media-centre/eating-disorder-statistics (accessed 9 August 2018).
71. David C. Giles and Jessica Close, 'Exposure to "Lad Magazines" and Drive for Muscularity in Dating and Non-dating Young Men', *Personality and Individual Differences* 44 (2008), pp. 1610–16, p. 1611.
72. Featherstone, 'Body, Image and Affect in Consumer Culture'.
73. prothinspo.com (n.d.). Available at http://www.prothinspo.com/proanadistractions.html (accessed 9 April 2015).

74. Anon., 'Pro Ana Tips and Tricks To Lose Weight {Tips & Diet Plan}', n.d. Available at https://theproanatips.com/ (accessed 6 February 2020; no longer available).
75. Tiqqun (Collective), *Preliminary Materials*, p. 129.
76. Mulvey, *Visual and Other Pleasures*, p. 14.
77. Tiqqun (Collective), *Preliminary Materials*, p. 17.
78. Ibid., p. 19.
79. Susie Orbach, *Hunger Strike: The Anorectic's Struggle as a Metaphor for Our Age*, 2nd edn (Harmondsworth: Penguin, 1993), p. 68.
80. Ibid., p. 79.

Bibliography

Allen, Kelly, '*Love Island*'s Malin "I had £7K of Surgery to Look Good on Social Media": She Had It *All* done for Instagram and Snapchat', *Heat* 932 (22–28 April 2017), pp. 12–14.

Allen, Kelly, 'Snapchat Surgery Hits the UK', *Heat* 932 (22–28 April 2017), p. 15.

Anon., 'Pro Ana Tips and Tricks To Lose Weight {Tips & Diet Plan}', n.d. Available at https://theproanatips.com/ (accessed 6 February 2020; no longer available).

Apter, Emily, *Feminizing the Fetish – Psychoanalysis and Narrative Obsession in Turn-of-the-Century France* (Ithaca, NY: Cornell University Press, 1993).

Baudrillard, Jean, *The Consumer Society: Myths and Structures*, trans. Chris Turner, 2nd edn (London: Sage, 1998) [*La société de consommation* (Paris: Gallimard, 1970)].

Beat Eating Disorders, 'Statistics for Journalists', n.d. Available at https://www.beateatingdisorders.org.uk/media-centre/eating-disorder-statistics (accessed 9 August 2018).

Bordo, Susan, *Unbearable Weight: Feminism, Western Culture, and the Body*, 2nd edn (Berkeley and Los Angeles, CA: University of California Press, 2004).

Döring, Nicola, Anne Reif and Sandra Poeschl, 'How Gender-Stereotypical Are Selfies? A Content Analysis and Comparison with Magazine Adverts', *Computers in Human Behaviour* 55 (2016), pp. 955–62.

Farey-Jones, Daniel, 'Hello Boys Voted Greatest Poster Ever Created', 31 March 2011. Available at http://www.campaignlive.co.uk/article/hello-boys-voted-greatest-poster-ever-created/1063405# (accessed 26 August 2016).

Featherstone, Mike, 'Body, Image and Affect in Consumer Culture', *Body and Society* 16/1 (2010), pp. 193–221.

Freud, Sigmund, 'Fetishism', in A. Richards (ed) *On Sexuality: Three Essays on the Theory of Sexuality and Other Works*, trans. James Strachey (London: Penguin Books, 1991), pp. 345–57 ['Fetischismus', *Almanach* (1929), pp. 17–24].

Giles, David C. and Jessica Close, 'Exposure to "Lad Magazines" and Drive for Muscularity in Dating and Non-dating Young Men', *Personality and Individual Differences* 44 (2008), pp. 1610–16.

Gill, Rosalind, 'Postfeminist Media Culture: Elements of a Sensibility', *European Journal of Cultural Studies* 10/2 (2007), pp. 147–66.
Gill, Rosalind, 'Empowerment/Sexism: Figuring Female Sexual Agency in Contemporary Advertising', *Feminism and Psychology* 18/1 (2008), pp. 35–60.
Gill, Rosalind, 'Beyond the "Sexualisation of Culture" Thesis: An Intersectional Analysis of "Sixpacks," "Midriffs" and "Hot Lesbians" in Advertising', *Sexualities* 12/2 (2009), pp. 137–60.
Goffman, Erving, *Gender Advertisements* (New York: Harper Torchbooks, 1976).
Haug, Wolfgang Fritz, *Critique of Commodity Aesthetics: Appearance, Sexuality and Advertising in Capitalist Society* (Cambridge: Polity Press, 1986), trans. Robert Bock, 8th edn.
Iqani, Mehita and Jonathan E. Schroeder, '#Selfie: Digital Self-portraits as Commodity Form and Consumption Practice', *Consumption Markets and Culture* 19/5 (2016). Available at http://dx.doi.org/10.1080/10253866.2015.1116784 (accessed 5 January 2016).
Kaplan, Louise J., 'Fits and Misfits: The Body of a Woman', *American Imago* 50/4 (1993), pp. 457–80.
Marx, Karl, *Capital* (New York: Random House, 1906) [*Das Kapital, Kritik der politischen Ökonomie* (Hamburg: Verlag Otto Meissners 1867)].
McRobbie, Angela, 'Young Women and Consumer Culture', *Cultural Studies* 22/5 (2008), pp. 531–50.
McRobbie, Angela, 'Reflections on Feminism and Immaterial Labour', *New Formations* 70 (2010), pp. 60–76.
Mulvey, Laura, *Visual and Other Pleasures*, 2nd edn (Basingstoke: Palgrave Macmillan, 2009).
Murray, Derek Conrad, 'Notes to Self: The Visual Culture of Selfies in the Age of Social Media', *Consumption Markets and Culture* 18/6 (2015), pp. 490–516. Available at http://dx.doi.org/10.1080/10253866.2015.1052967 (accessed 13 August 2015).
Nixon, Sean, *Hard Looks: Masculinities, Spectatorship and Contemporary Consumption* (London: UCL Press, 1996).
Orbach, Susie, *Hunger Strike: The Anorectic's Struggle as a Metaphor for Our Age*, 2nd edn (Harmondsworth: Penguin, 1993).
Power, Nina, 'She's Just Not That into You', *Radical Philosophy* 177 (2013). Available at https://www.radicalphilosophy.com/reviews/individual-reviews/rp177-shes-just-not-that-into-you (accessed 12 May 2016).
prothinspo.com, n.d. Available at http://www.prothinspo.com/proanadistractions.html (accessed 9 April 2015).
Rocamora, Agnès, 'Personal Fashion Blogs: Screens and Mirrors in Digital Self-portraits', *Fashion Theory* 15/4 (2011), pp. 407–24.
Sapiro, Virginia, *A Vindication of Political Virtue: The Political Theory of Mary Wollstonecraft* (Chicago: The University of Chicago Press, 1992).
Tiqqun (Collective), *Preliminary Materials for a Theory of the Young-Girl* (Los Angeles, CA: Semiotext(e), 2012).
Weigel, Moira and Mal Ahern, 'Further Materials toward a Theory of the Man-Child', *The New Enquiry*, 2013. Available at https://thenewinquiry.com/further-materials-toward-a-theory-of-the-man-child/ (accessed 12 May 2016).

CHAPTER 7
MAKING *LEMONADE?*: BEYONCÉ'S PREGNANCIES AND THE POSTFEMINIST MEDIA GAZE

Maureen Lehto Brewster

When Demi Moore bared her pregnant belly on the cover of *Vanity Fair* in 1991, it induced – for better or for worse – a new representational standard for the female body. This seminal image, and the genre of maternity photography it helped inspire, represents persistent, conflicting ideals and anxieties regarding femininity and pregnancy. Though they have helped to liberate the pregnant body from centuries of culturally imposed secrecy, these images have also placed it under increased surveillance: the gaze of postfeminist media culture,[1] which has swiftly sexualized, commodified and disciplined it via media and fashion.[2] This chapter will discuss how this media gaze, and its standard of fashionable pregnant beauty, requires celebrity mothers to adopt a self-reflexive gaze, to monitor and discipline their unruly maternal bodies. It argues that pregnancy is not only something that is 'done' – through repetitive acts of the body, fashion and media – but, more importantly, that it is something that can be done *wrong*.[3] Entertainment and tabloid media outlets breathlessly follow Pippa Middleton as she 'flaunts [her] eight-month baby bump'[4] while running errands and tell readers about how Jessica Simpson 'showed off [her] baby bump' on Instagram.[5] Such rhetoric frames the celebrity baby bump as an object for public affection and consumption, but when celebrity bodies or their narratives do not comply – when they 'do' pregnancy wrong – they are subject to intense scrutiny and shame. Few celebrities are more aware of this than Beyoncé Giselle Knowles-Carter. Her 2011 pregnancy, which she only selectively revealed to the public, was hounded by conspiracy theories that she had hired a surrogate to carry daughter Blue Ivy. To this day, a vocal minority on the internet insists that the singer utilized a prosthetic belly to literally perform a fake pregnancy.

When Beyoncé announced her second pregnancy on 1 February 2017 in an elaborately staged Instagram post, it quickly broke the record for the most 'liked' photograph on the social media platform.[6] Signed 'The Carters', the post allowed the couple to 'share [their] love and happiness' with the world on their terms, or perhaps more accurately, Beyoncé's terms – that is to say, perfectly lit and artfully posed by artist Awol Erizku. The image features Beyoncé calmly staring down at the viewer, baring her pregnant belly in front of a lush, floral throne. The image was later revealed to be part of an album of maternity photographs, a veritable art history course of religious and mythological references: there are allusions to Venus and Madonna, but also to the Yoruban fertility goddess Oshun.[7] This open display of her body and personal life seemed to herald a newly public Beyoncé, offering a sharp contrast to her secretive first pregnancy.

When viewed in this context, Beyoncé's social media practices during her second pregnancy appear to be a response to the gaze of the so-called *pregnancé conspiracé*[8] of 2011: a means of rewriting and reclaiming control over her star image.[9] While that first pregnancy invited a conspiracy that questioned the authenticity of her stardom, body and maternity, she used her social media presence to perform a strategically 'public' second pregnancy. Beyoncé's digital and sartorial self-fashioning are thus framed in this chapter as 'practices of the self'[10] – as methods of framing her pregnant body within cultural discourse – and also as a means to hone her star image via a transmedia narrative[11] that spans stage, screen and social media. This chapter will compare the mediation and self-fashioning of Beyoncé's pregnancies, arguing that her shifting approach to self-representation between the two pregnancies exemplifies her internalization and reproduction of postfeminist norms regarding the pregnant body. Refashioned to reflect historical and contemporary representations of pregnancy, Beyoncé's body emerges as a disciplined object that neatly fits into the established discourse of acceptable pregnancy performance – constructing an image that she, perhaps paradoxically, invokes to reclaim her body's authenticity. Ultimately, this chapter will argue that Beyoncé is appropriating the visual language of modern celebrity pregnancy to reframe her pregnancy narrative, illustrating the symbolic power of the postfeminist media gaze upon the celebrity body.

Making a postfeminist pregnancy

The pregnant body has evolved as an object in feminist discourse since the 1970s. Reproductive rights took centre stage in Second-Wave feminism, with activists arguing that access to contraception and abortion – and, for women of colour, 'the right to have and support their children' – were central to achieving gender equality.[12] Feminist scholarship in this period also aimed to re-centre the embodied knowledge and subjectivity of women in debates about reproductive rights and motherhood.[13] The result of these efforts can be seen in contemporary postfeminist culture, in which 'motherhood (for white, middle-class women, anyway)' is presumed to be 'a matter of choice' rather than a predestined role.[14] Ironically, postfeminist discourse often presents 'traditional' choices – domesticity and motherhood in particular – as a means of resolving 'the most intractable problems' of modern life.[15] Postfeminist media discourse has framed this 're-traditionalized' narrative of 'highly-stylized [and sexualized] femininity' as 'personal choice rather than obligation'.[16] In this modern, panoptic framework of individuation and personal responsibility, a 'well-kept home and well-kept body' have become signifiers of 'achieved adult femininity'.[17] As reproductive rights have increasingly eroded under the Trump administration, it can be argued that this 'obsessive' surveillance of the pregnant body (and in particular, the pregnant celebrity body) in postfeminist media culture has not only impacted the internalization of these social norms but also 'enable[d] biopolitical governance of women's bodies for conservative ends'.[18]

Of course, the female body in celebrity culture is subject to intense scrutiny even before the advent of pregnancy. Though 'surveillance of women's bodies constitutes perhaps the largest type of media content across all genres and media forms', it is the female celebrity body that receives the most 'excessive and punitive' criticism.[19] Bartky (1990) discusses how the systematic surveillance, discipline and punishment of women's bodies recall Foucault's (1977) writings on visibility and power in *Discipline and Punish*, which refer to the penal structure of the panopticon to illustrate 'power relations in the everyday lives of men'.[20] Bartky extends this definition to consider the effects of patriarchy as an institutionally unbound, panoptic force upon women, referencing the discipline of the female body into specific physical and ornamental configurations:[21] a patriarchal – though not always male – gaze. It functions to encapsulate women within regimes of self-care and surveillance to create a 'new gender regime' of beauty and domesticity: 'body projects' by which women's bodies are constitutive of their identity[22] and their ability to 'make the right choices'.[23]

This model of feminine beauty leaves little room for error; yet at the same time, postfeminist media culture has embraced the pregnant body, which is in many ways a direct contradiction to the slender, contained model policed in so much of entertainment journalism. The maternal body represents the formless and uncontained, signifying matter – unbound, unfinished and in a state of constantly becoming.[24] This bodily transgression, in which the feminine borders of the body are disrupted, is exacerbated by the moral 'flaws' of the pregnant body, which as Imogen Tyler (2011) notes has been 'indelibly marked by sex'.[25] This physical and moral deviance evokes comparison to the fat body, another contradiction to normative feminine embodiment – a failed body project.[26]

These narratives of physical and moral deviance have long impacted representations of pregnancy in popular culture. When Lucille Ball decided to make her pregnancy into a storyline for her character on *I Love Lucy* (1951–57), she couldn't even say the word 'pregnant' – she was 'expecting' instead, her body obscured beneath loose, girlish maternity clothing.[27] The storyline did little to challenge representations of the pregnant body as clinical or subversive over the next few decades. When Demi Moore appeared in the aforementioned 'More Demi Moore' cover for *Vanity Fair*, shot by photographer Annie Leibovitz for the magazine's August 1991 issue, only her eyes were visible on news stands – the rest of her nude, pregnant body was 'demurely' covered by paper, demonstrating that pregnancy was still somewhat taboo in popular culture.[28] In the image, Moore is bare save for the glint of her diamond jewellery; though her eyes avoid the camera, her slight smile and careful posture suggest an awareness of the viewer's gaze and the controversy she was courting.

Discussing 'the shift from abjection to idealization' seen in the 'More Demi Moore' image, Tyler links the increasing visibility of the pregnant body not only to celebrity culture but also to postfeminist notions of self-care and personal choice.[29] In the '"bump chic" generation', Tyler argues, 'pregnancy is not an embarrassing or abject physical state but an opportunity to have a completely different fashionable and sexy body shape'. This depends, however, on the presentation of a 'taut … "perfect little bump"',[30] which is difficult for many women to achieve. Postfeminist media culture has repackaged the pregnant body as 'pregnant beauty',[31] which effectively limits female celebrities to two acceptable models of femininity: fit and trim or fit and pregnant. A great deal of tabloid and media coverage is dedicated to establishing the distance between 'fat' and 'pregnant' and to convey the amount of physical discipline required to maintain such distance even while pregnant. The public is left with a narrative of celebrity pregnancy that emphasizes the sanctity of the disciplined, fit, sexualized female body and recognizes pregnant beauty as an alternative body of desire – but only for a limited time and only when celebrity mothers play by all of the rules.

Negotiating a private pregnancy

As sociologist Meredith Nash discusses, pregnancy requires the 'constant renegotiation of "public" and "private" discourses in light of the obsessive cultural surveillance of pregnant bodies'.[32] With the advent of social media, the exposure of the pregnant body – celebrity or not – has become commonplace and even mundane, blurring the boundary between public and private for expecting mothers. Maternity photography has proliferated online, where images are shared among family and friends; particularly creative or moving images may even go viral. Search parenting blogs, Pinterest, Facebook or Instagram feeds to see photographs of women in fields and forests, on beaches and bedcovers – even, memorably, *en pointe* in a tutu – all prominently displaying their taut, rounded bellies. Though mothers to be are encouraged to be creative with their photographs,[33] most of these images conform to the visual rhetoric of what I call 'bump culture', to smooth and objectify the 'bump' as a fashionable and disciplined accessory.[34] As both the objects and enforcers of the gaze, they are truly 'the perfect product'.[35]

While many celebrities are keen to perform their pregnancies in the public eye, the extreme surveillance of the pregnant body has resulted in a growing number of celebrity mothers who prefer to hide from the spotlight entirely; a notable example is Kylie Jenner, who publicly announced her pregnancy and shared personal images only after the February 2018 birth of her daughter, Stormi Webster. In the post, called 'a masterclass [*sic*] in how to publicly strategize the private and intimate phenomenon of motherhood', the reality television star and cosmetics mogul apologized for keeping fans 'in the dark' during her pregnancy, explaining that she chose to keep it private in order to 'prepare for this role of a lifetime in the most positive, stress free, and healthy way i [*sic*] knew how'.[36] Jenner simultaneously released an eleven-minute documentary video of her pregnancy and birth, showing her fans the pregnancy announcement, baby shower and carefully selected glimpses of her pregnant body that they had missed in her absence from social media.

The subtext of Jenner's announcement – that pregnancy in the public eye is negative, stressful and unhealthy – feels reminiscent of the treatment that her older half-sister, Kim Kardashian West, received in the press during her two pregnancies; vilified for her fashion and weight, Kardashian West has since described pregnancy as 'the worst experience of [her] life', not only because she felt 'gross' but also because of her insecurities about her body: 'I just always feel like I'm not in my own skin.'[37] Her discomfort was likely amplified by the tabloid headlines trumpeting her '200-lb. nightmare'[38] caused by her supposed binge eating habits and exacerbated by her form-fitting maternity fashion. As her body literally spilled out of the borders of her tight dresses and designer heels, Kardashian West was unable to perform 'pregnant beauty', and her body was reclassified as 'fat'.[39] If Jenner's pregnancy was a master class in how to negotiate a private pregnancy, Kardashian West's was a master class in why one might be necessary.

The sisters' experiences emphasize how the maternal body, as another contradiction to established standards of physical fitness, is an unbound body to be reshaped and disciplined in celebrity culture; such discipline has historically taken place both upon the body, by virtue of maternity fashion, and more importantly by the representations of those fashioned maternal bodies in the media. The pregnancies of Kylie Jenner and Beyoncé Knowles-Carter, however, demonstrate that the maternal body can be further reshaped via its representation on social media. While Jenner was perhaps preventative in her tightly controlled pregnancy narrative – by only selectively revealing her pregnant body and fashion, she neatly avoided the negative media attention that Kardashian West received about both – I argue that Beyoncé's use of social media to selectively perform her second pregnancy is a direct response to the narrative of her first pregnancy and represents not only an awareness of but an internalization of the media's gaze. In this context, her maternity 'album' can thus be seen as a self-reflexive attempt to regain control and reclaim the authenticity of both her body and her celebrity image.

The *pregnancé conspiracé*

Beyoncé's first pregnancy was nearly as invisible as Jenner's; although she was often snapped by paparazzi and made multiple public appearances, she shared very little of her pregnancy with fans. Her reluctance to display her pregnant body ended up feeding perhaps one of the most persistent celebrity conspiracy theories in contemporary popular culture. This *pregnancé conspiracé* has thrived online, where theorists debate the relative lack of photographs of a pregnant Beyoncé during 2011; they also note some inconsistencies in the size and shape of her belly in the few photographs that do exist, as well as discrepancies in her reported due date.[40] At the core of the theory is footage of an October 2011 interview with Australia's *Sunday Night*, which appeared to show Beyoncé's belly 'deflating' as she sat down. Viewers – from online commenters to 'mommy' bloggers to television personality Wendy Williams – also noted her stance in the film stills from the video, which they argued is often avoided by pregnant women due to potential back strain.[41] But why would Beyoncé go to so much trouble to fake her pregnancy? Some theories – that she was raising either husband Jay Z or father Mathew Knowles's illegitimate child – seem very far-fetched. More plausible is that the performer, who had spoken and even sung about a past miscarriage, hired a surrogate because she was unable to carry a baby. Less kind, but ultimately more powerful, is the rumour that she hired a surrogate because she was unwilling to subject her body – '#Flawless' as it is – to the physical toll that pregnancy would take on her body. More simply, many of the conspiracy theorists believed she would rather use a surrogate than risk weight gain and stretch marks.

Beyoncé called the controversy 'so stupid' and said that the fabric of her dress had folded – 'Does fabric not fold?'[42] But with few images to counteract these claims, and still further evidence to be found in Beyoncé's established narrative as a 'notoriously tight-lipped' and perfectionist performer, there are still many people who firmly believe that Beyoncé did not carry her first child.[43] These rumours were so persistent that a large portion of Beyoncé's 2013 HBO special, *Life Is But a Dream*, is dedicated to the display of film footage and photographs from her pregnancy with Blue Ivy. In the film, she addresses the 'crazy' rumours in a confessional, directly to the camera: 'I guess there are some crazy celebrities in this world, so we get a bad rep, but … um … to think I would be that vain.'[44] I thus argue that the film is a response to the *pregnancé conspiracé* and its implicit charges of opacity, vanity and inauthenticity against Beyoncé. It is permeated by a self-reflexive gaze that seems particularly attuned to her authenticity, whether as a performer or as a mother: it is gratuitous in its persistent use of 'raw' footage of Beyoncé singing, practising dance moves in a hotel hallway and, most notably, baring her growing belly in the mirror.

That last moment, a self-filmed diary entry, feels the most responsive to the conspiracy theorists: it shows Beyoncé in a bathroom, talking about her upcoming MTV VMAs appearance and how '[her] baby may be debuting itself on [*sic*] the awards.'[45] The sequence first shows her bared belly, then cuts to a shot centred on her face and shoulders, with her belly below the camera's view; the last frame shows Beyoncé shifting the camera to show that '[she's] going to be a mommy', so that it can once again capture her belly in profile.

Unlike the more composed confessional that narrates the rest of the film, the shaky laptop footage feels intimate, captured spontaneously by Beyoncé herself. This narrative framing and the use of 'home video footage' build a 'rhetoric of authenticity', similar to that described by Meyers (2009) in her analysis of the docuseries *Britney and Kevin: Chaotic* (2005). Like *Chaotic*, Beyoncé's *Life Is But a Dream* is 'not simply a revelation of an essential "real person" [… but rather] a disclosure of a way of being a celebrity, a way of coping with its pressures [… via] a self-conscious personal project'.[46] The style of the image is also crucial: by presenting her pregnant belly, taut, bared and in profile, the footage conforms to normative visual discourse of 'pregnant beauty' in celebrity culture. It also resolves a key point of contention for conspiracists: that there weren't enough clear images of Beyoncé's pregnant body. Bared publicly at last, her belly is presented as material evidence of her body's authenticity to refute claims of surrogacy. This reinforces the performative nature of Beyoncé's pregnancy (and indeed of celebrities in general): they are real only to the extent that they are performed within the confines of the postfeminist media gaze. Put more simply, the film shows that the authenticity of Beyoncé's pregnancy could only be legitimized when it conformed to the standards of bump culture.

Though *Life Is But a Dream* attempts to use the visual language of celebrity pregnancy to counter the *pregnancé conspiracé*, its contrived nature did little to dispel the rumours, at least among true believers. Sceptics noted that you 'never see a full, clear shot of Beyoncé's pregnant, swanlike body' in the film and that 'when her body is shown in full, it's in grainy, black and white footage in which her face is shadowed'.[47] Without such documentation during her 2011 pregnancy, these conspiracy theorists had already assembled a viable narrative of Beyoncé's pregnancy with their remaining tools: their understanding of contemporary celebrity pregnancy, her established star image and the few images of her pregnant body that were left for consumption.

It was, in hindsight, a perfect storm. In a cultural moment where the female celebrity body is routinely subject to excessive and punitive surveillance and criticism, and where celebrity pregnancy is largely mediated as a negotiation of bodily anxieties, the notion that any celebrity would opt to forgo the 'earthly … material [and] visceral'[48] process of pregnancy – and all of its attendant bodily transformations and media invasiveness – seems reasonable. When the celebrity in question is Beyoncé, whose star image is built upon various media and self-presented narratives that portray her as powerful, secretive and calculated, it is equally reasonable to question her readiness to sacrifice her meticulously maintained body to maternity. Given her careful self-fashioning and mediation and the magnitude of her celebrity, it is also easy to assume that she would have both the financial means and the control needed to perform a fake pregnancy. The stilted intimacy of *Life Is But a Dream*, with its constant assertions of Beyoncé's authenticity as an entertainer, relied so heavily on depictions of her as an all-powerful triple threat that it backfired in its attempts to convey the authenticity of her pregnant body. I argue that the persistence of this conspiracy informed Beyoncé's decision to bare her body at the start of her second pregnancy, though it can also be attributed to her shifting strategy of self-representation and star image.

Making *Lemonade*?

Beyoncé's controlled management of her career, and ultimately of her celebrity narrative, has given her an unprecedented amount of power over her music and star image.[49] Frequently referred to as 'Queen Bey' in the media as well as among her millions of fans, she has become someone closer to a religious icon than your everyday pop star. Such worship is rooted as much within Beyoncé's near-mythological background as it is the authenticity of her performances. Groomed for celebrity by her father, Mathew Knowles, who served as her manager until 2011, young Beyoncé trained by running a mile while singing ('so I would be able to perform on stage without being exhausted'[50]) and worked her way up from girl groups to solo stardom. Her 2008 marriage to rapper and businessman Shawn 'Jay-Z' Carter made her one half of what is now a 1.2 billion USD (927 million GBP) couple.[51] Despite their extravagant wealth and fame, their day-to-day lives remain secret; while occasional moments of strife are leaked in gossip pages, the majority of public knowledge about their relationship and family life is now available only through the media they produce – namely, in their music and social media accounts.[52]

This lifetime immersion in the business of celebrity has made Beyoncé particularly aware of her own image: she has employed a 'visual director' since 2005 to follow and document her 'every waking moment' and has a personal archive to document her career, from photographs of her childhood girl group Girls Tyme to diary recordings that she made on her laptop.[53] She is also keenly attuned to the mediation and management of her image in the press: she rarely gives interviews, and even when granted, they are often taped or conducted via email. The singer famously served as *Vogue*'s September 2015 cover star, gracing its pages in glorious, posed colour without speaking a word; rather than the typical profile or interview, the magazine ran a piece 'about her star quality' written '[without] contact from her camp'.[54] She is, as Matthew Schneier notes in his *New York Times* article about the *Vogue* feature, 'seen but not heard'.[55]

Because she rarely gives interviews, it is her social media use – and, of course, her music – that speaks for her, allowing her to craft the sensation of intimacy on her terms by strategically 'dropping' glimpses of her carefully guarded personal life. Because she has continued to eschew interviews and appearances, her music and social media – both controlled by her – are the primary media texts used to construct her star image. Social media allows celebrities to communicate and commodify their own celebrity image, bypassing traditional media channels to give fans what feels like a truly authentic representation of their private life. Marwick and boyd's (2011) study of celebrity engagement on Twitter argues that the social media site gives fans the 'appearance and performance of backstage access to the famous', in part because the site '[provides] the possibility of actual interaction' through user 'mentions' and messaging.[56] Instagram has a similar 'parasocial dynamic',[57] not only via direct lines of communication but for the literal glimpse it offers into a celebrity's 'private', 'real' life. Curiously, Beyoncé doesn't seem as interested in portraying authenticity as she is in creating a fantasy. While many public figures have utilized social media interaction to display dramatic, perhaps catastrophic transparency, Beyoncé uses media to perform what I would call radical privacy, releasing glimpses of her life to fans in carefully managed, highly edited bursts. She wields this privacy both creatively, in the release of her music, and in her personal life, where she uses photography-sharing platforms like Instagram and Tumblr as a means of selective self-representation to make her own 'self-conscious personal project',[58] through which she can present a glamourized version of 'authenticity' to fans.

Beyoncé uses Instagram to 'fashion [herself] for the screen'[59] as Queen Bey, enabling her to craft a career that is somehow as dazzling in its publicity as it is shrouded in secrecy. Her mostly inactive Twitter account and once-thriving Tumblr have been all but left behind in favour of Instagram, an image-based application that arranges photographs in a grid on a sleek, mobile-friendly interface. Beyoncé's Instagram posts are not just static images of her life and style: she often uses collages and animations, drawing inspiration from pop art and street art to 'play a very sophisticated game of dress-up with herself'.[60] While many celebrity Instagram accounts are constructed to document the user's 'everyday' life and feel intimate, Beyoncé's posts are far more 'thoughtful and complex', released in series of three so that they are neatly aligned in her grid. The layered references and identities in the images 'tease' viewers with their opacity, allowing the performer to fashion, refashion and even evade her narrative.[61]

The 'open-ended', documentary-style format of Instagram, coupled with its emphasis on photography over text, 'intensifies the importance of self-presentation' for casual users as well as celebrities, as Marwick (2015) argues.[62] Meanwhile, Warfield's (2014) analysis of self-taken images, or 'selfies', reveals that they encourage feelings of self-assessment and performance: she argues that selfies make their subjects into 'self-conscious thespians'[63] and describes how those subjects draw upon photographic 'tropes and conventions' to present themselves in 'favorable ways' to an online audience – in short, to create a mediatized version of themselves. The term 'mediatization' refers to the pervasive influence of the media and its transformation of 'social reality', in not only how 'institutions and agents ... practices and experiences' are transmitted but how they are actually 'performed and constituted'.[64] Rocamora (2017) argues that mediatization has altered self-fashioning in everyday life: she reframes Warfield's 'performing subjects' as mediatized subjects, who are 'practiced to appear online, as an image to be shared and circulated on a digital screen, and so [need] to be fashioned accordingly'.[65] Rocamora proposes that these screens are Foucauldian 'mirrors', arguing that they operate as technologies of the 'networked self'.[66] As a 'practice' or [perhaps literal] 'technology' of her networked self, I argue that Beyoncé's use of Instagram enables her to 'constitute' herself within social media discourse; it allows her to 'bring into congruence' the gaze of the media with her own reflexive gaze and fashion herself accordingly. Following Foucault, Nixon (2003) discusses 'techniques of looking' or the 'acquired *acts* of looking which cite and reiterate the ways of looking formally coded' in media.[67] In her consideration of fashion via Foucauldian theory, Entwistle (2000) describes how it 'stimulates ways of thinking and acting on the self', which are then articulated by the process of self-fashioning.[68] 'Practices of the self' can thus be used not only to investigate the relationship between subject and discourse but also to discuss the actual *practices* that are used to produce the subject; I use the term to describe how Beyoncé uses both fashion and social media to reflexively produce herself. Her Instagram account is thus an integral part of how 'Beyoncé' – the imagined, mediatized version of the real person – is created and consumed.[69]

Her strategy of radical privacy reached its zenith in the audiovisual album *Lemonade* (2016), an ode to black femininity that explored themes of race, religion, trauma and resilience.[70] The hour-long film explores such themes through a central story of infidelity, casting Beyoncé as a woman scorned, navigating the anger and grief of her lover's betrayal in full audiovisual splendour. It was touted as 'Beyoncé's most outwardly personal work to date', reportedly addressing years of tabloid speculation about Jay Z's rumoured infidelity or perhaps even that of her own father, whose affair with an actress ended his relationship with Beyoncé's mother, Tina Lawson.[71] Crucially, however, though the lyrics frame the singer's struggles within a troubled relationship, the film '[ties] the personal with the communal with the national, showing the sacrifice of self [that black women] do for others, including [their] country'.[72] The film features numerous black female celebrities, which helps to expand the narrative beyond Beyoncé's experiences. However, it is the inclusion of three lesser-known faces that best exemplify black femininity and resilience: Sabryna Fulton, Gwen Carr and Lezley McSpadden, each of whom lost a son to police brutality.[73] They appear in a film sequence for the song 'Freedom', holding photos of their slain children. In her critique of *Lemonade*, feminist theorist bell hooks (2016) writes that these and other 'diverse', 'utterly aestheticized' representations of black femininity construct a 'powerfully symbolic black female sisterhood that resists invisibility'.[74] However, she questions the film's 'simplified worldview' and depiction of female violence and victimhood, arguing that it 'glamorizes' and 'does not resolve' a 'world of gendered cultural paradox and contradiction'.[75] hooks points out that *Lemonade* is ultimately a 'commodity' selling 'Beyoncé as star', as representative of 'the art of money making' as it is of artistic expression.[76] While the film thus 'shifts the gaze of white mainstream culture',[77] it must still be acknowledged as a 'self-conscious personal project',[78] a way to strategically mediatize Beyoncé's personal life for public consumption. hooks's review highlights the film's deliberate presentation of a narrative that is at once deeply personal and yet carefully communal – a 'way to know the present and invent the future' of black female representation[79] that, in typical Beyoncé style, creates an illusion of intimacy on her terms.

Lemonade concludes on a hopeful note with the song 'All Night', as smiling couples (including Lawson with her new husband and Beyoncé with Jay) fill the screen after finding their 'salvation' in true love.[80] It is hard to avoid reading Beyoncé's second pregnancy in the same light, as yet another visual album; as Vanessa Friedman notes, her maternity photography follows the *Lemonade* playbook, using religious and mythological themes to portray pregnancy as something to be worshipped.[81] In her initial announcement photograph, Beyoncé wears a gauzy, sea foam veil similar to that of the Virgin Mary; her embrace of her pregnant belly feels reminiscent of the many Medieval and Renaissance depictions of Mary with the baby Jesus. Yet her grip – her fingers resting both upon her belly and also curling beneath it, near the pubis – recalls both Botticelli's and Titian's depictions of Venus, and her direct gaze complicates an asexualized reading of the image. Clad in lingerie and kneeling before a floral throne, she is simultaneously the Virgin and a pin-up Venus, both highlighting and deconstructing the 'double entanglement'[82] of this binary in cultural representations of the pregnant body.

Through photographer Awol Erizku's lens, the images invoke religious iconography and pan-African colours to celebrate and centre Beyoncé's black identity, proudly displaying her body as a twenty-first-century, Instagram-ready religious icon, saturated in golden light and 'likes'. Such imagery cements the popular imagination of the performer as Queen Bey, a goddess who presides over stage and mobile phone screens with beauty, grace and power. Produced with a similar visual character and by the same creative staff as *Lemonade*, the maternity photographs almost appear to be out-takes from the film. One photograph features Beyoncé swimming, her pregnant body swathed in golden fabric that swirls around her. The image recalls both the womb and the video sequence for *Lemonade*'s 'Hold Up', which starts with the singer submerged underwater and later features her in a ruffled, ochre Roberto Cavalli dress, baseball bat swinging and ready for vengeance.[83] Another photograph, shot in black and white, features Beyoncé draped in sheer fabric, hair loose and curly beneath a floral crown. Dripping wet and cradling her belly, her pose is reminiscent of both 'More Demi Moore' and a bathing Titian goddess; the image also echoes the frequent presence of water within *Lemonade*, in which it was used to symbolize baptism, death and resurrection. These dramatic visual and thematic similarities to *Lemonade* position the maternity album as continuation of that story: as an epilogue that depicts the salvation of Beyoncé and Jay Z's relationship, an immaculate conception that resolves all marital sin. When read in this way – as part of a transmedia narrative of Beyoncé's personal and professional lives – the maternity album can thus be seen as a means of stabilizing the performer's star image after the turbulence of *Lemonade* – a rebirth of their marriage, lush and verdant once more.

The images also serve to stabilize her pregnancy narrative. Notably, her belly is bared in nearly all of the pictures, which are also rife with symbols of femininity and fertility. Her posture and fashioning are anchored in both art history and the visual language of the baby bump throughout the album, using a variety of representational strategies to do so: there are crowns, flowers and plenty of diaphanous fabric, but also Blue Ivy, who kisses her mother's belly like so many future siblings in maternity photography before her. Because they conform to the visual rhetoric of the baby bump, the images serve as proof of Beyoncé's pregnancy, all thoughts of *conspiracé* forgotten. Whether kneeling on a vintage Porsche[84] stuffed with flowers, lounging on a chaise or floating underwater, Beyoncé bares her pregnant belly and stares down the viewer, a deity of pop culture inviting reverence – and daring any lingering conspiracy theorists to doubt the validity of *this* pregnancy.

After the release of the maternity album, Beyoncé continued to post images of her pregnancy to Instagram, seemingly opting to 'flaunt' rather than hide her body; though these images were not necessarily candid – they were often staged and heavily edited – they tacitly acknowledged the power of the 'Bump Watch'. In the images, we finally see Beyoncé's 'pregnant, swanlike body'[85] in full colour, bare and smooth and beautiful. The maternity album, while certainly beautiful and remarkable for its artistic quality, thus demonstrates the power of the postfeminist media gaze and the self-reflexive surveillance it imposes upon the pregnant celebrity body. It was only by complying with that gaze – by submitting the glossy, perfectly styled, spectacular images of pregnant beauty – that Beyoncé was, perhaps ironically, able to convince the public that her second pregnancy was real.

As the distance between the embodied reality of pregnancy and its stylized performance in fashion, media and celebrity culture continues to increase, social media seems poised to allow expectant mothers like Beyoncé the opportunity to use the spectacle to their advantage: negotiate a sense of privacy while also positioning both their pregnancy and motherhood as desirable, beautiful and authentic. It is the inauthenticity of these representations, of course, that makes them so dangerous – it was Debord, after all, who warned of the hypnotic, destructive power of the spectacle, a 'concrete version of life', where 'the liar has lied to himself'.[86] In postfeminist media culture, pregnancy is somehow both more visible and yet less authentic than ever before. The spectacular flow of baby bumps on social media and in tabloid media has rewritten the natural, visceral pregnant body into taut, pregnant beauty, enabling a self-reflexive regime of bodily discipline not only of the body itself but also of its mediation and styling. A growing number of celebrities and influencers are working to subvert these postfeminist norms regarding motherhood and the body. Former supermodel Chrissy Teigen was celebrated for 'keeping it real' when she posted a photograph of herself wearing mesh postpartum underwear to her Instagram account in May 2018.[87] British actress Jessie Cave's Instagram account captures the humour and chaos of raising small children, showing her pumping breast milk and changing diapers in public bathrooms. Even Beyoncé has become more candid about her maternal body: in her interview with *Vogue* for the magazine's September 2018 issue, she describes embracing her 'FUPA', or 'fat upper pubic area', after her second pregnancy.[88] All images of her postpartum body have, however, erased the 'little mommy pouch' she lovingly mentions in the interview. Though the singer was praised for promoting 'self-love and self-care',[89] her self-representations during pregnancy and postpartum almost exclusively upheld the visual discourse of pregnant beauty, rather than that of body positivity.

Overall, Beyoncé's pregnancy narrative demonstrates the performative quality of postfeminist pregnancy and its reliance upon repetitive, discursive acts as performed by the media, the public and celebrity mothers alike. This narrative also highlights, however, Beyoncé's skilful mastery of these discourses and her ability to appropriate them to work within and even rewrite her star image. By interweaving the themes of *Lemonade* with those of art history, religion and African culture, she uses them to resolve lingering marital tension and solidify a new vision of black excellence and artistry; equally important, however, is the revelation of her body, smoothly disciplined to absolve her from the *pregnancé conspiracé*. When viewed as a means of transmedia storytelling, Beyoncé's maternity album ultimately works to demonstrate the authenticity of her second pregnancy, bringing her body, as well as her performance of femininity and pregnancy, into congruence with the postfeminist media gaze. While her first pregnancy was shrouded in secrecy and conspiracy, her second is awash with flowers and golden light, a performance of pregnancy that follows the rules of normative pregnant beauty and publicity – that is, like Beyoncé herself, seen but not heard.

Notes

1. Rosalind Gill, 'Postfeminist Media Culture: Elements of a Sensibility', *European Journal of Cultural Studies* 10/2 (2007).
2. Maureen Lehto Brewster, 'Bump Watch: Fashioning Celebrity Pregnancy as Performance and Product', *MA Thesis*, The New School, New York, 2014. See

also Renee Ann Cramer, *Pregnant with the Stars: Watching and Wanting the Celebrity Baby Bump* (Redwood City, CA: Stanford University Press, 2016).

3. I refer indirectly here to Judith Butler's concepts of performance and performativity. See Judith Butler, 'Performative Acts and Gender Constitution', in H. Bial (ed), *The Performance Studies Reader* (London: Routledge, 2004), pp. 154–66.
4. Emma Osborne, 'Heavily Pregnant Pippa Middleton Flaunts Eight-Month Baby Bump Weeks before Due Date', *OK! United Kingdom*, 27 September 2018. Available at https://www.ok.co.uk/celebrity-news/1476428/pippa-middleton-pregant-baby-bump-pictures-due-date-husband-james-matthews (accessed 1 December 2018).
5. Jessica Vacco-Bolanos, 'Pregnant Jessica Simpson Shows Off Baby Bump in First Photo since Announcing Her Pregnancy: Pic', *Us Weekly*, 18 September 2018. Available at https://www.usmagazine.com/celebrity-moms/news/pregnant-jessica-simpson-shows-off-baby-bump-see-the-pic/ (accessed 1 December 2018).
6. The record was later broken by soccer star Cristiano Ronaldo and, coincidentally (as of April 2018), Kylie Jenner's pregnancy announcement. See Rebecca Farley, 'Kylie Jenner Just Beat Beyoncé for Most Liked Instagram & There's Only One Solution', *Refinery29*, 7 February 2018. Available at https://www.refinery29.com/2018/02/190184/kylie-jenner-more-likes-than-beyonce-instagram (accessed 29 April 2018).
7. Doreen St. Felix, 'A Love Profane: On *Lemonade*, Beyoncé's Visual Album', MTV News, 28 April 2016. Available at http://www.mtv.com/news/2874454/beyonce-lemonade-a-love-profane/ (accessed 18 June 2017).
8. I wish I had invented this pithy term for the Beyoncé surrogate conspiracy, but it is borrowed from Gawker. See Gabriella Bluestone, 'Black Bag: Did Beyoncé Fake Her Pregnancy?', Gawker (blog), 26 March 2015. Available at http://blackbag.gawker.com/did-beyonce-fake-her-pregnancy-1693597363 (accessed 4 June 2017).
9. I use this term in reference to the theoretical model as defined by Richard Dyer. See *Stars*, 2nd edn (London: BFI, 1998).
10. I use this term, along with 'technologies' of the self, to describe these acts by which celebrities constitute themselves in social media and fashion discourses. See Michel Foucault, 'Self-Writing', in P. Rabinow (ed), *Ethics: Subjectivity and Truth* (London: Penguin, 2000), pp. 207–22.
11. I use this term to describe a narrative constructed with, and across, multiple media channels. See Leigh Edwards, 'Transmedia Storytelling, Corporate Synergy, and Audience Expression', *Global Media Journal* 12/20 (Spring 2012), pp. 1–11.
12. Sara Hayden and D. Lynn O'Brien Hallstein (eds), *Maternity in an Era of Choice: Explorations into Discourses of Reproduction* (Plymouth, UK: Lexington Books, 2010), p. xxiii.

13. See Kathy Davis, *The Making of Our Bodies, Ourselves: How Feminism Travels across Borders* (Durham, NC: Duke University Press, 2007); Adrienne Rich, *Of Woman Born: Motherhood as Experience and Institution* (New York: W. W. Norton, 1976); Wendy K. Kolmar and Frances Bartkowski (eds), *Feminist Theory: A Reader*, 3rd edn (Boston: McGraw-Hill Higher Education, 2010).
14. Hayden and O'Brien Hallstein, *Maternity in an Era of Choice*, p. xxvi. See also Angela McRobbie, 'TOP GIRLS?: Young Women and the Post-feminist Sexual Contract', *The Journal of Cultural Studies* 21/4–5 (2007), p. 721.
15. Diane Negra, *What a Girl Wants?: Fantasizing the Reclamation of the Self in Postfeminism* (New York: Routledge, 2008), p. 7.
16. McRobbie, 'TOP GIRLS?', p. 723.
17. Ibid., p. 118.
18. Cramer, *Pregnant with the Stars*, p. 19.
19. Gill, 'Postfeminist Media Culture: Elements of a Sensibility', p. 149.
20. Michel Foucault, *Discipline and Punish* (Harmondsworth: Penguin, 1977), p. 205.
21. Sandra Bartky, 'Foucault, Femininity, and the Modernization of Patriarchal Power', *Femininity and Domination: Studies in the Phenomenology of Oppression* (New York and London: Routledge, 1990), p. 65.
22. Chris Shilling, *The Body and Social Theory* (London: Sage, 2003).
23. McRobbie, 'Post-feminism and Popular Culture', p. 261.
24. See Lynda Nead, *The Female Nude: Art Obscenity and Sexuality* (London: Routledge, 2011); Francesca Granata, *Experimental Fashion: Performance Art, Carnival and the Grotesque Body* (London: I.B. Tauris, 2017); and Mary Russo, *The Female Grotesque: Risk, Excess and Modernity* (New York: Routledge, 1995).
25. Imogen Tyler, 'Pregnant Beauty: Maternal Femininities under Neoliberalism', in R. Gill and C. Scharff (eds), *New Femininities: Postfeminism, Neoliberalism and Subjectivity* (Hampshire: Palgrave Macmillan, 2011), p. 27.
26. Kathleen LeBesco, *Revolting Bodies?: The Struggle to Redefine Fat Identity* (Boston: University of Massachusetts Press, 2004), p. 3. [Editors' Note: See also Lauren Downing Peters's chapter in this volume for discussion of the fat body in the self-portraiture of Jen Davies.]
27. Tove Hermanson, 'Lucille Ball, Style Icon… In Spite of Herself', *Worn Through* (blog), 16 August 2011. Available at http://www.wornthrough.com/2011/08/16/lucille-ball-style-icon-in-spite-of-herself/ (accessed 15 May 2017).
28. Imogen Tyler, 'Skin Tight: Celebrity, Pregnancy and Subjectivity', in S. Ahmed and J. Stacey (eds), *Thinking through the Skin* (London: Routledge, 2001), pp. 69–83.

29. Tyler, 'Pregnant Beauty', p. 23.
30. Tyler (2011) references a *New York Magazine* article by Laurie Abraham, which discusses the 'freshly minted group neurosis' regarding pregnancy weight gain and the possibly damaging pursuit to avoid it. See 'The Perfect Little Bump', *New York Magazine*, 27 September 2004. Available at http://nymag.com/nymetro/health/features/9909/ (accessed 22 June 2017).
31. Tyler, 'Pregnant Beauty', p. 27.
32. Nash, 'Making "Postmodern" Mothers', p. 3.
33. This guide aims to help expectant mothers get the 'perfect pics' and 'show off that adorable baby bump': Ashley Neuman, '39 Ways to Nail a Stunning Maternity Photo Shoot', *The Bump*, March 2018. Available at https://www.thebump.com/a/best-maternity-photos (accessed 22 June 2017).
34. The term 'baby bump' itself denotes a distinction between the mother and her body; this linguistic shift has helped make it 'the new Birkin', a reference to the exclusive Hermès handbag. See Brewster, 'Bump Watch', and Renee Ann Cramer, 'The Baby Bump Is the New Birkin', in M. Jolles and S. Tarrant (eds), *Fashion Talks: Undressing the Power of Style* (Albany, NY: SUNY Press, 2012), pp. 53–65.
35. Laura Mulvey, 'Visual Pleasure and Narrative Cinema', in P. Erens (ed), *Issues in Feminist Film Criticism* (Bloomington and Indianapolis: Indiana University Press, 1990), p. 36.
36. Anna Freeman, 'Kylie Jenner and the Ultimate Performance of Privacy in a Post-selfie Era', *Dazed and Confused*, 8 February 2018. Available at http://www.dazeddigital.com/life-culture/article/38944/1/kylie-jenner-social-media-pregnancy-privacy (accessed 3 April 2018).
37. Kardashian West explained that she didn't enjoy 'one moment' of pregnancy in a post called 'How I Really Feel about Being Pregnant' on her website and app. See Lindsay Kimble, 'Kim Kardashian West: "Pregnancy Is the Worst Experience of My Life"', *People Babies* (blog), *People Magazine*, 5 October 2015 (3:35 pm). Available at http://celebritybabies.people.com/2015/10/05/kim-kardashian-west-pregnancy-worst-experience/ (accessed 22 April 2018).
38. Kardashian West was vilified via meme as well: a viral image set compared her to a killer whale. Mary Kate Frank and Sarah Grossbart, 'Kim and Kate's Baby Weight Battles', *US Weekly*, 22 April 2013, no. 949, pp. 54–9. See also Michelle Ruiz, 'Why Was America So Mean to Pregnant Kim Kardashian?', *Vogue Culture* (blog), 31 May 2015 (6:05 pm). Available at https://www.vogue.com/article/kim-kardashian-pregnant-media-hate (accessed 12 August 2018).
39. Brewster, 'Bump Watch'.
40. Bluestone, 'Did Beyoncé Fake Her Pregnancy?'
41. Ibid.
42. Anya Leon and Alexis Chiu, 'Beyoncé: Surrogacy Rumors Were "Just Crazy"', *People Babies* (blog), *People Magazine*, 29 April 2012 (10:00 am). Available

at http://celebritybabies.people.com/2012/04/29/beyonce-most-beautiful-woman-surrogate-rumors/ (accessed 17 May 2017).

43. Gawker seems to be one of the main hubs of this conspiracy. See Rich Juzwiak, 'Beyoncé Has Never Been Less Convincing about the Veracity of Her Pregnancy Than She Was in Her Own Movie', *Gawker* (blog), 18 February 2018 (2:21 pm). Available at http://gawker.com/5985096/beyonce-has-never-been-less-convincing-about-the-veracity-of-her-pregnancy-than-she-was-in-her-own-movie (accessed 17 May 2017).
44. *Life Is But a Dream*, directed by Ed Burke, Beyoncé Knowles-Carter, and Ilan Benatar (2013; London: BBC Worldwide, 2013), DVD.
45. Ibid.
46. See Erin Meyers, '"Can You Handle My Truth?": Authenticity and the Celebrity Star Image', *The Journal of Popular Culture* 42/5 (October 2009), p. 902. See also Andrew Tolson, 'Being Yourself: The Pursuit of Authentic Celebrity', *Discourse Studies* 3/4 (2001), pp. 443–57.
47. Juzwiak, 'Beyoncé Has Never Been Less Convincing ...'.
48. Russo, *The Female Grotesque*, p. 1.
49. Dyer, *Stars*, p. 60.
50. Asha Chowdary, 'Beyoncé to Fight Childhood Obesity', *The Times of India*, 17 June 2011. Available at https://timesofindia.indiatimes.com/entertainment/hindi/music/news/Beyonce-to-fight-childhood-obesity/articleshow/8888356.cms (accessed 10 March 2018).
51. While rumours suggested that Jay Z hyphenated his last name to include Beyoncé's surname, the couple or their management never officially confirmed it; I therefore use his name as it is most frequently reported. That such rumours exist points to Beyoncé's perceived status and star image. See Tanza Loudenback, 'Jay Z Is the Richest Hip Hop Artist in the World but He'd Be Nothing without Beyoncé – Here Are the 7 Richest Power Couples', *Business Insider*, 1 March 2018. Available at http://www.businessinsider.com/worlds-richest-power-couples-2017-11#beyonc-and-jay-z-3 (accessed 25 April 2018).
52. Jeff Nelson, 'A Detailed Timeline of Beyoncé and JAY-Z's Relationship', People Music (blog), *People Magazine*, 4 April 2018. Available at http://people.com/music/beyonce-jay-z-relationship-timeline/ (accessed 28 April 2018).
53. Amy Wallace, 'Miss Millenium: Beyoncé', *GQ*, 10 January 2013. Available at https://www.gq.com/story/beyonce-cover-story-interview-gq-february-2013 (accessed 4 April 2018).
54. By 2018, she had graduated to negotiating editorial control over the magazine's September issue as part of her cover appearance. See Matthew Schneier, 'Beyoncé Is Seen but Not Heard', *The New York Times*, 19 August 2015. Available at http://www.nytimes.com/2015/08/20/fashion/beyonce-is-seen-but-not-heard.html?smid=tw-nytimes&smtyp=cur (accessed 10 June 2017). See also 'Beyoncé's Buzzed-About September 2018 "Vogue" Cover Is Here

[Updated]', *Fashionista News* (blog), 6 August 2018. Available at https://fashionista.com/2018/08/beyonce-vogue-magazine-september-issue-2018 (accessed 10 August 2018).

55. Schneier, 'Beyoncé Is Seen but Not Heard'.
56. See Alice Marwick and danah boyd, 'To See and Be Seen: Celebrity Practice on Twitter', *Convergence: The International Journal of Research into New Media Technologies* 17/2 (2011), pp. 139–58.
57. These relationships are 'para-social' due to their one-sided nature, typically between fans and celebrities; Turner's discussion about the often spiritual nature of these connections is intriguing given the religious references in Beyoncé's maternity photographs. See Graeme Turner, *Understanding Celebrity* (London: Sage, 2004), pp. 92–4.
58. Meyers, 'Can You Handle My Truth', p. 902.
59. See Agnès Rocamora, 'Mediatization and Digital Media in the Field of Fashion', *Fashion Theory* 21/5 (2017), pp. 505–22.
60. Professor Kinitra Brooks of the University of Texas at San Antonio, among other Beyoncé experts, discusses the singer's control of her image via social media, noting that it feels particularly powerful in the light of black women's historical lack of control over their image and representation. See Emilia Petrarca, 'Beyoncé Is the Leonardo da Vinci of Instagram', *The Cut*, 6 November 2017. Available at https://www.thecut.com/2017/11/beyonce-is-instagrams-leonardo-da-vinci.html (accessed 8 April 2018).
61. Ibid.
62. See Alice Marwick, 'Instafame: Luxury Selfies in the Instagram Economy', *Public Culture* 27/1 (2015), p. 143.
63. See Katie Warfield, 'Making Selfies/Making Self: Digital Subjectivities in the Selfie', in *Conference of the Image and the Image Knowledge Community* (Berlin: 2014), pp. 3–4. Available at https://arcabc.ca/islandora/object/kora%3A39?solr_nav%5Bid%5D=5906a926a644e5be0a54&solr_nav%5Bpage%5D=0&solr_nav%5Boffset%5D=1 (accessed 11 January 2019).
64. Rocamora, 'Mediatization and Digital Media', pp. 507–8.
65. Ibid., p. 516.
66. Ibid., p. 515.
67. Sean Nixon, 'Exhibiting Masculinity', in S. Hall (ed), *Representation: Cultural Representation and Signifying Practices* (London: Sage, 2003), p. 323.
68. Joanne Entwistle, *The Fashioned Body: Fashion, Dress and Modern Social Theory* (Cambridge: Polity, 2000), p. 26.
69. Foucault, 'Self-Writing', p. 221.
70. See *Lemonade*, directed by Beyoncé Knowles-Carter, Kahlil Joseph and Todd Tourso (2016; New York: HBO).

71. See Joe Coscarelli, 'Beyoncé Releases Surprise Album "Lemonade" after HBO Special', *The New York Times*, 23 April 2016. Available at https://www.nytimes.com/2016/04/24/arts/music/beyonce-hbo-lemonade.html?_r=0 (accessed 19 June 2017).
72. Clover Hope, 'Lemonade Is Beyoncé's Body and Blood', *Jezebel* (blog), 25 April 2016 (1:10 pm). Available at http://themuse.jezebel.com/lemonade-is-beyonces-body-and-blood-1772819494 (accessed 25 May 2018).
73. The singer later invited these women to walk the red carpet with her at the 2016 MTV Video Music Awards. See Jonah Engel Bromwich, 'Beyoncé Shares V.M.A. Red Carpet with Mothers of Black Lives Matter', *The New York Times*, 29 August 2016. Available at https://www.nytimes.com/2016/08/29/arts/music/beyonce-vma-black-lives-matter.html (accessed 7 December 2018).
74. See bell hooks, 'Moving beyond Pain', *The Bell Hooks Institute* (blog), 9 May 2016. Available at http://www.bellhooksinstitute.com/blog/2016/5/9/moving-beyond-pain (accessed 22 November 2018).
75. Ibid.
76. Ibid.
77. Ibid.
78. Meyers, 'Can You Handle My Truth', p. 902.
79. hooks, 'The Oppositional Gaze', p. 203.
80. Beyoncé, 'All Night', YouTube Video, 6:21, 30 November 2016. Available at https://youtu.be/gM89Q5Eng_M (accessed 15 May 2017).
81. See Vanessa Friedman, 'Beyoncé 3.0: The Maternal Ideal', *The New York Times*, 27 April 2017. Available at https://www.nytimes.com/2017/04/27/fashion/beyonce-serena-williams-pregnancy-goals.html?_r=0 (accessed 18 May 2017).
82. McRobbie, 'Post-feminism and Popular Culture', p. 255.
83. Beyoncé, 'Hold Up', YouTube Video, 5:16, 4 September 2016. Available at https://youtu.be/PeonBmeFR8o (accessed 15 May 2017).
84. Of course, the internet knew what kind of car it was. See Jason Torchinsky, 'Beyoncé Chose a Porsche 914 for That Famous Pregnancy Photo', Jalopnik (blog), 2 February 2017. Available at http://jalopnik.com/beyonce-chose-a-porsche-914-for-that-famous-pregnancy-p-1791915161 (accessed 14 June 2017).
85. Juzwiak, 'Beyoncé Has Never Been Less Convincing ...'.
86. Instagram (and indeed all social media) would horrify Guy Debord but it probably wouldn't surprise him. See Guy Debord, *Society of the Spectacle* (New York: Zone Books, 1994), p. 2.
87. See Heather Marcoux, 'Chrissy Teigen + mesh underwear is the postpartum real talk all moms need to hear', *Motherly* (21 May 2018). Available at https://www.mother.ly/news/chrissy-teigen-keeps-it-real-in-mesh-panties (accessed 5 December 2018).

88. See Beyoncé Knowles-Carter, 'Beyoncé in Her Own Words: Her Life, Her Body, Her Heritage', *Vogue* (6 August 2018). Available at https://www.vogue.com/article/beyonce-september-issue-2018 (accessed 28 November 2018).
89. See Erica Smith, 'Beyoncé Wrote a Love Letter to the FUPA', *The Cut* (6 August 2018). Available at https://www.thecut.com/2018/08/beyonce-vogue-september-issue-fupa.html (accessed 10 December 2018).

Bibliography

Abraham, Laurie, 'The Perfect Little Bump', *New York Magazine*, 27 September 2004. Available at http://nymag.com/nymetro/health/features/9909/ (accessed 22 June 2017).

Allen, Robert C, 'From Film and History: Theory and Practice', 1985, in L. Braudy and M. Cohen (eds), *Film Theory and Criticism* (New York: Oxford University Press, 2004), pp. 606–19.

Bluestone, Gabriella, 'Black Bag: Did Beyoncé Fake Her Pregnancy?', *Gawker* (blog), 26 March 2015. Available at http://blackbag.gawker.com/did-beyonce-fake-her-pregnancy-1693597363 (accessed 4 June 2017).

Butler, Judith, 'Performative Acts and Gender Constitution', in H. Bial (ed), *The Performance Studies Reader* (London: Routledge, 2004), pp. 154–66.

Chowdary, Asha, 'Beyoncé to Fight Childhood Obesity', *The Times of India*, 17 June 2011. Available at https://timesofindia.indiatimes.com/entertainment/hindi/music/news/Beyonce-to-fight-childhood-obesity/articleshow/8888356.cms (accessed 10 March 2018).

Coscarelli, Joe, 'Beyoncé Releases Surprise Album "Lemonade" after HBO Special', *The New York Times*, 23 April 2016. Available at https://www.nytimes.com/2016/04/24/arts/music/beyonce-hbo-lemonade.html?_r=0 (accessed 19 June 2017).

Cramer, Renee Ann, 'The Baby Bump Is the New Birkin', in M. Jolles and S. Tarrant (eds), *Fashion Talks: Undressing the Power of Style* (Albany, NY: SUNY Press, 2012), pp. 53–65.

Cramer, Renee Ann, *Pregnant with the Stars: Watching and Wanting the Celebrity Baby Bump* (Redwood City, CA: Stanford University Press, 2016).

Davis, Kathy, *The Making of Our Bodies, Ourselves: How Feminism Travels across Borders* (Durham, NC: Duke University Press, 2007).

Debord, Guy, *Society of the Spectacle* (New York: Zone Books, 1994).

Dyer, Richard, *Stars*, 2nd edn (London: BFI, 1998).

Edwards, Leigh, 'Transmedia Storytelling, Corporate Synergy, and Audience Expression', *Global Media Journal* 12/20 (Spring 2012), pp. 1–11.

Entwistle, Joanne, *The Fashioned Body: Fashion, Dress and Modern Social Theory* (Cambridge: Polity, 2000).

Farley, Rebecca, 'Kylie Jenner Just Beat Beyoncé for Most Liked Instagram & There's Only One Solution', *Refinery29*, 7 February 2018. Available at https://

www.refinery29.com/2018/02/190184/kylie-jenner-more-likes-than-beyonce-instagram (accessed 29 April 2018).

Fashionista, 'Beyoncé's Buzzed-About September 2018 "Vogue" Cover Is Here [Updated]', 6 August 2018. Available at https://fashionista.com/2018/08/beyonce-vogue-magazine-september-issue-2018 (accessed 10 August 2018).

Foucault, Michel, *Discipline and Punish* (Harmondsworth: Penguin, 1977).

Foucault, Michel, 'Self-Writing', in P. Rabinow (ed) *Ethics: Subjectivity and Truth*, trans. R. Hurley et al. (London: Penguin, 2000), pp. 207–22.

Frank, Mary Kate and Sarah Grossbart, 'Kim and Kate's Baby Weight Battles', *US Weekly*, 22 April 2013, no. 949, pp. 54–9.

Freeman, Anna, 'Kylie Jenner and the Ultimate Performance of Privacy in a Post-selfie Era', *Dazed and Confused*, 8 February 2018. Available at http://www.dazeddigital.com/life-culture/article/38944/1/kylie-jenner-social-media-pregnancy-privacy (accessed 3 April 2018).

Friedman, Vanessa, 'Beyoncé 3.0: The Maternal Ideal', *The New York Times*, 27 April 2017. Available at https://www.nytimes.com/2017/04/27/fashion/beyonce-serena-williams-pregnancy-goals.html?_r=0 (accessed 18 May 2017).

Granata, Francesca, *Experimental Fashion: Performance Art, Carnival and the Grotesque Body* (London: I.B. Tauris, 2017).

Hampp, Andrew and Jason Lipshutz, 'Beyoncé Unexpectedly Releases New Self-titled "Visual Album" on iTunes', *Billboard*, 13 December 2013. Available at https://www.billboard.com/articles/columns/the-juice/5827398/beyonce-unexpectedly-releases-new-self-titled-visual-album-on (accessed 8 May 2017).

Hayden, Sara, and Lynn O'Brien Hallstein (eds), *Contemplating Maternity in an Era of Choice: Explorations into Discourses of Reproduction* (Plymouth, UK: Lexington Books, 2010).

Hermanson, Tove, 'Lucille Ball, Style Icon … In Spite of Herself', *Worn Through* (blog), 16 August 2011. Available at http://www.wornthrough.com/2011/08/16/lucille-ball-style-icon-in-spite-of-herself/ (accessed 15 May 2017).

hooks, bell, *Black Looks: Race and Representation* (London: Routledge, 2014).

hooks, bell, 'Moving beyond Pain', *The Bell Hooks Institute* (blog), 9 May 2016. Available at http://www.bellhooksinstitute.com/blog/2016/5/9/moving-beyond-pain (accessed 22 November 2018).

Hope, Clover, 'Lemonade Is Beyoncé's Body and Blood', *Jezebel* (blog), 25 April 2016 (1:10 pm). Available at http://themuse.jezebel.com/lemonade-is-beyonces-body-and-blood-1772819494 (accessed 25 May 2018).

Juzwiak, Rich, 'Beyoncé Has Never Been Less Convincing about the Veracity of Her Pregnancy Than She Was in Her Own Movie', *Gawker* (blog), 18 February 2013 (2:21 pm). Available at http://gawker.com/5985096/beyonce-has-never-been-less-convincing-about-the-veracity-of-her-pregnancy-than-she-was-in-her-own-movie (accessed 17 May 2017).

Kimble, Lindsay, 'Kim Kardashian West: "Pregnancy Is the Worst Experience of My Life"', *People Babies* (blog), 5 October 2015 (3:35 pm). Available at http://celebritybabies.people.com/2015/10/05/kim-kardashian-west-pregnancy-worst-experience/ (accessed 22 April 2018).

Knowles-Carter, Beyoncé, 'Beyoncé in Her Own Words: Her Life, Her Body, Her Heritage', *Vogue*, 6 August 2018. Available at https://www.vogue.com/article/beyonce-september-issue-2018 (accessed 28 November 2018).

Kolmar, Wendy K., and Frances Bartkowski (eds), *Feminist Theory: A Reader*, 3rd edn (Boston: McGraw-Hill Higher Education, 2010).

LeBesco, Kathleen, *Revolting Bodies?: The Struggle to Redefine Fat Identity* (Boston: University of Massachusetts Press, 2004).

Lemonade, directed by Knowles-Carter, Beyoncé, Joseph, Kahlil and Tourso Todd (2016; New York: HBO, 2016), DVD.

Lehto Brewster, Maureen, 'Bump Watch: Fashioning Celebrity Pregnancy as Performance and Product', *MA Thesis*, The New School, New York, 2014.

Leon, Anya and Alexis Chiu, 'Beyoncé: Surrogacy Rumors Were "Just Crazy"', *People Babies* (blog), 29 April 2012 (10:00 am). Available at http://celebritybabies.people.com/2012/04/29/beyonce-most-beautiful-woman-surrogate-rumors/ (accessed 17 May 2017).

Life Is But a Dream, directed by Burke, Ed, Knowles-Carter, Beyoncé, and Benatar, Ilan (2013; London: BBC Worldwide, 2013), DVD.

Loudenback, Tanza, 'Jay Z Is the Richest Hip Hop Artist in the World but He'd Be Nothing without Beyoncé – Here Are the 7 Richest Power Couples', *Business Insider*, 1 March 2018. Available at http://www.businessinsider.com/worlds-richest-power-couples-2017-11#beyonc-and-jay-z-3 (accessed 25 April 2018).

Marcoux, Heather, 'Chrissy Teigen + Mesh Underwear Is the Postpartum Real Talk All Moms Need to Hear', *Motherly*, 21 May 2018. Available at https://www.mother.ly/news/chrissy-teigen-keeps-it-real-in-mesh-panties (accessed 5 December 2018).

Marwick, Alice, 'Instafame: Luxury Selfies in the Information Economy', *Public Culture* 27/1 (2015), pp. 137–60.

Marwick, Alice, and danah boyd, 'To See and Be Seen: Celebrity Practice on Twitter', *Convergence: The International Journal of Research into New Media Technologies* 17/2 (2011), pp. 139–58.

McRobbie, Angela, 'Post-feminism and Popular Culture', *Feminist Media Studies* 4/3 (2004), pp. 255–64.

McRobbie, Angela, 'TOP GIRLS?', *Cultural Studies* 21/4–5 (2007), pp. 718–37.

Meyers, Erin, '"Can You Handle My Truth?": Authenticity and the Celebrity Star Image', *The Journal of Popular Culture* 42/5 (2009), pp. 443–57.

Mulvey, Laura, 'Visual Pleasure and Narrative Cinema', in P. Erens (ed), *Issues in Feminist Film Criticism* (Bloomington and Indianapolis: Indiana University Press, 1990), pp. 28–40.

Nash, Meredith, *Genders and Sexualities in the Social Sciences: Making "Postmodern" Mothers: Pregnant Embodiment, Baby Bumps and Body Image* (Houndsmills, GBR: Palgrave Macmillan, 2012).

Nead, Lynda, *The Female Nude: Art Obscenity and Sexuality* (London: Routledge, 2011).

Negra, Diane, *What a Girl Wants?: Fantasizing the Reclamation of Self in Postfeminism* (Kentucky: Routledge, 2008).

Nelson, Jeff, 'A Detailed Timeline of Beyoncé and JAY-Z's Relationship', People Music (blog), *People Magazine*, 4 April 2018. Available at http://people.com/music/beyonce-jay-z-relationship-timeline/ (accessed 28 April 2018).

Neuman, Ashley, '39 Ways to Nail a Stunning Maternity Photo Shoot', *The Bump*, March 2018. Available at https://www.thebump.com/a/best-maternity-photos (accessed 22 June 2017).

Ovalle, Priscilla Peña, 'Resounding Silence and Soundless Surveillance, From TMZ Elevator to Beyoncé and Back Again', *Sounding Out* (blog), 9 September 2015. Available at https://soundstudiesblog.com/2014/09/15/resounding-silence-and-surveillance-from-tmz-elevator-to-beyonce-and-back-again/ (accessed 13 April 2018).

Petersen, Anne Helen, *Scandals of Classic Hollywood: Sex, Deviance and Drama from Golden Age of American Cinema* (New York: Plume, 2014).

Petrarca, Emilia, 'Beyoncé Is the Leonardo da Vinci of Instagram', *The Cut*, 6 November 2017. Available at https://www.thecut.com/2017/11/beyonce-is-instagrams-leonardo-da-vinci.html (accessed 8 April 2018).

Reed, James, 'Beyoncé's Surprise Release a Stroke of Marketing Genius', Critic's Notebook (blog), *The Boston Globe*, 16 December 2013. Available at https://www.bostonglobe.com/arts/music/2013/12/16/beyonce-calculated-masterpiece-marketing-and-album-that-blissfully-organic/BcqjYeVfotaBZt0bPwRfFJ/story.html (accessed 15 June 2017).

Rich, Adrienne, *Of Woman Born: Motherhood as Experience and Institution* (New York: W. W. Norton, 1976).

Rocamora, Agnès, 'Mediatization and Digital Media in the Field of Fashion', *Fashion Theory: The Journal of Dress, Body and Culture* 21/5 (2017), pp. 505–22.

Rojek, Chris, *Celebrity* (Chicago, IL: Reaktion Books, 2001).

Ruiz, Michelle, 'Why Was America So Mean to Pregnant Kim Kardashian?', *Vogue Culture* (blog), 31 May 2015 (6:05 pm). Available at https://www.vogue.com/article/kim-kardashian-pregnant-media-hate (accessed 12 August 2018).

Russo, Mary, *The Female Grotesque: Risk, Excess and Modernity* (New York: Routledge, 1995).

Schneier, Matthew, 'Beyoncé Is Seen but Not Heard', *The New York Times*, 19 August 2015. Available at http://www.nytimes.com/2015/08/20/fashion/beyonce-is-seen-but-not-heard.html?smid=tw-nytimes&smtyp=cur (accessed 10 June 2017).

Smith, Erica, 'Beyoncé Wrote a Love Letter to the FUPA', *The Cut*, 6 August 2018. Available at https://www.thecut.com/2018/08/beyonce-vogue-september-issue-fupa.html (accessed 10 December 2018).

St. Felix, Doreen, 'A Love Profane: On Lemonade, Beyoncé's Visual Album', *MTV News*, 28 April 2016. Available at http://www.mtv.com/news/2874454/beyonce-lemonade-a-love-profane/ (accessed 18 June 2017).

Tolson, Andrew, 'Being Yourself: The Pursuit of Authentic Celebrity', *Discourse Studies* 3/4 (2001), pp. 443–57.

Torchinsky, Jason, 'Beyoncé Chose a Porsche 914 for That Famous Pregnancy Photo', *Jalopnik* (blog), 2 February 2017. Available at http://jalopnik.com/

beyonce-chose-a-porsche-914-for-that-famous-pregnancy-p-1791915161 (accessed 14 June 2017).
Turner, Graeme, *Understanding Celebrity* (London: Sage, 2001).
Tyler, Imogen, 'Skin Tight: Celebrity, Pregnancy and Subjectivity', in S. Ahmed and J. Stacey (eds), *Thinking through the Skin* (London: Routledge, 2001), pp. 69–83.
Tyler, Imogen, 'Pregnant Beauty: Maternal Femininities under Neoliberalism' in R. Gill and C. Scharff (eds), *New Femininities: Postfeminism, Neoliberalism and Subjectivity* (Hampshire: Palgrave Macmillan, 2011).
Wallace, Amy, 'Miss Millennium: Beyoncé', *GQ*, 10 January 2013. Available at https://www.gq.com/story/beyonce-cover-story-interview-gq-february-2013 (accessed 4 April 2018)
Warfield, Katie, 'Making Selfies/Making Self: Digital Subjectivities in the Selfie', in *Conference of the Image and the Image knowledge Community* (Berlin: October, 2014). Available at https://arcabc.ca/islandora/object/kora%3A39?solr_nav%5Bid%5D=5906a926a644e5be0a54&solr_nav%5Bpage%5D=0&solr_nav%5Boffset%5D=1 (accessed 11 January 2019).

PART III
LOOKING AT THE 'OTHER'

CHAPTER 8
LOOKING FAT IN A SLENDER WORLD: THE DIALECTIC OF SEEING AND BECOMING IN JEN DAVIS'S *ELEVEN YEARS*

Lauren Downing Peters

In 2002, Brooklyn-based photographer Jen Davis trained her camera's lens on a new subject: herself. Shy and struggling with her body image, the decision to become her own subject placed Davis at the margins of her comfort zone; however, what began with a one-off self-portrait of the artist sitting on a South Carolina beach quickly evolved into an intimate, years-long exploration of how one navigates a slender world while inhabiting a fat body. Yet, as the series evolved, so too did Davis herself. After undergoing bariatric surgery in 2011, nine years into the project, Davis lost a remarkable 110 pounds.

The resulting photographic series titled *Eleven Years* (2002–13) documents her bodily transformation with unflinching honesty. Mundane as they are extraordinary, in the photographs Davis can be glimpsed variously ordering from a late-night hot dog stand or hanging up her laundry to dry. Most frequently, however, Davis captures herself in the confines of her bedroom and bathroom as she naps, towels off after a shower or unclasps her bra. In the most literal sense of the term, the series is autobiographical; arguably, however, the most arresting photographs in the series are those that are removed from any clear or obvious social or domestic context. In these photographs, her body is cropped to the point of abstraction, the focus placed singularly on the fleshy layer of fat that enshrouds her bony frame.

Perhaps because Davis's own unruly and imperfect body does not fit neatly within the Western art historical tradition in its flouting of the construct of bodily perfection, critics have almost universally deemed *Eleven Years* a daring, if not audacious, series of self-portraits. In the journal *Aperture*, for instance, Rod Slemmons describes Davis's work as 'courageous'.[1] Elsewhere within the popular media, Davis's work has been frequently co-opted as a weight loss success story, being described by Diana Spechler in *O, The Oprah Magazine* as a journey towards finding her most 'beautiful' and 'desirable' self[2] and in the feminist magazine *Bustle* as a body of work that makes the viewer want to 'cheer for a woman who struggled and found happiness in spite of it all'.[3] Certainly, these photographs are explicitly about Davis's body and the complex relationship between body image and the cultural gaze – a point which Davis herself confirms in numerous interviews.[4] Reducing her body of work to a weight loss success story, however, is far too simplistic. Moreover, doing so reifies the hegemony of the normativizing male gaze and thereby illustrates what Jessica Evans has described as the manifest tendency in Western culture to render the fat body as 'other' and, more specifically, to pathologize or medicalize fatness.[5]

In this chapter, I therefore aim to offer a critical re-reading of *Eleven Years* through the lens of Fashion Studies – or the interdisciplinary study of the history, theory and culture of fashion and dress. In doing so, I draw upon the sociologist Joanne Entwistle's insights that 'human bodies are *dressed* bodies' (emphasis in original) and that the body, dress and the self should not be 'perceived separately but simultaneously, as a totality'.[6] By turning the focus to Davis's dress and dress practices, it becomes possible to glimpse how clothing is strategically employed throughout the series to exacerbate the apparent unruliness of her flesh and likewise how dress provokes bodily insecurities. Indeed, the artist's dissatisfaction with her body is palpable in photographs in which she captures herself in the act of getting dressed or glancing in a mirror – her eyes lingering on the points at which her clothing cuts uncomfortably into her too soft flesh. In addition to Davis's own self-critical gaze, however, there are other gazes present within *Eleven Years*, not least of which being that refracted from her full-length mirror, which itself functions as a proxy for a critical, normativizing gaze that mandates that women's bodies be 'tight, contained, under control [and] with firm margins'.[7] With my focus on Davis's dress and dress practices, what I am therefore interested in here is how garments simultaneously provoke in the viewer feelings of pity and disgust.

Verging on the surreal, these potent images recall in many ways Hans Bellmer's photographs of contorted and disembodied doll parts from the late 1930s, Irving Penn's voluptuous, tightly cropped nudes from the late 1940s and especially the monumental and, at times, unsettling paintings of obese bodies by Lucian Freud from the 1990s. In particular, however, Davis's work seems to reference a feminist canon of art making and scholarship dating to the 1990s, and oftentimes referred to as the 'corporeal turn', that placed emphasis on how we both know and *know through* the body.[8] Within this context, the work of Jenny Saville was exemplary for the extent to which the artist disembodied, fetishized and examined fat flesh for its material and textural qualities. In working within this tradition, Davis's series is subversive in its rejection of both Western beauty norms and historical conventions for depicting the nude body as orderly and shaped by underlying scientific laws within the Western canon of art. As Kenneth Clark has written, because the classical body is such a mainstay of Western art, 'we are immediately disturbed by wrinkles, pouches and other small imperfections, which, in the classical scheme, are eliminated'.[9] Building upon this point, Lynda Nead further argues that the artistic nude is a cultural construct, one which 'shores up' the female body by sealing its orifices and preventing 'marginal matter from transgressing the boundary dividing the inside [and] the outside'.[10]

In exploring this fraught artistic terrain and how Davis's work fits within it, this chapter draws upon a matrix of theories and conceptual frameworks that address the multiple gazes present within Davis's work and which speak to the problematics surrounding looking at and imaging the fat body in Western visual culture.[11] Among them, I draw upon Laura Mulvey's conceptualization of the gendered gaze so famously laid out in her seminal essay 'Visual Pleasure and Narrative Cinema' (1975), Michelle Meagher's notion of the 'aesthetics of disgust' (2003), Laura Marks's theory of 'haptic visuality' (2000) and, more generally, Michel Foucault's discussion of the panoptic gaze (1975). The aim here is to illustrate how, to borrow Efrat Tseëlon's phrasing, 'the act of representation modifies the nature of the represented object'.[12] Building upon this idea, I argue that images of fat women do not only reveal the tensions and contradictions of looking fat in a slender world but actually play a central role in shaping the physical experience of fat embodiment. Within this context, paying heed to the role that dress plays in Davis's work provides an additional opportunity to consider the fragile dialectics that exist between *seeing* and *becoming* and of *looking* and *being looked at* in the constitution of fat, female embodiment.

Subverting the gaze in *Eleven Years*

While her photography most clearly references the aforementioned works of Jenny Saville, Lucien Freud and Irving Penn, Davis also aligns her work with that of the Dutch genre painter Johannes Vermeer. Throughout *Eleven Years*, a gradually shrinking Davis is arrested in a number of ordinary and intimate moments, such as towelling her hair after a shower or tangled in bed with a lover. In these scenes, she is bathed in beams of golden sunlight that, quite literally, cast new light on simple everyday tasks. Indeed, Davis herself suggested in an interview that 'the light is what dictates the narrative of the picture'.[13] However, the presence of windows and doors that act as framing devices in many of the photographs further drive the narrative by heightening their psychological appeal and, importantly, casting viewers as voyeurs.[14]

What at first glance may seem like snapshots of spontaneous moments, however, are actually heavily composed still lifes in which Davis is the principal subject. In a 2014 interview with John Pilson, Davis explains how, at the beginning, 'I would often photograph in real time, responding to an emotional state that I was experiencing. [As the series wore on, however, I became] more deliberate – setting things up, finding the perfect interior, the perfect light, the perfect color relationships.'[15] It is in these later photographs that Davis began to more seriously consider the contours and curvatures of her flesh and what it means to be a fat woman in modern America. As Davis became more confident in her artistic practice after joining the Yale MFA photography programme, a single photograph could take her hours or even days to compose; however, even if the viewer knows that these photographs are less straight documents than composites, there is an air of autobiographical honesty that pervades her work.

Davis initially set about photographing herself out of a deep desire to, in her words, 'turn the gaze onto myself, to look inward, giving space to create a representation of myself that I did not even understand'.[16] The first photograph in the series foreshadows her coming transformation. Titled *Pressure Point* (2002), it captures Davis in a vulnerable moment as she sits self-consciously on a South Carolina beach, fidgeting with her toes and conspicuously covered up in black shorts and a tank top alongside tanned, slender, less covered up and more obviously carefree beachgoers (Figure 6). Within this scene, Davis renders her body as one that is unfit for public consumption, her fleshy curves flouting the requirements of the proverbial beach body. Over the ensuing eleven years, Davis would cultivate a persona that was at once autobiographical and an amalgam of the experiences of other fat women in America whose bodies uncomfortably vacillate between the poles of invisibility and hypervisibility.[17] This vulnerability, and the deeply human desire to both see and be seen, is perhaps what makes Davis's photographs so susceptible to multiple interpretations and, to women especially, so deeply relatable.

Just as the fat, female body is 'liminal' or semiotically unstable,[18] so too is *Eleven Years* to the extent that it both continuously reveals and challenges the gender dynamics of the gaze. In her essay 'Visual Pleasure and Narrative

Figure 6 Jen Davis, *Pressure Point* (2002). Copyright Jen Davis, courtesy Lee Marks Fine Art.

Cinema', Mulvey describes the male gaze as that which reifies the patriarchal social order 'in which man can live out his fantasies and obsessions [...] by imposing them on the silent image of woman still tied to her place as bearer of meaning, not maker of meaning'.[19] As Mulvey, drawing upon Freud's conceptualization of 'scopophilia', goes on to explain, this gaze is almost always sexual in nature for the manner in which the female body is 'subject to a controlling and curious gaze'.[20] She argues that there is an essential eroticism to the act of voyeurism in which the viewer is transmuted into a proverbial Peeping Tom. Although Davis positions the viewer as a voyeur in many of her photographs, what they ultimately seem to be about is how Davis, a woman, sees herself refracted through a normativizing cultural gaze that upholds a slender beauty ideal. As she explains in numerous interviews, Davis explicitly seeks to subvert the male gaze through her professed desire to 'look inward' to better understand herself rather than measuring herself against an illusory construct. At the same time, however, Davis also remarked that the inspiration for *Pressure Point* – and thereafter the rest of the series – was simultaneously driven by an underlying desire 'to be looked at' and a deep longing for 'recognition and visibility' from the opposite sex.[21]

Mulvey's conceptualization of the male gaze has become an invaluable touchstone for scholars – mainly within the fields of art history and women's and gender studies – to critique the gender dynamics (and imbalances) at play in the making of images of and about women. I argue, however, that there are clear limitations to Mulvey's formulation of the gendered gaze – especially when it comes to interpreting images of the fat, female body. As Samantha Murray has written, in Western society the fat, female body exists as a gross parody of female sexuality, or 'a distortion of contemporary paradigms of feminine beauty and desirability', and is a body that is regarded as 'uncared for, uncultivated and [...] as a body that has failed as the subject of aesthetics'.[22] Hers is the grotesque body, which, as Francesca Granata drawing on the writings of Mikhail Bakhtin has written, is an 'open, unfinished body, which is never sealed or fully contained, but is always in the process of becoming and engendering another body'.[23] With her large, leaky body rendered other or ancillary to the otherwise orderly and contained feminine ideal, the fat woman is neither permitted to experience sexual pleasure nor is she imagined (or imaged) as a sexual being. As Hannele Harjunen points out, the male gaze has been identified by feminist scholars from Susan Bordo to Naomi Wolf as being a crucial force in the proliferation of images of hyper-sexualized and slender female bodies within Western visual culture, which thereby perpetuate women's feelings of bodily dissatisfaction and, more distressingly, foment disordered eating.[24] To this end, it could be argued that Mulvey's male gaze is an inherently normativizing one, which naturally takes as its object a slender body.

What then are we to make of images of bodies that do not expressly pander to this normativizing gaze? And more specifically, what models exist for the interpretation of the fat, female body – a body that is less a source of pleasure than it is a spectacle – within Western society?

In her discussion of female spectatorship, Mary Ann Doane argues that masquerade can be used by artists as a technique to deflect the male gaze by creating distance between the viewer and object. As she explains, 'To masquerade is to manufacture a lack in the form of a certain distance between oneself and one's image.'[25] Feminist works that resist the male gaze are therefore those in which 'the woman uses her own body as a disguise'.[26] Drawing upon this notion, it could be argued that part of what makes *Eleven Years* so important and so challenging is the extent to which it humanizes the fat experience by foregrounding fat sexuality. In other words, even as Davis touches upon fat stereotypes – a point that will be discussed at greater length below – she also presents the fat, female body as it is rarely seen: *as an object of desire*. Yet even as the series might stand as a meditation on fat sexuality, Davis's non-normative body prevents her from being turned into a conventional sex object – especially in the photographs that were taken prior to her weight loss. Within these images, Davis's fat effectively steels her against the male gaze, thereby permitting more nuanced ways of looking. To borrow the language of the historian Richard Klein, her fat is rendered 'a cancerous growth [...] inessential to the body or its image'.[27] One could even argue that throughout the series, Davis's fat is rendered a prop of sorts – a suit of flesh, worn on the outside of her inside that hides a more slender person that resides within and which is slowly liberated throughout the progression of the series.

While Davis is ostensibly the object of a gaze (if not the male gaze per se), at the same time, her non-normative body permits her to resist the objectification that Mulvey describes in her essay. Certainly, one gets the sense that Davis is unaware of the viewer's gaze and is therefore not entirely in control of her image; yet, rather than a source of male pleasure in the manner Mulvey discusses, Davis's body is rendered a spectacle. It does not fit neatly into any pre-existing archetypes of female beauty nor is it a body that is typically idealized within Western visual culture at this moment in time. She is neither 'the girl' of fashion photography[28] nor is she the supple reclining nude of art history.[29] Her photographs also do not sit easily alongside the overtly theatrical self-portraits of other women photographers like Cindy Sherman or Hannah Wilke – artists who have been discussed in other contexts as performing a female gaze[30] – to the extent that Davis professes her own desire to be an object of male lust. To borrow the words of Roxane Gay, the fat woman's body is 'unruly' and therefore resists clear definition,[31] and, to a certain extent, much the same could be said about Davis's work. While the male and female gaze are both alternately present, and at multiple levels, throughout her work, there is also a third gaze that has gone unacknowledged. What, however, is this third gaze?

Considering the third gaze

One proposal comes from Jessica Evans who in her essay, 'Feeble Monsters: Making up Disabled People' (1999), explains how, in visual culture, disabled people tend to be 'screened out' or else occur in a limited number of medicalized roles. Within these contexts, Evans explains how the 'physical or mental impairment [becomes] the defining feature of a person to such an extent that it makes a character less than a whole character: it subtracts from personhood and undercuts one's status as a bearer of culture'.[32] What we have left when the disabled person is constructed through the lens of the medical gaze is a representation of an individual who is, at once, and perhaps paradoxically, a source of both pity and fear: *pity* because we feel sorry for the person affected by the disability and *fear* because we experience anxiety about the possibility of becoming similarly afflicted. This psychological splintering, Evans writes, reflects our alienation from the disabled individual and further entrenches their status as 'other'.[33]

The medical gaze Evans describes above is, I argue, an apt framework through which we may consider how the fat, female body is represented in Davis's work, as well as within visual culture at large. Indeed, as mentioned previously, images of fat bodies within Western visual culture tend to vacillate between the poles of hypervisibility and invisibility and are therefore conspicuously absent within neutral or positive contexts – a phenomenon that, as Kathleen LeBesco points out, speaks to the extent to which fat people have been constructed as symbols of social and physical disability in the West.[34] As a result, Adrienne Hill argues that fat people are frequently absent within Western visual culture as 'thinking subjects' and are instead made hypervisible as 'objects constantly subject to a prurient, disapproving gaze'.[35] To phrase it somewhat differently, amid escalating fears over the global obesity epidemic, the fat body has been pathologized through what I would argue is a non-gendered, equal-opportunity, fat-hating gaze that both reflects and perpetuates 'longstanding prejudices against fat people as lazy, incompetent and unattractive in [...] American culture'.[36] Drawing upon Evans's discussion of how disabled bodies are represented in the media, it is not a stretch to suggest that obesity has become a disability in its own right. This, in turn, has had a great effect on how fat people are visualized within the media, when they are present at all.

Building upon this notion, Charlotte Cooper coined the phrase 'the headless fatty phenomenon' to describe a pervasive visual trope in which fat individuals are photographed without their consent, either from behind or with their faces cropped out of the frame.[37] In such images, the camera focuses morbidly on the degree to which the fat body does not fit within the architectures and rhythms of modern life: T-shirts nestle into the creases between fat rolls, too-full bellies overflow from airline seats and ponderous hindquarters swallow bicycle seats. Most often, headless fatties can be seen in advertisements for diet drugs and weight loss regimens or, more often, illustrating sensational news articles about the obesity crisis in the West. In such images, Cooper argues that fat people are robbed of their individual agency and, in the process, are rendered as 'objects, as symbols, as a collective problem, as something to be talked about'.[38] Through the headless fatty phenomenon, the fat person becomes little more than a physical manifestation of illness, disease and decay. Different from the disabled body, however, the fat body is rarely a source of pity.

In her own work, Michelle Meagher has considered how images of fat people cause the body to recoil through the feeling of '*experiencing oneself as disgusting*' (emphasis in original).[39] Meagher describes Jenny Saville's larger-than-life paintings of obese bodies as simultaneously unsettling and captivating. They do not so much redefine the boundaries of beauty, she argues, as much as they reveal an 'aesthetics of disgust', which emerges from 'a system of cultural ideals that often compels women to see their bodies in a distorted and negative manner'.[40] Indeed, in a fat-phobic culture that so marginalizes non-normative bodies, Meagher argues that the reflexive response that viewers have to Saville's paintings – but also to more contemporary artwork of and about the fat, female body from the likes of Laura Aguilar and Sarah Sitkin – emerges from a deep-seated desire 'to render oneself distinct from that which disgusts'.[41] The body as depicted in these artists' work plays with the gaze; it is a gross caricature of obesity that reveals 'what lurks in the feminine imagination' – a representation, perhaps, of how women see themselves but not necessarily as they are seen.[42] To this end, the aesthetics of disgust exemplify the female gaze or how women internalize images of the slender ideal against which they always measure their perceived corporeal excesses and shortcomings. Somewhat unfortunately, however, Meagher points out how these disturbing paintings ultimately constitute 'a feminist recuperation of the female form' that is bound up in feelings of shame and self-loathing.[43] In the bruised and puckered flesh of Saville's, Aguilar's and Sitkin's nudes, female spectators see their own corporeal flaws even as they recoil in disgust.

However, the medical gaze and the aesthetics of disgust have recently been countered by a growing body of imagery that draws upon the tropes of Classical painting in the romanticization of the fat, female body. Over the past decade or so, in concert with the rise of the body positivity movement,[44] there has been what can only be described as a pervasive tendency for fashion photographers to depict fat models in some state of undress – the most recent instance of which being the highly controversial images of model Tess Holliday on the cover of the UK edition of *Cosmopolitan*. In these images, which appear in both high fashion magazines and mainstream women's magazines alike, the plus-size model is rendered a classical and frequently reclining, beauty – her ample proportions recalling the masterworks of Peter Paul Rubens, from whom the euphemism 'Rubenesque' was coined. As Leah Sweet argues, such depictions of the fat, female body 'communicate messages of size acceptance and/or fat pride and legitimize the insertion of fat bodies into mainstream structures of visibility'.[45] Such depictions of female fatness seek to redefine the boundaries of beauty by objectifying and fetishizing fat, female bodies. However, as plus-size fashion has gone mainstream, it is as if the fashion and beauty industries have overreached in their attempts to offset the extent to which the fat body has become associated with disorder and disease by re- or over-sexualizing the fat, female body. Within this context, the fat, female body has become the exoticized other, occupying a domain at the other end of the spectrum, far from the ectomorphic ideal embodied by the fashion model and much to the exclusion of 'average' and 'in-between' bodies. Some have hailed the sudden visibility of the romantic, voluptuous body within the fashion media as a victory; however, Sweet argues that such images are 'nostalgic' and preclude 'nuanced discussions of how fat intersects with issues such as race, gender and ability'.[46] Indeed, these depictions ultimately uphold a white, Western beauty norm, albeit slightly enlarged.

As a result, the fat body is rarely seen in neutral or positive contexts, existing on the one hand as a symbol of social and physical disability and on the other as a sexualized object of male desire. Through images such as these – images in which the fat, female body uncomfortably wavers between the poles of hypervisibility and invisibility – the fat woman's body weight becomes her defining characteristic, thereby undercutting her status as a bearer of culture by rendering her as an object of pity and shame. Somewhat differently, however, in the work of Jen Davis, the fat, female body is depicted as it is rarely seen: as ordinary. Yet, the ordinariness of these images does not preclude the fact that they have multiple layers and evidence multiple gazes or ways of looking. Indeed, Davis's approach suggests that she is hotly aware of how bodies like hers are seen, or rather, it is something that she learned as the series progressed. As she told the *New York Times* in 2012, 'I had wanted to see what the outside world saw when they looked at me.'[47] One therefore gets the sense that, throughout the series, Davis is toying with the viewer's expectations of what a fat body should look like and what a fat body can do in her appropriation of the medical gaze – an effect that is heightened by the presence (and absence) of clothing.

Re-fashioning the gaze

In some of the earliest photographs in the series – namely those that were taken prior to 2007 when she moved to New Haven to pursue her MFA – Davis seems to knowingly indulge the viewer's morbid curiosities about the experience of fat embodiment. In her 2002 photo *Maxwell Street*, for instance, Davis pictures herself placing an order at a late-night Chicago hot dog stand. Rendered a shapeless silhouette against a grimy yellow backdrop of perforated steel, this is an image with a predictable punchline – one that fulfils stereotypes pertaining to fat people's ignorance and lack of dietary self-control. It is also, however, one of the few images in which Davis turns away from the camera. By obscuring her face, she effectively strips herself of her identity and becomes just another headless fatty – a stock image of obesity. Here, Davis seems to appropriate the medical gaze while also subverting it by proving that she is in on the joke. Indeed, this image could appear in any news story about the Western weight crisis.

In other examples of her early work, however, Davis more pointedly satisfies the viewer's latent and somewhat perverse desire to experience what it feels like to be burdened with excess flesh as she explores the aesthetics of disgust described by Meagher above. The physicality of some of these images is undeniable – a feeling that is only heightened, I argue, by her strategic use of dress objects. In her 2002 self-portrait *Ascension*, for instance, we see Davis captured in a moment in which she appears to be pushing herself up from a seated position – the arms of the taupe chair in which she was sitting only barely visible at the perimeter of the image (Figure 7). The photo

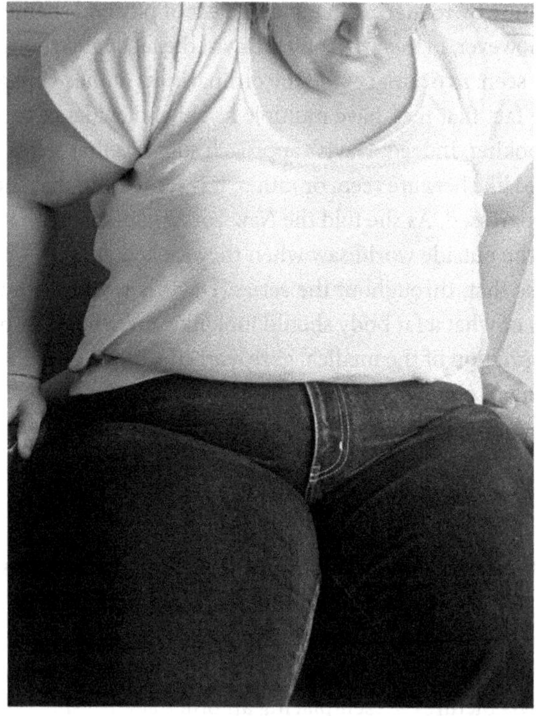

Figure 7 Jen Davis, *Ascension* (2002). Copyright Jen Davis, courtesy Lee Marks Fine Art.

tightly cropped around her midsection, Davis's physical exertion but also her discomfort are made manifest. This effect is only heightened by the tightness of her blue jeans and by the ill fit of her white T-shirt that stretches around and under her belly fat and which is itself unnaturally bisected by the tight waistband of her jeans. In this image, the all-American uniform of a white T-shirt and jeans – a symbol of easy, carefree dressing – is transformed into a vice that constricts her movement and adds another layer of difficulty to what, for many, is a task that is completed effortlessly, countless times throughout the day. What Davis so poignantly captures in this image is the fat experience that viewers inured to the visual discourses of the obesity epidemic almost expect to see: the body physically burdened by its own weight – its unruly margins defiantly pressing against the seams of garments not made to withstand the excesses of this body. The title of the photo – *Ascension* – only affirms this by framing this simple act as something verging on biblical.

The fleeting moment that is arrested in *Ascension* brings to mind Umberto Eco's essay 'Lumbar Thought' (1976) in which the philosopher reflected on how, after gaining weight, his suddenly too-tight jeans restricted his movements and subdivided his body into two independent zones: one free above the waist and one constricted and thereby identified with the denim. His body subdivided, Eco noted how 'my movements, my way of walking, turning, sitting, hurrying were different [...]. I lived in the knowledge that I had jeans on [...]. I lived for my jeans, and as a result I assumed the exterior behavior of one who wears jeans'.[48] This experience created what he deemed an 'epidermic self-awareness', or a state in which he grew self-aware about 'the relationship between my pants and me and the society we live in' and especially the lengths to which women go to conform their bodies to the whims of fashion.[49] In *Ascension*, one gets the distinct sense that her movement is inhibited by her tight, albeit fashionable, jeans and that she is epidermically self-aware of the extent to which her body does not conform to a slender ideal materialized through her too-tight clothing.

Figure 8 Jen Davis, *Conforming* (2002). Copyright Jen Davis, courtesy Lee Marks Fine Art.

Ana Carden-Coyne and Christopher E. Forth argue that the condition of fatness is fundamentally an affliction of the abdomen and, as such, it has become a favoured, if hotly political, site of self-fashioning.[50] Drawing upon this notion, it could be argued that while different body shapes have gone in and out of vogue over the centuries – with hips being exaggerated with the use of bustles and panniers and the bust being variously exaggerated or reduced by brassières and binders, for instance – the belly has rarely been the object of attempts to increase or exaggerate its size. In women especially, an hourglass silhouette is a hallmark of femininity.[51] In her 2002 photo *Conforming*, Davis seems to further explore her own epidermic self-awareness while also making a commentary on the difficulties of getting dressed while fat (Figure 8). Much as in *Ascension*, in *Conforming*, we see Davis embroiled in another sartorial struggle – this time to close a pair of trousers which appear to be a couple of sizes too small for her or, alternatively, for which she is several sizes too big. With the fly gaping wide open, her belly button and underwear clearly visible through the gap, it is difficult to imagine that she could ever close them. Attesting to how mass-manufactured, standard size garments are a powerful medium that give shape to the standard body,[52] this image viscerally illustrates the difficulties of getting dressed as a fat woman whose unruly body exceeds the spectrum of standard sizes; however, it also reveals her deep-seated desire to conform to this standard, as the title suggests, or to quite literally *fit in*. Indeed, the title evokes Davis's need to physically fit her body to the trousers, but also a deeper, more complicated desire to fit into a normative model of feminine embodiment, materialized here again through a garment.

Lacking the compositional richness and Davis's deft use of natural lighting, these photographs stand apart from others within *Eleven Years*. With their intense, almost medical focus on the body, they provoke in the viewer a different response – one that is visceral and embodied. In staring at these images, one can almost feel one's own waistband constrict. Writing specifically about film, Laura Marks writes about images that bear the capacity to provoke a tactile response in the viewer or what she deems 'touching through the eye'.[53] Although often blurry or unclear, 'haptic images', she explains, destabilize the supremacy of pictorial representation by relying upon forms of 'nonvisual knowledge, embodied knowledge, and experiences of the senses, such as touch, smell and taste'.[54] While Marks's focus is specifically on film, a similar idea could be applied to the still image, too. Marco Pecorari applies this notion to his discussion of 'haptic fashion images', which foreground the textures of fabrics or the blurry swish of a dress over the high gloss of canonical fashion imagery. Such images, he writes, 'do not only convey signs of the dress, but also mime the tactile sensation [of wearing a garment]'.[55] Pecorari further argues that the success of haptic fashion images ultimately hinges upon the viewer's embodied knowledge or experience of wearing clothing. This embodied knowledge is ultimately what makes these images so highly evocative: they provoke in the viewer a tactile memory that is frequently airbrushed or Photoshopped out of fashion photography, but which is perhaps all too familiar to the average consumer.

Both within and through these images, Davis defines, reconstructs and subverts the limited cultural lenses through which her stigmatized body and bodies like hers are viewed. Much like Jenny Saville, Davis does not seek to create beautiful images; rather, she dabbles in the aesthetics of disgust by creating photographs that, to borrow the language of Meagher, are 'viscerally difficult'.[56] Much as with Mulvey's male gaze in which the viewer is able to identify with a character on screen, so too can viewers try on a proverbial fat suit through the simple act of looking at Davis's photographs. While Meagher argues that such 'difficult' images bear in them the capacity to '[propose] new modes of feminine embodiment',[57] it could more simply be argued that they speak to a mode of embodiment that is all-too familiar to women who struggle to navigate the minefield of standardized dress while inhabiting a non-standard body.

Seeing and being seen

After 2007, however, there occurs a discernible shift in Davis's work. Rather than exploring the aesthetics of disgust and indulging the viewer's appetite for the spectacle of the fat, female body, her portraits turn inwards and become decidedly more self-meditative and narrative. In many of these images, Davis's full-length mirror and medicine cabinet recur as tools that permit a doubling of the gaze through which the viewer is afforded an opportunity to look at Davis looking at herself in what could be theorized as a Foucauldian performance of self-surveillance in the service of prevailing beauty ideals.[58] In her self-portrait *Untitled No. 37* from 2010, for instance, Davis captures herself gazing in her bathroom vanity mirror. As in many of her other photographs, the warm early evening light perfectly frames her face as she performs a private ritual, likely familiar to many female viewers. Absorbed in her own reflection, she poses and contorts her profile to better embody a normative feminine ideal or an image of a future self. Just a year after this photo was taken, Davis underwent Lap Band surgery – a decision that was partially informed by the version of herself that she had seen captured on film for the previous nine years and with whom she had grown so dissatisfied. Of this decision, Davis explained to the *New York Times*, 'I realized that I didn't want to wake up in this body at 40.'[59] In *Untitled No. 37*, Davis therefore depicts herself on the precipice of undergoing a drastic transformation as she turns the gaze onto herself – assessing her appearance with a new, unflinching intensity while also perhaps test-driving a new identity.

As Sabine Melchior-Bonnet writes in her book *The Mirror* (2001), the mirror is transformative in that it permits the individual to engage in a slippery 'dialectic of being and seeing [by appealing] to the imagination, introducing new perspectives and anticipating other truths'.[60] Continuing, she explains how the mirror permits one to 'observe oneself, to measure oneself, to dream oneself and to transform oneself [...] beyond the cultural stigmas long attached to looking at one's self'.[61] Fashion theorist Van Dyk Lewis has similarly described the performances that women enact in private in front of their full-length bedroom mirrors through which they attempt 'to reconcile the imagined body with [their] actual body shape' by tensing and flexing their muscles in an attempt to embody [their] mental reflections of a perfect or ideal body.[62] By doing so, women respond to fashion's demands for 'the constant activity of the transformative figure' by creating a fleeting image of a future body.[63] In *Untitled No. 37* but also in earlier works such as *Untitled No. 4* (2004), Davis captures this dialectic of 'being and seeing', or perhaps more appropriately, of *seeing and becoming* – a doubled gaze that is further compounded by the looming presence of the normativizing cultural gaze – or the invisible yardstick of beauty ideals against which she seems to be measuring herself in her private performance of a future self.

In another example from 2007 titled *Untitled No. 24*, the viewers take the place of the mirror, in front of whom Davis stands un-self-conscious with her hands clasped atop her head while donning a black bra, underwear and sheer pantyhose (Figure 9). Much as in *Ascension* and *Conforming*, Davis employs dress in this photograph to exacerbate the degree to which her body fails to conform to the Western ideal of beauty. Her flat-footed stance, fleshy, pale midsection, stretch-marked skin and dead eyes negate the sexual overtones of her black lingerie and seductive pose. As Tucker writes in her essay about Davis's work, in this photo, she seems resigned to the fact that she is 'not playing the sexual game successfully'.[64]

In a later photograph titled *Untitled No. 47*, however – one which was taken a year after her Lap Band surgery in 2012 – a markedly thinner Davis stands again in front of a full-length mirror, donning black lingerie and a

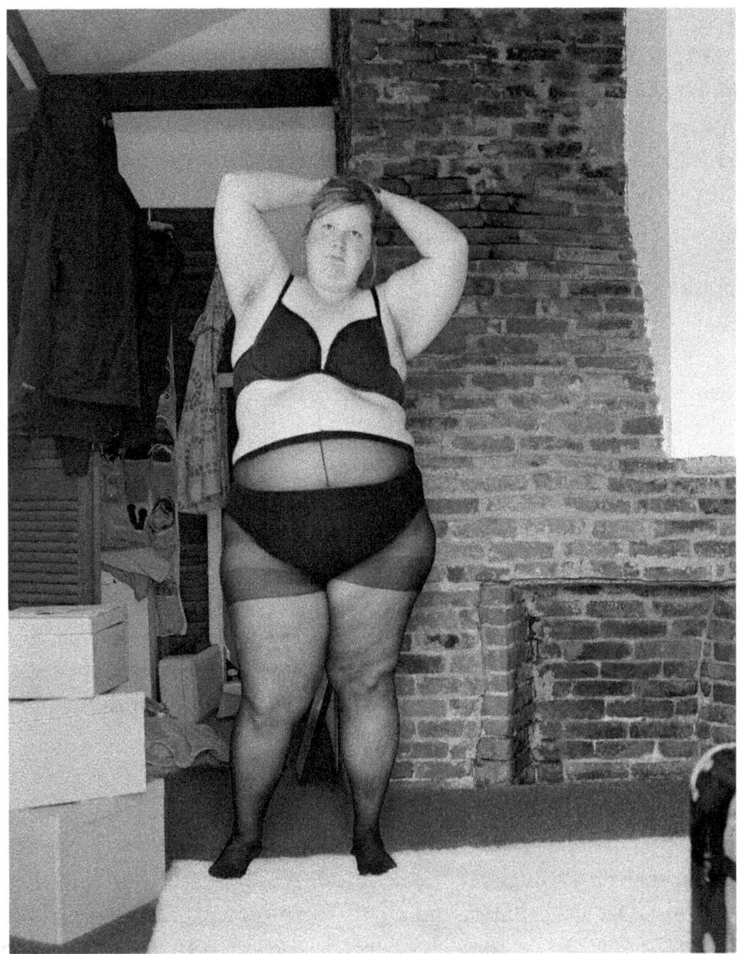

Figure 9 Jen Davis, *Untitled No. 24* (2007). Copyright Jen Davis, courtesy Lee Marks Fine Art.

new haircut. In contrast to the previous image, Davis's gaze seems more contented, if not confident, as she assesses her thinning frame. Different from the 2007 photograph, *Untitled No. 47* more closely resembles so-called 'fatshion' photographs which, as Majida Kargbo has written, resignify fat 'beyond the future conditional' by rendering the fat, female body as 'a gendered body, a desiring body, a livable body, a body who does not function only as the shamed other'.[65] Said somewhat differently, although Davis might still be perceived as 'fat' in this photograph, her gaze suggests that she has reached a place in which she is content with her curves. Indeed, it is notable that in photographs dating to after Davis's weight loss there seems to occur another shift. In these photographs, the viewer is more likely to encounter the artist in the company of men, as in *Tim and I* (2012), *Aldo and I* (2013) and *Pablo and I* (2013) in which Davis turns her self-critical gaze onto her lovers while framing herself as the object of the male gaze and of male desire.

Conclusion

As the above analysis demonstrates, Jen Davis's challenging and thought-provoking work is implicitly about the gaze and specifically about the multiple gazes to which the fat, female body is subject. To draw again upon Efrat Tsëëlon's quote with which I opened this chapter, in this series, it is possible to see how 'the act of representation modifies the nature of the represented object'.[66] Through the intrepid act of turning her camera's lens onto herself, Davis sought to see her body as others saw it. In the process, she found herself acquiescing to the normativizing gaze of culture as she pursued an aggressive and controversial weight loss procedure. As mentioned previously, however, to reduce the series to a weight loss success story is to miss out on an opportunity to understand the processes through which the fat, female body is fashioned.

In *Eleven Years*, Davis presents the fat, female body as we are not accustomed to seeing it. Unlike the overly sexualized images of plus-size models that abound in the fashion press or the headless fatties that litter evening news broadcasts, Davis's work presents a more stable and empathetic depiction of fat embodiment and all the pressures that are brought to bear on the fat, female body. To this end, it is perhaps not a stretch to argue that Davis's work provides a new lens or 'gaze' through which we might be able to understand the experience of fat, female embodiment *as a process*, or as a complex relay in which the cultural gaze is internalized and, thereafter, materialized on the body through various practices and performances of self-assessment and self-fashioning.

Notes

1. Rod Slemmons, 'Jen Davis Body Image', *Aperture* 182 (2006), pp. 30–7.
2. Diana Spechler, 'Coming into Focus: 3 Photos That Will Change How You Think about Your Body 2012', *O, The Oprah Magazine* (September 2012).

Available at http://www.oprah.com/health/jen-davis-self-portraits-weight-loss-and-photography/all (accessed 13 January 2019).

3. Emma Cueto, 'Photographer Jen Davis' Eleven Years' Photo Series Discusses Body Acceptance and Fat Shaming', *Bustle*, 21 May 2014. Available at https://www.bustle.com/articles/25292-photographer-jen-daviseleven-years-photo-series-discusses-body-acceptance-and-fat-shaming (accessed 13 August 2018).
4. Maia Booker, 'Jen Davis's Self-Portraits Offer Eleven Years of Self-Scrutiny: A Weighty Study of Beauty', *The New Republic*, 17 June 2014. Available at https://newrepublic.com/article/118222/jen-davis-photos-eleven-years-self-portraits-exploring-body-image (accessed 13 August 2018); Jen Davis and John Pilson, 'Torch Songs and Love Scenes', in J. Davis (ed), *Eleven Years* (Berlin: Kehrer Heidelberg, 2014), pp. 27–9; Kate Salter, 'Jen Davis Interview: The Skin I Was In', *The Telegraph*, 17 March 2013. Available at https://www.telegraph.co.uk/culture/photography/9930597/Jen-Davis-interview-The-skin-I-was-in.html (accessed 13 August 2018).
5. Jessica Evans, 'Feeble Monsters: Making Up Disabled People', in J. Evans and S. Hall (eds), *Visual Culture: The Reader* (London: Sage, 1999), pp. 274–88.
6. Joanne Entwistle, *The Fashioned Body: Fashion, Dress & Modern Social Theory* (Cambridge: Polity, 2001), p. 6, p. 10.
7. Alison Adam, 'Big Girls' Blouses: Learning to Live with Polyester', in A. Guy, E. Green and M. Banim (eds), *Through the Wardrobe: Women's Relationships with Their Clothes* (Oxford: Berg, 2001), p. 40.
8. For an overview of this shift, see Maxine Sheets-Johnstone, 'Introduction', in M. Sheets-Johnstone (ed), *The Corporeal Turn: An Interdisciplinary Reader* (Exeter: Imprint Academic, 2009), pp. 1–16.
9. Kenneth Clark, *The Nude: A Study in Ideal Form* (Princeton: Princeton University Press, 1990), p. 7.
10. Lynda Nead, *The Female Nude: Art, Obscenity and Sexuality* (Abingdon and New York: Routledge, 1992), p. 6.
11. In taking this stance, I reject the biological determinism of fatness and instead frame it as a cultural construct.
12. Efrat Tseëlon, *The Masque of Femininity: The Presentation of Woman in Everyday Life* (London: Sage, 1995), p. 3.
13. Davis and Pilson, 'Torch Songs', p. 28.
14. Anne Wilkes Tucker, 'Looking for Narrative', in J. Davis (ed), *Eleven Years* (Berlin: Kehrer Heidelberg, 2014), p. 113.
15. Davis and Pilson, 'Torch Songs', p. 27.
16. Ibid.
17. Adrienne Hill, *Spatial Awarishness: Queer Women and the Politics of Fat Embodiment*, PhD diss. (University of Bowling Green, 2009), p. 15.
18. Katariina Kyrölä and Hannele Harjunen, 'Phantom/Liminal Fat and Feminist Theories of the Body', *Feminist Theory* 18/2 (2017), pp. 99–117.

19. Laura Mulvey, 'Visual Pleasure and Narrative Cinema', in L. Braudy and M. Cohen (eds), *Film Theory and Criticism: Introductory Readings* (New York: Oxford University Press, [1975] 1999), p. 834.
20. Ibid., p. 835.
21. Davis and Pilson, 'Torch Songs', p. 27.
22. Samantha Murray, 'Locating Aesthetics: Sexing the Fat Woman', *Social Semiotics*, 14/3 (December 2004), p. 237.
23. Francesca Granata, *Experimental Fashion: Performance Art, Carnival and the Grotesque Body* (London: I.B. Tauris, 2017), p. 1.
24. Hannele Harjunen, *Neoliberal Bodies and the Gendered Fat Body* (London: Routledge, 2017), p. 88.
25. Mary Ann Doane, 'Film and the Masquerade: Theorising the Female Spectator', *Screen*, 23/3–4 (September 1982), p. 82.
26. Ibid.
27. Richard Klein, 'Fat Beauty', in J. Evans Braziel and K. LeBesco (eds), *Bodies Out of Bounds: Fatness and Transgression* (Berkeley: University of California Press, 2001), p. 27.
28. Paul Jobling, '"Alex Eats," a Case Study in Abjection and Identity in Contemporary Fashion Photography', *Fashion Theory* 2/3 (1998), pp. 209–24.
29. John Berger, *Ways of Seeing* (New York: Penguin, [1972] 2008), p. 64.
30. Judith Williamson, 'Images of "Woman" – The Photographs of Cindy Sherman', *Screen* 24/6 (1983), pp. 236–41.
31. Roxane Gay, *Hunger: A Memoir of (My) Body* (New York: HarperCollins, 2017), p. 4.
32. Evans, 'Feeble Monsters', p. 275.
33. Ibid., p. 284.
34. Kathleen LeBesco, *Revolting Bodies: The Struggle to Redefine Fat Identity* (Amherst: University of Massachusetts Press, 2004), p. 75.
35. Hill, 'Spatial Awarishness', p. 15.
36. Lauren Downing Peters, '"Fashion Plus": Pose and the Plus-Size Body in Vogue, 1986–1988', *Fashion Theory* 21/2 (2017), pp. 175–99.
37. Charlotte Cooper, 'Headless Fatties', *CharlotteCooper.net*, 1 January 2007. Available at http://charlottecooper.net/fat/fat-writing/headless-fatties-01-07/ (accessed 13 August 2018).
38. Ibid.
39. Michelle Meagher, 'Jenny Saville and a Feminist Aesthetics of Disgust', *Hypatia* 18/4 (Winter 2003), p. 24.
40. Ibid., p. 25.
41. Ibid., p. 33.

42. Ibid., p. 34.
43. Ibid., p. 36.
44. Lauren Downing Peters, *Stoutwear and the Discourses of Disorder: Constructing the Fat, Female Body in American Fashion in the Age of Standardization*, PhD diss. (Stockholm University, 2018), p. 363.
45. Leah Sweet, 'Fantasy Bodies, Imagined Pasts: A Critical Analysis of the "Rubenesque" Fat Body in Contemporary Culture', *Fat Studies* 3/2 (2014), p. 131.
46. Ibid., p. 132.
47. Miki Meek, 'Seeing Yourself as Others Do', *New York Times*, 26 April 2012. Available at https://lens.blogs.nytimes.com/2012/04/26/seeing-yourself-as-others-do/ (accessed 13 August 2018).
48. Umberto Eco, 'Lumbar Thought', in U. Eco (ed), *Travels in Hyperreality*, trans. William Weaver (San Diego, New York and London: Harvest, 1986), p. 192.
49. Ibid., p. 193.
50. Ana Carden-Coyne and Christopher E. Forth (eds), *Cultures of the Abdomen: Diet, Digestion, and Fat in the Modern World* (New York: Palgrave Macmillan, 2005), pp. 1–2.
51. This notion is exemplified by the pervasiveness of corsets, girdles and, later, body shapers – all of which cinch the waist and create an hourglass silhouette – as the foundations of women's dress from the last half of the sixteenth century onwards. See Valerie Steele, *The Corset: A Cultural History* (New Haven: Yale University Press, 2003).
52. Ingrid Jeacle, 'Accounting and the Construction of the Standard Body', *Accounting Organizations and Society* 28/1 (2003), pp. 357–77.
53. Laura Marks, *The Skin of the Film: Intercultural Media, Embodiment, and the Senses* (Durham and London: Duke University Press, 2000), p. 161.
54. Ibid., p. 2.
55. Marco Pecorari, *Fashion Remains: The Epistemic Potential of Fashion Ephemera*, PhD diss. (Stockholm University, 2016), p. 200.
56. Meagher, 'Jenny Saville', p. 24.
57. Ibid.
58. This idea is drawn from the writings of Michel Foucault and specifically his notion of panopticism. See Michel Foucault, *Discipline and Punish: The Birth of the Prison*, trans. Alan Sheridan (New York: Vintage Books, 1995), p. 205.
59. Meek, 'Seeing Yourself'.
60. Sabine Melchior-Bonnet, *The Mirror: A History*, trans. Katharine H. Jewett (New York: Routledge, 2001), pp. 156–7.
61. Ibid., p. 157.

62. Van Dyk Lewis, 'Sizing and Clothing Aesthetics', in S.P. Ashdown (ed), *Sizing in Clothing: Developing Effective Sizing Systems for Ready-to-Wear Clothing* (Manchester: Woodhead, 2007), p. 315.
63. Ibid.
64. Tucker, 'Looking for Narrative', p. 114.
65. Majida Kargbo, 'Toward a New Relationality: Digital Photography, Shame, and the Fat Subject', *Fat Studies: An Interdisciplinary Journal of Body Weight and Society* 2/2 (2013), p. 161.
66. Tseëlon, *The Masque of Femininity*, p. 3.

Bibliography

Adam, Alison, 'Big Girls' Blouses: Learning to Live with Polyester', in A. Guy, E. Green and M. Banim (eds), *Through the Wardrobe: Women's Relationships with Their Clothes* (Oxford: Berg, 2001), pp. 39–53.

Berger, John, *Ways of Seeing* (New York: Penguin, [1972] 2008).

Booker, Maia, 'Jen Davis's Self-Portraits Offer Eleven Years of Self-Scrutiny: A Weighty Study of Beauty', *The New Republic*, 17 June 2014. Available at https://newrepublic.com/article/118222/jen-davis-photos-eleven-years-self-portraits-exploring-body-image (accessed 13 August 2018).

Carden-Coyne, Ana and Christopher E. Forth (eds), *Cultures of the Abdomen: Diet, Digestion, and Fat in the Modern World* (New York: Palgrave Macmillan, 2005).

Clark, Kenneth, *The Nude: A Study in Ideal Form* (Princeton: Princeton University Press, 1990).

Cooper, Charlotte, 'Headless Fatties', *CharlotteCooper.net*, 2007. Available at http://charlottecooper.net/fat/fat-writing/headless-fatties-01-07/ (accessed 13 August 2018).

Cueto, Emma, 'Photographer Jen Davis' Eleven Years' Photo Series Discusses Body Acceptance and Fat Shaming', *Bustle*, 21 May 2014. Available at https://www.bustle.com/articles/25292-photographer-jen-daviseleven-years-photo-series-discusses-body-acceptance-and-fat-shaming (accessed 13 August 2018).

Davis, Jen and John Pilson, 'Torch Songs and Love Scenes' in J. Davis, *Eleven Years* (Berlin: Kehrer Heidelberg, 2014), pp. 27–9.

Doane, Mary Ann, 'Film and the Masquerade: Theorising the Female Spectator', *Screen*, 23/3–4 (1982), pp. 74–88.

Eco, Umberto, 'Lumbar Thought' in U. Eco, *Travels in Hyperreality*, trans. William Weaver (San Diego, New York and London: Harvest, 1986), pp. 191–6.

Entwistle, Joanne, *The Fashioned Body: Fashion, Dress & Modern Social Theory* (Cambridge: Polity, 2001).

Evans, Jessica, 'Feeble Monsters: Making Up Disabled People"', in J. Evans and S. Hall (eds), *Visual Culture: The Reader* (London: Sage, 1999), pp. 274–88.

Foucault, Michel, *Discipline and Punish: The Birth of the Prison*, trans. Alan Sheridan (New York: Vintage Books, 1995).

Gay, Roxane, *Hunger: A Memoir of (My) Body* (New York: HarperCollins, 2017).
Granata, Francesca, *Experimental Fashion: Performance Art, Carnival and the Grotesque Body* (London: I.B. Tauris, 2017).
Harjunen, Hannele, *Neoliberal Bodies and the Gendered Fat Body* (London: Routledge, 2017).
Hill, Adrienne, *Spatial Awarishness: Queer Women and the Politics of Fat Embodiment*, PhD diss., University of Bowling Green, 2009.
Jeacle, Ingrid, 'Accounting and the Construction of the Standard Body', *Accounting Organizations and Society* 28/1 (2003), pp. 357–77.
Jobling, Paul, '"Alex Eats", A Case Study in Abjection and Identity in Contemporary Fashion Photography', *Fashion Theory* 2/3 (1998), pp. 209–24.
Kargbo, Majida, 'Toward a New Relationality: Digital Photography, Shame, and the Fat Subject', *Fat Studies: An Interdisciplinary Journal of Body Weight and Society* 2/2 (2013), pp. 160–72.
Klein, Richard, 'Fat Beauty', in J. Evans Braziel and K. LeBesco (eds), *Bodies Out of Bounds: Fatness and Transgression* (Berkeley: University of California Press, 2001), pp. 19–38.
Kyrölä, Katariina and Hannele Harjunen, 'Phantom/Liminal Fat and Feminist Theories of the Body', *Feminist Theory* 18/2 (2017), pp. 99–117.
LeBesco, Kathleen, *Revolting Bodies: The Struggle to Redefine Fat Identity* (Amherst: University of Massachusetts Press, 2004).
Lewis, Van Dyk, 'Sizing and Clothing Aesthetics' in S.P. Ashdown (ed), *Sizing in Clothing: Developing Effective Sizing Systems for Ready-to-Wear Clothing* (Manchester: Woodhead, 2007), pp. 309–27.
Marks, Laura, *The Skin of the Film: Intercultural Media, Embodiment, and the Senses* (Durham and London: Duke University Press, 2000).
Meagher, Michelle, 'Jenny Saville and a Feminist Aesthetics of Disgust', *Hypatia* 18/4 (2003), pp. 23–42.
Meek, Miki, 'Seeing Yourself as Others Do', *New York Times*, 26 April 2012. Available at https://lens.blogs.nytimes.com/2012/04/26/seeing-yourself-as-others-do/ (accessed 13 August 2018).
Melchior-Bonnet, Sabine, *The Mirror: A History*, trans. Katharine H. Jewett (New York: Routledge, 2001).
Mulvey, Laura, 'Visual Pleasure and Narrative Cinema', in L. Braudy and M. Cohen (eds), *Film Theory and Criticism: Introductory Readings* (New York: Oxford University Press, [1975] 1999), pp. 833–44.
Murray, Samantha, 'Locating Aesthetics: Sexing the Fat Woman', *Social Semiotics* 14/3 (2004), pp. 237–48.
Nead, Lynda, *The Female Nude: Art, Obscenity and Sexuality* (Abingdon and New York: Routledge, 1992).
Pecorari, Marco, *Fashion Remains: The Epistemic Potential of Fashion Ephemera*, PhD diss., Stockholm University, 2016.
Peters, Lauren Downing, '"Fashion Plus": Pose and the Plus-Size Body in Vogue, 1986–1988', *Fashion Theory* 21/2 (2017), pp. 175–99.
Peters, Lauren Downing, *Stoutwear and the Discourses of Disorder: Constructing the Fat, Female Body in American Fashion in the Age of Standardization*, PhD diss., Stockholm University, 2018.

Salter, Kate, 'Jen Davis Interview: The Skin I Was In', *The Telegraph*, 17 March 2013. Available at https://www.telegraph.co.uk/culture/photography/9930597/Jen-Davis-interview-The-skin-I-was-in.html (accessed 13 August 2018).

Sheets-Johnstone, Maxine, 'Introduction', in M. Sheets-Johnstone (ed), *The Corporeal Turn: An Interdisciplinary Reader* (Exeter: Imprint Academic, 2009), pp. 1–16.

Slemmons, Rod, 'Jen Davis Body Image', *Aperture* 182 (2006), pp. 30–7.

Spechler, Diana, 'Coming into Focus: 3 Photos That Will Change How You Think about Your Body', *O Magazine*, September 2012. Available at http://www.oprah.com/health/jen-davis-self-portraits-weight-loss-and-photography/all (accessed 13 January 2019).

Steele, Valerie, *The Corset: A Cultural History* (New Haven: Yale University Press, 2003).

Sweet, Leah, 'Fantasy Bodies, Imagined Pasts: A Critical Analysis of the "Rubenesque" Fat Body in Contemporary Culture', *Fat Studies* 3/2 (2014), pp. 130–42.

Tseëlon, Efrat, *The Masque of Femininity: The Presentation of Woman in Everyday Life* (London: Sage, 1995).

Wilkes Tucker, Anne, 'Looking for Narrative', in J. Davis (ed), *Eleven Years* (Berlin: Kehrer Heidelberg, 2014), pp. 113–15.

Williamson, Judith, 'Images of "Woman" – The Photographs of Cindy Sherman', *Screen* 24/6 (1983), pp. 236–41.

CHAPTER 9
RE-READING THE QUEER FEMALE GAZE IN THE 1990S: SPECTATORSHIP, FASHION AND THE DUALITY OF IDENTIFICATION AND DESIRE

Catherine Baker

Among feminists revisiting ideas of the female gaze in the 1990s, some film and fashion scholars started explaining a contradictory but surprisingly common queer experience: desiring the object of the gaze and wanting to look like them at the same time. While heteronormative culture would expect desires about how the self should look and desires involving attraction to flow along opposite channels of gender presentation (one masculine and one feminine), in many queer lives they do not. Indeed, the conflation of 'wanting to have' and 'wanting to be' has become commonplace in queer art and media – yet it was, and is, supremely confusing to young queer people forming their subjectivity in heteronormative surroundings without knowing this as a queer experience. Work on queer spectatorship and the fashioned female body by authors such as Jackie Stacey, Caroline Evans, Lorraine Gamman and Reina Lewis captured this simultaneity of identification and desire better than any previous approach to gaze theory. Yet by restricting itself to women's gazes at fashioned *female* bodies, it did not account for everyday identifications with men's style that many queer women were already making and mid-1990s women's fashion invited. Nevertheless, this chapter argues, the conceptual tools for understanding identifications with masculinities within gaze theory's cycle of spectatorship and desire already existed – the literature just needed to realize such identifications could also matter to people who were not men. Present-day lesbian and queer women's digital culture, this chapter suggests, is more comfortable with this than feminist gaze theory has been to date.[1]

This chapter takes an autoethnographic approach to spectatorship and fashion, contrasting examples from 1990s popular culture with those from the present. I read and write about mid-1990s accounts of the 'lesbian gaze' knowing I am one of the queer women who was forming her subjectivity through spectatorship and fashion at that time – as a London teenager trying to understand why I was drawn to softly masculine women's fashion and whether I just wanted to *be like* or actually *be with* women who seemed to embody it better than me. Between 1994 and 1997, Caroline Evans and Lorraine Gamman were tracing queerly androgynous aesthetics seeping into mainstream advertising and explaining movies where homoerotic doublings and ambiguous stars all but demanded to be watched against the heteronormative grain.[2] Reina Lewis, with Katrina Rolley, was asking why lesbians enjoyed reading womenswear spreads in mainstream high-fashion magazines[3] and showing that the lesbian lifestyle magazine *Diva*, founded in 1994, used fashion spreads to offer the pleasure of an *openly* lesbian gaze.[4] I was encountering the same advertising and movies; I was learning what society considered aspirational and attractive from the same mainstream magazines; and I should have been among *Diva*'s reading public, had I ever dared confirm I was a lesbian by buying the magazine. The arguments in these scholarly texts about women, spectatorship and fashion implicitly call my own identifications and desires onto the page. In fact, they appeared just when I was noticing, then explaining away, my queerness and my own desires about how I wanted to be seen.

Nevertheless, my subjectivity was forming without any active spectatorship of lesbian media or participation in queer spectatorial communities, let alone any consciousness that feminists were already writing theory that could have explained my confusion. Unable or unwilling to interpret my own queer gaze towards fashion and fashionable women as anything more than 'noticing women I wanted to look like' (which seemed more socially acceptable), my 12- to 15-year-old self in 1994–7 did not realize I was perceiving a very specific moment in queer fashion history. This was a moment when Britpop fashion and 'lesbian chic'[5] were converging with what Evans and Gamman were already terming the lesbian 'subcultural' competences of recognizing style cues (haircuts, clothing, footwear, even movement) as clues to queerness.[6] I was ever more conscious that my spectatorship towards the fashioned female body involved identifications I then desired to have recognized. I bored, and sometimes alarmed, classmates and family by talking about how much I wanted to look like a particular pop star or even who looked more like her at school. Yet I tried to disavow the idea that this could be a *lesbian* gaze, which I believed had to involve wholly sexual desire.

I was, in fact, the very reader (and spectator) 'without a sense of the reality of other such readers' that Lewis and Rolley conjectured on the peripheries of the lesbian gaze: or, rather, I knew there *were* such readers, but did not (want to) recognize myself among them.[7] The mid-1990s studies rethinking the female gaze through queer women's spectatorship and fashion would have explained much of the cycle of spectatorship, identification, fashion and desire I was experiencing. Yet this very literature said surprisingly little about the everyday identifications with masculinities that informed some queer women's gender expression within that cycle, as my autoethnographic account shows. This oversight stands in contrast to the much greater ease with which contemporary queer women's digital culture talks about the same ideas.

Spectatorship and the duality of identification and desire

The notion that identification and desire can be complementary concepts, not opposites of each other, within spectatorship itself emerged from the psychoanalytically informed gaze theory of the 1980s and early 1990s and was central to Jackie Stacey's *Star Gazing: Hollywood Cinema and Female Spectatorship*, a study of British women's spectatorship towards 1940s–1950s British/US female film stars. This followed Stacey's earlier work on how desire and identification between women was represented *on* screen.[8] Surprisingly, *Star Gazing* seemed to describe my own experiences of spectatorship better than most 'lesbian' writing when I read it aged twenty-one, even though all Stacey's participants were heterosexual (as far as she knew).[9] Much of the pleasure of watching and identifying with stars, Stacey argued, stemmed from spectators' pleasure in recognizing some point of similarity between stars and themselves. Such recognition let them temporarily imagine a transformed self in the gap between similarity and difference where fantasy could occur. The pleasure of homoerotically perceiving identification with stars across bridges of resemblance was, in other words, 'available to *all* women', not even just lesbians – and certainly not just a 'misentangled', inexplicable part of *my* subjectivity.[10]

Feminist gaze theory up until Stacey had held that identification and desire were separate pleasures which had to run along differently gendered lines. Since Laura Mulvey's 'male gaze' essay in 1975,[11] feminists had used psychoanalysis to explain how cinema forced spectators to identify with an objectifying male gaze towards women, what pleasures women spectators could nevertheless experience and how avant-garde women film-makers strove to construct different gazes instead. Diana Fuss had applied psychoanalytical ideas of pleasure to close-up fashion photographs of women, arguing that they psychodynamically invited women to '"recover" the lost object' of the mother's face.[12] She termed the resultant contradiction between fashion's heteronormativity and its giving women 'cultural impunity' to gaze on other women a 'homospectatorial look'.[13] Fuss was not interested in lesbian spectatorship and ostensibly neither was Stacey – but Stacey's reworking of Lacanian psychoanalysis in gaze theory created more space for lesbian and queer spectators to exist.

To explain her participants' accounts of watching female film stars, Stacey turned to the 'projection' and 'introjection' theory of another psychoanalyst, Melanie Klein.[14] Klein had understood the formation of the self as a cycle of 'projective identification' where individuals first project emotions and desires onto others, then absorb qualities of the ideal other so they can regard them as belonging to the self.[15] Stacey used this cycle to explain why her participants also described pleasures and practices of identification away from the screen, which she saw as equally important expressions of the spectatorial gaze's interplay between identification and desire.[16] Many participants remembered they had bought particular clothes or perfumes, or done certain things with their hair, because of associations with stars they identified with;[17] these 'extra-cinematic' practices afforded, if successful, all-important recognition by others of the individual's identification with the star.[18] Such a cycle exemplifies how identificatory desires for resemblance or transformation, and for its recognition, can permeate from the moment of spectatorship into individuals' ongoing embodied and socially constituted identity performances through fashion and dress. These are 'an intimate aspect of the experience and presentation of the self', as fashion theorist Joanne Entwistle reminds us.[19] They are, for queer women, the affects behind what Lisa Walker had already termed the politics of 'looking like what you are'.[20]

One might think, given Teresa de Lauretis's objections to Stacey's earlier work on dynamics of identification and desire between women in film, that scope for Stacey's frameworks to offer insights into lesbian gazes might be limited.[21] Stacey had argued in 1987 that films like *All About Eve* (1950) and *Desperately Seeking Susan* (1985), representing intense identifications and desires between women, 'offer[ed] particular pleasures' to women spectators which centred on 'active' female desire, beyond the bounds of the normative heterosexual male gaze.[22] De Lauretis contended these films only contained 'simple narcissistic identification', not active desire, and could not contribute to 'conceiving another kind of sexuality for women and between women' or establishing 'material, physical [...] lesbian desire'.[23] This dispute reverberated into 1990s reassessments of the lesbian gaze through spectatorship and fashion. De Lauretis seemed to imply, Evans and Gamman wrote, 'that Stacey ha[d] "desexualised" the lesbian spectator, and [...] made the case for female narcissism, rather than erotic contemplation of women by women'.[24] They weighed this critique against Stacey's suggestion that, psychoanalytically, 'all forms of looking are [already] sexually charged'.[25]

Stacey rather than De Lauretis, I suggest, offered a gaze theory that left more space to accommodate the slippage between 'wanting to have' and 'wanting to be (or become)' which has confused so many queer experiences of spectatorship. De Lauretis believed heteronormative patriarchal structures prevented dominant cultural representations depicting 'women desiring women' sexually: instead, such desires were forced into unsatisfying ersatz forms, including 'the desire of one woman to be like, or to be, another, with positive or negative connotations of narcissistic and role-model identification [...] or rivalry'.[26] The structures De Lauretis opposed did, and do, constrain queer women from expressing desire and seeing women like themselves represented in terms they recognize. And yet her argument assumed the boundary between desire-as-identification-and-aspiration and desire-as-attraction had to be impassable. But these very desires blur, breaching that boundary, in questions like 'Do you want to look like her or be with her?' – the kind of strapline that the queer women's website Autostraddle imagined, in a 2017 feature, would characterize a world where 'women's magazine covers were aimed at queer women'.[27] That question has long been a lesbian and queer cliché – and theorizing this duality of identification *and* desire helped Evans, Gamman, Lewis and Rolley explain the place of spectatorship and fashion in 'the' lesbian gaze.

Even these significant texts, however, reveal important silences today. These were, tacitly, texts about queering white women's gazes, sometimes briefly considering the racialized politics of exoticism.[28] More structural considerations of how race intersected with gender in women spectators' subject positions were left to black feminists like bell hooks and Z. Isiling Nataf until E. Ann Kaplan's study of the 'imperial gaze' in film.[29] The 1990s texts' queerness was explicitly gay and lesbian rather than bisexual and dwelled on transvestism as Mulveyan metaphor more than embodied trans experience;[30] they did not explain how far lesbian media and subcultural competences included or excluded bisexual and trans women, nor posit lesbians who did not desire sex.[31]

Moreover, even though Jack Halberstam was about to name 'female masculinities' as a distinct set of gender presentations,[32] the 1990s texts reflected remarkably little of many queer women's everyday identifications with masculinities or their desires to embody those in ways that might sometimes be legibly queer or sometimes deniable as such. Shannon Keating, editor of Buzzfeed LGBT, was certainly not alone in retrospectively realizing she was 'not the only lesbian who'd once had a serious thing for Jack Dawson', Leonardo DiCaprio's floppy-haired character in *Titanic* (1997);[33] neither was I. Such everyday points of identification with masculinities – and with androgynously styled women who appeared legible as embodying them – were widely circulating through mainstream popular culture in the 1990s. They reached a much broader audience, especially among young people, than the avant-garde subcultural settings where the literature has given queer women's identifications with masculinities greater presence.

When men embody these styles and embodied performances, heteronormativity would expect women to regard them through a gaze structured by heterosexual desire. But this is not the only gaze women can turn on embodied and fashioned masculinities: such performances of masculinity are also potential points of identification for women who do not romantically or sexually desire men and indeed some who do. While the 1990s literature wrote solely of the 'lesbian' gaze, some (though not all) bisexual women consider that they have shared some spectatorial experiences and cultural reference points in common with 'lesbian' culture, while being attracted to stars and characters of other genders too. The uncertainty of identification and desire in bisexual women's spectatorship often stems from believing that identifying with stars of a certain gender means you cannot also be attracted to them and that you must choose between a straight or lesbian orientation, even when your own spectatorial experiences tell you that neither of those would be correct.

From this platform, therefore, this chapter rethinks the queer female gaze. Its theoretical starting point is that, as Stacey argued, the affects of identification can extend beyond the moment of spectatorship into extra-cinematic practices of self-fashioning where identifications and resemblances can be offered up for recognition (or, sometimes, pleasurably half-concealed). Within this continuum of spectatorship and fashion, everyday and mainstream expressions of masculinity are among the objects of many queer women's entanglements of identification and desire: indeed, 1990s fashion cultures made them particularly available to women just when film and fashion scholars were reconceptualizing the 'lesbian' gaze.

Masculinities and the queer female gaze in the 1990s

The mid-1990s literature which, I suggest, reframed the cycle of spectatorship, identification, fashion and desire in the female gaze glimpsed, but often lost sight of, the potential for masculinities to become imaginative resources in this cycle for queer women.[34] Stacey, for instance, had written that some of *Star Gazing*'s participants 'did mention male stars, and others wrote of their frustration at not being asked about male stars', suggesting that, in narrating their subjectivity, they had also wanted to speak of watching men.[35] Lewis, exploring lesbian gazes towards several photographic genres, including avant-garde art, advertising and fashion, showed that 'butch' and androgynous aesthetics (often reworking certain culturally constructed masculine archetypes) were signs that enabled lesbian readers to 'recognize a (recently constructed) narrative of the lesbian past along with popular looks from the lesbian present'.[36] The 'genderfuck' performance and photography that inspired and sometimes involved queer theorists like Halberstam was close to the conceptual centre of queer revisitations of the gaze, even though it was on the social margins outside academia and queer scenes.

Such avant-garde artists were interested in entanglements of identification and desire towards masculinities as felt by people who had not been raised as men. Often, these were entanglements they experienced themselves. Halberstam's examples included a 1995 show by the performance artist Peggy Shaw ('You're Just Like My Father'), 'reworking and improving' her family's masculinities into one which was 'part and parcel of her lesbianism', and Catherine Opie's 1991 photo-series 'Being and Having', a name directly evoking the constitutive queer elision of wanting to be the other (or to become like them) and wanting to sexually or romantically 'have' them.[37] Evans and Gamman's chapter ended with three 1992 images by the photographer now called Del LaGrace Volcano, showing a buzz-cut androgynous model ('Jack', 'Jackie' or 'Jax') topless in military and naval uniform.[38]

These photographs illustrated the chapter's argument that queer representations were those which 'disturb[ed] stable definitions' of gendered identity and caused Butlerian 'gender trouble'.[39] From the back, Jax's clothes, hair and musculature signalled a young man, embodying militarized masculinities that were easily legible as an object of gay male desire; from the front, the breasts Jax revealed in removing a khaki T-shirt showed the model's body would be read as 'actually' female through a cisnormative lens. The ambiguity of genderfuck, Evans and Gamman argued, exemplified the subjectivity of spectatorship and the fluidity of identifications with and across gender that queer (and non-queer) spectators might make.[40] These subcultural reworkings of masculinities were key reference points in revisiting the queer gaze.

And yet, focusing only on the avant-garde (despite its significance to subcultural insiders and many cultural producers) ignores the mainstream popular culture most spectators experience most of the time.[41] These spectators include those who do not yet understand queerness as a collective identity or wish to take it on, even if already exercising a gaze they may later recognize as queer. Queer geographers and historians also emphasize wider circles of queer experiences and behaviours that exist beyond the metropolitan centres of avant-garde queer art, literature, theory and sociability.[42] Numerically speaking, far fewer queer women's identificatory and desiring gazes fell on Volcano's or Opie's photographic subjects than on Britpop's androgynous celebrities or the young DiCaprio. Moreover, queer spectators newly realizing – or resisting – their positions as queer spectators would encounter mainstream points of identification and modes of embodiment before avant-garde ones. Here, my own situated knowledge as a queer spectator in the mid-1990s starts interweaving with the very literature that would later help me understand it.

Fashion and the homoerotics of resemblance: A connection is (almost) made

In the contradictory mid-1990s, when my own queer subjectivity formed, 'lesbianism' was a culturally visible phenomenon, the frequently queer signifier of androgyny was in fashion and mainstream popular culture expressed repeated cultural anxieties over the queer female gaze. The notion that queer women could even have shared experiences of spectatorship, or that an academic discipline was theorizing these, was beyond my everyday experience. Although my middle-class, intellectual parents supported what they would probably have called 'gay rights', the all-girls' private school I attended on a government-funded Assisted Place had an organizational culture I experienced as institutionally homophobic, exacerbated by the state homophobia of 'Section 28' (in force 1988–2003 in England and Wales) precluding staff discussing homosexuality. ('School', Walker writes of lesbian narratives, 'both allows and contains the possibility of lesbianism': mine certainly did both.)[43] As far as I knew, women's practices of looking and women's practices of fashion should not have had anything to do with women's desire for women, even though I found them commingled. Simultaneously, Reina Lewis was understanding the dynamics of lesbians looking at magazines' fashion photographs as 'a mode of narcissistic identification with the beautiful woman in the image which [...] produces a desire both to be and to have the displayed woman': such identification was a fantasy of being like her, having her and being gazed *at*.[44] I would have got into, and caused, far less trouble, if my own experiences of (gender)queer identification, spectatorship and desire had been so legible to me as queer.

Two modes of desire between women did reach me. One was the heavily sexualized early 1990s version of butch–femme exemplified by Cindy Crawford and k.d. lang's 1993 *Vanity Fair* cover, echoed elsewhere in fashion and advertising.[45] I knew I didn't want style to code me as 'feminine', and I was fascinated by women who looked the same as me (or, rather, like I might want to), not women who embodied more femininity than me. If lesbian desire could only be a butch–femme dyad with women either occupying one embodied and desiring position or the other, I *couldn't* be a lesbian (I believed), even though I was starting to be called one. Demonstrably 'butch' lesbian subcultural styles visible in mainstream media did not appeal to me either, because they were less 'fashionable' than I aspired to be.[46] The only other script available to me for understanding a homoerotics of resemblance, rather than difference, was the idea that one woman wanting to look like another signified dangerous obsession, which had recently been revived in popular consciousness by the 1992 thriller *Single White Female*. The film's antagonist is driven first to assume her flatmate's appearance, then try to kill her, through an obsessional gaze of desiring to resemble and replace another woman for whom she implicitly experiences repressed desire. This was 'the double movement of a lesbian visual pleasure wherein the viewer wants both to be and to *have* the object'[47] turned against itself: put two homoerotically doubled women on screen, I understood, and sooner or later someone must end up with a stiletto in the eye.

This mode of emplotting what Olu Jenzen calls 'the trope of lesbian *Doppelgangers*' – with mainstream cinema dooming one or both to literal or symbolic death – pathologizes 'dissident sexuality', positioning homosexuality as antisocial, predatory and deadly.[48] Heteronormative frameworks of desire, we understand, cannot accommodate reciprocal attraction to resemblance. Indeed, since a reciprocal attraction to resemblance undoes heteronormative difference on the level of embodied gender expression, it might be even more unsettling than women's desire towards other women itself. Such a pathologization of the queer female gaze, I would suggest, exemplified the decade's cultural anxiety over lesbians just as mainstream media were making them more visible. If the very question of how attraction between women worked was uncomfortable and threatening to heteronormative society, queer desire based on resemblance not difference was even more so. It is little wonder 1990s magazines rarely sexualized fashion images which harnessed 'the long lesbian tradition of eroticized sameness' as much as images remediating butch–femme.[49]

My formative experiences of queerness, therefore, were intertwined with spectatorship and fashion at a time when 'lesbian' desire and the homoerotics of resemblance were highly charged topics and when fashion's boundaries of gender expression were particularly hard to discern (Suede's Brett Anderson, Blur's Alex James, Pulp's Jarvis Cocker and Elastica's Justine Frischmann all wore the same long fringe and tight polyester shirts).[50] In 1994, I had started wondering why I enjoyed watching Celine Dion on *Top of the Pops* so much (in retrospect, her suits and short hair at the time made her seem styled as the straight k.d. lang, and her early 1990s videos showed her delivering the camera many lingering glances, a queer subtextual convention – I would later realize – in Hollywood film).[51] By 1995–6 I had realized that among my year group at school (where, unusually for Britain, we had no uniform), particularly among the popular and largely upper-middle-class group whose acceptance I wanted, girls often praised classmates' fashionable identity performances by comparing them to certain popular stars (including Justine from Elastica, particularly admired for attending our school) (Figure 10).

By this time, I had also internalized, from teachers and classmates who saw any expression of women's desire for other women as intrusive, that talking about wanting to form deep female friendships was alarming. Through fashion, conversely, I had understood it was acceptable (and not even lesbian) to be interested in how other women looked because one aspired to look like that too: as Lewis and Rolley wrote in 1996,

> From an early age women are encouraged to develop a potentially obsessive concern with their own and other women's appearance. One of the primary socially sanctioned – and indeed quintessentially feminine – mediums through which women develop this skill is the fashion magazine.[52]

Wanting to look like another woman was socially sanctioned, while being attracted to another woman was not – and, indeed, I lived in a household

Figure 10 Justine Frischmann and Elastica (1995). Photo by Mick Hutson/Redferns via Getty Images.

where fashion magazines were so unthreatening my grandmother had written for them, whereas making classmates afraid you were attracted to them would make the school phone home. Finally, with increasing disregard for how others were feeling and increasing willingness to meet other people's worst expectations, I brought what were rightly serious disciplinary consequences on myself at the end of 1997. After several warnings to stop trying to get the attention of a classmate I admired for performing the same look I aspired to more successfully than me, I appeared one October morning with what was readily recognizable as the same centre-parted, long-fringed hairstyle and the same brown TopShop shirt.[53] (I would never have admitted then that her style reminded me of young *male* stars like DiCaprio as well.) (Figure 11).

Feminist insights into the queer female gaze would eventually show me that my ambiguous feelings over whether I was attracted to other women and/or wanted to look like them had been more ordinary than I thought.

Figure 11 Leonardo DiCaprio at the *Romeo and Juliet* Premiere (1996). Photo by Barry King/WireImage via Getty Images.

Stacey's description of 'extra-cinematic' identificatory practices – spectators 'engaging in some kind of practice of transformation of the self to become more like the star they admire, or to involve others in the recognition of their similarity with the star' – was 'normal' enough that even straight women did it (though of course some of the participants who mentioned their husbands could have been bisexual – a position *Star Gazing* did not account for).[54] Lewis's unequivocal naming of 'a lesbian visual pleasure wherein the viewer wants both to be and to *have* the object', meaning that 'lesbian responses [...] may be both objectifying *and* narcissistic (identificatory)', describes precisely the confusion of my own spectatorship when I believed these positions had to be separate.[55] The 1990s, both in fashion and in lesbian identity-making, were a moment when (Lewis writes elsewhere) 'identity [could] no longer be decoded from appearance'.[56] This surely made it even harder to understand whether my spectatorship and fashion practices *were* lesbian competencies: How could I have known whether I was attracted to a star if fashionable straight women wanted to dress like her too? And how was I meant to know what was 'just' fashion and what was lesbian or queer? The 1990s literature elaborating 'the' lesbian gaze unambiguously linked identification and desire – yet oddly skipped over the everyday identifications with, and desires to allusively embody, fashionable masculinities that could also form part of queer women's desiring and self-fashioning gaze.

Everyday identifications with masculinities and the queer female fashioned body

The theorizations of the female gaze reconsidered here made important advances by rejecting rigid oppositions of identification *or* desire. They showed instead that an aspirational desire to fashion the self to express a recognizable identification with the other, and romantic or sexual desire for the other, need not be mutually exclusive. As such, they even rescued the 'tradition of eroticized sameness' from the psychoanalytical stigmatization of narcissism.[57] Stacey's insistence that '[t]he love of the ideal [...] may express a desire to become more like that ideal, but this does not exclude the homoerotic pleasures of a love for that ideal' anticipates Jenzen's call for a 'radical narcissism' that reclaims the trope of the lesbian double from her doomed mainstream fate.[58] This is, at last, a model of female desire where I might belong: yet these revisitings of the lesbian gaze are still primarily concerned with femininities. The ways that some trans and non-binary authors, like CN Lester, describe their identifications with androgynous figures often speak more to me than texts about lesbian femininities, even though these authors have had to reject female gender identities imposed on them at birth and I have not.[59]

While Stacey reinvented the duality of identification and desire in women's spectatorship by investigating women's relationships with 'popular images of femininity', femininities are not the only form of gender expression with which queer women's spectatorship has been concerned:[60] the forming of queer women's subjectivities through spectatorship and fashion can also take in masculinities. Paradoxically, while collecting photographs and home-taped video clips of (reassuringly straight) women stars with short hair and androgynous personas, I consciously avoided collecting images of men who resembled women I was fascinated by, such as DiCaprio, the young David Beckham, or the Verve's Richard Ashcroft circa 'Bittersweet Symphony'. (Many queer British people my age might add Placebo's Brian Molko – but his music probably struck me as too sexual to have anything to do with me.) I had internalized heteronormativity and cisnormativity enough (intersecting with aesthetics of whiteness) to know I should not be experiencing the same gaze towards men as I did towards women, whatever that gaze was. And yet, as Judith Butler and then Halberstam were already theorizing,[61] masculinities are not solely points of identification for men. A hinge for theorizing identification with masculinities into queer female spectatorship, however, exists in the cultural history of masculinities – and especially the work of Graham Dawson, who was applying Melanie Klein's theories of projection and introjection to his own research just when Stacey was applying them to hers.

Dawson's work on twentieth-century British men's and boys' identifications with masculinities points to the broader historical-political context in which individuals' subjectivities form, but also creates an unexpected articulation with feminist gaze theory. Dawson's *Soldier Heroes*, published (like *Star Gazing*) in 1994, addressed narratives of imperial adventure and 'soldier heroes' (like Lawrence of Arabia or comic-book Second World War infantrymen) in British public memory, exploring how these produced white British imperial masculinities through the stories and games young boys identified with – including his 1950s boyhood self.[62] Dawson was interested in how boys and men 'locate[d] themselves imaginatively' within their social worlds, what narratives of masculinity they identified with and what masculine-coded 'tastes and desires' they wished to be recognized as having as a result.[63] Indeed, his notion of aspirational identification was very close to Stacey's when he wrote that '[m]en may wish and strive to become the man they would like to imagine themselves to be'.[64] Importantly for understanding how militarism and imperialism have permeated everyday life, one 'hegemonic form of masculinity' that dominant cultural representations train men to identify with has been, since at least the 1850s, the 'soldier hero'.[65]

Using Klein, Dawson delves deeper into the affective dimensions of identification than Stacey, describing identity formation as a cycle where the self internalizes aspects of idealized fantasy figures ('imagos') into how it wants to be perceived in the social world.[66] He expands on Klein, however, by exploring how cultural representations are 're-introjected' *into* the self's internal world, to be brought back out into the external world through practices of dress.[67] For him, these had included the cowboy hats he wore in childhood family photographs and the check shirt he had come to like after his mother told him cowboys wore them (indeed, he realized while writing, he still often wore them as an adult).[68] Another cycle of spectatorship, identification, fashion and desire, Dawson argued, led to men and boys internalizing military and imperial masculinities into their own lived identities simultaneously with imperial whiteness. Within this cycle – from reading comics and watching films, through solo imaginative play, to social recognition through costume – '"who I can imagine myself to be" becomes inseparable from "who they will recognise me as"'.[69] The same affective dynamics thus seem to explain men's identifications with military masculinities and women's identifications with Hollywood stars.

Except, of course, men need not just identify with masculinities and women need not just identify with femininities. And some spectators are neither women nor men at all. Some scholarship does already explore how people who are *not* men engage in imagination, identification and fantasy towards hegemonic masculinities like the soldier hero, especially in traditionally masculine institutions like the military itself.[70] Queer women, and other people whom society has assigned a 'female' body but who sense that they do not match what heteronormativity and cisnormativity expects that body to look like and do, can find these identifications particularly fascinating. Studies in the 1990s did indeed often discuss cross-gender identifications with masculinity and performances of masculinity in BDSM and leather subculture: Anna Marie Smith, for instance, wrote about lesbians 'going beyond tentative appropriations from gay male culture to take up explicitly gay male-identified positions' in *A Queer Romance*.[71] Some people whose identity or art was named 'lesbian' in these texts would later disaffiliate from female names and pronouns, while others continued to understand themselves within the category of 'woman'.[72] When Stacey mentions some women in her research also wished she had asked about male stars, my own situated knowledge wonders 'What was it they wanted to tell you?' Perhaps their stories about spectatorship, identity or fashion had not fitted into her questionnaire.

For queer spectators even more than others, watching film, TV and music videos and seeing fashion images are frequently a search for ways in which they (we) might belong: they seek scripts that could make their desired embodied and fashioned performances socially intelligible or 'legible' and learn how society might view the desires they express or name.[73] Indeed, such spectatorial experiences are frequently among the ways that queer people later realize they have shared experiences (the ingredients of shared identities) with others. Understanding identifications with masculinities within the queer female gaze does not mean reviving early gaze theory's totalizing assumption that cinema only offered women the spectatorial subject positions of heterosexual men. Rather, it allows gaze theory to explore identifications with masculinities and masculine style that women have made in understanding how they want to look, to be recognized by others and to fashion their embodied selves. Contemporary digital culture has, indeed, made such identifications more recognizable as shared queer experiences.

Queer women's digital culture, spectatorship and community

For intertwined social, political and technological reasons, contemporary digital culture has altered the conditions in which spectators form and express identifications and interpret their desires. The implications of such changes for queer subjectivities are part of the uneven distribution of risk with which queer subjects negotiate legibility and illegibility through dress.[74] A teenager who was queer today in broadly the same ways as me, with safe enough internet access, would be forming their subjectivity in different circumstances (which LGBTQ-phobic governments tightening control over digital and educational spaces could nevertheless force 'back'). Firstly, they would have access to more representations that implicitly and fundamentally validate queer identities, not just representations framing them as social problems. Secondly, queer online media would be letting them find out about and join a participatory culture of intersectional queer media critique.[75] They might thus learn much more easily about ideas of 'the gaze' and access or produce sophisticated criticism about how queer people form subjectivities through identifying with stars, characters and images, much more readily than most young people embedded in 1990s media cultures (despite a few participating in queer and fandom-related spaces via 1990s web technology). Indeed, digital media and user-generated content has afforded queer and especially trans youth access to knowledge, resources and community (often including the very ideas of *being* trans, non-binary or genderqueer) beyond anything their 1990s counterparts encountered.[76]

The queer women's website Autostraddle (covering popular culture, fashion, relationships and other topics common to women's lifestyle magazines) is one such space, where writers discursively create community by referring to everyday and spectatorial experiences they imply their readers share – exemplifying 'the discursive construction of a shared lesbian identity' through language.[77] As an Autostraddle reader now older than four-fifths of its audience (in its 2016 reader survey[78]), I am regularly struck by how casually its articles refer to experiences that once caused me deep, irreconcilable confusion – not least the 'Fashion Identity Crisis: Do You Want to Look Like Her or Be with Her?' question posed by its imaginary queer women's magazine covers in 2017.[79] Autostraddle readers are permitted to understand that the answer is just as likely to be 'both', just as Lewis's references to lesbian culture's 'tradition of eroticized sameness' let readers recognize their own desires.[80] In the 1990s, I had understood such blurring of identification and desire as meaning I was not even what society thought of as a lesbian. Here, instead, the ambiguity figures as a trope through which lesbians and other queer women might recognize themselves, producing community as readers take up the invitation to identify with what the article describes. The same Autostraddle author, several weeks later, offered readers her light-hearted 'Weird But Legal Fashion Idea: Copy Outfits Leonardo DiCaprio Wore in the 90s':

> We're working on solid ground. Decade-hopping to rip styles is straight out of the Professional Fashion Editor handbook. Recycled trends aren't coincidences! [...] Dressing as Leonardo DiCaprio is a meta gay experience. Who was many a baby queer's crush if not Leo f'in DiCaprio, his assessable, pretty face speaking to hidden sensibilities?[81]

Eleven of the fifty-one comments are from users remembering times when they had worn clothes or haircuts that looked like his or remarking that they were wearing them that day. (I might have commented that in 1997 I had had the same haircut much less successfully, occasionally wore one picture's flexicomb headband and was now wondering if these photographs had inspired TopShop to sell a brown polyester shirt.) The same casual acknowledgement that many queer women form their identifications with style through men's as well as women's fashion inspired Autostraddle's editor to riff on the masculine-of-centre lesbian comedian Cameron Esposito's tweet that 'they finally made Kens that look like my ex-girlfriends!!' and produce a list of '75 lesbian Ken dolls, ranked by lesbianism'.[82] The illustrated list invited readers to view each doll's outfit and hair through subcultural competences of reading how they would appear on a queer woman's body, guided by comments from an Autostraddle writers' discussion ('She looks like somebody Jenny Schecter [from the 2004–9 US lesbian drama *The L Word*] would have dated for an episode or two'; 'I'd date her'; 'i probably wore this exact thing in high school tbh'). So many readers 'recognized our exes, our current partners, and our selves in these dolls' ('We laughed, we grimaced, we tagged our friends who most reminded us of Lesbian Ken #18') that a follow-up gallery of readers' photographs two weeks later collected 'more than 150 photos of queers dressed as Ken (and a few Barbies!)'.[83] While more serious Autostraddle sections would problematize over-identifying queer women's identities with any one mode of style, these light-hearted commentaries still suggest that online vernacular (self-conscious) understandings of 'lesbian style' have outstripped gaze theory in disentangling gender expression from gender identity and in recognizing masculinities as ingredients of queer women's self-fashioning.

Conclusion

This chapter's situated account of forming a queer subjectivity through spectatorship and fashion reflects two then-confusing aspects of that subjectivity that prevented me recognizing myself in mainstream representations of 'lesbianism' in the 1990s, but which gaze theory has dealt with in dramatically different ways. The queerness of attraction to resemblance, and the potential for the desire to resemble the other and be loved by the other to coexist in the same gaze, was already emerging in the 1990s through Stacey's and Lewis's work. Stacey's interest in 'forms of otherness between women characters which are not merely reducible to sexual difference, so often seen as the sole producer of desire',[84] might have troubled celebrations of lesbian identity which primarily centred on sexual pleasure and cisgender female bodies. Yet it offers more to models of queer women's identity which (like the subject positions Autostraddle's editors have constructed for their reading community) refuse to be constrained by cisnormativity and which accommodate asexual queer experience by recognizing that desire for the other can be experienced in more than just sexual ways.[85]

Acknowledging queer women's identifications with masculinities and their reworkings of masculine style as part of the queer female gaze towards popular culture and fashion, however, raises issues of feminist politics that gaze theory has scarcely grappled with. Just as feminists researching war can succumb to the tempting fallacy that women are more naturally inclined towards peace, feminist gaze theory has hardly even attempted to theorize women's potential complicity in the identifications with militarism and its embodiments that troubled Dawson. The eroticized 'female' military masculinities (or, rather, military masculinities embodied by non-cis-male bodies) that Volcano projected into the 'Jax' series nevertheless hint at an affective politics of queer women's identifications with masculinities that scholars have traced more thoroughly in avant-garde queer art than in the everyday domains where more queer lives have been lived.[86] Rethinkings of feminist gaze theory have already explained the commingling of desire to resemble the other and attraction to the other that queer women have often recognized as a shared experience. But until now they have made much less of identifications with fashioned, popular-cultural and archetypal masculinities in understanding the queer female gaze.

Notes

1. This paragraph uses 'lesbian and queer' here to avoid foreclosing potentially overlapping bisexual or genderqueer spectatorial experiences. The chapter refers to 'lesbian' theorists and communities where they use this label and 'queer women' when describing spectatorial/identificatory experiences bisexual women might share. It does not make collective claims about non-binary people's or trans men's spectatorship.
2. Caroline Evans and Lorraine Gamman, 'The Gaze Revisited, or Reviewing Queer Viewing', in P. Burston and C. Richardson (eds), *A Queer Romance: Lesbians, Gay Men and Popular Culture* (London: Routledge, 1995), pp. 13–56, 47.
3. Reina Lewis and Katrina Rolley, 'Ad(dressing) the Dyke: Lesbian Looks and Lesbians Looking', in P. Horne and R. Lewis (eds), *Outlooks: Lesbian and Gay Sexualities and Visual Cultures* (London: Routledge, 1996), pp. 178–90.

4. Reina Lewis, 'Looking Good: The Lesbian Gaze and Fashion Imagery', *Feminist Review* 55 (1997), pp. 92–109.
5. Ann M. Ciasullo, 'Making Her (in)visible: Cultural Representations of Lesbianism and the Lesbian Body in the 1990s', *Feminist Studies* 27/3 (2001), pp. 577–608, 582.
6. Evans and Gamman, 'Gaze', pp. 35–6.
7. Lewis and Rolley, 'Ad(dressing)', p. 189.
8. Jackie Stacey, 'Desperately Seeking Difference', *Screen* 28/1 (1987), pp. 48–61.
9. Jackie Stacey, *Star Gazing: Hollywood Cinema and Female Spectatorship* (London: Routledge, 1994).
10. Ibid., p. 29 (emphasis in original).
11. See Laura Mulvey, 'Visual Pleasure and Narrative Cinema', *Screen* 16/3 (1975), pp. 6–18.
12. Diana Fuss, 'Fashion and the Homospectatorial Look', *Critical Inquiry* 18/4 (1992), pp. 713–37, p. 722.
13. Ibid., p. 713.
14. Stacey, *Star Gazing*, pp. 228–9.
15. Ibid., p. 229.
16. Ibid., p. 230, quoting Juliet Mitchell (ed), *The Selected Works of Melanie Klein* (Harmondsworth: Penguin, 1986), p. 20.
17. Ibid., pp. 206–7.
18. Ibid., p. 159. This felt, I thought when first reading this phrase, like the sort of word my headmistress might have put in a letter home, telling me to stop being fascinated by wanting to look like other women.
19. Joanne Entwistle, *The Fashioned Body: Fashion, Dress and Modern Social Theory*, 2nd edn (Cambridge: Polity, 2015), p. 10.
20. Lisa Walker, *Looking Like What You Are: Sexual Style, Race, and Lesbian Identity* (New York: NYU Press, 2001).
21. See Karen Hollinger, 'Theorizing Mainstream Female Spectatorship: The Case of the Popular Lesbian Film', *Cinema Journal* 37/2 (1998), pp. 3–17.
22. Stacey, 'Difference', p. 53. *All About Eve*, like *Single White Female* (1992), sublimates a potentially homoerotic female gaze (aspiring to resemble an object of desire) into an obsessional gaze motivated by desire to eliminate and replace the other.
23. Teresa de Lauretis, 'Film and the Visible', in Bad Object-Choices (ed), *How Do I Look?: Queer Film and Video* (Seattle, WA: Bay Press, 1991), pp. 223–63, pp. 259, 262.
24. Evans and Gamman, 'Gaze', p. 34.
25. Ibid., p. 34.

26. De Lauretis, 'Film', p. 229.
27. Erin, 'If Women's Magazine Covers Were Aimed at Queer Women, pt. 3', *Autostraddle*, 3 March 2017. Available at https://www.autostraddle.com/if-womens-magazine-covers-were-aimed-at-queer-women-pt-3-369912/ (accessed 9 December 2018). The US-based Autostraddle, founded in 2009, has become the largest online lifestyle website created for and by queer women: 'What Is Autostraddle?', *Autostraddle*, n.d. Available at https://www.autostraddle.com/about/ (accessed 9 December 2018).
28. Lewis and Rolley, 'Ad(dressing)', p. 185.
29. bell hooks, *Black Looks: Race and Representation* (Boston, MA: South End Press, 1992), pp. 115–32; Z. Isiling Nataf, 'Black Lesbian Spectatorship and Pleasure in Popular Cinema', in P. Burston and C. Richardson (eds), *A Queer Romance*, (Routledge: London, 1995), pp. 57–80; E. Ann Kaplan, *Looking for the Other: Feminism, Film and the Imperial Gaze* (London: Routledge, 1997). Later publications cited these, e.g. Lewis and Rolley, 'Ad(dressing)', p. 183.
30. See, for example, Cherry Smyth, 'The Transgressive Sexual Subject', in Burston and Richardson (eds), *A Queer Romance*, (Routledge: London, 1995), pp. 123–43, p. 126; contrast Nataf, 'Spectatorship', p. 60.
31. The nearest thing was about to be Halberstam's theorization of the 'stone butch': Judith Halberstam, *Female Masculinity* (Durham, NC: Duke University Press, 1998), pp. 118–28.
32. Ibid., p. 14.
33. Shannon Keating, 'How Jack from "Titanic" Launched a Thousand Lesbian Awakenings', *Buzzfeed LGBT* (19 December 2017). Available at https://www.buzzfeed.com/shannonkeating/leo-and-the-lesbians (accessed 9 December 2018).
34. I follow Raewyn Connell (*Masculinities*, 2nd edn (Cambridge: Polity, 2005)) in understanding 'masculinities' as different socially recognized types of masculinity.
35. Stacey, *Star Gazing*, p. 16.
36. Lewis and Rolley, 'Ad(dressing)', p. 188.
37. Opie's subjects, short-haired, masculine-presenting models from 'dyke, transgender and S-M communities', wore the handlebar moustaches of contemporaneous gay masculine style: Halberstam, *Female Masculinity*, pp. 31–3.
38. Evans and Gamman, 'Gaze', pp. 41–5.
39. Ibid., p. 46.
40. Ibid., p. 49.
41. Hollinger, 'Theorizing', p. 6.
42. See Gavin Brown, 'Homonormativity: A Metropolitan Concept That Denigrates "Ordinary" Gay Lives', *Journal of Homosexuality* 59/7 (2012), pp. 1065–72, p. 1068.

43. Walker, *Looking*, p. 146.
44. Lewis, 'Looking', pp. 94–5.
45. See Joyce D. Hammond, 'Making a Spectacle of Herself: Lesbian Visibility and k.d. lang on Vanity Fair's Cover', *Journal of Lesbian Studies* 1/3–4 (1997), pp. 1–35; on theorizing butch–femme in the late 1980s, see Sue-Ellen Case, 'Towards a Butch–Femme Aesthetic', *Discourse* 11/1 (1989), pp. 55–73.
46. On 1990s butch camp and fashionably androgynous lesbian style, see Adam Geczy and Vicki Karaminas, *Queer Style* (London: Bloomsbury Academic, 2013), pp. 37–48.
47. Lewis and Rolley, 'Ad(dressing)', p. 181, emphasis in original.
48. Olu Jenzen, 'Revolting Doubles: Radical Narcissism and the Trope of Lesbian *Doppelgangers*', *Journal of Lesbian Studies* 17/3–4 (2013), pp. 344–64, p. 347.
49. Lewis and Rolley, 'Ad(dressing)', p. 189.
50. As Ruth Holliday noted in 2001, 'the visible distinction between straight and lesbian women was becoming eroded since androgyny had been embraced by mainstream youth culture' (Ruth Holliday, 'Fashioning the Queer Self', in J. Entwistle and E. Wilson (eds), *Body Dressing* (Oxford: Berg, 2001), pp. 215–32. See Wendy Fonarow, *Empire of Dirt: The Aesthetics and Rituals of British Indie Music* (Middletown, CT: Wesleyan University Press, 2006), pp. 206, 214, on the Britpop scene's gendered spectatorship discourses towards Frischmann, able to 'whip the hormones of otherwise heterosexual females into a frenzy' according to music magazines (neither they nor Fonarow considered non-heterosexual female spectators).
51. See Richard Dyer, 'Homosexuality and Film Noir', *Jump Cut* 16 (1977), pp. 18–21.
52. Lewis and Rolley, 'Ad(dressing)', p. 179.
53. Even as unexpected echoes of my own queer experience go in fashion/spectatorship literature, Joanne Entwistle's reference to fashion communicating that '"this winter, brown is the new black" [...] in the winter of 1997' is almost uncomfortably so: Entwistle, *Body*, p. 245.
54. Stacey, *Star Gazing*, p. 159.
55. Lewis and Rolley, 'Ad(dressing)', p. 181.
56. Lewis, 'Looking', pp. 108–9.
57. Lewis and Rolley, 'Ad(dressing)', p. 189.
58. Stacey, *Star Gazing*, p. 175; Jenzen, 'Doubles'.
59. Lester, for instance, writes: 'Joan of Arc was my hero [as a child], and I had an active fantasy life in which I was transformed into a stern and androgynous warrior with elaborate armour, and a white steed' (CN Lester, *Trans Like Me: A Journey for All of Us* (London: Virago, 2017), p. 85) – my gender identity differs from theirs, but we overlap here. Experiencing a gaze similar to mine would also

be even more confusing for trans lesbians whose desired gender expression as women runs masculine-of-centre, who need to disentangle their gaze as trans women from what cisnormative society expects would be their gaze as men: see Hannah Rossiter, 'She's Always a Woman: Butch Lesbian Trans Women in the Lesbian Community', *Journal of Lesbian Studies* 20/1 (2016), pp. 87–96.

60. Stacey, *Star Gazing*, p. 209.
61. Judith Butler, *Gender Trouble: Feminism and the Subversion of Identity* (London: Routledge, 1990); Halberstam, *Female Masculinity*.
62. Graham Dawson, *Soldier Heroes: British Adventure, Empire and the Imagining of Masculinities* (London: Routledge, 1994).
63. Ibid., p. 22.
64. Ibid., p. 23.
65. Ibid., p. 24.
66. Ibid., p. 33.
67. Ibid., p. 47.
68. Ibid., pp. 260, 263.
69. Ibid., p. 261.
70. See Nina Rones and Kari Fasting, 'Theorizing Military Masculinities and National Identities: The Norwegian Experience', in R. Woodward and C. Duncanson (eds), *The Palgrave International Handbook of Gender and the Military* (London: Palgrave Macmillan, 2017), pp. 145–62, p. 150.
71. Anna Marie Smith, '"By Women, for Women and about Women" Rules OK?: The Impossibility of Visual Soliloquy', in P. Burston and C. Richardson (eds), *A Queer Romance*, (Routledge: London, 1995), pp. 199–215, 212.
72. See C. Jacob Hale, 'Leatherdyke Boys and Their Daddies: How to Have Sex without Women or Men', *Social Text* 52–53 (1997), pp. 223–36; Gayle Rubin, 'Of Catamites and Kings', in S. Stryker and S. Whittle (eds), *The Transgender Studies Reader* (Durham, NC: Duke University Press, 2006), pp. 471–81.
73. Lewis's later work on Muslim women's fashion uses social 'legibility' directly: Reina Lewis, 'Veils and Sales: Muslims and the Spaces of Postcolonial Fashion Retail', *Fashion Theory* 11/4 (2007), pp. 423–41, p. 425. See Walker, *Looking*.
74. Shaun Cole and Reina Lewis, 'Introduction: Seeing, Recording and Discussing LGBTQ Fashion and Style', *Fashion, Style and Popular Culture* 3/2 (2016), pp. 149–56, p. 153.
75. See Alexander Cho, 'Default Publicness: Queer Youth of Color, Social Media, and Being Outed by the Machine', *New Media and Society* 20/9 (2018), pp. 3183–200.
76. Lauren B. McInroy and Shelley L. Craig, 'Transgender Representation in Offline and Online Media: LGBTQ Youth Perspectives', *Journal of Human Behavior in the Social Environment* 25/6 (2015), pp. 606–17, p. 613.

77. See Lucy Jones, 'Lesbian Identity Construction', in K. Hall and R. Barrett (eds), *The Oxford Handbook of Language and Sexuality* (Oxford: Oxford University Press, in press).
78. Riese, 'This Is You: Some Things the 2016 Autostraddle Survey Told Us about You', *Autostraddle*, 10 July 2017. Available at https://www.autostraddle.com/welp-here-you-are-some-things-the-2016-autostraddle-survey-told-us-about-you-383173/ (accessed 9 December 2018).
79. Erin, 'Covers'.
80. Lewis and Rolley, 'Ad(dressing)', p. 189.
81. Erin, 'Weird But Legal Fashion Idea: Copy Outfits Leonardo DiCaprio Wore in the 1990s', *Autostraddle*, 29 March 2017. Available at https://www.autostraddle.com/weird-but-legal-fashion-idea-copy-outfits-leonardo-dicaprio-wore-in-the-90s-374323/ (accessed 9 December 2018).
82. Cameron Esposito, 'They Finally Made Kens That Look Like My Ex-girlfriends!!', Twitter, 20 June 2017. Available at https://twitter.com/cameronesposito/status/877172393034137600 (accessed 23 April 2018); Riese, '75 Lesbian Ken Dolls, Ranked by Lesbianism', *Autostraddle*, 21 June 2017. Available at https://www.autostraddle.com/75-ken-dolls-ranked-by-lesbianism-383518/ (accessed 9 December 2018).
83. Vanessa, 'Your "Lesbian Ken" Community Photo Gallery Is Here', *Autostraddle*, 6 July 2017. Available at https://www.autostraddle.com/autostraddles-lesbian-ken-community-photo-gallery-384500/ (accessed 9 December 2018).
84. Stacey, 'Difference', p. 53.
85. See Ela Przybylo and Danielle Cooper, 'Asexual Resonances: Tracing a Queerly Asexual Archive', *GLQ* 20/3 (2014), pp. 297–318.
86. See Judith Halberstam, *In a Queer Time and Place: Transgender Bodies, Subcultural Lives* (Durham, NC: Duke University Press, 2011).

Bibliography

Brown, Gavin, 'Homonormativity: A Metropolitan Concept That Denigrates "Ordinary" Gay Lives', *Journal of Homosexuality* 59/7 (2012), pp. 1065–72.

Butler, Judith, *Gender Trouble: Feminism and the Subversion of Identity* (London: Routledge, 1990).

Case, Sue-Ellen, 'Towards a Butch–Femme Aesthetic', *Discourse* 11/1 (1989), pp. 55–73.

Cho, Alexander, 'Default Publicness: Queer Youth of Color, Social Media, and Being Outed by the Machine', *New Media and Society* 20/9 (2018), pp. 3183–200.

Ciasullo, Ann M., 'Making Her (in)visible: Cultural Representations of Lesbianism and the Lesbian Body in the 1990s', *Feminist Studies* 27/3 (2001), pp. 577–608.

Cole, Shaun, and Reina Lewis, 'Introduction: Seeing, Recording and Discussing LGBTQ Fashion and Style', *Fashion, Style and Popular Culture* 3/2 (2016), pp. 149–56.

Connell, Raewyn, *Masculinities*, 2nd edn (Cambridge: Polity, 2005).

Dawson, Graham, *Soldier Heroes: British Adventure, Empire and the Imagining of Masculinities* (London: Routledge, 1994).

De Lauretis, Teresa, 'Film and the Visible', in Bad Object-Choices (ed), *How Do I Look?: Queer Film and Video* (Seattle, WA: Bay Press, 1991), pp. 223–63.

Dyer, Richard, 'Homosexuality and Film Noir', *Jump Cut* 16 (1977), pp. 18–21.

Entwistle, Joanne, *The Fashioned Body: Fashion, Dress and Modern Social Theory*, 2nd edn (Cambridge: Polity, 2015).

Erin, 'If Women's Magazine Covers Were Aimed at Queer Women, pt. 3', *Autostraddle*, 3 March 2017. Available at https://www.autostraddle.com/if-womens-magazine-covers-were-aimed-at-queer-women-pt-3-369912/ (accessed 9 December 2018).

Erin, 'Weird But Legal Fashion Idea: Copy Outfits Leonardo DiCaprio Wore in the 1990s', *Autostraddle*, 29 March 2017. Available at https://www.autostraddle.com/weird-but-legal-fashion-idea-copy-outfits-leonardo-dicaprio-wore-in-the-90s-374323/ (accessed 9 December 2018).

Esposito, Cameron, 'They Finally Made Kens That Look Like My Ex-girlfriends!!', Twitter, 20 June 2017. Available at https://twitter.com/cameronesposito/status/877172393034137600 (accessed 9 December 2018).

Evans, Caroline, and Lorraine Gamman, 'The Gaze Revisited, or Reviewing Queer Viewing', in P. Burston and C. Richardson (eds), *A Queer Romance: Lesbians, Gay Men and Popular Culture* (London: Routledge, 1995), pp. 13–56.

Fonarow, Wendy, *Empire of Dirt: The Aesthetics and Rituals of British Indie Music* (Middletown, CT: Wesleyan University Press, 2006).

Fuss, Diana, 'Fashion and the Homospectatorial Look', *Critical Inquiry* 18/4 (1992), pp. 713–37.

Geczy, Adam, and Vicki Karaminas, *Queer Style* (London: Bloomsbury Academic, 2013).

Halberstam, Judith, *Female Masculinity* (Durham, NC: Duke University Press, 1998).

Halberstam, Judith, *In a Queer Time and Place: Transgender Bodies, Subcultural Lives* (Durham, NC: Duke University Press, 2011).

Hale, C. Jacob, 'Leatherdyke Boys and Their Daddies: How to Have Sex without Women or Men', *Social Text* 52–53 (1997), pp. 223–36.

Hammond, Joyce D., 'Making a Spectacle of Herself: Lesbian Visibility and k.d. lang on Vanity Fair's Cover', *Journal of Lesbian Studies* 1/3–4 (1997), pp. 1–35.

Holliday, Ruth, 'Fashioning the Queer Self', in J. Entwistle and E. Wilson (eds), *Body Dressing* (Oxford: Berg, 2001), pp. 215–32.

Hollinger, Karen, 'Theorizing Mainstream Female Spectatorship: The Case of the Popular Lesbian Film', *Cinema Journal* 37/2 (1998), pp. 3–17.

hooks, bell, *Black Looks: Race and Representation* (Boston, MA: South End Press, 1992).

Jenzen, Olu, 'Revolting Doubles: Radical Narcissism and the Trope of Lesbian *Doppelgangers*', *Journal of Lesbian Studies* 17/3–4 (2013), pp. 344–64.
Jones, Lucy, 'Lesbian Identity Construction', in K. Hall and R. Barrett (eds), *The Oxford Handbook of Language and Sexuality* (Oxford: Oxford University Press, in press).
Kaplan, E. Ann, *Looking for the Other: Feminism, Film and the Imperial Gaze* (London: Routledge, 1997).
Keating, Shannon, 'How Jack from "Titanic" Launched a Thousand Lesbian Awakenings', *Buzzfeed LGBT*, 19 December 2017. Available at https://www.buzzfeed.com/shannonkeating/leo-and-the-lesbians (accessed 9 December 2018).
Lester, C. N., *Trans Like Me: A Journey for All of Us* (London: Virago, 2017).
Lewis, Reina, 'Looking Good: The Lesbian Gaze and Fashion Imagery', *Feminist Review* 55 (1997), pp. 92–109.
Lewis, Reina, 'Veils and Sales: Muslims and the Spaces of Postcolonial Fashion Retail', *Fashion Theory* 11/4 (2007), pp. 423–41.
Lewis, Reina, and Katrina Rolley, 'Ad(dressing) the Dyke: Lesbian Looks and Lesbians Looking', in P. Horne and R. Lewis (eds), *Outlooks: Lesbian and Gay Sexualities and Visual Cultures* (London: Routledge, 1996), pp. 178–90.
McInroy, Lauren B., and Shelley L. Craig, 'Transgender Representation in Offline and Online Media: LGBTQ Youth Perspectives', *Journal of Human Behavior in the Social Environment* 25/6 (2015), pp. 606–17.
Mulvey, Laura, 'Visual Pleasure and Narrative Cinema', *Screen* 16/3 (1975), pp. 6–18.
Nataf, Z. Isiling, 'Black Lesbian Spectatorship and Pleasure in Popular Cinema', in P. Burston and C. Richardson (eds), *A Queer Romance: Lesbians, Gay Men and Popular Culture* (London: Routledge, 1995), pp. 57–80.
Przybylo, Ela, and Danielle Cooper, 'Asexual Resonances: Tracing a Queerly Asexual Archive', *GLQ* 20/3 (2014), pp. 297–318.
Riese, '75 Lesbian Ken Dolls, Ranked by Lesbianism', *Autostraddle*, 21 June 2017. Available at https://www.autostraddle.com/75-ken-dolls-ranked-by-lesbianism-383518/ (accessed 9 December 2018).
Riese, 'This Is You: Some Things the 2016 Autostraddle Survey Told Us about You', *Autostraddle*, 10 July 2017. Available at https://www.autostraddle.com/welp-here-you-are-some-things-the-2016-autostraddle-survey-told-us-about-you-383173/ (accessed 9 December 2018).
Rones, Nina, and Kari Fasting, 'Theorizing Military Masculinities and National Identities: The Norwegian Experience', in R. Woodward and C. Duncanson (eds), *The Palgrave International Handbook of Gender and the Military* (London: Palgrave Macmillan, 2017), pp. 145–62.
Rossiter, Hannah, 'She's Always a Woman: Butch Lesbian Trans Women in the Lesbian Community', *Journal of Lesbian Studies* 20/1 (2016), pp. 87–96.
Rubin, Gayle, 'Of Catamites and Kings', in S. Stryker and S. Whittle (eds), *The Transgender Studies Reader* (Durham, NC: Duke University Press, 2006), pp. 471–81.

Smith, Anna Marie, '"By Women, for Women and about Women" Rules OK?: The Impossibility of Visual Soliloquy', in P. Burston and C. Richardson (eds), *A Queer Romance: Lesbians, Gay Men and Popular Culture* (London: Routledge, 1995), pp. 199–215.

Smyth, Cherry, 'The Transgressive Sexual Subject', in P. Burston and C. Richardson (eds), *A Queer Romance: Lesbians, Gay Men and Popular Culture* (London: Routledge, 1995), pp. 123–43.

Stacey, Jackie, 'Desperately Seeking Difference', *Screen* 28/1 (1987), pp. 48–61.

Stacey, Jackie, *Star Gazing: Hollywood Cinema and Female Spectatorship* (London: Routledge, 1994).

Vanessa, 'Your "Lesbian Ken" Community Photo Gallery Is Here', *Autostraddle*, 6 July 2017. Available at https://www.autostraddle.com/autostraddles-lesbian-ken-community-photo-gallery-384500/ (accessed 9 December 2018).

Walker, Lisa, *Looking Like What You Are: Sexual Style, Race, and Lesbian Identity* (New York: NYU Press, 2001).

'What Is Autostraddle?', *Autostraddle*, n.d. Available at https://www.autostraddle.com/about/ (accessed 9 December 2018).

CHAPTER 10
KILLER LOOKS: MARLENE MCCARTY'S *MURDER GIRLS*

Rosa Nogués

> *Marlene Olive wrote poetry. She dreamed of being a prostitute or a model. She toyed with the occult and tried to convince her friends that she was a witch. She liked David Bowie, platform shoes, hip hugger jeans, and lots of makeup. Her mother did not. Her mother kept the curtains in their upper middle-class neighborhood house shut tight. Her mother spent a lot of time in bed. Her mother called her a slut. […] Marlene had been a chubby, well protected child brought up in private schools until her parents moved to Marin County. Freed from school uniforms, she found herself to be a young woman that attracted the other sex. She liked that. Her mother didn't. Her new found sexuality yielded power and control. She liked her boyfriend Chuck because he would do anything for her. […] One night her father was out. Her boyfriend snuck into the house. Marlene took a hammer and bashed her mother's head in while she was sleeping.*[1]

Marlene Olive: Fashioning a body image

The quotation is an extract from the text accompanying the large drawing of Marlene Olive ('Marlene Olive – June 21, 1976', 1995–7) by the artist Marlene McCarty. In the drawing, Olive stares directly at the viewer, defiantly and arrogantly, almost contemptuously. She is sitting on the floor with her legs crossed, relaxed, unbothered, with her hands carefully resting on her ankles. Her enigmatic expression is rendered even more ambiguous by the large scale of the drawing – 96 x 60 inches – her face standing well above the viewer's head. We have to step back to see the full portrait and when we do, Marlene Olive is staring right at us, her mouth caught between a smile and a smirk. Even if the accompanying text had not been read, there is a menacing edge to the figure. She appears poised and impassive, calm yet expectant, returning our look in a calculated manner, the precision of McCarty's pencil marks intensifying Olive's calculating glare. She knows that we are looking. She knows that we know. And the monumental scale in which she is presented fills her expression with a contained menace. The defiance of her stare contrasts starkly with the softness of her features, carefully and tenderly rendered by a light, yet precise, pencil mark. Her hair is dark and long, flowing naturally down her body. Her trousers are unbuttoned, letting the darkness of her pubic hair show. The only other dark mark on the drawing are Olive's nipples. Although we see the outline of a shirt, it looks transparent, unable to cover the girl's body. And, as if she knew this, she carefully lays her hands at the precise spot where her genitals are. The gesture implied oscillates between shame and titillation (Figure 12).

Figure 12 Marlene McCarty, *Marlene Olive – June 21, 1976* (1995–7). Courtesy of the artist.

The piece is part of McCarty's series called *Murder Girls*, which she started in the mid-1990s, depicting real-life girls who had committed matricide. Each portrait refers to an actual killing, and the specific details of each are always offered in a matter-of-fact tone, like in the text above. All drawings are rendered in large scale, in pencil and ballpoint pen, setting out a stark tension between the scale and the medium. The blue ink of the ballpoint pen weighs heavily on the viewer's reading of the image. And despite the fact that some, like Olive's, are drawn in pencil only, they all exhibit, in their choice of medium and drawing style, an amateurish, almost juvenile, quality. Were it not for the scale of the works, we could be looking at an adolescent's private drawings, at their high school doodles. McCarty was directly referencing portraits she had made of herself when she was a teenager, which she found when clearing out her things in her parents' house. They were made with 'graphite and terribly tightly rendered, with all the teenage angst of hoping to make it look like a pretty version of me'.[2] The drawing of Marlene Olive echoes this type of adolescent obsessive engagement with one's self-image in another way. It is made up of different images cut out from fashion magazines, evoking the way that teenage girls would superimpose their faces on fashion images or fill the walls of their rooms with these images: 'I remember the collages I hung on my bedroom walls [...]. The very idea of my self was worked out by slicing and dicing and recombining images from Vogue.'[3] McCarty evokes here how the girl's sense of self, her ego, is constructed in relationship to the images of women that surround her; how she fashions her own sense of self by cutting and pasting images from fashion magazines. The girl's idea of femininity takes shape in relation to these fashion images, which, by and large, reproduce the normative character of femininity within the patriarchal regime of sexual difference. McCarty's drawings attest to the role that glossy fashion images, and consumer culture more generally, play in the cultural construction of certain forms of femininity and the shaping of young women's sense of identity and embodiment in relation to them.

This reading clearly echoes the feminist critique of representation that takes shape around Laura Mulvey's important essay, 'Visual Pleasure and Narrative Cinema', at the centre of this publication and constitutes the critical context that informs McCarty's drawing series. In the decade of the 1990s the interpretation of images of women was largely overdetermined by this feminist critique of representation, which, over the two previous decades, had laid bare the function of these images in preserving and reproducing the patriarchal regime of sexual difference within the social and cultural orders. The figure of the castrated woman as the fetishized materialization in visual culture of the subjected position of women in patriarchy, elaborated by Mulvey, provided a means to understand not only the various conscious and unconscious sexually specific meanings being mobilized by the images but also the sexually specific nature of the structure of vision itself, where the woman on screen or in the photograph was forever and inevitably fated to the object position. The central premise of this feminist critique of representation was the fact that cultural practices participate in the construction of sexed subjectivities according to the patriarchal regime of sexual difference, and the critical exercise that it performed consisted in the analysis of the operation and function of representational practices in reproducing the patriarchal order. It was not only the proliferation and ubiquity of images of women, and their function in reproducing a specific form of femininity, that feminist critics were concerned with but also, and more significantly, the specific dynamic of identification and fantasy that constituted sexually specific positions within the visual field.

Mulvey's theory of the 'male gaze', albeit substantially critiqued and revised, provided an important framework within which to engage with and analyse images as well as the sexual structure that determined the conditions of their viewing and their possibilities of meaning. Her argument in 'Visual Pleasure and Narrative Cinema' develops from a particular understanding of Jacques Lacan's theory of the mirror stage, which she extends to the cinema viewer. Similar to the way Lacan theorizes the constitution of the infant's ego in relation to the misrecognition of and identification with the specular image in the mirror stage, Mulvey claims the (male) cinema spectator identifies with the hero on screen. In a similar process, the adolescent girl interiorizes the fashion image as ideal and constructs her femininity around these images, the normative character of which guarantees the reproduction of the patriarchal regime of sexual difference. The significant insight of feminist criticism here is how images of women produce woman as image.

To insist on the representation of the female body, as McCarty does in this series, within this critical context, and from a feminist position, is significant. It is also a fundamental part of any critical engagement with the represented body in the drawings. It is against the backdrop of this feminist critique of representation that McCarty's drawings offer us an alternative mode of engaging with the represented female body. My argument develops from Mulvey's theory and is likewise rooted in Lacanian psychoanalytic theory, yet departs from it significantly: rather than focus on the role that the mirror stage plays in constituting the ego and the subject's imaginary, I will look to the notion of Other *jouissance* and the particular understanding of the body that it proffers.

One significant problem in 'male gaze' theory as it was originally articulated is that it was premised on a disembodied observer as viewing eye, where the 'gaze' originates. Yet, Lacan's psychoanalytic theory not only does not support the positing of such a disembodied observer; on the contrary, it clearly presents and argues for the corporeal dimension of the observer as it is manifested, and summoned, in the visual field itself. The dynamic of vision at the centre of the 'male gaze' theory is thus clearly limited to the act of looking, to the action of the viewing eye, and not that of the gaze, a concept that is clearly misconstrued when it is conflated with the singular viewing position postulated by the 'male gaze' theory. In 'Nervous Theory: The Troubling Gaze of Psychoanalysis in Media Studies', Craig Saper gives a useful, albeit selective, overview of the criticism raised against 'male gaze' theory.[4] According to Saper, it was precisely the conflation of eye and gaze in the theory's appropriation of Lacanian concepts, the misconstrued interpretation and mobilization of Lacan's notion of the gaze, that attracted the bulk of the criticism. As Saper put it, 'The gaze [was] in trouble.'[5] And, as his essay succeeded in demonstrating, the trouble stemmed precisely from the fact that 'the gaze [was] troubling'.[6] For the gaze, in its psychoanalytic specificity, is that which *disrupts* vision. It refers precisely to that which *destabilizes* and collapses viewing positions, problematizing perception itself.[7] And hence, it is easy to see how its appropriation by feminist and film theory on the terms outlined in Mulvey's text was fundamentally problematic.

My main objective here, however, is not to challenge or invalidate 'male gaze' theory for its theoretical inaccuracies. These kinds of exercises have already been amply rehearsed, and Saper's essay offers a good overview of this.[8] For the fact remains that despite its theoretical faults and flaws, 'male gaze' theory constituted and continues to constitute an important paradigm of visuality for feminist theory, as the publication of the present volume attests. The understanding of the function and visual structure of images of women continues to be overdetermined by the notion of an objectifying, fetishizing form of looking. The magnitude and intensity of the criticism that 'male gaze' theory has elicited are no doubt testament to its immense influence and prevalence. In what follows, my argument will lay out how, in engaging with the represented female body, it might prove more fruitful and less limiting to shift the focus away from the notion of the 'male gaze', and its fetishizing and objectifying determinations, and problematize the concept of sex itself. Following Lacanian theory, which provides the stepping stone for Mulvey's theory by establishing the formation of the ego and the subject's imaginary in relationship to the mirror image, I will instead turn my attention to Lacan's later problematization of sex itself with the notion of sexuation. The concept of *jouissance*, as that form of enjoyment tied to the body and to the subject's (phallic) inscription in the symbolic, provides the means to trace an engagement with the female body not as castrated (as in 'male gaze' theory) but as suggestive of an Other *jouissance*. The body then becomes the ultimate radical Other.

Could our relationship to the image, especially in the case of women, be understood not as a form of self-surveyance, self-objectification and fetishization *à la* Berger, or narcissism, but maybe in terms of looking for an assurance in the image? We will see how in the drawing of Marlene Olive, we could interpret her determined and obsessive look in the mirror as a way of seeking a specific assurance in the image, just before her murderous psychotic break is about to occur, when her body is being inundated by *jouissance*. And precisely because this is not a (phallic) *jouissance*, inscribed in the symbolic via castration, which results in a body fragmented into partial drives and erogenous zones, could we not be in the presence of another, an Other, body?

Looking at fashion

For the adolescent girl, who is fashioning and constructing her self-image by cutting and pasting fragments from a variety of fashion images, and identifying with them, the resulting body image is a precariously put together composite of fragments, cut up and fetishized. The 'fashion gaze', responsible for the initial fragmentation and fetishization of the female body, is internalized and the girl's relationship to her own body is mediated by this gaze. John Berger's insight that woman, in surveying herself through the cultural (masculine) lens, or gaze, turns herself into an object of vision – an image – is here still relevant. Despite the fact that, as many critics have rightfully argued, fashion magazine images are predominantly addressed to and directed exclusively to women, thus claiming for these images a 'feminine gaze', it is hard to situate the fashion image outside of the fetishizing and objectifying dynamic of looking that Mulvey's concept of the male gaze encapsulates.

On this point my argument differs from certain readings of the fashion image as capable of resisting and even subverting its patriarchal determinations. The debate is slightly reminiscent of the claim that 'positive images' of women can be found and produced within patriarchal culture, images which somehow escape their inscription within the patriarchal order and which provide 'positive' points of identification for women. The argument against this position, as it was articulated already back in the feminist debates during the 1970s and 1980s, is that it is the representational order itself which is patriarchally determined – the problem is not limited to the 'content' of images, it is to do with the way the image itself produces a specific structure of looking, where the woman is always relegated to the object position – and hence, all representations are inscribed within the patriarchal order.[9] Given the observed fascination of women with the fashion image, a number of feminist scholars have attempted to understand this fascination in terms of empowerment and control rather than of the capture of women's subjectivities within the patriarchal representational order. The inherent difficulty of engaging with images, objects or processes through the lens of psychoanalysis lies in the fact that the latter is concerned with the unconscious. And so, when we point to the significance of representation in the constitution of the subject, given the central role played by the mirror image (in the mirror stage, which is temporal as well as structural), we are not claiming that an active engagement between the infant and their image is taking place. Within the Lacanian narrative this takes place on the level of the unconscious. The argument that the subject is somehow capable of controlling her (unconscious) relationship to certain forms of representation, and resist the fetishizing and objectifying determinations of certain images, is thus difficult to maintain. Any kind of voluntaristic understanding of the subject's psychic process is going to be deeply problematic in terms of psychoanalytic theory.

A different strategy for engaging with the fashion image as resisting its ideological and normative determinations is present in Alison Bancroft's *Fashion and Psychoanalysis: Styling the Self*, which analyses the world of fashion (as a creative practice rather than an industry) in its relationship to the image, femininity, identity and the female body, among other aspects, in terms of psychoanalysis. Bancroft claims that fashion, while not capable of completely undoing the patriarchal system of which it is a fundamental part, can indeed have a disruptive function, 'subvert[ing] from within'.[10] In her reading of the fashion image, she posits that some contemporary fashion photography, such as the work of Nick Knight, in presenting a distorted, non-naturalistic image of the body, replicates the fragmented experience of the body before the mirror stage provides the unified body image for the child to identify with and gain a sense of (a unified) ego. Bancroft places these photographs within the pre-symbolic realm, offering a 'site of resistance to dominant cultural […] models of femininity', and awards them the capacity to contribute to the 'dissolution of the subject'.[11] Bancroft rightfully emphasizes the significance of representation in the Lacanian narrative, yet she seems to then interpret this in voluntaristic terms (' … representations interact with the inquiring psyche'), claiming that this offers grounds to refute Berger's classic critique of representation in patriarchy as producing woman as (passive) object (of the look).[12] However, Berger is discussing the social and political determinations and effects of cultural representations, and his analysis is both valid and accurate as the starting point that it in fact offered and definitely not refuted by the psychoanalytic understanding of representation – quite the contrary, as feminist theory has demonstrated, the fact that representation is key in the constitution of the subject makes the analysis of cultural representations of women both urgent and necessary.

Furthermore, the 'fragmented body' that Bancroft posits at the centre of the mirror stage (that is grounds for her claim that fashion photography, in reproducing this fragmentation, is a 'representation of the processes of subjectivity'[13]) is not a represented body and cannot be understood in terms of representation (I would argue that it is not even a *body* as such – the body itself comes to be as image in the mirror image as ideal (whole/unified), and then again in language, as marked by the Other). The psychoanalytic approach to the body is limited to the way that the analysand's body is marked by the Other, by language and the symbolic order. 'Man is not a body' is Lacan's basic proposition according to Colette Solers, 'man has a body', he is 'given a body' by language.[14] It is precisely in terms of the way that different, isolated parts of the body are invested with signification and take on a specific meaning that psychoanalysis accounts for the subject's body. The paralysis of the hysteric, unexplained pains, the anorexic's refusal are all brought about by the signifier, by language. 'Words are caught up in all the body images that captivate the subject; they may "knock up" the hysteric, be identified with the object of *Penisneid*, represent the urinary flow of urethral ambition, or represent the feces retained in avaricious *jouissance*.'[15] This relation between the subject and the Other, the specific way of bearing the Other's mark, is determined by loss. The subject comes to be, as such, within the field of the Other, upon entering the symbolic order and accessing language. And in doing so, a lack is instituted at the core of the subject by a specific form of loss, that is, castration. This fundamental lack constitutes one of the basic principles of psychoanalysis.

The body, as it is articulated in psychoanalysis, holds a very specific and paradoxical position, markedly distinct from non-psychoanalytic accounts of the body, whether more biologically or more sociologically oriented.[16] The body in psychoanalysis is clearly not the anatomical body/organism of biology, and so the 'fragmentation' that Bancroft posits against the image of wholeness and unity that the mirror image provides is the uncoordinated, uncontrolled, dependent experience of the child, who at this stage lacks the sense of a unified embodied experience. The role of representation – in its interiorized ideal form, an ideal ego – is precisely to disavow this lack of control and coordination, and to provide a sense of unity and wholeness.

In my reading, Berger's and Mulvey's critique is still central. In the images of glossy fashion magazines, the representation of the body of woman is fetishized and spectacularized, and the girl looking at these images interiorizes this objectifying gaze and the relationship to her own body is established at a distance (what Holland et al. have termed a 'disembodied femininity'[17]). Her self-image is constructed in terms of this image world – the world of consumerism – as sexual commodity. In the collage that serves as referent for *Marlene Olive* (Figure 13) this identificatory relation between the young woman and the fashion image as ideal – the specular ideal of Lacan's mirror stage – is laid bare and at work. And yet, as I advanced above, McCarty's portrait suggests a further way of thinking about the representation of the girl's body: not as the fetishized body of the fashion gaze but as the body of *Other jouissance*. Beyond a framework within which to interpret the function of representation in the production of subjectivities under patriarchy, psychoanalytic theory offers a radical problematization of the concept of sex. The Lacanian concept of sexuation is neither the biological category associated with anatomy nor the sociological category to do with gender, but rather articulates the relationship between the speaking subject and her *jouissance*. It offers a conception of sex distinctly divorced from anatomical determinations which can thus offer an interesting, albeit challenging, perspective to feminist theory.

The violence of the look

Going back to the narrative informing Marlene Olive's portrait, it is important to underscore the contrast that is established between the disturbing tale of the girl's murderous and brutal violence towards her mother, and the intimacy of the artist's drawing gesture. The careful and precise lines, the

Figure 13 Marlene McCarty, *Marlene Olive*, Collage (1994–6). Courtesy of the artist.

familiar shade of blue of the BIC ballpoint pen, provide the portrait with an air of familiarity that draws the viewer in. Identifying that particular adolescent stage in their own personal history, the viewer is then confronted with the violence of the girl's killing. The matter-of-fact tone of the written narrative effectively highlights the brutality of the murders, by sparing us no details, and intensifies the viewer's discomfort before the portrait. The ambiguity of the artist's gesture, overlaying these brutal acts with an air of familiarity, again replicates the ambiguity of the girl's expression. This is an ambiguity that reflects a very precise psychic dichotomy. According to Lacan:

> The aggressive drive, which resolves itself in murder, appears to be the affliction that lies at the basis of psychosis. We could call it unconscious, which means that the intentional content that translates it into consciousness cannot manifest itself without a compromise with the social demands internalised by the subject, that is to say, without a camouflage of motives that constitutes precisely the whole delirium.
>
> But this drive is itself imprinted by social relativity: it always has the intentionality of a crime, almost always that of revenge, frequently the sense of punishment, that is to say, a sanction from the social ideals, sometimes, in the end, it identifies with the accomplished act of morality, it has the significance of an expiation (self-punishment).[18]

Although McCarty initially limited her project to girls who had murdered their mothers, soon after she extended it to girls who, alone or with the help of their boyfriends or siblings, had murdered both of their parents, and at times, their whole family. In all of the cases, however, it is the murder of the mother that lies at the heart of the crime. Moreover, it is, according to McCarty, the fraught and complex relationship between mother and daughter that determines the brutality and transgressive nature of the crime: 'The girls were blossoming sexual beings while their mothers could see their own sexuality waning. In all cases there was an extreme (though often unacknowledged) power struggle between the girls and their mothers.'[19] The reasons for the murders vary, but as Lacan points to in the quotation above, they often displayed the features of an act of revenge and punishment on the mother, usually an overbearing, domineering and punishing figure.

The quotation is from Lacan's analysis of the famous crime of the Papin sisters, which took place in 1933, in the French town of Le Mans.[20] Christine and Léa Papin, maids at the Lancelin house, battered Mme. Lancelin and her daughter Geneviève to death, repeatedly cutting their legs and, most significant and disturbing of all, tearing their eyes out while still alive. The sisters were tried for the murder and found guilty. The three psychiatrists called on as witnesses declared the women to be mentally healthy and thus responsible for their actions.[21] One other psychiatrist, called on in their defence, Dr Logre, claimed otherwise and diagnosed the sisters, without having been allowed to personally examine them, as suffering from 'hysterical epilepsy, sexual perversion, and persecution mania'.[22]

Logre's conclusions were based on events both before the crime and after, when the sisters were arrested and imprisoned separately. Some time before the events of February 1933, the sisters had gone to the local authority, the mayor of Le Mans, M. Le Feuvre, alleging that they were being persecuted. The incident, clearly a paranoid symptom, which in the psychoanalytic clinic is indicative of psychosis, is significant in that the sisters appealed to the town's mayor, a surrogate figure of the mother, given the homophony in French between mayor, '*maire*', and mother, '*mère*'.[23] Interestingly, the sisters used to secretly refer to Mme. Lancelin as '*maman*', mom. The sisters' own mother, Clémence, was both domineering and unloving. She was an overbearing figure who had a strong impact on the sisters' upbringing, despite the fact that both of them had lived most of their lives away from her.[24] Christine, the older of the two sisters, spent the early years of her life under the care of her father's sister Isabelle and, after the couple's divorce, during which Clémence claimed that Gustave, her husband, had sexually abused the couple's oldest daughter, Emile, the eldest daughters were housed in an orphanage, while Léa, the youngest, went on to be cared for by her uncle. After the sisters' arrest, during the months prior to the trial, Christine's poor mental health became blatantly obvious. She had several hallucinatory episodes, showed signs of depression, refused to eat, engaged in exhibitionism and on one occasion tried to gouge out her own eyes, after which she was kept in a straitjacket. The sexual nature of the strong connection between the two sisters, which was remarked on by Logre in his conclusions, was made evident when, during the one time when they were reunited, Christine took off her blouse and said to Léa: 'Say yes! Say yes!'[25] During this time, Christine is also reported to have claimed that in another life she had been her sister's husband. Shortly after, however, Christine gave up trying to be imprisoned with her sister and never again mentioned her name.

Lacan's article appeared in the surrealist publication *Le Minotaure* in December 1933, only three months after the trial and conviction of the Papin sisters. It was only in November of 1932 that he had defended his thesis on the case of another psychotic, *Aimée*. Her real name was Marguerite Pantaine, and in April 1931 she was admitted to the Hospital of Saint Anne, where Lacan was undertaking his psychiatric training, after she had attempted to kill a famous Parisian theatre actress with a kitchen knife. Lacan examined her and diagnosed paranoid psychosis, after which he spent the following year treating her, making of her the clinical case at the centre of his doctoral thesis. It is also noteworthy, in terms of his approach to the Papin crime, that only a year before the event, in 1932, he had translated Freud's text on paranoia, 'Some Neurotic Mechanisms in Jealousy, Paranoia and Homosexuality',[26] and started his own analysis with Rudolph Loewenstein. In his patient's diagnosis Lacan said: 'In her victim, Aimée strikes out at her exteriorized ideal', wrote Lacan, the actress representing 'what [she] herself wanted to be'. Could this be exactly what Marlene Olive is doing when she attacks and kills her mother? Could she not be staging an attack against the 'exteriorized ideal' that we see in the collaged image, an ideal constructed not only in relation to the fragmentary fashion images against which her sense of self and embodiment is shaped but also in relation to her mother's enforcement of a particular form of 'proper' celibate femininity?

Psychosis and the mother's *jouissance*

> *Jim Olive, her father, adored her. He ran his own struggling business, but his most important job was peacemaker between Marlene and her mother.*[27]

In Lacanian psychoanalysis, psychosis is characterized by the lack of the paternal function in the subject's psychic structure. As opposed to neurosis, which is the effect of repression, in psychosis the main operation is that of foreclosure, *Verwerfung*. This means that something is not symbolized,[28] something is 'refused', 'expelled'[29] from the symbolic world. In psychosis the Oedipus complex is not complete, something is missing from it,[30] 'the subject refuses access to his symbolic world to something that he has nevertheless experienced, and which in this case is nothing other than the threat of castration'.[31] It is of course in the father's prohibition that this threat is manifested, in the father's *No!*, what Lacan calls the No/Name-of-the-Father[32] which, by effectively mediating between mother and child, provides access to the symbolic order. In psychosis, this paternal function is missing. The Name-of-the-Father is foreclosed from the subject's symbolic dimension, leaving a hole in the symbolic order.[33] With the paternal function missing from the subject's psyche, the mediation between mother and child, which the father function effects as symbolic pact, is not there. This has direct consequences in terms of the subject's capacity to relate to the mother and her *jouissance*. The subject is left unable 'to escape or set a limit to the mother's *jouissance*'.[34]

The few commentaries on McCarty's *Murder Girls* have interpreted the acts committed by the girls in the series as 'pathetic'[35] acts of rebellion, a tragic escalation of 'quite common situations of conflict'.[36] The family dynamics which gave rise to the crimes are understood to be 'average' and common,[37] typical of the process of individualization and socialization that is puberty and the girls as simply being unable to restrain their murderous impulses.[38] These kinds of readings are indicative of the need to imbue the act with a meaning that transcends the crime itself, to understand the act. Likewise, in the case of the Papin sisters, commentators at the time insisted on interpreting the double murder as an effect of class struggle.[39]

But this is not the type of interpretative exercise with which we are concerned here. My claim is that McCarty's piece suggests the possibility of a different kind of engagement with it, not in terms of making sense of the image, of understanding the girl's motives and actions, but rather in terms of the represented body. In psychosis, the body and the specific disturbances that the body undergoes are central. These have to do with a form of *jouissance* that takes over the body. In the Papin crime, the significance of the body is clear. The sisters stripped Geneviève of her clothing, slashed both their mistresses' bodies, left their thighs looking 'like meat being made ready for the oven',[40] hit their heads with a hammer and a pewter jar, and tore out their eyes. Both Christine and Léa had their period at the time of the attack, as well as Geneviève, her menstrual blood 'mingling' with the blood 'gushing' from both her and her mother.[41] When Christine was later asked about having disrobed Geneviève, she said: 'I was looking for something that would make me stronger.'[42]

The Papin crime, and Lacan's interpretation of it as a symptom of psychosis, read in parallel to the *Murder Girls* provides the context from which to engage with the represented bodies in McCarty's drawings. Our interpretative exercise is not centred around making sense of the crimes or diagnosing the real-life murder girls, but is rather linked to the way the construction of their bodies in the portraits reflects the disturbances of the psychotic body, a specific disturbance of *jouissance*.

The body of Other *jouissance*

Marlene Olive's pose in 'Marlene Olive – June 21, 1976' (see Figure 12) is especially significant within McCarty's *Murder Girls* series.[43] She is looking straight ahead, and her body is carefully framed within the surface of the paper in a long upright rectangle, clearly suggestive of a full-body mirror reflection, something which her inquisitive and defiant stare reinforces. In the other portraits of the series, even in the cases when the subjects are looking straight at the viewer, the pose is never so direct and fully contained within the rectangle of the frame. For instance, in *Barbara and Jennaleigh Mullens*, who shot their parents eight times while they were sleeping, the sisters are portrayed as if they had been caught in the middle of a playful game, their pose and smiles typical of a family snapshot. In Olive's portrait, however, her body is carefully positioned in the centre, fully contained within the borders of the paper. The possibility that this work is reproducing a mirror reflection is supported by the fact that Olive is also the only one of the *murder girls* to be self-consciously covering a part of her body, a gesture that suggests her awareness of her own nakedness, of the fact that her clothes are not covering her sexed body.

Could there be a sense of shame in this gesture of covering up? This is no doubt the prevalent interpretation in those commentators who read Olive as acting out a specific motive or fantasy and thus being capable of feeling the guilt and shame that such an act, in the social order, merits. In contrast to this, might not the gesture instead have something to do with the stability of the image? Covering the genitals suggests a way of preserving the unity of the body, sought in the mirror image, which the genitals somehow disturb. Although, in Olive's portrait, the subject has been successful in covering up this dark disturbance, echoed in the flowing hair and the dark nipples, in the other portraits in the *Murder Girls* series, this point of instability in the image has been clearly marked. In the portrait of Patty Columbo, for instance, the girl's genitals are visible through the dress, yet the combination of lines and surfaces marking the texture of the dress and the girl's own body imbues this area of the drawing with a distinctly uncanny quality. As opposed to the rest of the drawing, rendered in clear and precise lines tracing the recognizable contours of the girl's body, hair and clothes, in the genital area different shapes float about. The borderline between the two levels of representation in the drawing, so clear in the rest of the portrait, loses specificity in the genital area, effectively drawing the viewer's attention to this section of the portrait. This disturbing quality is likewise unmistakable in a later portrait (2004) of Olive, 'M26 (Marlene Olive – June 22, 1975)' (Figure 14). The girl is shown reclining on a surface. The intensity and unsettling quality of the stare mimics the earlier portrait, but unlike then, her legs this time are wide open. The movement and darkness of her hair again contrast starkly with the stillness and softness of the rest of the portrait, and just like in the

Figure 14 Marlene McCarty, *M26 Marlene Olive – June 22, 1975* (2004). Courtesy of the artist.

earlier portrait, the darker elements of the drawing stand out: Olive's hair, her nipples, a pendant around her neck, a bracelet on her left hand and a short, thick, simple line for her genitals. The graphic quality of this line, echoing tongue-in-cheek teenage drawings in a school's bathroom door, or graffiti defacing advertising photographs in the city's streets, suggests that rather than belonging to the portrait, it is an element that has been added on. And like a phallus, crassly drawn on the photograph of a public figure, this line marks precisely the absence of what it represents. Together with the other, darker features in Olive's body, it belongs to a different order than the rest of the portrait. Like the pendant and the bracelet, which belong to the same order in the drawing, Olive's sexual characteristics, her nipples and her genitals, are elements that do not belong to Olive's body. They are adornments, external objects that have been added on, stuck on to her body. Yet they are an integral part of the body. These are the Other's marks on the body, the signifiers marking the body as female.

This alienated relationship between the subject and her own genitals is, according to psychoanalyst Frédéric Declercq, an ordinary occurrence, easy to verify in simple observation. Little children approach their own genitals as if they did not belong to their body, 'as if they were some kind of attribute stuck to the rest of their body'.[44] This is closely connected to what can later develop into the feelings of modesty and shame. In his article, Declercq recalls Lacan's discussion in his seminar of 1974–5, *RSI*, of a film that the child psychoanalyst Jenny Aubry had shown him in relation to his theory of the mirror stage. The film showed little children in front of a mirror, and one particular child, 'I no longer know whether it was a little girl or a little boy – it is even quite striking that I no longer remember',[45] catches Lacan's attention. The child, in front of the mirror, covers their genitals with their hands. Lacan sees in this gesture a confirmation of his postulate of the function of the mirror stage, which provides the child with a sense of unity – (mis)recognized in the image in the mirror reflection – which their body, uncoordinated due to its prematurity, lacks. The gesture of covering up indicates the threat to that unity of the body that the sight of the genitals poses for the child. It is a gesture of 'elision',[46] to remove 'what was perhaps a phallus or perhaps its absence'[47] from the image. Declercq links this act of covering up with the alien quality of the genitals, which the child removes and erases from the image because 'they don't fit in',[48] they cannot be contained within the unified image in the mirror, precisely because they threaten that very unity. This anecdote leads Lacan to the following statement: 'The phallus then is the Real.'[49] The specific theoretical weight of this statement is very carefully contextualized within the framework guiding Lacan's discussion in the seminar, namely the relation and specific form of interaction between the three orders of the Imaginary, the Real and the Symbolic. Significant for our purposes is the relation that he establishes between this phallus as Real and *jouissance*, as 'the Real [...] with respect to this phallus'.[50] It is thus *jouissance* itself that troubles the child and which threatens the unity of the image.[51]

Interestingly, an obsessive way of looking at their reflection in the mirror – suggested in Olive's portrait – is typical of psychotics. It is given the name of 'mirror sign' and is found to be more prevalent right before the psychotic delusion is about to occur. The constant looking at the mirror, which sometimes can last for hours, provides in these cases a form of reassurance in the image. According to the French psychiatrist Paul Abély, who coined the term, the mirror sign 'is a more or less apprehensive/anxious response to a change the psychotic felt inside of him'.[52] This 'inside of him' is, according to Declercq, *in* the body. The psychotic looks at her body's reflection in the mirror to get a sense of reassurance in the face of a bodily disturbance, which, for Declercq, is caused by an excessive *jouissance*: 'the subject is destabilized by an intrusion of *jouissance* in the body'.[53]

The foreclosure of the Name-of-the-Father has several consequences for the psychotic's relation to her body and the type of *jouissance* that she experiences. As opposed to neurosis, in which, as Bruce Fink reminds us, 'the body is dead'[54] in terms of it being 'overwritten by the symbolic',[55] in the psychotic subject, the symbolic function has not intervened, thus leaving the subject without any defence or mediation to curtail the *jouissance* of the (m)Other. The phallic investment in the different parts of the body where the partial drives will operate does not take place in the psychotic's body, and so, *jouissance*, unmarked and unlimited by the symbolic, 'is erratic and spreads all over the body',[56] thus leaving the body 'inundated by *jouissance*'.[57] In the psychotic, 'it is not the subject who enjoys, it is the body.'[58]

The body as radical other

Sexuation and aetiology tie up in the work of psychosis.[59]

Psychotic *jouissance* was one of the earlier names that Lacan gave to what he later called *Other jouissance*.[60] This is a form of *jouissance* linked to the feminine position, produced by castration together with phallic *jouissance*, as the latter's beyond. As a *jouissance* beyond the phallus, it points to the limit of the phallus, of phallic inscription and phallic signification. This does not imply that a different *jouissance* is available to women, as some commentators have inferred. The notion that women have access to a mystical kind of sexual enjoyment is again part of the mythical construction of femininity in patriarchy as a natural determination. The feminine position, Lacan argues, could be taken up by both men and women.

In not being limited by the phallus, Other *jouissance* points to a *jouissance* 'beyond the signifier',[61] a *jouissance* 'of the body at the subject's expense'.[62] This, of course, is reminiscent of the body disturbances we identified in psychosis in the section above, when the psychotic found her body overrun by *jouissance*. In that instance, we suggested that it was not the subject who enjoyed (in terms of *jouir*) but rather the body. Other *jouissance* points specifically to the question of the Other. In Geneviève Morel's words, 'We have to understand that "Other *jouissance*" refers to the Other [...]. The Other is always the locus of an absolute alterity for the subject.'[63] It is this alterity that Other *jouissance* alludes to, as that which lies beyond the phallus, beyond the symbolic. The fundamental element in the structure of the feminine is the signifier of the lack in the Other, S(Ⱥ). It is in relation to this that Other *jouissance* must be understood. S(Ⱥ) points to a radical alterity, to that which is not marked by phallic signification: 'femininity [...] poses the question of the Other'.[64] The body of Other *jouissance* is thus a body marked by this radical alterity: 'And no wonder [...] that in the final analysis, the Other (in all the senses of the term) of whom Lacan speaks is, for the subject, basically the body.'[65]

McCarty's drawings on the one hand suggest a powerful critique of the role that fashion images play in shaping young women's sense of self and embodiment, which goes on to determine the murderous rage that ends in matricide. The girls attack the 'exteriorized ideal' represented in the collaged self-image and kill it (an ideal constructed not only in terms of the fragmentary and fetishized fashion images but also in terms of the mother's enforcement of a 'proper' femininity) in an act of self-punishment, as Lacan remarked in the case of the Papin crime. The idealized body, the body of the mother (real or surrogate as in the case of the Lancelin mistresses) is attacked, cut up and (re)turned to its fragmented state. On the other hand, McCarty's work points precisely to the relationship of alterity to one's own body developed above. The body represented is the body as the effect of Other *jouissance*. Here the possibility of a *jouissance* beyond the phallus is invoked. In tracing the similarities to psychotic *jouissance*, where the phallus does not at all intervene and cut out the various erogenous zones, the bodily dimension of this *jouissance* is highlighted. It is a *jouissance* that overruns the body, that inundates the body 'at the expense of the subject'. *Jouissance* is *of* the body. The body produced is a body that enjoys. This is not the body as the organic whole that anatomy traces, which is always an imaginary myth. The specificity of the feminine position in Lacan's theory of sexuation points very precisely to the relationship to the signifier of the lack in the Other, S(Ⱥ). This then implies a relationship of radical alterity to the body, where the body in effect constitutes the radical Other. The body represented is thus sexed not in an anatomical sense but in terms of its determination by *jouissance*. The work thus points to a radical dissociation of sex from the anatomical specificity of the body.

The consequences of this radical problematization of sex for a feminist criticism of art and culture more generally are both difficult and provocative. On the one hand, the necessity and urgency to continue to reveal and subvert the role that representational practices, such as the fashion image, play in (re)producing a specific social order determined by the patriarchal regime of sexual difference that produces specific forms of femininity and positions women in a subordinate position cannot be denied. Given the strength and effectiveness of these images in prescribing and reinforcing specific forms of femininity according to the patriarchal order, the analysis of the role that these images play in determining the way that we look at them and in the constitution of subjectivities is still a primary concern of feminism. The inherent patriarchal violence in these images, the objectification and detached relationship to one's own body that they enforce, is echoed in the killer rage that these forms of ideal femininity can produce. Marlene Olive's staring at her own reflection in the mirror suggests this killer look, both in terms of the matricide that will effectively destroy the enforced ideal of femininity embodied and reproduced by her mother, and also in terms of the reading provided in these pages. It offers us another way of engaging with the represented body. The precarious nature of the patriarchal regime of sexual difference is both veiled and denied if the specific nature of sex – dissociated from the myth of the two sexes of the sexual relation – is not itself questioned. What would it mean to kill the current understanding of sex, to abandon the idea of sex regulated by sexual difference (the psychic interpretation of anatomical facts) and understand sex to be instead determined by the particular access that each of us, speaking beings, manages to establish to that form of being that is *jouissance*?

Notes

1. Marlene McCarty, *Where Is Your Rupture?*, ed. L. Kotz (The Swiss Institute, New York, 1998) [exhibition catalogue], p. 9. An extract of this text, with slight variations, is also found in Maud Lavin, 'Marlene McCarty's *Murder Girls*', in C. Grant and L. Waxman (eds), *Girls! Girls! Girls! in Contemporary Art* (Bristol and Chicago: Intellect, 2011), p. 93. I have followed the text in the exhibition catalogue, adding 'house' after 'neighborhood' to correct a possible typo in the text, after contrasting it with the extract in Lavin.
2. Ana Finel Honigman, 'Sex and Death: Interview with Marlene McCarty', *ArtSlant* (2013). Available at www.artslant.com/ny/articles/show/36498-sex-and-death-interview-with-marlene-mccarty (accessed 20 May 2017).
3. Jennifer Kabat, 'Rules of Attraction: The Uncomfortable World of Marlene McCarty', *Frieze*, 159 (2013).
4. Craig Saper, 'Nervous Theory: The Troubling Gaze of Psychoanalysis in Media Studies', *Diacritics* 21/4 (1991), pp. 33–52.

5. Ibid., p. 33.
6. Ibid.
7. 'We must think paradoxically about the gaze. The distinction is crucial. If we do not understand the difference between a positivism of paradoxes and paradoxical thinking, then we fall prey to formalism and turn Lacanian psychoanalytic theory into an empirical method of reading texts. The gaze, as the remainder of this essay will explain, unsettles empiricism and sets in motion the (re)appearance of gaps, fadings, and flickerings in our perception and understanding.' Saper, p. 43.
8. See Joan Copjec, 'The Orthopsychic Subject: Film Theory and the Reception of Lacan', *October* 49 (1989), pp. 53–71.
9. See Griselda Pollock, 'What's Wrong with Images of Women?', *Screen Education* 24 (1977), pp. 25–34.
10. Alison Bancroft, *Fashion and Psychoanalysis: Styling the Self* (London: I.B. Tauris, 2012), p. 5.
11. Ibid., p. 16.
12. Ibid., p. 28.
13. Ibid., p. 43.
14. Colette Soler, '*El cuerpo en la enseñanza de Jacques Lacan*' [The Body in Jacques Lacan's Teaching], *Estudios de psicosomática*, vol. 1, ed. Vera Gorali (Buenos Aires: Atuel-cap, 1993), pp. 93–105 (p. 97).
15. Jacques Lacan, 'The Function and Field of Speech and Language', in *Écrits*, trans. Bruce Fink (New York and London: W. W. Norton, 2002), p. 248.
16. In principle, psychoanalysis, in its therapeutic specificity, rejects the body explicitly. In the psychoanalytic clinic the body of the patient, of she who suffers, is clearly left out of the therapeutic process, even when the symptoms it is expected to resolve take place on the body, in the form of paralysis, pain, spasms, and so on. As Lacan reminds us in the introductory session of *Seminar 8*, no medical bodily examination is necessary previous to undergoing psychoanalysis. The specific reality of the body as organism is not taken into consideration. Anatomy is explicitly left out. And yet, on the other hand, psychoanalysis gets underway as both therapy and theory, in order precisely to understand and treat the hysteric body. It is the bodily manifestations of the hysteric's symptoms that psychoanalytic therapy, as 'talking cure', proves capable of isolating and resolving. And precisely because of the non-organic nature of these symptoms, because no physiological explanation can account for the emergence and persistence of the symptoms – 'hysteria behaves as though anatomy did not exist' (Freud, 'Some Points for a Comparative Study of Organic and Hysterical Motor Paralyses', *The Standard Edition 1*, pp. 155–72 (p. 169)) – psychoanalysis is able to foreground a significant feature of the body which the organicist conception does not address, namely the body's relation to language: '[hysteria] takes the organs

in the ordinary, popular sense of the names they bear' (ibid.). And it is in this relation that psychoanalysis finds its specificity and its relevance.

17. Janet Holland et al., *The Male in the Head: Young People, Heterosexuality and Power* (London: The Tufnell Press, 1998).
18. Jacques Lacan, 'Motifs du crime paranoïque. Le crime des soeurs Papin' [Motives of a Paranoic Crime. The Crime of the Papin Sisters], *Minotaure* 3/4 (1933), p. 26 [photographs of the article available at www.papinsisters.tripod.com/lacan.html (accessed 22 January 2012)].
19. Honigman, 'Sex and Death'.
20. The case has been famously portrayed in numerous books, articles, plays and films, such as Jean Genet's *Les Bonnes* of 1947, and, more recently, Claude Chabrol's *La Cérémonie* of 1995.
21. A good account of the crime and subsequent analyses of it can be found in Rachel Edwards and Keith Reader, *The Papin Sisters* (Oxford: Oxford University Press, 2001).
22. Elisabeth Roudinesco, *Jacques Lacan. An Outline of a Life and a History of a System of Thought* (Cambridge and Malden: Polity Press, 1999), p. 63.
23. Francis Dupré, *La 'Solution' du Passage à l'Acte. Le Double Crime des Soeurs Papin* (Toulouse: Erès, 1984), quoted in Edwards and Reader, *The Papin Sisters*, p. 11.
24. It was their mother, Clémence, who dictated where they were to live during their childhood years. When Christine attempted to follow in the footsteps of her older sister, Emile, and live in a convent, Clémence refused. She was also responsible for placing them in the Lancelin home as maidservants.
25. '*Dit-moi oui! Dit-moi oui!*', in Edwards and Reader, *The Papin Sisters*, p. 12. According to Edwards and Reader, some accounts report Christine 'exposing her private parts and fondling her breasts', but as they point out, this is not supported by any evidence. It nevertheless attests to the reception by the media at the time of the relationship between the two sisters.
26. Sigmund Freud, 'Some Neurotic Mechanisms in Jealousy, Paranoia and Homosexuality', *The Standard Edition* 18, pp. 221–32.
27. Marlene McCarty, *Marlene Olive – June 21, 1975*, 1995–7 (extract), in Lavin, 'Marlene McCarty's *Murder Girls*', p. 93.
28. Jacques Lacan, *El seminario de Jacques Lacan. Libro 3: Las psicosis, 1955–1956*, trans. Juan-Luis Delmont-Mauri and Diana Silvia Rabinovich (Buenos Aires, Barcelona and México: Paidós, 1984), p. 119.
29. 'What is it about when I talk about *Verwerfung*? It is about the refusal, the expulsion, of a primordial signifier to the exterior darkness [...]'. Lacan, *El seminario* 3, p. 217.
30. 'In a psychosis something did not work, essentially something was not finished in the Oedipus complex.' Ibid., p. 287.

31. Ibid., pp. 23–4.
32. In French *non/nom-du-père* plays with the homophony between *non*, 'no', and *nom*, 'name'. The Name-of-the-Father thus alludes to both the prohibition of incest, the *No!* of the father, and the symbolic dimension of the father's name – to accept the latter means to enter the symbolic order, given that it is a purely symbolic position: 'The attribution of procreation to the father can only be the effect of a pure signifier, of a recognition, not of the real father, but of what religion has taught us to invoke as the Name-of-the-Father.' Jacques Lacan, 'On a Question Prior to Any Possible Treatment of Psychosis', in *Écrits*, pp. 445–88 (p. 464).
33. Lacan, *El seminario 3*, p. 225.
34. Judith Feher-Gurewich, 'The *Jouissance* of the Other and the Prohibition of Incest: A Lacanian Perspective', *Other Voices: The (e)Journal of Cultural Criticism* 1/3 (1999). Available at www.othervoices.org/1.3/jfg/other.php (accessed 28 November 2012).
35. Lavin, 'Marlene McCarty's *Murder Girls*', p. 90.
36. Annette Schindler, 'Marlene McCarty', in Kotz (ed), *Marlene McCarty What Is Your Rupture?*, p. 4.
37. 'Who has not, at one time or another, felt a killing rage towards her own mother?' Lavin, 'Marlene McCarty's *Murder Girls*', p. 90.
38. In her text part of the exhibition catalogue *What Is Your Rupture?* Annette Schindler literally states that it is not about psychosis: 'Yet none of these murders can be considered psychotic.' Schindler, 'Marlene McCarty', p. 4.
39. See, for example, Simone de Beauvoir's take on it: 'In its broad outline, the tragedy of the Papin sisters was immediately clear to us. In Rouen, as in Le Mans, and perhaps even among the mothers of my pupils, there were no doubt women who deducted the cost of a broken plate from their maid's wages, who put on white gloves to find forgotten specks of dust on the furniture: in our eyes, they deserved death a hundred times over. [...] One must accuse their childhood orphanage, their serfdom, the whole hideous system set up by decent people for the production of madmen, assassins and monsters. The horror of this all-consuming machine could only be rightfully denounced by an exemplary act of horror: the two sisters had made themselves the instruments and martyrs of a sombre form of justice.' Simone de Beauvoir, *The Prime of Age*, trans. Peter Green (London: Deutsch, Wiedenfeld and Nicolson, 1963) p. 108.
40. Edwards and Reader, *The Papin Sisters*, p. 11.
41. Ibid.
42. Roudinesco, *Jacques Lacan*, p. 63.
43. It was in fact with Olive that McCarty started the series.

44. Frédéric Declercq, 'Lacan's Concept of the Real of *Jouissance*: Clinical Illustrations and Implications', *Psychoanalysis, Culture & Society* 9 (2004), pp. 237–51 (p. 238).
45. Lacan, *The Seminar of Jacques Lacan, Book 22: R.S.I. 1974–75*, trans. Cormac Gallagher. Available at www.lacaninireland.com/web/published-works/seminars/ (accessed 10 December 2012), Session of 11 March 1975, p. 102.
46. Ibid., p. 103.
47. Ibid.
48. Declercq, 'Lacan's Concept'. p. 238.
49. Lacan, *Seminar 22*, p. 103.
50. Ibid.
51. In his article, Declercq reminds us that Freud too took note of this disturbance in the child's relation to its genitals: 'Because of the *jouissance* it generates, [Little Hans's] so-called "widdler" is so strange to him that he attributes penises to everything except human beings. [...] Lacan makes a revealing pun about this. [...] he says that infantile sexuality is not in fact auto-erotic, but *hetero*-erotic.' Declercq, 'Lacan's Concept', p. 238.
52. Paul Abély, 'Le signe du miroir dans les psychoses et plus spécialement dans la démence prérrce', *Annales médico-psychologiques* 1 (1930), p. 33. Cited in Declercq, 'Lacan's Concept', p. 241.
53. Declercq, 'Lacan's Concept', p. 241.
54. Bruce Fink, *A Clinical Introduction to Lacanian Psychoanalysis, Theory and Technique* (Cambridge, MA and London: Harvard University Press, 1999), p. 97.
55. Ibid., p. 88.
56. Declercq, 'Lacan's Concept', p. 242.
57. Fink, *A Clinical Introduction*, p. 97.
58. Declercq, 'Lacan's Concept', p. 240.
59. Ernesto Piechotka, 'Psychosis: Sex, Gender or Symptom?' in M. Bassols (ed), *Sexuation and Sexuality, Psychoanalytical Notebooks*, 11 (2003), pp. 61–6 (p. 63).
60. Paul Verhaeghe, *Beyond Gender: From Subject to Drive* (New York: Other Press, 2001), p. 89.
61. Verhaeghe, *Beyond Gender*, p. 92.
62. Ibid.
63. Geneviève Morel, *Sexual Ambiguities*, trans. Lindsay Watson (London: Karnak, 2011), p. 149.
64. Serge André, *What Does a Woman Want?*, trans. Susan Fairfiled (New York: Other Press, 1999), p. 259.
65. Ibid., p. 260.

Bibliography

André, Serge, *What Does a Woman Want?*, trans. Susan Fairfield (New York: Other Press, 1999).

Bancroft, Alison, *Fashion and Psychoanalysis: Styling the Self* (London: I.B. Tauris, 2012).

Copjec, Joan, 'The Orthopsychic Subject: Film Theory and the Reception of Lacan', *October* 49 (1989), pp. 53–71.

de Beauvoir, Simone, *The Prime of Age*, trans. Peter Green (London: Deutsch, Wiedenfeld and Nicolson, 1963).

Declercq, Frédéric, 'Lacan's Concept of the Real of *Jouissance*: Clinical Illustrations and Implications', *Psychoanalysis, Culture & Society* 9 (2004), pp. 237–51.

Edwards, Rachel, and Keith Reader, *The Papin Sisters* (Oxford: Oxford University Press, 2001).

Feher-Gurewich, Judith, 'The *Jouissance* of the Other and the Prohibition of Incest: A Lacanian Perspective', *Other Voices: The (e)Journal of Cultural Criticism* 1/3 (1999). Available at http://www.othervoices.org/1.3/jfg/other.php (accessed 28 November 2012).

Fink, Bruce, *A Clinical Introduction to Lacanian Psychoanalysis, Theory and Technique* (Cambridge, MA and London: Harvard University Press, 1999).

Freud, Sigmund, 'Some Neurotic Mechanisms in Jealousy, Paranoia and Homosexuality', in *The Standard Edition of the Complete Psychological Works of Sigmund Freud*, trans. and ed. James Strachey (London: Vintage, 2001), vol. 18, pp. 221–32.

Freud, Sigmund, 'Some Points for a Comparative Study of Organic and Hysterical Motor Paralyses', in *The Standard Edition of the Complete Psychological Works of Sigmund Freud*, trans. and ed. James Strachey (London: Vintage, 2001), vol. 1, pp. 155–72.

Holland, Janet et al., *The Male in the Head: Young People, Heterosexuality and Power* (London: The Tufnell Press, 1998).

Honigman, Ana F., 'Sex and Death: Interview with Marlene McCarty', *ArtSlant*, 2013. Available at www.artslant.com/ny/articles/show/36498-sex-and-death-interview-with-marlene-mccarty (accessed 20 May 2017).

Kabat, Jennifer, 'Rules of Attraction: The Uncomfortable World of Marlene McCarty', *Frieze* 159 (2013).

Kotz, Liz (ed), *Marlene McCarty, Where Is Your Rupture?* (New York: The Swiss Institute, 1998).

Lacan, Jacques, *El seminario de Jacques Lacan. Libro 3: Las psicosis, 1955–1956*, trans. Juan-Luis Delmont-Mauri and Diana Silvia Rabinovich (Buenos Aires, Barcelona and México: Paidós, 1984).

Lacan, Jacques, *Écrits*, trans. Bruce Fink (New York and London: W. W. Norton, 2002).

Lacan, Jacques, 'Motifs du crime paranoïque. Le crime des soeurs Papin' [Motives of a Paranoic Crime. The Crime of the Papin Sisters], *Minotaure* 3/4 (1933), p. 26 [photographs of the article available at http://papinsisters.tripod.com/lacan.htm (accessed 22 January 2012).

Lacan, Jacques, *The Seminar of Jacques Lacan, Book 22: R.S.I. 1974–75*, trans. Cormac Gallagher. Available at www.lacaninireland.com/web/published-works/seminars/ (accessed 10 December 2012).

Lavin, Maud, 'Marlene McCarty's Murder Girls', in C. Grant and L. Waxman (eds), *Girls! Girls! Girls! in Contemporary Art* (Bristol and Chicago: Intellect, 2011), pp. 87–106.

Piechotka, Ernesto, 'Psychosis: Sex, Gender or Symptom?' in M. Bassols (ed), *Sexuation and Sexuality, Psychoanalytical Notebooks*, vol. 11 (2003).

Pollock, Griselda, 'What's Wrong with Images of Women?', *Screen Education* 24 (1977), pp. 25–34.

Roudinesco, Elisabeth, *Jacques Lacan. An Outline of a Life and a History of a System of Thought* (Cambridge and Malden: Polity Press, 1999).

Saper, Craig, 'Nervous Theory: The Troubling Gaze of Psychoanalysis in Media Studies', *Diacritics* 21/4 (1991), pp. 33–52.

Soler, Colette, '*El cuerpo en la enseñanza de Jacques Lacan*' [The Body in Jacques Lacan's Teaching], *Estudios de psicosomática*, vol. 1, ed. Vera Gorali (Buenos Aires: Atuel-cap, 1993.

Verhaeghe, Paul, *Beyond Gender: From Subject to Drive* (New York: Other Press, 2001).

INDEX

Abély, Paul 243
Abraham, Laurie 164 n.30
activism 2, 10, 13–14, 16, 18
Advanced Style blog 11
adverts/advertisements 134, 136, 140
  fat body in 183
  male bodies in 126, 139
  models in Dolce and Gabbana 131–2, 141
  Wonderbra 1994 advert ('Hello Boys') 128–9
'aesthetics of disgust' 177, 183–5, 189
agency 9, 42, 62, 69, 102, 133, 139, 183
  representational 15
  sexual 14
  wearer (dress) 55, 57–8, 67, 71
Aguilar, Laura 183–4
Ahern, Mal 124
Ahkam-e Negah Kardan ("The commandments for looking") 88
Alinejad, Masih 95 n.18
Allen, Jennifer. *See* Quilla Constance
'ambient gaze' 6, 55–6, 61–2, 71
Amir-Ebrahimi, Masserat, 'Weblogistan' 92
Anderson, Brett 208
Andersson, Malin 136
androgynous aesthetics 200, 204–6, 212
Apter, Emily 135
Arena magazine 126–7
Ashcroft, Richard 212
ASMR (autonomous sensory meridian response) 50
'athletic nervosa' disorder 138
Aubry, Jenny 243
autoerotic scopophilia 39–40, 51 n.5
Autostraddle website 215–17, 219 n.27
averted gaze 88
Azoulay, Ariella 110

Baer, Hester 17
Baker, Catherine 10
Baker, Josephine 89–91
Ball, Lucille, *I Love Lucy* 150
Bal, Mieke 22 n.51
Baloch, Qandeel (murder of) 14–15, 25 n.107
Bamdad, Badr ol-Moluk 81
Bancroft, Alison
  Fashion and Psychoanalysis: Styling the Self 4, 233–4
  'fragmentation' 234–5
Banet-Weiser, Sarah 17
Barthes, Roland 57, 106
Bartky, Sandra 149
Bartlett, Djurdja, *Fashion and Politics* 26 n.130
Baudrillard, Jean 52 n.6
  The Consumer Society 124
Beattie, Trevor (1994 Wonderbra campaign) 128
beauty 5, 10, 20 n.31, 85, 107–8, 110, 123, 127, 131, 135, 138, 149, 159, 181
  fashion and 102, 184
  fat-phobic 104
  ideals of 134, 177, 180, 184, 189–90
  myths 44
  'pregnant beauty' 147, 150, 152, 154, 160–1
  and sexuality 115
Beckham, David 212
bell hooks 10, 18, 158, 203
Bellmer, Hans 41, 176
Benjamin, Walter, on flâneur 132–3
Bentham, Jeremy 89
Berger, John 232–3, 235
  Ways of Seeing 3
Beyoncé 165 n.51. *See also* Jay Z
  black body 14, 158–9
  cover star for *Vogue* (2015) 156
  'fat upper pubic area' (FUPA) 161
  'hiphop feminism' 13–14
  Lemonade album 158–9, 161

Life Is But a Dream 153–5
maternal/pregnant body 147–8, 152, 154, 158–9, 160–1
postpartum 161
pregnancé conspiracé of 2011 147–8, 152–5, 161
privacy 155–6
use of Instagram 156–7
binary/binaries 4, 36–7, 49, 103, 107, 159
black feminism 9–10, 14, 158–9, 203
Black Lives Matter movement 13
Blue Ivy 147, 153, 160
#bodyhairdontcare hashtag 16
Boissonnas, Sylvina 83
Bordo, Susan 111, 137, 180
boudoir photography 17
client testimonials 102–3, 109, 112–13
and confident selfhood 104–6
nudity 109
pornographic aspect of boudoir 108
queer 103
relationship between photographer and client 106–15
Bourdieu, Pierre 5
boyd, danah 156
Brewster, Maureen Lehto 14
Britney and Kevin: Chaotic docuseries 154
Britpop 200, 206, 220 n.50
Brown, Wendy, 'extramarket morality' 115
Bruzzi, Stella 20 n.29
Burgin, Victor 39–40
'Jenni's Room: Exhibitionism and Solitude' 38, 42–3
Burns, Anne 17
Bustle feminist magazine 175
butch–femme 207–8
Butler, Judith 8, 101, 162 n.3, 212 *See also* performativity

Campbell, Colin 59
Carden-Coyne, Ana 188
Carr, Gwen 158
Cartesian dualism 5, 58–9
Cavalli, Roberto 159
Cave, Jessie 161
celebrity pregnancy 147–8, 150–2
'pregnant beauty' 150, 154, 160
Chasseguet-Smirgel, Janine 137
Chong Kwan, Sara 6
cisnormativity 13, 212–13, 217
Clark, Kenneth 177
Classen, Constance 60
Close, Jessica 138
Clout, Lucy, *Shrugging Offing* 49–51
Cocker, Jarvis 208
Cohen, Ari Seth 11
Cole, Shaun 58
Colomina, Beatriz, *Publicity and Privacy* 90
Conor, Liz 112
consumer culture 2, 16–17, 123–4, 139
contemporary 124, 129–30, 136, 139
female 125, 127–9, 139–40
male 125, 127
neoliberal 16
sexual commodity 235
subjectivity 132–3, 135
support from social networking sites 134
control 14, 17, 42–5, 64, 82, 180, 214, 233, 235
gaze/look 36–7, 51 n.5, 89–90, 180
image 155–6, 166 n.60, 181
panoptic 11, 134
patriarchal 139
sexual desire 80
visible/invisible 57, 67
Cooper, Charlotte 183
cosmetic/plastic surgery 136–7
Crawford, Cindy 207
Crenshaw, Kimberlé 9
'critical gaze' 10–11
cultural gaze 176, 180, 190, 192
Cultural Studies approach 18
'curiosity' 4

Dant, Tim 70
Davis, Jen 11, 185
Ascension (2002) 185–8
bariatric surgery 175
Conforming (2002) 187–8
Eleven Years (2002–13) 175–82, 188, 192
'epidermic self-awareness' 187–8
Lap Band surgery 189–90
Maxwell Street (2002) 185
Pressure Point (2002) 178–80
re-fashioning gaze 185–9
self-critical gaze 192
Untitled No. 4 (2004) 190
Untitled No. 24 (2007) 190–1

Untitled No. 37 (2010) 189–90
Untitled No. 47 (2012) 190–1
weight loss 175–6, 181, 192
Dawson, Graham 217
identity formation 213
military and imperial masculinity 213
Soldier Heroes 212
de Beauvoir, Simone 84
Debord, Guy 160, 167 n.86
Declercq, Frédéric 242–3, 250 n.51
De Lauretis, Teresa 202–3
'desire' 13, 61, 92, 101, 133, 199, 207–8, 211
identification and 199–204, 211–12, 215
lesbian 203, 207–8
object of (body) 51 n.5, 127–9, 181, 184
patriarchal codes of 139–40
sexual 43, 80, 200, 211
towards masculinities 205
DiCaprio, Leonardo 10, 204, 206, 210, 212
Dietrich, Marlene 41
digital culture of queer women 214–16
digital feminism 2–3, 13, 17–18
'digital sisterhood' 13
Dion, Celine, *Top of the Pops* 208
direct gaze 88–9, 159
disability impairment 182–5
dissecting gaze 17, 123, 135–9, 141
Diva lesbian lifestyle magazine 200
Doane, Mary Ann 40–1, 45, 47
masquerade 181
'A Phantasmagoria of the Female Body: The Work of Cindy Sherman' 41
Dolce and Gabbana adverts, models in 131–2, 141
Döring, Nicola 134
'double act' on visuality 6, 35, 50
doubled gaze 189–90
'dress' 55–6, 58–9, 65, 80, 176
'modest dressers' 85
women's sensory experiences of 62–5
'dudeoir' 115 n.1
Dyer, Richard 162 n.9

Eco, Umberto, 'Lumbar Thought' 187
Edwards, Rachel 248 n.25
Eicher, Joanne B. 55
Elastica rock band 208–9
Elias, Ana Sofia 104
embodiment 15, 48, 58–61, 72 n.17, 112, 150, 177, 185, 188–9, 192, 206, 217, 229, 239, 245
empowerment 7, 14, 16, 18, 45, 102, 140
in consumer culture 128–9
with sexualization and commodification 130
sexual liberation 129
Entwistle, Joanne 24 n.88, 56, 58–9, 157, 176, 202, 220 n.53
Erizku, Awol 148, 159
Esposito, Cameron 216
Evans, Adrienne 17, 101
Evans, Caroline 6, 10, 199–200, 203, 205
Evans, Jessica 176
'Feeble Monsters: Making up Disabled People' 182
exhibitionism 37–40, 43. *See also* Ringley, Jennifer
Extreme Makeover television programme 136–7

fabric 61, 66–7, 69, 153, 159–60, 188
Facebook 2, 13, 15, 95 n.18, 151
faith-related fashion 85
Family Protection Law (1967), Iran 79–81
fashion
fashion gaze 232
fashion magazines 10, 207, 209, 232, 235 (*see also specific magazines*)
fashion photography 9, 181, 184, 189, 202, 233–4 (*see also* photographs/photography)
gendering of 63
and homoerotics of resemblance 206–11
symbolic production of 6
Fashion and Dress Studies 56–7, 59
Fashion Studies 4, 6, 18, 23 n.75, 176
fat body 2, 9–11, 104, 111, 138, 150, 152, 161, 175–6, 184
Davis's work (*see* Davis, Jen)
in modern America 178
in Western visual culture 177, 180
Fatehrad, Azadeh 12
Departure Series 77
Favaro, Laura 111
'confidence chic' 105, 108
Featherstone, Mike 135–6
'athletic nervosa' disorder 138
female body 4, 15–16, 36, 41, 126, 130, 213

ageing body 3, 11
in celebrity culture 149, 154, 160
disabled body 182–4
disciplined modern 80
fashioned 2–3, 10–11, 18, 93, 199–200, 211, 227–32
fat (*see* fat body)
fragmented body 234–5
grotesque 180
hypervisibility of bodies 2, 11–12, 85, 93, 178, 182, 184
maternal/pregnant bodies 147–50, 152, 160 (*see also* pregnancy)
of Other *jouissance* 240–4
as radical other 244–6
sexualization of 102, 150
and subjectification 103, 110
transgression 150
veiled body 11–12, 91–2 (*see also* hijab in Iran)
'female gaze' 7–8, 181–2, 203, 211–12. *See also* 'male gaze'
aesthetics of disgust 183
homoerotic 218 n.22
in 1990s 199, 201, 205–6
queer 36, 204–5, 207, 210, 214, 217
religious gaze 15
female genital mutilation (FGM) 42
'female masculinities' 204
FEMEN movement 2, 13
feminism/feminist 1–2, 7, 51, 104, 125, 181
activism 2, 8–10, 13–14, 18
'ageing femininities' 10–11
black 9–10, 14, 158–9, 203
digital (*see* digital feminism)
femininity (*see* femininity)
hashtag (*see* hashtag feminism)
hiphop 13–14
intersectionality in 2, 9–18
and Islam 84
and misogyny 17–18
movements 2, 13
protests 2, 13, 82–3
scholarship 13, 18
social change 8, 18, 37, 65
on 1936 'Unveiling' 82
#feministselfie Twitter hashtag 17
femininity 5, 8, 12, 15, 41, 130, 150, 160, 229–30, 245–6
'achieved adult femininity' 149
'ageing femininities' 10
black 158 (*see also* black feminism)
lesbian 212
masquerade 43, 50
maternal 87
neoliberal 102
'passive' adult 4
and pregnancy (*see* pregnancy)
fetishism 5, 17, 20 n.31, 37–8, 41, 45, 129, 139
fetishistic scopophilia 123
hyperfocalization 135
Fink, Bruce 244
Fletcher, John 41
'formulaic female sexualities' 134
Forth, Christopher E. 188
Foucault, Michel 7–8, 101, 157
Discipline and Punish: The Birth of the Prison 149
panoptic gaze 11, 149, 177
Fourth Wave feminism. *See* digital feminism
Fraser, Nancy 16
FreeTheNipple campaign 13
Freud, Lucian 176–7
Freud, Sigmund 3, 9
'lotus feet' (Chinese custom) 129
scopophilia 37, 39–40, 51 n.5, 91, 179
'Three Essays on the Theory of Sexuality' 37
Friedman, Vanessa 158
Frischmann, Justine 208–9
Frosh, Paul 111
Fulton, Sabryna 158
Fuss, Diana 20 n.18, 201–2

Gamman, Lorraine 6, 199–200, 203, 205
The Female Gaze: Women as Viewers of Popular Culture 9
'subcultural competences' 10
Garb, Tamar 1
Gaugele, Elke, *Fashion and Postcolonial Critique* 26 n.130
Gawker blog 165 n.43
Gay, Roxane 181
gaze 36. *See also* 'looking'; *specific gazes*
evolution of 3–9
gender 1, 9, 23 n.71, 57–8, 124–5, 130, 134, 205, 212–13, 216
bisexual 203–4, 211, 217 n.1
cisgender (non-transgender) women 103, 217
equality 13, 125, 149
expression 201, 207–8, 212, 216, 221 n.59

gendered gaze 177–8, 180
'genderfuck' 205
gendering of clothing 63
heterosexual 103, 113–14, 128–30, 201–2, 204, 214
homosexuality 206–7
inequality 37, 123
and sexuality 8–9, 15, 42
transvestitism 4
Giles, David 138
Gill, Rosalind 10, 104, 106, 111
'confidence cult' 105
depictions of male bodies 126
on empowered young woman (1990s) 128
'midriff' 128, 130, 134
'Post-postfeminism?: New Feminist Visibilities in Postfeminist Times' 14
Gilman, Sander L. 10
Goffman, Erving 134
Gottschalk, Simon 57
Gram, Sarah 134
Granata, Francesca 180
Grosz, Elizabeth 41, 47
Becoming Undone 45–6

Hadimioglu, Çagla 86
Hagan, Sean O', 'new lad' 126–7
hair 16, 88, 138, 159, 177, 202, 205, 210, 212, 215–16, 228, 241–2
Halberstam, Jack 204–5, 212
haptic visuality 5–6, 35, 46–9, 51, 67, 188
Harjunen, Hannele 180
hashtag feminism 2, 13–14, 17, 25 n.99
#bodyhairdontcare 16
#feministselfie 17
#Flawless 153
#thinspiration 137
#YesAllWomen 13
Haug, Wolfgang Fritz 128
heteronormative culture 10, 200, 202–4, 208, 212–13
desires 199, 207
patriarchal structures 203
psychoanalytic 8
sexual display 129
hijab in Iran 78–84
andaruni (inner part) 87
biruni (outer part) 87
derivation of 80
fashion and 79, 85
forms of covering 80
'hijabisation of behaviour' 80
Hill, Adrienne 182
'hiphop feminism' 13–14
Hirsch, Ann 43–4
Scandalishious YouTube video series 43
vaginal canals video 44
Holliday, Ruth 220 n.50
Holliday, Tess 184
Howes, David 60, 63
'hyperfocalization' 17, 135, 138

I am Malala campaign 14
imperial gaze 203
Instagram 2, 14, 25 n.116, 134, 136, 147, 151, 156–7, 159–61, 167 n.86
interdisciplinary approach 7
Iqani, Mehita 134
Iran, veiled body in. *See* veil (chador) in Iran (post-revolutionary)
Irigaray, Luce 5, 62

James, Alex 208
Jay Z 153, 155, 158–9, 165 n.51. *See also* Beyoncé
Jenks, Christopher 92
Jenner, Kylie 151–2
Jenzen, Olu 207, 211
Jermyn, Deborah, 'Pretty Past It' 11
Jones, Amelia 110
The Feminism and Visual Culture Reader 10, 23 n.75
Jordanova, Ludmilla 91
jouissance (enjoyment) 39, 232, 239–40
Other *jouissance* 4, 231–2, 235, 240–5
psychotic 244–5

Kaplan, E. Ann 203
Kaplan, Louise 137
Kardashian West, Kim 151–2, 164 nn.37–8
Kargbo, Majida 191
Keating, Shannon 204
Khoi, Musavi 88
Khomeini, Ayatollah 82, 84
on act of looking 88
on veiling 77–8
Klein, Melanie 202, 212–13
Klein, Richard 181
Knight, Nick 233
Knowles-Carter, Beyoncé. *See* Beyoncé
Knowles, Mathew 153, 155

Lacan, Jacques 3, 8–9, 202, 237, 243
  jouissance (*see jouissance* (enjoyment))
  'The Mirror-Stage' 3–4, 37, 230, 233, 235, 243
  Papin sisters crime 237–40, 245
  psychoanalysis (*see* psychoanalysis/psychoanalytic approach)
  sexuation 235
  subjectification 110
Laing, Morna 21 n.48
lang, k. d. 207–8
Lawson, Tina 158
LeBesco, Kathleen 182
Lefebvre, Henri, *The Production of Space* 86
Leibovitz, Annie 150
Lennox, Annie 14
lesbian/lesbianism 103, 206, 211, 213, 215–17, 221 n.59
  'butch' 207
  desire 203, 207–8
  'lesbian chic' 200
  lesbian gaze 10, 199–205, 211
  and queer 217 n.1
Lester, CN 212, 220 n.59
Lewis, Reina 10, 24 n.88, 79, 199–200, 208, 216
  faith-related fashion 85
  hypervisibility 12
  legitimization 15
  lesbian gaze 203, 205, 207, 211, 215
  Modest Fashion: Styling Bodies, Mediating Faith 85
  space for women 10
Lewis, Van Dyk 190
Loaded style magazine 127
'looking' 1–3, 10, 42, 78, 135. *See also* spectatorship
  active/passive 3, 35–6, 39
  direct gaze 88–9
  disinterested 5
  at fashion 232–5
  and feeling 8
  haptic 6, 47, 188
  in Iranian society 85–93
  mutual exchange of gazes 42
  new politics of 9–18
  relational 110–15
  violence of look 235–9
Loos, Adolf, *Looking at the Pool through a Fixed Window* 89–91
lover's gaze 113–14
Lurie, Alison 58–9

magazines 10, 102, 125, 184, 208–9, 215, 229, 232, 235
  Arena 126–7
  Bustle 175
  Diva 200
  F-Magazine 84
  Heat 136
  i-D magazine, 'The Female Gaze Issue' 7, 21 n.48
  Loaded style 127
  New York Magazine 164 n.30
  The Oprah Magazine 175
  Vanity Fair 147, 150, 207
  Vogue 156, 161, 229
magnifying gaze 135–9
'male gaze' 2, 6, 55, 106, 176, 181–2, 202, 231. *See also* 'female gaze'; masculine/masculinity
  feminist critiques of 56, 62–5
  mahrem (unlawful)/*namahrem* (lawful) 86
  male lookers in Iran 86–7, 95 n.28
  at mixed-sex parties in Iran 88
  Mulvey's work on 1, 3, 9, 35–7, 78, 105, 179–80, 189, 201, 230, 232
  'self policing narcissistic gaze' 129
'Man Repeller' blog 2, 19 n.13
Marks, Laura U. 5–6, 48–9
  electronic video analyses 46–7
  'haptic visuality' 177, 188
  The Skin of the Film 5
Marshment, Margaret, *The Female Gaze: Women as Viewers of Popular Culture* 9
Martin, Gina 18
Marx/Marxism/Marxist 3, 123
Marwick, Alice 156–7
masculine/masculinity 4, 8, 41, 199, 204, 212
  contemporary gay style 219 n.37
  female identifications with 211–14
  male body 126, 130, 139
  men's sensations of dress 66–7
  military and imperial 213
  'new man'/'new lad' 126
  and queer female gaze (1990s) 205–6
Mason, Jennifer 61
'masquerade' 6, 35, 40–1, 43, 45–7, 49, 181
McCarty, Marlene 3, 235, 237, 245, 246 n.1

drawings of 'Marlene Olive' (*see* Olive, Marlene)
Murder Girls 229, 240–1
McRobbie, Angela 9, 104, 128
McSpadden, Lezley 158
Meagher, Michelle 185, 189
'aesthetics of disgust' 177, 183
media gaze 147, 152, 160
'mediatization' 157
medical gaze 182, 184–5
Melchior-Bonnet, Sabine, *The Mirror* 190
Merleau-Ponty, Maurice 6, 58–9
Meyers, Erin 154
Middleton, Pippa 147
Milani, Farzaneh 87
Miller, Daniel 63
Millett, Kate 82
Mirzoeff, Nicholas, *The Feminism and Visual Culture Reader* 10, 23 n.75
modernity 81, 92
misrecognition 107, 111, 114, 230
Mohammad Reza Shah 78–9, 81. *See also* Reza Shah
Family Protection Law (1967) 79–80
Moore, Demi (cover for *Vanity Fair*) 147, 150
moral police 78, 80, 88–9
Morel, Geneviève 244
Mouvement de libération des femmes (MLF) 83
Mouvement de libération des femmes iraniennes - année zéro documentary 83
Mulard, Claudine 83
Muller, Michelle 83
Mulvey, Laura 1–2, 9, 16, 40, 50–1, 131, 181, 235. *See also* 'male gaze'
Afterthoughts on "Visual Pleasure and Narrative Cinema" 4, 7
Death 24x a Second: Stillness and the Moving Image 2, 12
on female bodies 125–6
'feminization' of film 12
Fetishism and Curiosity 87
heteronormative analysis 37
on heyday of Hollywood cinema 37
'A Phantasmagoria of the Female Body: The Work of Cindy Sherman' 41
veiled body 12
'Visual Pleasure and Narrative Cinema' 1–2, 4, 20 n.31, 35, 123, 125, 129, 139, 177–9, 229–30
Murray, Derek Conrad 15–16, 133
'pin-up' style selfies 134
selfies *vs.* self-portraiture 15–17
Murray, Samantha 180
'My Stealthy Freedom' online movement 85, 95 n.18

Naficy, Hamid, *Veiled Visions/Powerful Presences: Women in Post-revolutionary Cinema: The New Iranian Cinema* 78, 91
Nakadate, Laurel 6, 44–6
narcissism/narcissistic identification 16, 36, 44, 203
autoerotic 40
gaze 90
for male and female 37, 203
primitive phase 39
radical 211
Nash, Jennifer 9
Nash, Meredith 151
Nataf, Z. Isiling 203
National Unity of Women's Associations (Iran) 83
Nawai, Shahin 83–4
Nead, Lynda 177
Negra, D. 142 n.9
Negrin, Llewellyn 6, 59
neoliberalism 2, 14, 16–17, 102–4. *See also* postfeminism/postfeminist
feminine subject 102, 105, 112, 115
'technology of sexiness' 101
Nixon, Sean 8, 126, 133
Hard Looks: Masculinities, Spectatorship and Contemporary Consumption 132
'new lad' 127
'techniques of looking' 157
Nogués, Rosa 3–4

objectified/objectifying/objectification 6, 18, 108, 246
gaze 102, 109, 115 n.1, 126, 181, 184, 201, 211, 231–2, 235
medium of photography 114
sexually 77, 101, 106, 140
obsessional gaze 9, 207, 218 n.22, 232, 243

ocularcentrism 5, 56
Offbeat Bride blog 103, 107–8
O'Grady, Lorraine 10
Olive, Marlene 241, 246
  fashioning body image 227–32
  'M26 Marlene Olive – June 22, 1975' (2004) 241–2
  'Marlene Olive,' (1994–6) 236
  'Marlene Olive – June 21, 1976' (1995–7) 228, 240
  violence of look 235–9
online abuse of women 42
Opie, Catherine 206
  'Being and Having' photoseries 205
optical visuality 6, 35, 46–7
Orbach, Susie 141
Orgad, Shani 106, 111
  'confidence cult' 105
Other, The 14–15, 231–2, 234–5, 240–5
Owens, Craig 110

Parkins, Ilya 17
Parsay, Farrakhroo 79
Paterson, Mark 64
patriarchal society 6, 105, 123, 234
  female sexuality in 42, 203, 229–30, 233, 246
  gaze 35, 51, 63, 149, 179
  old new patriarchal 125–30
  'psychical obsessions' 9
  social codes of desire 139–40
Pecorari, Marco 188–9
Penn, Irving 176–7
performance 45, 162 n.3, 190, 202, 204
  exhibitionistic 40
  fashionable identity 208
  'genderfuck' 205
  of masculinity 213
  pregnancy 148, 160–1
  Quilla Constance's 47
  of self-surveillance 189
  of sexual agency 14
  Tyler's dance 43
  Willson's work on 23 n.71
performativity 8, 42, 101, 162 n.3. *See also* Butler, Judith
Peters, Lauren Downing 11
Pham, Minh-Ha T. 17
Phipps, Alison 13
photographs/photography 11. *See also* Davis, Jen
  boudoir (*see* boudoir photography)
  of clothing 62
  fashion 9, 181, 184, 189, 202, 233–4
  'fatshion' 191
  intimate 101
  maternity (baby bump) 147–8, 151, 158–60
  'popular misogyny' 17–18
  thinspiration 138–9
  'upskirting' 18
Pilson, John 178
Pink, Sarah 62
plus-size fashion/model 184, 192
Poeschl, Sandra 134
postfeminism/postfeminist 127
  media gaze 14, 147, 149–50, 154, 160–1
  pregnancy 14, 148–52, 161
Power, Nina 124
pregnancy 147–50, 152, 160
  'baby bump' 160, 164 n.34
  celebrity (*see* celebrity pregnancy)
  maternity (baby bump) photography 147–8, 151
  postfeminist 14, 148–52, 161
  private 151–2
Preliminary Materials for a Theory of the Young Girl (Tiqqun) 124–5, 139–40
  and selfie subjectivities 130–5
pro-ana (pro-anorexia) eating disorder 137–8
pro-eating disorder websites 137–8
'projective identification' 202
psychoanalysis/psychoanalytic approach 4, 7–9, 36–7, 139, 201–2, 230–1, 233–5
  Marxism and 123
  psychosis and mother's *jouissance* 239–40
  therapeutic specificity 247 n.16
public/private divide 13, 18, 56, 78, 81–2, 86–7, 92–3, 151, 156

'Queen Bey.' *See* Beyoncé
queer gaze 36, 199–201, 203–4, 206
  digital culture of queer women 214–16
  female fashioned body 211–14
  female gaze 204–7, 210, 214
Quilla Constance 6
  Pukijam 47–9, 51

'radical narcissism' 211
RAISE Our Story (street style) blog 17
Reader, Keith 248 n.25
Reif, Anne 134
religious dress code 85
Rey, Sylviane 83
Reza Shah 78–9. *See also* Mohammad Reza Shah; veil (chador) in Iran (post-revolutionary)
  speech in support of women 81
  1936 'Unveiling' 81–2
  Western-style dress code 81
Riegl, Aloïs 5, 46
Riley, Sarah 17, 101
Ringley, Jennifer 6, 44
  JenniCam 38–9, 42–4
  voyeurism and exhibitionism 38–40
Roach-Higgins, Mary Ellen 55
Rocamora, Agnès 7, 64, 132–4, 157
Rodino-Colocino, Michelle 25 n.99
Rolley, Katrina 10, 200, 203, 208
Romeo, Francesca 15
Rubens, Peter Paul 184
Ruggerone, Lucia 58, 63

Saper, Craig, 'Nervous Theory: The Troubling Gaze of Psychoanalysis in Media Studies' 231
Saville, Jenny 176–7, 183–4, 189
Scharff, Christina 104
Schecter, Jenny, *The L Word* 216
Schindler, Annette 249 n.38
Schneier, Matthew 156
Schroeder, Jonathan E. 134
Second-Wave feminism 2, 13, 16, 37, 127, 130, 139, 148
self-critical gaze 176, 192
self-fashioning process 157, 211, 216
selfies (and self-portraiture) 15–17
  on fashion blogs 132
  'imperfect' 136
  'pin-up' style 134
  and 'thinspiration' 123
  Warfield's analysis of 157
self-reflexive gaze 147, 152–3, 160
self-regarding gaze 135, 137, 140
sensory approaches to dress 57–62. *See also* 'dress'
  atmosphere of dressed body 55–6, 61, 70
  fashion 57, 60
  non-visual aspects of dress 62–3, 70
  senses and sensory behaviour 60
sexual liberation 17, 102, 128–9
shame 17, 78, 88, 101, 147, 184–5, 191, 228, 241, 243
Shaw, Peggy 205
Shayegan, Dariush 91
Sherman, Cindy 15, 41, 50, 181
Silverman, Kaja 65
Simmel, Georg 9, 55, 60–1, 65
Simpson, Jessica 147
Sitkin, Sarah 183–4
Slemmons, Rod 175
SlutWalk movement 2, 13–14
Smith, Anna Marie, *A Queer Romance* 213
Smith, Mark M. 70
Snapchat surgery 136, 140
'social constructivist' approach 58
social gaze 55–6, 65–71
social media 7, 18, 133–8, 140–1, 148
  exposure of pregnant body 151, 160
  hashtag feminism on 2, 13
  for self-representation 133, 152
  study of celebrity engagement 156
  visibility on 14–15
Solers, Colette 234
space
  fashion magazines as 10
  Islamic conceptualization of 86
  Lefebvre's forms of 86
  online 13–14, 17–18, 50–1
  public space in Iran 82, 86–7, 92–3
  transitional 39, 42–3
Spechler, Diana 175
spectatorship 1–4, 6–9, 18, 214. *See also* 'looking'
  bisexual women's 204
  cinematic 13
  and fashion 199–200, 203–4, 208, 211–12, 216
  female 4, 7, 20 n.29, 37–8, 40–1, 184, 212
  identification and desire 201–5, 212
  intersectional 9
  lesbian (*see* lesbian gaze)
  queer (*see* queer gaze)
spot-squeezing YouTube videos 50, 53 n.33
Stacey, Jackie 199, 202–3, 211, 213–14, 216
  'extra-cinematic' 211
  identification and desire 204, 212

Star Gazing: Hollywood Cinema and Female Spectatorship 201, 205, 211
Sternberg, Josef Von 41
stigma 189–90, 211
Stormi Webster 151. *See also* Jenner, Kylie
surface
consumer culture 123–4
denigration of 63
looking 6, 46–7
masculine body 126
surveillance 36, 78, 89, 147, 154, 160
obsessive 149, 151
self- surveillance 16, 134–5, 189
Sweet, Leah 184
Sweetman, Paul 65
Synnott, Anthony 60

Taleghani, Mahmoud 84
Tasker, Yvonne. 142 n.9
Taylor, Lou 58
Teigen, Chrissy 160–1
10 Years Younger television programme 136–7
'Thinspiration' 17, 138, 141
anorexic body of 141
photographs 138–9
selfies and 123
and thinspo 137
Throp, Mo 6, 36–42, 44–9, 51
Tiqqun 124–5, 127, 131, 135, 139–40
Titton, Monica, *Fashion and Postcolonial Critique* 26 n.130
'trans' 3, 10, 103, 203, 211, 215, 217 n.1, 220–1 n.59
transitional space 39, 42–3
transvestitism 4, 203
Tseëlon, Efrat 58, 177, 192
Tucker, Anne Wilkes 190
Tyler, Bonnie, 'Total Eclipse of the Heart' 43
Tyler, Imogen 150, 164 n.30

Ungers, Oswald 91
uprising of women in Iran 82–4

Vannini, Phillip 57
veil (chador) in Iran (post-revolutionary). *See also* Reza Shah
compulsory dress code (1979) 77–8, 80
feminism and Islam 79, 84, 92
hijab (*see* hijab in Iran)
Iranian Revolution (1979) 80
'looking' in 85–92
protest on strict dress code 82–3
public space in 82, 86–7, 92–3
transgression 92
1936 'Unveiling' 81–2
women's movement 83–4
Venus (painting by Botticelli and Titian) 159
Vermeer, Johannes 177
video artists 6, 35, 41–2
Clout 49
and digital technology 49
Hirsch (*see* Hirsch, Ann)
Nakadate 44–5
Quilla Constance 6, 47
Ringley (*see* Ringley, Jennifer)
virtual gaze 36
vision 5, 35–6, 41, 61
haptic visuality 5–6, 35, 46–9, 51, 67, 188
optical visuality 6, 35, 46–7
visual culture 3, 9, 46, 127, 230
Western 177, 180–2
Volcano, Del LaGrace 206
buzz-cut androgynous model 205
voyeurism 36–8, 41–3, 51 n.5, 91, 180. *See also* Ringley, Jennifer

Walker, Lisa 202
Walsh, Maria 6, 35–8, 40–4, 46–52
Warfield, Katie 157
Waskul, Dennis D. 57
Weidhase, Nathalie 14
Weigel, Moira 124
Weinstock, Tish 22 n.62
Welsh, Irvine, *The Acid House* 36
White, Michele 101, 104, 106, 113
Wilke, Hannah 181
Williams, Wendy 153
Willson, Jacki 23 n.71
Wilson, Elizabeth 64
Wilson, Emma, *Visual Pleasure at 40* 5
Winnicott, Donald. W. 39
Wolf, Naomi 180
Wollstonecraft, Mary 127
Wonderbra 1994 advert ('Hello Boys'), Beattie's 128–9
Woodward, Sophie 58
Woolley, Dawn 16–17

#YesAllWomen Twitter hashtag 13
Young, Iris Marion 62–4
Young, Shelagh 22 n.50

www.ingramcontent.com/pod-product-compliance
Lightning Source LLC
Chambersburg PA
CBHW050411280326
41932CB00013BA/1814